AIRSHIP
DESIGN, DEVELOPMENT
AND DISASTER

AIRSHIP

DESIGN, DEVELOPMENT AND DISASTER

JOHN SWINFIELD

CONWAY

For Bridgit
Airship would not have sailed without her

A Conway Maritime book

© John Swinfield, 2012

First published in Great Britain
in 2012 by Conway,
an imprint of Anova Books Company Limited,
10 Southcombe Street,
London W14 0RA
www.anovabooks.com
www.conwaypublishing.com

John Swinfield has asserted his moral right to be
identified as the author of this work.

British Library Cataloguing in Publication Data:
A catalogue record for this book is available from
the British Library

ISBN 9781844861385

Anova Books Company Ltd is committed to
respecting the intellectual property rights of
others. We have made all reasonable efforts to
ensure that the reproduction of all content on
these pages is included with the full consent of
the copyright owners. If you are aware of any
unintentional omissions please contact the
company directly so that any necessary corrections
may be made for future editions. Full details of all
the books can be found in the Bibliography.

Editing and design by David Gibbons
Printed in China by Everbest

To receive regular email updates on forthcoming
Conway titles, email conway@anovabooks.com
with Conway Update in the subject field.

Front endpaper: It all began in 1783 with a hot-
air balloon created by Joseph and Etienne
Montgolfier, paper manufacturers in Annonay,
some forty miles from Lyons, in France's Rhone
Valley. Wondrous and diverse were the machines
that followed. (Library of Congress)

Rear endpaper: A colossal spider's web. The
ambitious interior framework of a giant Barnes
Wallis airship under construction c.1920s.
(SSPL/Getty Images)

CONTENTS

THE NEWS ALL THE TIME
LARGEST HOME-DELIVERED CIRCULATION
LARGEST ADVERTISING VOLUME

MAdison 2345
The Times Telephone Number
Connecting All Departments

IN TWO PARTS — 54 PAGES
Part I — GENERAL NEWS — 28 Pages

TIMES OFFICES
202 West First Street
And Throughout Southern California

Los Angeles Times

EQUAL RIGHTS
LIBERTY UNDER THE LAW — TRUE INDUSTRIAL FREEDOM

ZEPPELIN BLAST KILLS THIRTY-FIVE

Giant Dirigible Blazing Wreck

Airship Blows Up on Its Arrival at Lakehurst Airport From Germany; Passengers Leap From Burning Ship

LAKEHURST (N. J.) May 6. (AP)—Germany's great silver Hindenburg, the world's largest dirigible, was ripped apart by an explosion tonight that sent her crumpling to the naval landing field a flaming wreck with horrible death to about a third of those aboard her.

Exactly how many died was still in dispute as the flames licked clean the twisted, telescoped skeleton of the airship that put out from Germany seventy-six hours before on its opening trip of the 1937 passenger season.

The American Zeppelin Company, through its port representative, Harry Bruno, placed the death toll at thirty-four of the ninety-seven aboard. The company listed ten

Other news and wirephotos of the Hindenburg disaster will be found on Pages 2, 3, 8, 9, 10 and 4-6 of this section of The Times.

of the thirty-six passengers and forty-three of the sixty-one-man crew as the disaster's survivors.

Allen Hagaman of Lakehurst, who was watching the landing at the mooring mast, also was killed, raising known toll to thirty-five.

ESTIMATES RANGE TO FORTY

These figures were at slight variance with unofficial estimates of the number of dead which ranged up to forty.

In the crowded hospitals in neighboring communities many of the survivors were in critical condition, a number suffering from excruciating burns.

Some were so gravely injured, among them Capt. Ernst Lehman, that the last rites of the Roman Catholic Church were administered to them.

Lehman, skipper of the ship's 1936 flights, made the ill-fated flight as an observer. Capt. Max Pruss, the commander, was listed among the injured survivors.

CAUSE OF BLAST MYSTERY

What caused the fearful blast, just at the moment the great craft was being moored, no one knew. The explosion occurred at the rear and some observers believed a spark of static electricity following a mooring rope from the ground set off the highly inflammable hydrogen. Other reports indicated a backfiring motor might have sent a flash of flame into a minute gas leak.

Storms and buffeting headwinds had delayed the huge ship far behind her schedule for the maiden trip, and ordered boxes in the early evening to keep the unexpected rendezvous with disaster.

The ground crew of sailors, soldiers and marines moved out into the field to handle her landing ropes.

PASSENGERS IN GAY MOOD

Lower she nosed, her Diesel motors throttled down. Passengers, gayly waving at the crowd, lined the lounge windows which show like transparent slits in the great silver belly of the ship.

The spider-like web of landing ropes snaked down the little trap doors in the nose. Men of the ground crew grabbed them at the wooden crossbars.

It was 6:23.

Then came the terrific explosion, and brilliant yellow flames suddenly splashed out toward the stern and the rudder that bore the red-and-black Nazi swastika. The detonation tore the ship as if it were made of paper. The tail dropped earthward.

CRUMPLES DOWN IN FLAMES

The blunt nose bobbed up, hung a moment in the air and then crumpled toward the field, flames running along its sides and its fabric flaking off in big chunks.

Passengers and men of the crew were hurled through the silvered walls of the Hindenburg to the sandy ground below. The crowd receded in a panicky surge to the shout of "run for your lives." Navy men dashed into the flaming debris to make rescues.

Collapsing in a tangled mass of girders and aluminum beams, the ship was born by a series of secondary explosions, lesser in force than the first shattering blast. And the flames roared up in a red and yellow wall to envelop the ship.

The flames burned well into the night, despite the efforts of fire departments to quench them.

BLAST IN SHIP'S STERN

The explosion occurred in the No. 2 gas cell toward the stern of the ship, according to State Aviation Commissioner Gill Robb Wilson, who called the blast strange. The bright gas bag billowed into fierce flame as the explosion plummeted the ship to the airfield. Ground spectators said crew members in the stern of the ship never had a chance to escape.

Spectators shrieked and screamed as the explosion, apparently in the stern of the envelope, shattered the ship and she collapsed, falling in burning wreckage to the ground. Even after the first stunning explosion and the

Turn to Page 3, Column 1

BLASTS SEND GIANT BALLS OF FLAME SPURTING FROM AIRSHIP

Before the eyes of hundreds of horrified spectators, the giant dirigible Hindenburg exploded in mid-air with a terrific roar over the Lakehurst Naval Air Station yesterday at the completion of a trans-Atlantic journey from Germany. This remarkable picture was taken as one of several explosions sent giant balls of fire into the air from the descending gas bag. The huge Zeppelin was wrecked just as it was about to make fast to the mooring mast which is seen in the photograph.
(AP Wirephoto, Copyright, 1937, by Philadelphia Public Ledger)

C.I.O. Joins Film Strike

Labor Council Offer Rejected by F.M.P.C.; Shows to Be Picketed

The Hollywood film studio strike definitely still is on.

This fact was made clear yesterday by Charles Lessing, business agent for the striking Federated Motion Picture Crafts, who said his organization is not at all satisfied with the proposal of the Los Angeles Central Labor Council to end the current walkout.

"The strike will continue until the producers agree to a closed, or union, shop program," Lessing said.

It appeared that the newly formed Committee for Industrial Organization will take a hand, both locally and nationally, in the conduct of the strike, after a conference of Lessing and Verne Murdock of the F.M.P.C. and C. H. Myers

Turn to Page 4, Column 6

"In, The Times Today," index and summary of news and features, will be found on Page 2, Part I. Irwin S. Cobb's Observations appear on Page 4, Part I.

JURY QUIZZES MRS. SHELBY IN TAYLOR DEATH MYSTERY

Mrs. Charlotte Shelby, mother of Mary Miles Minter, yesterday dramatically denied that she murdered William Desmond Taylor.

She made her first denial before eighteen interested members of the Los Angeles county grand jury and told about a later to a crowd of newspapermen in the corridors of the Hall of Justice.

DAUGHTERS QUIZZED

"I was asked if I murdered Taylor and I had to tell them no," she asserted with passion.

She paused for breath and continued:

"They asked me if I had any idea who did it and I had to say no again."

Mrs. Shelby was the last of three witnesses to appear before the grand jury during the day. She was preceded by her two daughters, Mrs. Margaret Fillmore and Mary Miles Minter, former screen star.

NEW CLEWS HINTED

But despite Mrs. Shelby's statements that she was unable to throw any light on the reopened investigation of the thirteen-year-old murder of the motion-picture director, Dist. Atty. Eugene Williams hinted yesterday in presenting the evidence to the jurors, indicated that new material had been developed which may lead to a final solution of the case.

"Testimony given yesterday,

together with other information already in our possession, is going to lead to a complete recapitulation of the entire case," he declared. "The grand jury is obviously interested in what they heard and want the investigation continued."

Williams indicated that several

Turn to Page 15, Column 2

AGE-PENSION MEASURE VOTED

Assembly Unanimous on Liberalizing Bill

SACRAMENTO, May 6. (AP)—By unanimous vote of 70 to 0, the Assembly tonight passed the Hornblower bill liberalizing old-age pensions.

Under provision of the bill, the necessity of giving a lien on real property is removed, pensioners need not take the pauper's oath and it requires the payment, in full, of the $35 monthly pension without deductions for rent, but they are living rent-free.

Also, it permits pensioners to receive gifts or even up to a total of $15 additional a month before any deduction may be made from the pension allowance. The bill now goes to the Senate. (Other reports on yesterday's action in the Legislature will be found on Page 14, Part I.)

Survivor Tells Leap to Safety

Blasts Felt Only Slightly, Says One Aircraft Passenger

A survivor's account of the crash of the Zeppelin Hindenburg is given here by one of the passengers of the airship who suffered relatively few injuries.

BY HERBERT O'LAUGHLIN
Copyright, 1937, by the North American Newspaper Alliance, Inc.

LAKEHURST (N. J.) May 6. (Exclusive)—I was in my cabin, in the forward section of the Hindenburg, packing my belongings in preparation for the landing that seemed only minutes away, when I felt a slight tremor shaking the ship. That was an explosion that rent the tail of the airship, the first of the blasts that tore the dirigible apart, but in effect where I stood was like that of an air pocket.

Hearing people run past my door, I joined them to find the cause of the tremor. As I walked toward the promenade deck, a second tremor occurred.

There was very little confusion among the passengers, no screaming hardly any noise. Nobody knew what had happened and people were just curious.

When I reached the promenade deck the nose of the ship was about twenty feet above the

Turn to Page 10, Column 2

TENTATIVE LIST OF MISSING AND KNOWN CRASH SURVIVORS

LAKEHURST (N. J.) May 6. (Exclusive)—A tentative list of passengers still missing in the Hindenburg disaster and believed dead was compiled tonight as follows:

Rudolf Anders, Dresden.
R. Herbert Anders, Dresden.
Birger Brinck.
Hermann Doehner, Mexico City.
Donald Curtis, Chicago.
Edward Douglas, New York.
Fritz Erdman.
Otto C. Ernst, Hamburg, Germany.
Mrs. Ernst.
Moritz Feibusch, San Francisco.

LIST OF KNOWN SURVIVORS

Capt. Ernst Lehman, severe burns.
Capt. Max Pruss, severe burns.
Capt. Albert Sammt, burns.
Col. Nelson Morris, Chicago, injuries unknown.
Hans Vinhalt, injuries unknown.
Albert Summitt, injuries unknown.
Theodore Ritter, injuries unknown.

John Pannes, New York City.
Emma Pannes, New York City.
Otto Reichold, Vienna.
Ludwig Felber and Walter Bernhofer, members of the crew, died of burns in hospitals. They were the only crew members identified among the dead.
Hans Hugo, Leonard Jacobeon, Ray Stahler, William Stett and Franz Werner, crew members, were listed as missing and believed dead.

Philip Mangone, New York, injuries unknown.
George Hirschfeld, Bremen, Germany, injuries unknown.
William Leuchtenberg, injuries unknown.
Hans Hugo, injuries unknown.
Adolph Fischer, injuries unknown.
Carl Otto Clemens, Bonn, Germany, injuries unknown.
Mrs. Gertrude Adelt, injuries unknown.

Turn to Page 3, Column 5

PROLOGUE

At 7.25pm on 6 May 1937 the airship *Hindenburg* nosed cautiously towards the tip of her mooring mast in New Jersey, America. An ocean liner of the skies, her passage from Germany had been delayed by stormy weather and strong headwinds. Suddenly a billowing hydrogen fire erupted near her tail, devouring the ship with a terrible roar. In seconds her steel frame melted into a charred and twisted tangle. Passengers leapt from the promenade deck into the jaws of the inferno as the ship fell out of the sky, their screams drowned by the clamour and bellow of the conflagration. A reporter sobbed into his microphone and the world would recoil as the torment of the craft and the last moments of her passengers were flashed by newsreel around the globe.

Seven years before the calamity of the *Hindenburg* another wingless leviathan, the British airship *R101*, set sail for India on the most testing voyage any such vessel had undertaken. A seventh of a mile long, she floated upwards with a slow reluctance into the autumnal dusk of an early evening sky. Her five diesel engines throbbed, red and green navigation lights twinkled in the darkening heavens, white pin-pricks of light shone from torches waved by the crew in farewell to wives and children on the ground. Those aboard waved through the port-holes at the throng below. Before retiring to their bunks, tired from the excitements of the day, they watched the ground slide slowly away, the quickening gloom shrouding the ship's vast silver envelope. In the saloon they had a grand supper with fine wines, toasting the ship and their voyage with balloons of cognac. The asbestos smoking-room grew rich with the perfumed haze of the finest Havanas, the cigar-lighter chained to a feather-light table. Inches above their heads more than five million cubic feet of hydrogen in huge bags kept the craft aloft. The crew used a narrow gangway running bow-to-stern in the envelope, monitoring gasbags, fuel tanks and ballast controls. The engines and those who tended them were in small and deafening cars fastened like limpets to the ship's exterior; each engine drove a huge propeller. The fabric of its cover stretched for seven acres around a jigsaw of girders, a giant tent as gloomy and cavernous as a cathedral; inside was to be in the belly of a mammoth, dim yellow lamps casting pools of shadowy light. The girders groaned, the ship seemed alive. The wind had picked up, clawing at the fabric. The forecast warned of dangers ahead: a slow drizzle turning to rain, water streaming off the cover, making the ship heavier, urging her back towards the ground.

On the bridge in the control gondola the officers went about their business, warming the engines before opening them to full throttle, adjusting the angle of flight, keeping the nose up, spinning the ship's wheel, getting the feel of her, rudder, elevator and ailerons. Her captain, Flight Lieutenant Herbert Carmichael Irwin, known as 'Bird' to the ship's company, was a tall, quiet, dignified Irishman. On his issuing of the naval command 'Prepare to Slip', his ship had been liberated from its shackle at the pinnacle of the tower. She had shivered and trembled, a silver-skinned colossus scenting freedom, uncertain if to stay or to run. Her nose gently dipped, as if pulled back to earth by unseen wires. Water gushed from her belly, thousands of gallons of ballast, helping her to climb higher into the leaden sky, lifting her bows. She was pregnant with weight and overloaded. There was far to go and much to do. It was the start of a spectacular adventure, the culmination of a five-year building programme fraught with politics and controversy. She was sailing to Ismailia, in Egypt, where she would host a glittering aerial dinner for the finest in the land; later she would top up her tanks of diesel and water before continuing her four-thousand-mile passage to India.

This book is an examination of the faltering and calamitous history of the airship, the friction over control and deployment and the protracted and fractious manner in which the military toyed with a commercial proposition while trying to bend it to its own ends. It tracks the dismal progress of a British Imperial airship ensnared in government committees, its evolution hampered by inter-service chicanery culminating in a degree of government control unimagined by its progenitors, and which led to the intervention of the Ramsay MacDonald government and construction of the airship *R101*. The era saw unprecedented administrative upheaval in the services, the troublesome birth of the RAF and frequent changes of government and secretariat. *Airship* charts the history of these vessels from the continental pioneers of the late nineteenth century to Britain's airship stations in the First World War and the building in 1924–9 of the behemoth *R100* and its sister vessel the *R101*. It studies the crucial role of Count Zeppelin, the development of the Zeppelin airship in Germany as a bomber and reconnaissance craft, and the way the British Admiralty imitated German design. In Britain the airship was characterised by uncertain military involvement and political volatility. It was a time of strife: mass unemployment, the General Strike, in America the Wall Street Crash, all set against the growing shadow of tumult. Across Europe the airship cast its magic. In the United States fleets of airships took to the skies, culminating in two giant vessels, the *Akron* and her sister craft the *Macon*.

Threaded throughout these broadly chronological pages are the central themes and bold personalities of the era: it was a time of hope and despair, lofty expectations and cruel reality. Those dominant have been largely lost to history: Count Ferdinand von Zeppelin; Lord Thomson, Britain's suave air minister; Sir Sefton Brancker, the aviation chief whose party trick was to eat his monocle; George Herbert Scott, audacious pilot and inventor of the mooring mast; Sam Cody, American entertainer turned intrepid sky sailor; and Edward Maitland, airship commander and parachute pioneer. While many have been forgotten, some remain legendary, among them Barnes Wallis and the writer Nevil Shute. Throughout this quixotic interval the daring and resolve of those who built and sailed airships shines through, the memory of their creations burned into the pages of naval and aviation history.

ACKNOWLEDGEMENTS

To Bridgit for encouragement, patience and clarity; Anna and Dominic for everything; Sarah Palmer, Emeritus Professor Greenwich Maritime Institute, Greenwich University; Nigel Caley, his airship knowledge has been beyond price; Dr. John Sweetman, military historian; Dr. Giles Campion, editor *Dirigible*; Dr. Robin Higham, Kansas State University; Brad King, formerly of HMS *Belfast*; the late Tom Jamison, author, and Katrina; Sir Barnes Wallis's daughter, Dr. Mary Stopes-Roe, and Harry, her husband, with his own aviation lineage; Rebecca Atherstone for her grandfather's Log; Crispin Rope; Wendy Pritchard; Peter Davison, aviation historian. The Watts family: Arthur, Michael, Granville. For those of Pulham, Howden and Cardington: Susan Sampson, Chris Harper, Ron Fayres; Brian Carr; Pauline Hinton, Joan Williamson, Nick Durrant, Peter West, Sylvia Walker, Hilary Hardy, Mandy Rush, Sarah Rush, Michael Gaze, Jeffrey Bowles, Judy Alder, Mervyn Hickford, Margaret Griffiths, Sheila and Graham King, Pat Whitehead, Brian Gould, Kenneth Deacon, Peter Rix, Bernard Nield, Den Birchmore, Steve Walbridge. The late Hy Kurzner and Valerie, Suzanne Bell, Dick Richards, Robert Green, Philip Molineux. Staffs of the National Maritime Museum, the Fleet Air Arm Museum, Churchill Archives, National Archives, Airship Heritage Trust, Barnes Wallis Memorial Trust. Gordon Leith, the RAF Museum; Brian Riddle, National Aerospace Library. John Lee and Matthew Jones of Anova. There are myriad more. The list is too extensive to record each individual and institution. Their absence does not lessen my appreciation for their guidance and kindness over a protracted and demanding period.

A NOTE BY THE AUTHOR

My enchantment with the wingless leviathans that are the stars of this story began when I was a young reporter learning my craft on a weekly newspaper in Bedford. There I learned of the two mammoth airship sheds at Cardington, outside the town, where airship history had been forged. The sheds still stand, gaunt sentinels to a time long past. Later, after moving into broadcast journalism, I made a film for ITV about a small new airship at Cardington, the *Europa*, in which I was fortunate to fly – though I prefer sail, a description that mirrors more aptly the genesis of the airship. From the moment we rose with gentle serenity into a cloudless sky I was hooked, floating slowly over the soft undulations of the Bedfordshire countryside. Such an addiction has no known cure. More than three decades have passed. My career has taken me around the world and back, several times. Some memories have become misty with the years. But that day remains etched in my mind, fresh and sharp-edged as if newly minted. The airship was a siren whose call echoed across nations: Britain, Germany, France, Italy, America, Russia; from the silent wastes of the Arctic to the sultry rhythms of Latin America, each fell beneath her spell. There have been some fine airship histories to date. I follow in illustrious footsteps; if mine should inadvertently stray I can only beg clemency: in trying to distil truth from the swirl of opinion, divining fact from fiction, seeking clarity in the fog of decades long-elapsed, one can make errors. I have ducked from didactic witness and polemicist; in matters lighter-than-air there can be 'hot-air'. I have shrunk from the overly technical and mad-eyed enthusiasts whose eager fascination with the arcane can bewilder; kindly and well-meaning all of them. Some aficionada would have me give only one side of any story, wishing me to scribble in black and white when the world and its failings remain obdurately grey. I hope they recognise I have sought a balanced appraisal. As prejudice is not easily dislodged, such an ambition is unlikely to be realised; more likely it will merely confirm that which seasoned historians and airshipmen already know: the road to Hell is paved with good intentions.

COMPLEX LEVIATHANS

Rigid airships were the biggest of three different types of lighter-than-air craft. Their most obvious characteristic was size; behemoths that blocked out the sun, they were sometimes the length of an ocean liner and usually in the shape of a giant cigar or whale. Of other types the smallest was the blimp or non-rigid, entirely devoid of a skeleton; the second, the semi-rigid, had a keel, as with a surface ship, that ran the length of its envelope.

The immense covers of the big rigids were usually silver. They had a network of transverse and longitudinal girders around which the cover was stretched. It was stiffened and waterproofed with dope (with a smell familiar to model aircraft hobbyists). The correct time at which to dope an airship cover would become an issue of controversy.

Inside the envelope or cover were large gasbags filled with highly flammable hydrogen. The bigger and heavier the ship the more bags and the greater volume of gas it required to give it 'lift'. Later in airship development retard helium was used; though still lighter-than-air it is marginally heavier than hydrogen. But for most ships during a period of some three decades helium was expensive and unattainable. The purity of hydrogen was important: 'impure' hydrogen is less light and more prone to explosion. Hydrogen was regularly tested for its purity. Gasbags were fixed within the skeleton. As an airship sailed through the skies it was crucial to prevent the bags chafing on the metal frame or surging to and fro, which could jeopardise the sailing characteristics and the overall stability of the ship. Chafing might tear bags and cause them to leak, with all the attendant dangers; bags that leaked also reduced 'lift'. The method by which the bags were fastened to a ship was crucial, with copious research into the safest and most efficient way of fixing them; ships were entirely dependent on the way in which the degree of lift was transmitted from bags to vessel.

In the envelope ran a walkway from bow to stern. It permitted officers and crew to attend to their diverse technical and aeronautical duties. On bigger ships such as the *R100* and *R101*, designed for a large complement of crew and passengers, there were promenade decks, dining room, lounge, smoking room (astonishing given the explosiveness of the situation), sleeping cabins, washing and toilet facilities.

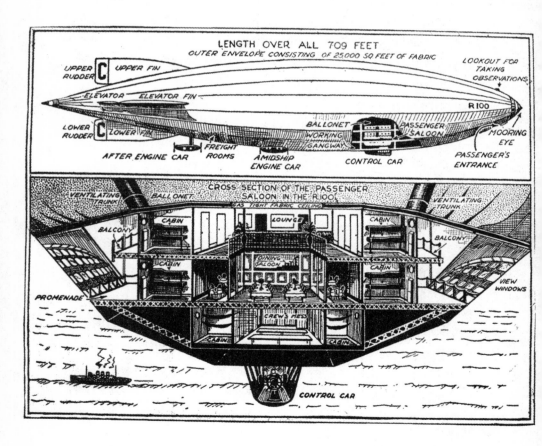

Beneath the belly of the ship was the control car. If a vessel wanted height it could jettison water ballast. If a commander wished to sail lower he might vent gas, making his craft heavier. Ships were driven by internal combustion engines driving propellers. Like aeroplanes and marine surface craft, airships had elevators, fins, ailerons and rudders. As in surface ships the job of an airship coxswain was one of many skilled jobs.

This is a simplified explanation of what could be a wayward and capricious vessel. To the untutored, the airship sounds straightforward. It resembled a mammoth whale. To some it was elegant, to others monstrous. Hydrogen gave lift, water provided ballast, engines drove propellers. But these were early years. Aeronautical knowledge was meagre. The complexities of stress and load were unexplored. Metallurgy and meteorology were in their infancy. Weather always had a hand in airship well-being. Ships were innovative. Those who mastered their construction and sailing showed an ingenuity and daring still startling today. There were myriad unknowns and variables: the way skeletons withstood, or failed to do so, the massive and hidden pressures of stress and load; unexplored forces exerted on gargantuan covers; the sometimes frightening manner in which gas could expand; the way vessels could rise above 'pressure-height' having grown light by heat from sun, sea or land; the opposite circumstances in cooler conditions, when ships became heavier, sometimes on night sailings, for instance, obliging ships to adopt a slight bows-up posture to maintain height, utilising – as with the wings of an aeroplane – the aerodynamic shape of the hull; the way for myriad reasons a ship could lose gas, making it heavy, on occasion causing it to plunge swiftly downwards in an anxious moment. Where appropriate to the text, technical explanations may be found in the notes and bibliography; the following glossary might further assist in unravelling the alchemy of the airship.

Contemporary illustration of the *R100*, showing some of the principal features of airship design.

GLOSSARY

Aerofoil: Plane-shaped to result in aerodynamic effect as a craft moves through the air.

Aerostat: Kite balloons and all lighter-than-air craft that are usually not navigable.

Air cooled: Engine cooled by its passage through air rather than by water in a water-jacket.

Airspeed meter: Air flowing through a right-angled 'pitot-tube' indicated the speed of a craft. Operators calculated differences in thin or dense 'slow' air dependent on altitude.

Altimeter: Aneroid (without liquid) barometer giving air pressure but crafted to show height. At lift-off barometric pressure changes could render inaccurate readings.

Ballast: Expelled to compensate for lost gas or heavy loads. Big ships had more than a dozen sacks each containing over 2,000 pounds of water released by an elevator man pulling a toggle in the control car. Some First World War German navy ships used sand.

Ballonet: Bag inside an airship designed to contain air to hold the shape of the envelope.

Bay: Any part or section of an airship contained between struts or frames.

Blimp: Name for small non-rigids. A variety of explanations for its origin include an RN officer in the First World War nipping the envelope and saying it made a 'blimp'-sounding noise.

Bow: Front end.

Bracing: Wires or struts tying and holding parts of the structure together.

Breeches: 500-pound water sacks (colossi like *Hindenburg* used bigger ones) underpant-shaped giving extra ballast for swift lightening in mooring, lift-off and emergencies.

Control car: Ship's bridge for commander, navigator, watch officers, elevator and rudder men. It incorporated a chart table, rudder and elevator wheels, ballast controls, engine-telegraph and a noise-free radio-compartment.

Crew: Similar, ranks, responsibilities as on seagoing ships. They included captain, navigators, engineers, radio operators and electricians. *Hindenburg* had 39 crew working an on-off watch system similar to maritime conventions.

Dope: Cellulose acetate in acetone used on the cover to tighten and make it water-repellant.

Dirigible: Any aerial craft based on lifting gas that can be steered through the air.

Drift: Route and distance from the original course determined by wind.

Duralumin: Light, strong aluminium alloy developed in 1903 and widely used in airships.

Dynamic Lift: Positive or negative force on the hull. With sufficient engine power, commanders could sail 'dynamically' at an angle to counter heaviness or lightness.

Elevator: Hinged flat flap fixed exterior at the tail. Operating up or down made the craft ascend or descend.

Engine cars: Cramped pods attached to the hull exterior housing engines and engineers.

Fins: Stabilising surfaces at the tail for vertical or horizontal sailing.

Fixed weight: All-in weight of airship structure and permanent installations.

Gasbag: Container in an airship for holding hydrogen or helium.

Gravity tanks: Permanent fuel tanks above each engine car feeding them fuel by gravity. Petrol was hand-pumped up to these engine-tanks from larger keel-sited tanks.

Gross Lift: Total lift of gas; equal to the weight of displaced air less weight of gas.

Hangar: Airship buildings; in nautical terms these are called sheds; hangars are for fixed-wing craft.

Helium: Helium is colourless, tasteless and odourless. It has very low boiling and melting points. It is used in cryogenics, deep-sea breathing apparatus, as a gas shield in robotic arc-welding and for growing silicon and germanium* crystals used to make electronic semiconductor devices. Helium is a by-product of natural gas and is now in plentiful supply. Fire was a hazard for hydrogen-airships. Helium is slightly heavier than hydrogen, which reduced airship lift, but it is immeasurably safer, being a retard, non-inflammable gas. With low density and low chemical reactivity, it is ideal for dirigibles but was not easily available in the airship era when the US had a monopoly.

Hydrogen: Inexpensive to make in a variety of ways. Inflammable, explosive if mixed with even tiny quantities of oxygen.

Inclinometer: Control-car apparatus indicating angle of incline or decline of an airship.

Kite-balloon: Captive balloon generally for reconnaissance designed to fly head-to-wind and made rigid by an internal air ballonet.

Landing ropes: On some airships mooring lines of 200 to 400 feet in the nose and along the keel which were dropped to the ground crew through hatches opened from the control car.

Longitudinals: Colossal main girders running the length of airships.

Main rings. Also called main frames. Polygons built of massive girders that acted as the principal transverse structural components in an airship. They were usually heavily braced with wires (but not on all ships) and set at regular intervals running the length of the vessel.

Mooring mast: Pioneered by legendary pilot G. H. Scott. Walking ships to or from sheds in wind could be disastrous. The mast, to which an airship could be moored, was portable, cheaper than huge steel sheds and enhanced utility. The USA preferred a 'stubby' version with the airship tail attached to a heavy moveable car.

---

* Germanium is a brittle grey element that is a semiconducting metalloid. It occurs principally in zinc ores and argyrodite: used in transistors, as a catalyst, and to strengthen and harden alloys.

Pressure height: Height at which falling atmospheric pressure allows lifting gas to expand and increase pressure inside the cells, which caused, in later ships, valves to open and emit gas. After climbing to a preselected pressure height, ships could ascend or descend to any altitude *below* this height without concern that gas would be released.

Rudder: Moveable vertical hinged flap sited at the tail used to steer to port or starboard.

Statascope: Instrument to monitor the rate of an airship's ascent or descent.

Static Lift: Lift without forward motion due entirely to the buoyancy of the gas.

Streamlining: Designers minimised resistance to help ships push through the air. All external appendages were shaped to aid aerodynamic efficiency.

Supercooling: This pertained usually at night with gas becoming cooler than surrounding air. If the density of gas increased, its lifting power was reduced.

Superheating: Reverse of the previous entry. Where the gas was warmer than the surrounding air, the density of gas was lessened and the lifting power became greater. This was often caused by heat from sun in the ship.

Trail rope: A rope that could be dropped from an airship to facilitate ground handling.

Thermometers: There were two: one measured air temperature, the other gas cell temperature. Using these crews could gauge lift. They were essential in dealing with the effects of superheating or supercooling.

Trim: If balanced, on an even keel or in trim, an airship's centre of gravity was directly under the centre of lift. If her nose was down she was 'trimmed at the bow'; if her tail was down she was 'trimmed by the stern'. If not level she would be described as being 'out of trim'.

Valve: This allowed gas to enter, exit or to be closed off in airship bags.

DRAMATIS PERSONAE

Arnstein, Dr. Karl (1887–1974) Born Prague. Airship designer. Savvy, ingenious, accomplished. Led team imported from Zeppelin in Germany to America by Goodyear chief Litchfield to build cutting-edge giant US airships *Akron* and *Macon*.

Atherstone, Grabowsky Noël (1894–1930) Born St. Petersburg. First officer *R101*. Joined Royal Navy 1913. Surface fleet 1914. Trained airship pilot 1917. First officer *R29* 1918. Rejoined RN 1919. Emigrated to Australia to farm sheep. In 1926 promoted Lieutenant Commander, RN Retd. Quit Austrialia. Joined *R101* programme Royal Airship Works Cardington. Maintained revelatory log *R101* construction and testing. Died aboard *R101*.

Bacon, Captain, later Admiral, Hugh Spencer Reginald (1863–1947). RN officer. Instrumental formation Naval Air Service. Technical, sophisticated, intellectual. Influential airship/submarine advocate, parallel technologies. First Inspecting Captain of Submarines; first captain of Fisher's *Dreadnought*. Fisher said Bacon had the best brain in the Navy. Member of Fisher's 'fishpond' comprising reformist RN officers.

Booth, Ralph (1895–1969) Commander *R100* on double Atlantic crossing. Ex-RN. In 1912 Midshipman. 1914 Sub-Lieutenant. 1915 RNAS airships. First World War captained non-rigids. 1918 First Officer *R24*. One-time commander Mullion airship station, Cornwall. 1925 RAF Squadron Leader after successful navigation of breakaway *R33*.

Brancker, Sir William Sefton (1877–1930) Director of Civil Aviation.

Generous, gregarious, monocle-wearing, raconteur, encouraging, energetic promoter military and civil aviation. Seemingly preferred fixed-wing to lighter-than-air craft. Died aboard *R101*.

Burney, Sir Charles Dennistoun (1888–1968) Ex-RN. Entrepreneurial, dogged, inventive, well-connected. Rich from invention of the paravane. Son of Admiral Sir Cecil Burney, second to Jellicoe at Jutland 1916. Tory MP. Formed Airship Guarantee Company, backed by Vickers, that built *R100* at Howden, east Yorkshire, England.

Cody, Samuel (1867–1913) Accomplished American-born kite and balloon expert, engineer, airship pilot, showman. In 1907 helped develop British army's first dirigible *Nulli Secundus*. Broke fixed-wing records. Killed in an aircraft of his own design.

Colmore, Reginald Blayney Basteel (1887–1930) Royal Airship Works (RAW) Director Airship Development. Airship devotee, contemplative, diplomatic, administrator. Former RN officer. Died aboard *R101*.

Du Plessis de Grenédan, Jean (1892–1923). French naval officer; talented commander of stricken French airship *Dixmude*, lost in storm with seven passengers and 43 crew.

Durr, Ludwig (1878–1956) Zeppelin's long-time leading designer. Unfairly criticised as ponderous provincial producing dull work; in reality tempered flair with experience, wisdom, prudence. Faithful Zeppelin servant during uncertain early years.

Eckener, Dr. Hugo (1868–1954) Count Zeppelin's heir. Citizen of the world. Former journalist. Droll, polished, inspiring. Chairman of Zeppelin, world's principal airship company. Consummate pilot, technologist, foremost airship ambassador.

Fisher, John Arbuthnot 'Jacky' Fisher (1841–1920). Admiral British Fleet. Mercurial, bellicose, reforming. Pugnacious supporter of 'new arsenal': airships, submarines, mines, torpedoes. Ordered successful non-rigids as First World War submarine spotters.

Fulton, Garland (1890–1974) US chief lighter-than-air division, Washington Bureau of Aeronautics. Far-seeing naval architect, aeronautical engineer. Oversaw construction of *Akron* and *Macon*. Intellectual, approachable, charming; vision about rigids and non-rigids, powerful airship supporter in Congress and US Navy.

Goddard, Victor (1897–1987) Ex-RN. Valiant airship pilot First World War. Dropped British agents from airship behind enemy lines. Commander Royal New Zealand Air Force; administrative head British Air Forces Burma and Malaya. Respected, technically fluent, friend of Barnes Wallis; later became expert in paranormal research.

Hunsaker, Jerome Clark (1886–1984) American, lambent, naval architect, aeronautical engineer, penetrating intellect, whip-smart theorist, lecturer, airship builder. Created first wind-tunnel Massachusetts Institute Technology. Compelling airship advocate.

Irwin, Herbert Carmichael 'Bird' (1894–1930) Dubliner. Commander *R101* on last voyage; on the fateful night it sailed over his Bedford home where Olivia, his wife of four years, lived. First World War sailed RNAS non-rigids and later RAF rigids. Seconded RAW Cardington. First-class athlete. Ran 1920 Olympics Belgium. Died aboard *R101*.

Lansdowne, Zachary (1888–1925) US Navy officer. Died as commander of USS *Shenandoah* (ZR1), which crashed 1925 over Ohio where he had been born. Talented and courageous airshipman who served first in US surface fleet. Attached First World War to British RNAS to learn about non-rigids. On *R34* first Atlantic sailing 1919.

Lehmann, Ernst (1886–1937) German navy officer. Played accordion and pig-skin swathed *Hindenburg* piano. Zeppelin bomber commander First World War. Employed by Zeppelin at Friedrichshafen, and joint Goodyear-Zeppelin project in US. Granted Zeppelin-control by Nazis. Died from burns in the *Hindenburg* disaster.

Litchfield, Paul (1875–1959) Far-seeing American capitalist. Chairman Goodyear airship company. Shrewd, influential. Imported 12 top German airship constructors into USA to build advanced US Navy airship giants *Akron* and *Macon*.

Mabry, Dale (1891–1922) Promising talent in American army's air service. Captain stricken Italian airship *Roma*, last hydrogen-ship bought by USA. *Roma* caught on power-lines in Norfolk, Virginia, killing 34 aboard including Mabry.

Maitland, Edward (1880–1921) Crucial in advancing British airships. Born leader, highly accomplished, courageous balloonist, parachute and airship pioneer. 1919 on *R34* for first transatlantic airship voyage. Died aboard *R38* when she broke up over the Humber.

Masterman, Edward (1880–1957). Unflappable airship pilot. Sailed 1916 first British *Rigid No.9*. Nonchalant, engaging, courageous. Ex-RN. Served RNAS First World War.

McCord, Captain Frank (1890–1933) American, commander ill-fated US aircraft-carrying airship *Akron*. Experienced ex-US navy surface officer. Perished aboard *Akron*.

Moffett, William (1869–1933). Revered US naval aviation leader. Open-minded, personable, natural leader, inspiring, courageous defender of innovation. Lauded chief of powerful Navy Bureau of Aeronautics. Persuasive airship lobbyist. Killed aboard *Akron*.

Nobile, Umberto (1885–1978). Italian semi-rigid designer, Polar pilot. With Norwegian Roald Amundsen on *Norge* voyage 1926. In 1928 Nobile's *Italia* crashed on second Polar voyage. During the search for survivors Amundsen died. Nobile hounded into Russian exile. Later reinstated as academic Naples University.

Pratt, Hartley B. Gifted airship engineer and designer. He and Barnes Wallis were youthful friends at J. S. White's shipyard, Cowes. Pratt's former employer, Vickers, recalled him to work on airships. Pratt asked Wallis to be his assistant, Wallis's first introduction to Vickers. Later Pratt became a tragic figure who took his own life.

Pruss, Max (1891–1960) German; Captain of *Hindenburg* on its final passage. Member of Nazi Party. Badly burned in inferno. Helped pull survivors from pyre.

Richmond, Vincent Crane (1893–1930) RAW. Assistant Director Airship Development, Technical (*R101* chief designer). Loyal, keen airship 'believer,' trained as structural engineer, lecturer, expert on doping covers. Died aboard *R101*.

Rope, Michael (1888—1930) RAW. Richmond's Chief Technical Assistant. *R101* designer in all but name. Gifted, meticulous, regarded in scientific and engineering circles as perhaps the most significant talent at Royal Airship Works. Died aboard *R101*.

Rosendahl, Charles (1892–1977). Ex-US Navy. Central to US airship programme. Heroic, well-liked, free-ballooned stricken *Shenandoah*'s dismembered bow to earth. Commander *Los Angeles*, first commander *Akron*. Officer on *Graf Zeppelin*'s record voyages. Commanding officer Lakehurst at the time of the *Hindenburg* catastrophe.

Santos-Dumont, Alberto (1873–1932). Brazilian; fun, flamboyant, appealing, dotty, technical. Gifted pilot, strong nerves, inventive and technically *au fait*. Personified much of the fable, acuity, eccentricity and daring central to lighter-than-air. Sailed round Paris in private airship. Died in sad and reduced circumstances.

Scott, George Herbert (1888–1930) RAW. Assistant Director Airship Development, Flying. Daring pilot. Invented mooring mast. Convivial, hated pomp or pretence. Bold airship advocate. Self-deprecatory, popular. Nonchalant air hid mathematical brain and resolution. Commander *R34* historic airship Atlantic crossing 1919. Died aboard *R101*.

Schutte, Johann (1873–1940) German naval architect. Formed Schutte-Lanz with timber specialist Karl Lanz. Built big, elegant, advanced airships. Mainly wood, subject to moisture and superseded by Zeppelin's more robust metal-framed craft.

Shute, Nevil Norway (1899–1960) Novelist, mathematician, pilot, engineer. Worked with Barnes Wallis as Chief Calculator *R100*. In *Slide Rule* wrote corruscating account of *R101*'s building. Established *Airspeed* aircraft company. World success as author.

Spiess, Joseph (1858–1917). Alsatian engineer, inventor of early rigid airship using hollow wooden beams.

Strasser, Peter (1876–1918) Led Zeppelin bomber raids. Driven, nerveless, misplaced fanatical belief in use of rigids as bombers. Proved international utility of long-range airships. Killed off Norfolk coast by British fighter on futile last Zeppelin raid on Britain.

Sueter, Murray (1872–1960) Ex-RN surface and submarine fleet. Innovative, outspoken, opinionated, Inspecting Captain Airships supervised fiasco-build

25

of first airship *Mayfly* (dubbed *Won't fly*). Instrumental in creating RNAS. Experimented with torpedoes dropped by aircraft. Later became Conservative MP.

Thomson, Christopher Birdwood (1875–1930) Air Minister in Ramsey MacDonald's Labour government. Suave, ambitious, aviation- and airship-besotted. Tipped as future Viceroy of India. Wide circle of friends across political and class divide. Died aboard *R101*.

Torres, y Quevedo, Leonardo (1852–1936) Spanish; civil engineer, versatile inventor, mathematician. Designed automatons, calculating machines, cable cars and *Astra-Torres* airships with French company Astra used by British and French in First World War.

Wallis, Sir Barnes (1887–1979) British polymath, acclaimed aeronautical engineer, scientist, inventor, famed for 'bouncing-bombs' in Second World War. Stellar career, often called genius. Designed advanced *R80* and airship *R100*, which sailed to Canada and back.

Watts, Granville (1898–1930). British airship engineer. Representative of the unknown legions of 'coal-face' sky-sailors. At Pulham, Howden, Cardington. On *R33*; in narrow escape and destruction of *R34*; sailed Canada *R100*. Poignant death.

Wiley, Herbert Victor (1891–1954) Indomitable US Navy airship captain. Escaped *Shenandoah*, *Akron* and *Macon* disasters. Commander *Los Angeles* airship. Graduate US Navy Academy. Went on to command Pacific destroyer squadron in Second World War.

Willows, Ernest (1886–1926) Built and sailed five airships. First in the UK to hold airship pilot's licence. Sailed airship from London to Paris 1910. *Willows IV* sold 1912 as *HM Naval Airship No. 2*. Died balloon accident Kempston near *R101* Cardington base.

Zeppelin, Ferdinand Graf von (1838–1917) Father of the airship. Popular, imaginative, strong-willed, energetic, optimistic. Aristocratic former army officer, endured string of calamities in determination to turn pipe-dreams and hot-air into a commercial reality.

1
THE BIRTH OF THE AIRSHIP

Pioneers

A model of the *R101* hangs today in the quiet of a Suffolk church. In a nearby town a chronicle of events that shook the world lies hidden in a bank vault. Golfers now play in a corner of east Yorkshire where aviation history was made. In south Norfolk is a muddied field where once a concrete apron lay. An alloy spar rests in the hall of a house in Birmingham, glinting in the morning sun, tactile and enigmatic as an abstract sculpture, feather-lightness adding to its mystery. A memorial in a Bedfordshire graveyard bears the names of those whose flights of fancy recognised no boundaries and whose horizons knew no limits. The reminders of an age long passed have all but disappeared: the era of the airship is no more. It took years before Britain caught up with the rest of Europe in its affection for the airship; when it did so its courtship was tentative and quarrelsome, its embrace brief and turbulent. From the first days of lighter-than-air, Britain had lagged behind Europe. Though pioneering work had been conducted in France, it was in Germany that the airship found its spiritual home. Large, rigid German airships, envelopes stretched taut around a metal frame, unlike non-rigids with envelopes inflated solely by the pressure of gas, were making regular military and commercial flights by 1914 and the start of the First World War. Sixty years before that the Frenchman Henri Giffard, in a non-rigid airship, flew the first powered vessel in the history of flight, a seventeen-mile journey by coke-fired, steam-driven airship on 24 September 1852.[1] Twenty years later Austrian Paul Hanlein built an airship twice the size of Giffard's, its engines so heavy they rendered his creation unworkable. In 1883 French brothers Gaston and Albert Tissandier constructed an airship powered by 24 batteries, but it was so weighty that control proved impossible. In 1884 *La France*, powered by lighter batteries and flown by Charles Renard and Arthur Krebs, achieved a sensational 14.5 miles an hour and proved highly manoeuvrable.[2]

The German Dr. Karl Woelfert experimented in 1888 with airships whose envelopes were filled with hydrogen, propelled by internal combustion engines developed by Otto and others.[3] In 1897, with his engineer Robert Knabe, Woelfert was killed when a flame from the exhaust, positioned perilously close to the gasbag, ignited the hydrogen.[4] In the same year, David Schwarz, an Austrian, developed the first rigid airship; but it was wrecked in Berlin on its maiden flight.

The fabled Brazilian aviator and engineer, Alberto Santos-Dumont (1873–1932) built his first airship in 1898, a cylindrical balloon with a gasoline engine.[5] He became the toast of Paris, a familiar sight flying around the Eiffel Tower, docking at his favourite café or, legend has it, mooring at his front door on the Champs-Elysées. After a distinguished career he committed suicide; he would die a nomad, broken, wandering from country to country, suffering from an incurable illness thought to be multiple sclerosis.[6] In 1903 the wealthy owners of a sugar refinery, the French Lebaudy brothers, Paul and Pierre, made the first controlled journey over a significant distance, flying thirty-eight miles in one hour and 41 minutes.[7]

All such exploits would be overshadowed by the endeavours of Count Ferdinand von Zeppelin.[8] A German cavalry officer born at Konstanz, in Württemberg on 8 July 1838, von Zeppelin was of French descent on his mother's side. His airship designs set the standard for years to come. He filled gas-bags with hydrogen and fastened them inside a cigar-shaped envelope of fabric stretched round a rigid frame. On 2 July 1900, aged 61, the exuberant Count flew his first craft from a water-borne dock near Friedrichshafen, on the northern side of Lake Constance near the borders with Switzerland and

Austria. At Friedrichshafen he would establish a factory destined to become the most successful airship works in the world.

His first ship, the *LZ1* (Luftschiff Zeppelin 1) was bigger than anything seen previously. It had 400,000 cubic feet of hydrogen and was powered by two Daimler engines. However, it was underpowered, which made the craft difficult to control. Zeppelin would grapple with a problem that tested other pioneers – trying to ascertain the correct combination of push that was delivered by the engines, and lift, primarily determined by the weight of craft, size of envelope and quantity and quality of gas.

Count Zeppelin epitomised the dashing aristocratic. Daring belied his age, and his popularity was enhanced by stoicism in overcoming a string of well-publicised mishaps. His company regularly teetered on the verge of bankruptcy, being rescued by public donations, newspaper appeals, a state lottery, aristocratic munificence and the seemingly endless fortitude of the eternally optimistic Count who had once been obliged to mortgage his wife's not inconsiderable estates. Von Zeppelin's second ship was also a failure, but it yielded information utilised in 1906 in the building of a third, more successful vessel. By 1924, when Britain's Airship Committee would stutter into being, Zeppelin was well established as the world's foremost airship constructor – and with 115 Zeppelins built and flown, the company was also far ahead of its French, Italian, Japanese and American rivals in technical competence and flying experience.

Another force in German airship development was the Danzig professor of theoretical naval architecture, Johann Schutte,[9] who in 1909 founded the Schutte-Lanz airship company. He studied parallels between airship and submarine design, informed in part by the influential naval architect William Froude and his pioneering stress experiments on marine hulls in the previous century.[10] Schutte chose to build his airships with plywood instead of metal frames. Douglas Robinson, the airship historian, makes a persuasive argument that Schutte's competition with Zeppelin was of such ferocity it quite blinded him to the obvious: wood is less strong than steel and absorbs humidity, making ships heavier if sailed over water, which most were. The choice of wood, and a marked preference by airship crews for the Count's creations, meant that Schutte would fail to match the global recognition of Zeppelin.[11]

There were continuous improvements in the design and construction of the Zeppelin, many due to Dr. Ludwig Durr (1878–1956), Zeppelin's principal engineer. Airships were a mix of the advanced and the archaic. Goldbeater's skin, based on a thin membrane from the intestine of a cow, was used to make the impervious gas bags in airship envelopes; their production was skilled, laborious and costly, many bags being needed, which necessitated vast herds of cattle. By 1914 the huge skeleton around which the cover was wrapped had undergone radical change: a new alloy, duralumin, had been developed. This challenged the use of steel and represented an important breakthrough, for duralumin was comparable in strength to soft steel but, crucially, only a third of its weight.[12]

British Military Balloons

Britain's airship development was never as auspicious as that of Germany. In the years prior to the First World War, Britain's military and political leaders had failed to recognise its potential. Consequently, Britain had lagged behind in terms of personnel, know-how and flying experience.[13] Nevertheless, in spite of trailing Germany in airships built and in the advantage of having a reservoir of people who had *flown* airships, Britain had quietly persisted with its own programme. Though devoid of an exponent with the popular zeal of Count Zeppelin, by 1900 recreational and military ballooning had become well established in Britain. Sporting events came under the auspices of the Aero Club, awarded its Royal title in 1910, while military ballooning was the responsibility of the Army's Royal Engineers based at Chatham, in Kent.[14]

The War Office established an operation to develop military ballooning at Woolwich, on the Thames in London, in 1878. Captain James Templer was appointed instructor in ballooning to the Royal Engineers. With a grant of £150, Britain's first military balloon, *Pioneer*, was built. A balloon school was established by the Royal Engineers in 1888 following military campaigns in the Sudan (1884–5) and Bechuanaland (1885). In each campaign, balloon sections were utilised by General Sir Charles Warren and General Sir Gerald Graham, VC, ex-Royal Engineer officers. Later, balloon units were despatched to South Africa and used for artillery observation at Ladysmith, Mafeking and Kimberley. A fourth unit was attached to the international force that included British and Indian sappers which occupied Peking during the Boxer Rebellion. Later this section moved to Roorkee where an elephant provided a holdfast for the experimental balloon section of the Bengal Sappers and Miners. Holdfasts were sometimes carried unexpectedly aloft – there were no reports of flying elephants, but the lifting power of balloons, and especially of airships, could always cause problems when it came to the tricky business of tethering them to earth. Following the Boer War in South Africa (1899–1902) man-flying kites and improved balloons and prototype airships were flown by both Sapper and infantry officers.[15]

Willows and HM Naval Airship No. 2

On the civilian front, Ernest Thompson Willows (1886–1926), the son of a Cardiff dentist, was an important innovator, but his sterling endeavours, as with many others, failed to achieve the recognition they deserved. Airship annals are littered with eidolons who were inventive, often brilliant engineers and passionate about lighter-than-air technology. Too often their myriad abilities and undiluted courage have passed without proper salute. As with several of his peers, Willows was bedevilled by a lack of funding. In 1910 he became the first to fly an airship from Britain to France across the Channel, and he is regarded by some as the true originator of the British non-rigid airship.

Willows built his first ship in 1905, when he was 19 years old, and on 5 August of that year made what was thought to be the first controlled flight in a British airship, flying from East Moors in Cardiff. It lasted for more than an hour. His craft was tiny compared with the behemoths that followed: it had a capacity of 12,000 cubic feet, a length of 72 feet and a diameter of 18 feet. The envelope was of silk with a gondola suspended beneath by struts and wires. It had a twin-cylinder 7-horsepower Peugeot engine; designed for a motorcycle, it powered a push-propellor. Though the ship was inspected by the War Office, no money or support was forthcoming. The inspection was conducted by Colonel J. E. Capper, destined to build his own reputation in aviation.

Willows' second ship was an improved and larger version of his first. It was powered by a JAP 30-horsepower air-cooled V8 engine, which drove two swivelling propellers mounted on either side of the gondola suspended beneath the envelope. The ship incorporated a further advance: the installation of a rudder, which gave some semblance of steering. This second ship was in turn enlarged, modified and rebuilt as the third Willows craft, *The City of Cardiff*. Willows flew it from London to Paris in 1910, the first crossing of the English Channel at night and the first from England to France. It was 120 feet long, 40 feet in diameter and had a gas volume of 32,000 cubic feet. The same JAP engine powered two six-foot propellers. The voyage was not without incident. Problems with the envelope caused Willows to land near Douai in the early hours of the morning, and a local French flier, Louis Breguet, helped repair the craft. Willows arrived in Paris on 28 December 1910 and celebrated New Year's Eve with a flight around the Eiffel Tower.

Willows demonstrated an early grasp of principles commonplace in ensuing years. His fourth ship, completed in 1912, was smaller than his third but more streamlined, measuring 110 feet in length, with a diameter of 20 feet and a gas capacity of 24,000 cubic feet. Beneath the envelope he built a keel from which was slung a two-man gondola. A 35hp Anzani engine drove two four-bladed steerable propellers. It was capable of 50 mph. Rejected by the army, it was bought by the Admiralty as a naval airship for £1,050 in September 1912.

In 1913 the Admiralty decided that its new airship was worthy of enlargement. It increased its gas capacity to 39,000 cubic feet and in the following year its two-seater gondola was replaced by a three-seat version. This proved an unsatisfactory configuration, an example of the Admiralty wrongfully assessing weight in ratio to power and the strength and capacity of the envelope. The envelope, though, was used as the prototype for the successful *SS* (*Sea*

Scout) class reconnaissance blimps in their U-boat surveillance role during the First World War.

During that war, at a factory in Cardiff, Willows built kite or barrage balloons. Willows was the first person in the UK to be awarded an airship pilot's certificate from the Royal Aero Club. On 23 August 1926 he was killed in a balloon accident at Kempston, in Bedford, close to Cardington, where so much airship history would be made in the ensuing years.[16]

Nulli Secundus

Military involvement continued. In 1906 Capper was made the head of the Army Balloon Factory at Farnborough, and in 1907, with Samuel Franklin Cody (1867–1913), he built Britain's first military dirigible, the *Nulli Secundus* ('Second to None'), one of three non-rigid airships he had helped develop. She made her maiden flight on 10 September 1907, and her first public appearance on 5 October when Capper and Cody flew from Farnborough to London. *Nulli Secundus* completed a passage over London before strong headwinds forced her to land at the Crystal Palace in Sydenham, south London. Her 50-mile flight lasted three hours and twenty-five minutes. At Crystal Palace she was deflated and transported back to Farnborough by road.

Cody was an American entertainer who would write his own impressive page in aviation history. He developed the steering gear and the engine of the *Nulli Secundus*. Cody (real name Cowdery) was born in Iowa in 1867. Much of his early life is a mystery, in part because of his tendency to fictionalise it. It is believed he had previously worked as a cowboy, frontiersman, travelling showman and playwright. At some point he had changed his name to forge an amusing, though spurious, link to William Cody, legendary as Buffalo Bill, the cowboy showman. Samuel Cody settled in England in 1896 and worked with the British army developing kites, airships and later aeroplanes. In 1906 he was made the Chief Kiting Instructor, developing the man-lifting kite system used by the British army for observation purposes.

Cody later designed his own aeroplane, Army Aeroplane No. 1. On 16 October 1908 he completed the first officially recognised manned flight in a powered aeroplane in England. He covered a distance of almost 1,400 feet in 27 seconds at an altitude of between 30 and 40 feet and won, in 1912, the Army military aeroplane trials held on Salisbury Plain. Cody was killed the following year, on 7 August 1913, when the *Cathedral V1* seaplane in which he was joy-riding with his passenger, the cricketer W. H. B. Evans, collapsed in mid-air. History has tended to concentrate on Cody's colourful personality and earlier career while overlooking his daring and technical elan. He was buried with full military honours in Aldershot Military Cemetery.[17]

Mayfly

In 1908 the reforming, mercurial First Sea Lord, was John Fisher, better known as 'Jacky' Fisher.[18] His protégé, the far-seeing Captain Reginald Bacon, was director of Naval Ordnance.[19] Fisher was one of Britain's few highly placed airship believers. He also championed the submarine, the principles of which had permeated airship thinking; Bacon and Captain Murray Sueter[20] had worked in torpedo development and had been heavily involved in the Vickers submarine development programme.[21] Sueter became Inspecting Captain of Airships between 1911 and 1914 and was head of the Admiralty Air Department from 1912 to 1915. In July 1908, Bacon drew up a plan he presented to Fisher, one of the Navy's most innovative thinkers. It was Fisher who transformed the navy from Victorian relic to modern fighting fleet; he and Winston Churchill would later become bitter foes, with accusations that Fisher's behaviour became irrational. Bacon's thesis effectively suggested the formation of a Naval Air Service. His revolutionary notion was that a Naval Air Assistant should join the Admiralty, and the War Office should make the advice of the Superintendent of the Balloon School available to the Admiralty; Vickers should be told to design and construct a rigid airship to be used by the Royal Navy for reconnaissance purposes.[22]

Bacon's proposals were examined in 1909 by the new and powerful Committee of Imperial Defence. After lengthy deliberations – nothing happened rapidly – the Committee recommended to the Cabinet that £35,000 be allowed in the Naval Estimates of 1909–10 to build Britain's first rigid airship.[23] By then, in August 1908, Vickers had already been asked by the Admiralty to build a rigid airship that would match the latest German Zeppelins. The frame was to be of duralumin, as were the those of the Zeppelins. Duralumin was an aluminium alloy, robust, less expensive and lighter than steel; it was invented in 1905 by Conrad Claussen, a German metallurgist, and Vickers bought the patent rights in 1910.[24]

The Admiralty demanded a fast airship of immense range, one that could stay aloft for at least 24 hours and be capable of distant offshore reconnaissance patrols. At one point it even wanted her to work in the Arctic – after laborious and expensive experiments with ratings using steam hoses, it was agreed that the best and cheapest way to rid an airship of snow was to brush it off: airship history is rich with straightforward solutions being passed over for alternatives that were expensive, complicated and prone to breakdown. The ship also had to carry the latest radio equipment, which was heavy, as was its gondola, being constructed of the finest Honduras mahogany. Most importantly for the Admiralty, the new British airship had to be an indubitably superior vessel to anything possessed by the German Navy.

British admirals were as sceptical of airships as they had been of submarines. Others were of the view that anything a German cavalryman could do British sailors could do better.[25] Each time the Admiralty changed its mind the costs rose. On 10 May 1911, Admiral Reginald McKenna, the First Lord of the Admiralty, said the price had risen from £35,000 to £40,876 17s 6d, plus £681 3s 5d for spare gear.[26] The Admiralty at the time (and for a lengthy period afterwards about airships in general) was incapable of making up its mind about the purpose of its new airship: each time it spied a new Zeppelin, bristling with innovation, it demanded changes in the specification of its own craft; there were so many alterations, it seems remarkable that the eventual price increase was not greater. Murray Sueter, a significant innovator in the arcane and frequently dangerous field of weapons development, supervised construction of the new craft. He received a number of depressing missives from the Admiralty saying, essentially, that it possessed very little faith in airships. Unsurprisingly, such communiqués further undermined the confidence of the constructors. Mr. L. G. Robertson, the marine manager at the Vickers shipyard at Barrow-in-Furness, on Britain's north-west coast, in which the ship, to be named *Mayfly*, was being built, became exercised by the unattainable ambitions of the Admiralty. Against the advice of Hartley Pratt, his assistant, Robertson dispensed with the keel.[27] Two years later, precisely as Pratt had predicted, the *Mayfly* (which never did) broke in two while being manhandled out of its shed on 24 September 1911.

The ambitions of the Admiralty had exceeded capability, a pattern that would become familiar in the future. However, Rear Admiral Frederick Sturdee,[28] who presided over the *Mayfly* inquiry, took a different view – he pronounced that *Mayfly* was clearly 'the work of a lunatic'. Sueter's riposte was equally robust: Sturdee's remark, he said, was 'hardly an unprejudiced judgement ... even before *Mayfly* the anti-air element in the Admiralty had been at least holding its own.'[29] The *Mayfly* (or the *Won't fly* as Churchill dubbed it) ended British airship development for five years, the first example of a faltering programme which would become characteristic. Meanwhile, the Italians, French and Germans forged ahead.

Rigid No. 9

In 1912 Sueter and Mervyn O'Gorman, superintendent of the Royal Aircraft Factory, were among those who were concerned that Britain had fallen behind: 'German airships have ... proved their ability to reconnoitre the whole of the German coastline on the North Sea. In any future war with Germany, except in foggy or stormy weather, it is probable no British war vessels or torpedo craft will be able to approach within many miles of the German coast without being discovered and reported to the enemy ... German airships have (already) covered a distance equal to the distance from Germany to the British coast without replenishing fuel ... it is difficult to exaggerate the value of this advantage to Germany ...'

Airship development resumed in Britain in 1913. The Admiralty had been exercised about reports detailing the success the German navy was having with its Zeppelins. But skills had been lost. Britain was devoid of technical skills and flying experience. Churchill also wanted development resumed. He wrote to Herbert Asquith, the Prime Minister, saying Britain should build its own airships, 'so that the art of making them is not wholly unknown to us'.[30] He urged that construction should start immediately: 'If we do not begin now we shall find ourselves in a helpless position, hopelessly behind everyone else ... we are already so far behind other countries we cannot afford to let more time slip away. These measures will not give us an air fleet comparable to those possessed by France and Germany: all they will do is put us in a position next year to make substantial advance in this new service.'[31]

In 1913 development was in the hands of a small Admiralty-Vickers team supervised by Sueter, who by then had become the director of the Naval Air Department. The general manager was Hartley Pratt, whose friend, Barnes Wallis, would become head of the drawing office.[32] The department had little to go on beyond snatched, grainy photographs of Zeppelins and drawings of a Zeppelin hastily prepared by Admiralty draughtsmen when it made a forced landing at Luneville, France, in April 1913.[33]

The first airship the team produced was *Rigid No. 9*. (Other airships built were non-rigids, which accounts for the non-consecutive numbering; non-rigid airships were devoid of the steel, later duralumin, frame of the bigger rigid airships, around which the envelopes were stretched.) *Rigid No. 9* flew on 27 November 1916. One of the few men in Britain with rigid airship flying experience, Commander Edward Alexander Dimsdale Masterman, RN, took the controls.[34] Masterman – with an insouciance characteristic of airshipmen – reported that the voyage had been uneventful bar *minor* problems. As the ship was being pulled from its shed its wheels had broken off due to a weak forging; this *minor* problem made for an inauspicious start but was insufficient to deter a flyer of Masterman's mettle. Sailing over Morecambe Bay, he noted his ship had failed to answer her helm: 'The auxiliary rudder control wheel in the aft gondola had buckled, the control wires had stretched ... the rudders were thus free to flap about.' Mid-air repairs, utilising cord cut from a gasbag, were expedited by Pratt. Masterman reported that the ship was heavy; it took him three minutes to turn her 180 degrees, giving a somewhat unsatisfactory turning circle with a diameter of one and a half miles.

Masterman reported the details to Sir Eustace Tennyson d'Eyncourt,[35] the Director of Naval Construction, who was responsible for the development of airships, and he passed them on to the Admiralty. The Admiralty accepted receipt of the airship 'even though she did not come up to specification ... we had to do this with the *No. 1 Holland* to do the diving trials. The lightening of the ship (should) be considered forthwith; the main object is to get this ship away from Barrow as soon as possible in order that work on the following ships can progress with all speed ... and also that flying experience can be gained with her.' The *Holland* was His Majesty's Submarine Torpedo Boat Number 1, *Holland 1*, the Royal Navy's first submarine, built in 1901 by Vickers at Barrow to a design by the anti-British, Irish-American engineer, John Philip Holland, the pioneer submarine designer.

Tennyson d'Eyncourt's representative on the test sailing of the airship had been refused passage because his presence would have made the ship too heavy. Tennyson d'Eyncourt, not a man to be tampered with, registered his not inconsiderable displeasure. With comic sang-froid the Admiralty, never likely to repent on such matters, informed him: 'The omission of the representative was very unfortunate ... however, personnel and ballast are only interchangeable within limits unless the former are prepared to be thrown overboard, if necessary.'[36]

Rigid No. 9 was Britain's first successful rigid airship. She was used mainly for crew training and sailed 198 hours before being scrapped in June 1918.[37] She had been completed in the autumn of 1916, more than three years after the order had been placed (five years from it being mooted) and less than two years before the end of the war.

The delays and procrastination that had hampered the building of *Rigid No. 9* came to typify airship construction. There were, in fairness, exceptional circumstances that also contributed to the airship's lengthy period of gestation: the first was a labour demarcation dispute and the second the Irish rebellion; the latter delayed the delivery of the flax used in the production of the netting that protected the gasbags. For three months before being scrapped on 28 June 1918, *Rigid No. 9* had hung idle in her shed at Pulham airship station in south Norfolk. Before her ignominious end she had flown more than 4,500 miles. She retains a significant place in airship development, but she was 'too heavy, too slow, too unwieldy and too late'.[38]

Sea Scouts

By August 1914, Britain had just six airships, of which only two were of operational value. They were used to patrol the Strait of Dover when the British Expeditionary Force crossed to France.[39] Churchill's frustration about the late delivery of airships is evident in a note he sent to the Second Sea Lord, Rear Admiral Sir Frederick Hamilton: 'The sanction [for airships] was obtained two months ago. Vickers informs me that they have no orders in writing but are proceeding on verbal orders. This matter ought to have been settled in a regular manner. Please report.'[40] In the belief that aeroplanes promised better value for money, Churchill – not unknown for changing his mind – did an about-turn from staunch supporter to rabid airship critic. As First Sea Lord, he had cancelled the Vickers No. 9 project in March 1915, causing yet a further hiatus in the development programme. The programme was restarted weeks later after Churchill's resignation in May 1915.[41]

The return of Jacky Fisher as the First Sea Lord in 1914 saw an airship expansion programme prompted by the German U-boat campaign. Fisher called for a fleet of small non-rigid airships to be built and deployed as reconnaissance vessels.[42] They were inexpensive and each took only a month to build.[43] Junior officers from the Grand Fleet and civilian engineers were drafted on to the airship reconnaissance programme.[44]

Sueter wrote that lessons learned from *Mayfly* and Rigid No. 9 proved invaluable in the construction of Jacky Fisher's fleet of scout ships which were in part designed by Michael Rope, who would subsequently play a significant role in the airship story. *Mayfly* taught airshipmen about fabrics for gasbags, how to make hydrogen and how to store it in portable plants. In strategic terms, Fisher's small, non-rigid airships, devoid of the skeletal frame of the bigger rigids, were an undoubted success when deployed as reconnaissance vessels and U-boat spotters. Fisher wrote: 'German submarine captains hated more than anything else our small airship patrols, not so much their bombs, but having their position given to surface craft in order that they could attack them. No food ships were sunk during the First World War when airships were on spotting patrols.'[45]

But while small airships were effective in reconnaissance, in attacking U-boats on their own they had only limited success. They worked better when cooperating with surface ships, as in the incident in 1918 when *U-115* was sunk off Sunderland. Airship *R29* spotted an oil leak from the U-boat and dropped a bomb to register the submarine's position. When the destroyer HMS *Ouse* arrived, *R29* dropped a second bomb and calcium flares. Three trawlers equipped with hydrophones and a second destroyer, HMS *Star*, joined the hunt and eventually destroyed the U-boat. For longer range reconnaissance and anti-submarine patrols, what were really needed were big rigid airships. Sir Eric Geddes,[46] First Lord of the Admiralty from 1917 to 1919, made this point to the War Cabinet. For strategic purposes, and because of their increasing sophistication, enemy submarines were operating farther out to sea. Geddes said that 'it was essential the Admiralty should have long flight machines to maintain an efficient patrol'.[47] Because of the time an airship could stay aloft, and its ability to hover, it was 'more effective than any other craft, on water or in the air, for reconnaissance and escorting convoys ... for which purpose they are essential'. An airship could search 100,000 square miles in 40 or 50 hours, far surpassing the reconnaissance abilities of a surface vessel.[48]

Zeppelins at War

Years before the First World War the German military recognised the potential of the airship. The first Zeppelin had been accepted by the German army in March 1909, six years after the first controlled, powered and sustained heavier-than-air flight by the American brothers Orville and Wilbur Wright at Kitty Hawk, North Carolina, in America.[49] On 28 June 1914 the assassination of

Archduke Franz Ferdinand of Austria, the heir to the throne of Austria-Hungary, was the immediate catalyst for the First World War. By August 1914 the German army had eight airships, and four requisitioned civilian airships;[50] 23 Zeppelins had been built and flown, plus another two craft from Schutte-Lanz. With the coming of conflict, Germany would concentrate on building big, long-range rigid airships to be deployed as bombers; the British, less knowledgeable about airships, chose to construct smaller, less ambitious non-rigids, used largely as reconnaissance craft over home waters.[51]

A flurry of telegrams on 6 and 7 November 1914 indicated the seriousness with which Winston Churchill, then First Lord of the Admiralty, took the threat of Zeppelin bombing. He won the agreement of General Joseph Joffre, the French Chief of Staff,[52] for British aeroplanes to fly from French territory on 21 November 1914 to bomb the Zeppelin production factory in Friedrickshafen. Two days later Churchill informed the House of Commons that Royal Naval Air Service aeroplanes had bombed the factory in 'a fine feat of arms'.[53] But the raid, however daring, had failed to cripple the Friedrickshaven works. Zeppelin raiders subsequently bombed London, Edinburgh and the Tyne in 1915 and 1916. The attacks caused alarm, loss of life and significant disruption.[54] 'People were terrified of Zeppelins. They were the H-bomb of the day.'[55] Civilians only knew of the presence of a Zeppelin when, without warning, its bombs exploded – with its engines cut, the Zeppelin could drift above the clouds in silent, unseen menace.

German lightweight Zeppelin 'height-climbers' were able to reach 22,000 feet, immune from British Sopwith Camel fighters, which could attain only 18,000 feet. The absence of high-flying fighters left Britain vulnerable. Novel suggestions were advanced to protect the country, especially London, from incursion by Zeppelin bombers. They included a notion by Admiral Robert Stewart Phipps Hornby, who hailed from a distinguished naval family, for an ambitious anti-Zeppelin curtain laced with grenades and suspended by fishing wire from small dirigibles, types of barrage balloons, which would float above the capital.[56] For hapless citizens below it might have been safer to let the Zeppelins do their worst.

A poster issued in Britain as the threat of German aerial attack became apparent.

Bombing runs for the Zeppelins meant a return journey of several hundred miles, often at night, sailing over the North Sea from moorings in Belgium or Kiel.[57] Such feats demanded high levels of competency, endurance and courage. Airships were difficult to manoeuvre, especially if heavily loaded with bombs. Navigation aids were primitive, officers and crews numb with cold in open gondolas.[58] Airship-bomber navigation was helped by developments in wireless, which made it possible to achieve a radio fix giving the precise location of an airship, but airship commanders were wary about breaking radio silence and compromising their principal advantage, that of stealth. Despite their scale, which made them beguiling targets for ground and air gunners, airships could still float softly away unseen and undetected. The ancient nautical art of dead-reckoning came into play: logging the speed at which an airship had sailed, for how long and in which direction; wind, though, could blow a craft miles off course, making a mockery of its supposed position. Their stealth and range, sailing at altitudes beyond the reach of fighters and taking full advantage of cloud cover, were tactics that helped to safeguard the Zeppelin. But height and cloud cover made their bombing campaigns woefully inaccurate. A tiny chariot, or cloud-car, was sometimes suspended by a slender cable wound 3,000 feet down into the sky below the belly of a ship. The cable doubled as a telephone link that allowed an observer in the midget gondola to talk to his ship – hidden far above him safe behind the clouds – and to direct the bombing. A Zeppelin pilot wrote that his observer was 'lowered half a mile below the ship and we ascended into the clouds ... he said he felt lonely down there; as he saw the big ship disappear from sight it seemed as if he were a disembodied spirit floating about in space ...'[59]

Airships utilised as bombers personified their naval heritage:

'They were more like warships than aeroplanes. The commander strode about his control cabin with binoculars around his neck while a coxswain steered the ship with a nautical-style wheel. Another coxswain monitored altitude and gas pressure. The engines were tended in flight by mechanics ... and a sailmaker checked for damage to the outer fabric ... the commander and his officers were constantly engaged in complex calculations about the airship's altitude. A variety of factors made the craft rise or fall ... when it rained, the water on the vast cover ... would increase its weight, making it lose height. Constant fine tuning of the ballast and gas pressure was needed to maintain a steady flight.'[60]

More powerful guns and high-flying fighters firing newly-developed incendiary bullets put paid to the Zeppelin threat. With hindsight it was imprudent to cast the airship as a bomber. Though raids brought death and destruction – in September 1915 a raid on London by the Zeppelin *L13* killed 22 people and injured 87 – in the terrible order of such things casualties caused were relatively light and merely helped stiffen resolve.[61]

Airships deployed as raiders were grossly impaired. Their flammability, scale, lack of agility and insufficient speed made them extraordinarily vulnerable. An aeroplane that managed to fly above an airship could drop bombs on its envelope, causing a conflagration from which few airship crew could escape. Being prey, also, to uncertain technology and the vicissitudes of weather meant forced landings became commonplace. Fog and wind were cursed by commanders who regularly lost London, let alone smaller targets.[62] Bad weather prevented the Zeppelin fleet from participating in the costly, but inconclusive, Battle of Jutland in 1916. Two months later Admiral Reinhard Scheer, Commander of the High Seas Fleet, included eight Zeppelins in his plan to attack the city of Sunderland on Britain's north-east seaboard: four scouted the North Sea looking for the Grand Fleet south from Scapa Flow, while the remainder reconnoitred waters off the Dutch and English east coasts.[63]

By 1917 the Germans had switched from using Zeppelins as bombers to Gotha aeroplanes which proved more deadly. Partly as a consequence of two Gotha raids on London in June and July of 1917, an elite Royal Flying Corps Sopwith Pup fighter squadron was recalled from the Western Front to stiffen Britain's home defences. Its presence was two-fold: to act as protector and to bolster civilian morale damaged by the Zeppelin terror and the enhanced effectiveness of the Gotha attacks.

Four airships took part in the final Zeppelin raid on Britain on 5 August 1918, in which Peter Strasser, the leader of the German Naval Division Zeppelin Command, was killed.[64] Strasser was shot down by Captain Robert Leckie, the gunner in a de Havilland DH4 fighter from Great Yarmouth air station. It was piloted by Major Egbert Cadbury of the chocolate dynasty.[65] The contest had been a duel of opposites. Cadbury was a dashing young officer, of a class decimated in the First World War; Strasser was intense, brooding, unswerving in his conviction that the Zeppelin would force Britain into submission. The collapse of the Zeppelin attack, and the death of Strasser, Germany's principal airship warrior, saw an end to German military airship exploits. Every commander needs good fortune. But Strasser's career had been dogged by ill luck. Among his crew he had the reputation of a Jonah. He had tried to persuade Scheer to pit his latest *L70* Zeppelins against London and New York. The *L70*s were formidable: almost 700 feet long, multi-engined with the ability to cross and re-cross the Atlantic. Each could carry a 4,000-kilogramme bomb load. Scheer rejected the plan; a fortnight later Strasser died in the final, futile Zeppelin raid on Britain.[66] During four years of war Zeppelins made 51 raids on Britain. They dropped 196 tons of bombs, killing 557 people and injuring another 1,358.[67] The toll on German airship crews was heavy; if a ship caught fire few would survive. Ships had sizeable crews and were heavily armed with machine-guns. Strasser's *L70*, in which he died, commanded by Kapitan-leutnant Johann von Lossnitzer, ended 'ablaze from stem to stern, its red-hot remains plunging into the North Sea'.[68]

At the conclusion of the First World War, Zeppelin crews, as with the German surface fleet at Scapa Flow, scuttled their airships; an inglorious conclusion to a bold, if injudicious campaign. It was unfortunate that the formative years of airship development coincided with conflict. War brought urgency to production and hastened airship refinement. But conflict would forever define the airship as a tool of the military, its capability judged as an instrument of war. The virtue of the airship as a giant transporter of passengers or cargo over great distances, an ability far ahead of anything offered by aeroplanes of the time, would remain largely untested for many years. Already, too, the airship was being seen as a competitor of the aeroplane; rivalry between contraptions which were heavier-than-air, and those such as the airship which were lighter, would damage the concept of the airship in the longer term. While conflict doubtless quickens innovation, an ability to soar to great heights in machines constructed to an astonishingly light and fragile template was a somewhat esoteric virtue and of minor merit in a post-war period in which the pursuit of safety and durability were paramount. If as much effort had been put into those considerations, as had been invested in utilising the airship as a raider, it might have had a more secure future. Sadly, such research would remain marginal while the airship was in the proprietorship of the military.

2

THE BRITISH AIRSHIP STATIONS

In the years that led up to the First World War, Kaiser Wilhelm II had taken Germany on a thunderous and bankrupting ride which could only result in an inevitable finale. The rapid completion of the Kiel Canal, ahead of schedule, which allowed the speeding up of maritime traffic between the Baltic and the North Sea, had been watched with foreboding by the British Admiralty. The Kaiser had embarked on a massive and costly expansion of his navy, appointing Admiral Alfred von Tirpitz as its chief and principal architect. Tirpitz had become a late believer in the submarine, having, like most surface commanders, been tardy and suspicious in his initial response to its evolution. The British Admiralty, recognising the menace of the growing German submarine fleet, and slowly beginning to appreciate the efficacy of using dirigibles to identify their presence, began building airship bases at strategic locations,* the first being constructed at Capel near Dover. By the summer of 1915 airship sheds were ready at Polegate, near Eastbourne, on Anglesey and at Luce Bay, near Stranraer in Scotland. These sites dominated the western end of the English Channel; allowed the guarding of the narrow channel between Stranraer and Larne in northern Ireland; and between Dublin and Holyhead. To work with the Grand Fleet, and to spot and harry U-boats attacking traffic on Britain's east coast, bases were established at East Fortune

* Twenty-eight British airship stations were established in the First World War, but one contemporary opinion is that there were as many as sixty; the author cannot verify the latter figure but is of the view that the remainder were not stations, but minor sub-stations or mooring-out sites.

near Edinburgh, Longside near Peterhead, Howden in east Yorkshire and Pulham St. Mary in south Norfolk.

Pulham

Pulham airship station in south Norfolk covered more than 500 acres. At its peak towards the end of the First World War it employed 3,000 people; indeed, if all part-time and ancillary workers are included it is feasible that as many as 5,000 were involved. An operation of such scale in a pastoral idyll was not without controversy and obliged the Admiralty to conduct its initial explorations in secrecy. In 1912 local land agents and surveyors, Thomas Gaze & Son, were told to discreetly acquire land in the area. Rumour had it that it was for sporting purposes; it was in the Admiralty's interest to nurture such gossip to allay local alarm. Jeffrey Bowles, former senior partner in the firm, said: 'Admiralty negotiations were with a predecessor, Clement Gaze. He was asked to conduct them in great secrecy. The cover story was that the land would be used to exercise horses.'[1] Land was acquired in Pulham St. Mary and the neighbouring village of Rushall.

By 1915 the Pulham site had been levelled by civilian contractors working with the Air Construction Corps, and the first complement of 100 Royal Navy personnel had moved in. Pulham was ideal: the landscape was relatively flat, almost devoid of trees, under-populated and located several miles inland, which helped in its protection from stray Zeppelin attacks.[2] East coast villages and towns were bombed by Zeppelins, some of which struggled to get home after raids on London in which they had been damaged. To lighten their load, allowing them to climb higher where they could sail in safety, they threw out redundant equipment or dropped any bombs they still had at random targets that lay beneath them on their homeward passage. By mid-1916 German floatplanes operating from occupied Belgium shot down two *Coastal* class airships, the *Pulham Pigs*. Their patrol work was later handed over to aeroplanes.

The Pulham airship shed was of wood. Its doors weighed 90 tons and had to be opened by an obsolete army tank, which was also used to tether airships.

On occasion the tank would be lifted into the air by a wayward ship, an indication of the lift such giants could exert. There are also stories of ground handlers clinging to mooring ropes before being hoist aloft, accidents that could sometimes result in injury and fatality. The size and weight of the shed doors meant they had to be assembled on the ground and raised into place by 200 men hauling on ropes reeved through pulleys at roof level. The shed initially housed four primitive ex-Army airships that had been handed over to the navy, and the first *Coastal* ship, the larger of the two early types to sail from Pulham, arrived in September 1915.[3] Two larger steel-framed sheds were built later for two bigger rigids – the *R23* (which had threatened to carry off the tank) and the *R26*, which arrived in September 1917.

The village of Pulham was transformed by the station's presence. Large numbers of women were employed stitching and repairing the fabric of the envelopes, or acting as messengers, clerks, gardeners and cooks. Several were employed as mechanics and engineers. Building an airship involved a workforce that was formed of 60 per cent women. Some lived in the immediate area, while others had to cycle long distances. Pulham included substantial accommodation: canteen, officers' mess, sick bay, dental clinic, workshops, gas and water plants. The arrival of an airship – perhaps as long as two football pitches – triggered excitement. Lorries drove round sounding klaxons, picking up a small army of 300 to 400 people who would help with the mooring. Docking could be precarious, especially in a capricious wind. Easterly winds in Norfolk can be cold and strong, as the wind sweeps in unhindered from the Russian Steppes. The mooring procedure might entail long hours clinging to ropes and wires for the hundreds of volunteers who comprised the ground handling-crew. Sometimes they had to haul the colossal ships across fields, over ditches and through hedges as they walked the vessels back to their sheds. Volunteers received five shillings for their exertions, a princely sum in an isolated corner of the country where employment was limited and rural poverty commonplace.[4]

In 1917 Edward Maitland was appointed commanding officer. For the previous two years he had been in command of the Kite Balloon Training

Section at Roehampton, Surrey. A devotee of lighter-than-air technology, Maitland was also a pioneer parachutist and instrumental in its development. Pulham station would become the headquarters of the Parachute Experimental Staff, 'who were testing somewhat rudimentary parachutes as a means of escaping from disabled airships and kite balloons. Nobody had yet thought of jumping from a moving aeroplane, it being deemed more practicable to attempt to land a crashing aeroplane, provided it was not on fire, than to launch oneself into space with only a silken umbrella to provide a dubious measure of safety.'[5] The small aircraft of the time had little spare room for parachutes – whereas the gondola of an airship offered a touch more stowage. Nigel Caley, the airship historian, wrote of Maitland: 'An utter legend ... adored by his men throughout the service ... closely involved in all aspects of airship development – including political lobbying. Renowned for jumping out of airships whenever the opportunity presented itself.' There is a story – perhaps apocryphal – of him parachuting out of *R32* over London in full evening dress for a dinner engagement, closely followed by his man. In airships he was the closest the British programme ever came to having a Hugo Eckener.[6*]

Pulham saw experiments with airships as aircraft-carriers. Sopwith Camel fighters, some built by the Boulton & Paul company in the nearby city of Norwich, were attached to a ship's belly prior to their release in mid-flight. Successful launches and retrievals were achieved. The purpose was two-fold: airships with fighters attached were more protected, while fighters limited by range could be launched over distant targets.

The chief experimental officer at Pulham was the legendary George Herbert Scott, pioneer of the mooring mast (see below) and later captain of *R34*, which made the first double crossing of the Atlantic in 1919. An outstanding personality of the airship years, he became the commanding officer at Pulham in 1920. He married the daughter of Archie Campbell, the managing director of Beardmore, the eminent Clydebank marine and later airship and engine builder. The airship historian Nigel Caley knows Scott's

---

* Dr. Eckener was a renowned German airshipman, universally regarded as the greatest airship captain.[7]

virtues: 'Scott ... [was] the most famous airship captain Britain produced ... witty and highly sociable ... a reputation for immense charm and good humour. Approachable to men from all walks of life, extremely modest when it came to his own achievements ... resourceful, unflappable. There were those who disapproved of Scott's lifestyle ... [who] perceived his relaxed nature to be a sign of laziness. Intense dislike of paperwork ... antipathy to pretension ... could deflate pretensions of the pompous with accuracy and irony.'[8]

Such stations as Pulham were important in guarding the Eastern seaboard where German submarines imperilled shipping and threatened to disrupt links with Britain's Belgian and French allies and with the neutral Netherlands and Scandinavia. Pulham's first operational ship, was thought to be a twin-engined *Coastal* with a five-man crew. Less agile than the small *Sea Scouts*, which were successful in locating submarines and mines, these were dubbed *Pulham Pigs* due to their flying characteristics and the yellowish-buff tones of their envelopes. Memorable, if inelegant, the name stuck, though later envelopes were coloured silver after being coated with dope pigmented with an aluminium powder.[9] *Sea Scout* (*SS*) airships were primitive with gas-tight (one hoped) envelopes and the nose stiffened by garden-canes. A small aeroplane fuselage was slung beneath, stripped of its wings, which bore the engine and a crew of three. They were intended as submarine and mine spotters. The *Coastal* class, known as the *Pulham Pigs*, had a fuselage or 'car' comprising two aeroplane fuselages mounted back to back with an engine at either end. They were difficult to sail, being slow and susceptible to wind. Their patrol area ran from Mablethorpe to Holland in the north, and Margate to Dunkirk in the south.

The Mooring Mast

Pulham was home to a pioneering innovation that would vastly enhance the practicality of the airship – the mooring mast, from which ships could more readily dock or embark. Gigantic mooring sheds were expensive, their construction slow and difficult, while the gargantuan amount of steel was costly and scarce, especially in wartime. A mast, pioneered by Scott, was quicker and cheaper to build and inordinately easier to dismantle and move. Large sheds such as those at Cardington, near Bedford, where Short Brothers, the aviation engineering company, had set up an airship subsidiary, were thus freed for construction and repair work.*

German airship commanders had long encountered problems trying to moor or take off from sheds (like surface ships, airships were docked in sheds, not hangars). They had to battle with the uncertainties of weather, of gusting winds and cross-currents. The mast helped ships to dock or to slip their moorings in adverse weather. The British army had experimented with a mast at Farnborough in 1912, but it was not until 1917 that the Admiralty decided that Vickers should build a 120-foot mast with a revolving top. It was originally going to be erected at the Vickers yard in Barrow, then at the Howden airship station, in east Yorkshire. But in May 1918 it was finally decided to construct it at Pulham, where it was erected in March 1919.

The delay from concept to installation typified the procrastination and muddle to which the service had become subject. Discounting political indecision, the delay had been caused by two considerations: the *R24* which had been chosen to experiment with the mast had to be redesigned with the addition of more ballast tanks, its nose stiffened with the addition of a novel coupling-and-winch system installed in its bow. Secondly, Pulham itself was not in a state of readiness: gas and water facilities were still to be installed, with main feeds brought to the masthead, together with electrical and telephone leads.

It was not until 11 July 1919 that *R24* finally moored at the mast. On 31 July she was returned to her shed for inspection and an overhaul. She was moored at the mast on two further occasions. By the end of 1921 the experiments, which also utilised *R33*, came to an abrupt, if temporary halt. But lessons learned from Scott's Pulham mast would be vital in the future, when a giant mast was built at Cardington, Bedfordshire, for a new chapter in the airship programme.[10]

---

* Cardington was later nationalised as the Royal Airship Works, but the community situated close to it is still known as Shortstown.

CIVIL AVIATION AIRSHIP STATION, PULHAM

Visit of Members of Parliament

JUNE 17th, 1921

Civil Airship G-F A A F (R 36) *at Experimental Mooring Mast, Pulham*

PROGRAMME

Leave Liverpool Street	9.50 a.m.
Arrive Diss (approx.)	12.17 p.m.
Cold Buffet	1.0 p.m.
Rendezvous at Mast after brief inspection of Station	3.15 p.m.
Ship leaves Mast	4.0 p.m.
Tea served on board	4.45 p.m.
Ship returns Mast	5.30 p.m.
Transport leaves Pulham	6.0 p.m.
Train departs Diss	6.50 p.m.
Train arrives Liverpool St.	9.17 p.m.

POINTS OF INTEREST

(1) German Airships L64 and L71.

(2) R33 (sister ship to R34, which crossed the Atlantic).

(3) Engineers' and Fabric Shops.

(4) Hydrogen Plant and Power House.

(5) Wireless and Meteorological Sections.

(6) Mooring Mast, with R36 anchored.

(7) Flight of R36 from and to the Mast.

The mooring mast at Pulham depicted in a programme for a visit by Members of Parliament to the station in 1921.

R33 and R34 at Pulham

These two celebrated airships, which first flew in 1919, are forever associated with Pulham. When the *R33* was being built, the Admiralty had benefited from a piece of good fortune. In September 1916 a German Navy Zeppelin, one of the most advanced ships, made a forced landing at Little Wigborough, near Mersea Island, Essex. (Confusingly, but coincidentally, it had been designated *L33*.) Though the crew of the Zeppelin tried to scuttle her – and managed to ignite her cover – the ship was seized by the British, who found to their glee that it was still in reasonable repair. For twenty weeks they poured over their prize, copying each feature, making detailed drawings, learning the secrets of German design. Consequently, *R33* and *R34* were modified to incorporate the newest German attributes. Tellingly, they were the first really successful British rigids – 'cloning' had paid off. The *R33* was built by Armstrong-Whitworth at Barlow, in north Yorkshire, while the *R34* was a Beardmore ship constructed at Inchinnan, Renfrewshire, Scotland.

While the *R34* would achieve international recognition (see page 71), its sister craft, the *R33*, may be described as the most fortunate, winning fame through a hair-raising excursion that caught the imagination of the nation. On a storm-tossed night in April 1925 it was torn from its mooring mast with only a skeleton crew aboard. With her nose in partial collapse and the first gasbag deflated, the crippled ship rode perilously low at the bow, wind and rain gusting in through the front section, skewing her angle of tilt towards the ground. The crew contrived to start the engines, allowing them to gain a little more height, and miraculously they managed to rig makeshift patching at the bow. Then the gale swept the vessel backwards out across the North Sea. In case the airship was forced into the water, a Royal Navy ship was despatched from Lowestoft, but the sea was so rough that it had to turn back. After five hours the crew of *R33* achieved a modicum of control, and she hovered until almost dawn before managing to limp home, crossing the Suffolk coast eight hours later and reaching Pulham at 13.50 hours. King George V honoured the crew with commemorative watches. The coxswain, Sergeant 'Sky' Hunt, received the Air Force Medal, which he insisted should be awarded to the crew as a whole.[11]

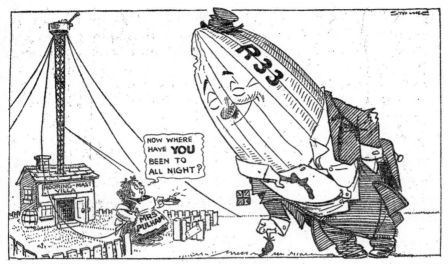

"BOYS WILL BE BOYS."

A cartoon that appeared following *R33*'s misadventures over the North Sea.

After the demise of airships the RAF used Pulham station during the Second World War to store explosives, petrol and detonators, and a unit there repaired ammunition containers and boxes. It was not until February 1958 that No. 53 Maintenance Unit was disbanded and the station closed as an RAF establishment. In 1962 the land was auctioned.[12] It was bought by Peter West of Church Farm, in the village of Brome, close to the station. His nephew lives in a house once occupied by George Herbert Scott and his wife. Mr. West said: 'We buried the six feet square concrete cubes used to tether the airships. Some were nine feet, used for the bigger ships. They said the land had been cleared of mines. But we still managed to blow a cultivator to pieces.'[13]

Howden

Howden in east Yorkshire would change as radically as Pulham when the Admiralty built an airship station three miles north of the town situated between the villages of Spaldington and Bubwith. By the end of September 1915 the Admiralty had purchased a thousand acres of farmland and had begun to construct a self-contained town. In employment terms it had a beneficial effect on Howden, famous in previous centuries for its Minster and horse-fair. Since its hey-day, its prosperity had diminished, mirroring the rundown of the nearby port of Goole. Townsfolk now found lucrative work at the station; those employed in its construction brought a fresh level of prosperity to Howden's hard-pressed tradespeople and its competing hostelries.

The station included a parade square, which subsequently doubled in size; it was termed, with naval correctness, the quarterdeck. Roads and a railway line were installed. Most airship personnel were accommodated in wooden huts, with officers housed in primitive brick-built bungalows. There was a cookhouse, garage, petrol station, chapel, YMCA, a meteorological hut, wireless hut and a pigeon loft – carrier pigeons on airships were used if the wireless broke down or if a ship had to ditch.

The site was dominated by three airship sheds: a large one for rigids and two smaller ones for non-rigids. There was a hydrogen plant, detonator and magazine stores, a fuel dump, workshops, compressor house, six gas-holders, a carpenters' shop and a blacksmiths' forge. Airships needed vast quantities of water for ballast, and water was also used to make hydrogen, which came under the auspices of the Admiralty Hydrogen Section. Opened in 1917, Howden hydrogen plant could produce 7,000 cubic feet of gas per hour. Three water wells were sunk and a pumping station and two water towers installed. Large concrete ducts carried hydrogen and water directly to the sheds.[14]

Howden's principal role was as an anti-submarine and training base between 1916 and 1920,[15] and it almost doubled in size in 1917 to cope with the new big rigid airships developed later. By 1919 it had the largest airship shed in the world. Of corrugated iron on a steel frame, it measured 750 feet with a clearance height of 130 feet at the doors. It was built by the Cleveland Bridge & Engineering company of Darlington for £232,662 and was big enough to house six Howden Minsters, the town's renowned twelfth-century church. Sub-Lieutenant Ralph Booth piloted the first airship flight into Howden in 1916 and the last out, in 1929, flying the Barnes Wallis-built *R100* on its maiden flight.

3
CONTROL, COMMERCIAL OPPORTUNITY AND CONTROVERSY

The reorganisation of the armed forces exacerbated rivalries between the services and did little to foster the advancement of the airship in Britain. 'The annals of the Royal Naval Air Service (or Fleet Air Arm) are in large measure a story of continuous controversy.'[1]

In 1910 the Admiralty had established its own Air Department, the primary task of which was to build airships. However, aeroplane development was also making great strides, and in 1911 the role of the Department was widened. As well as being responsible for lighter-than-air development, it would also cover fixed-wing creations, machines that were heavier-than-air. In 1912 its role was enhanced still further. With the Directorate of Military Aeronautics, which had been formed as a division within the War Office, the Admiralty was given joint responsibility for the Royal Flying Corps. To add to the confusion, the RFC had been split into two, providing a naval and a military wing.

A row erupted in 1912, when airship production had been brought to a close after the *Mayfly* fiasco, between Churchill, the First Lord of the Admiralty, and Admiral Sir Arthur Wilson, First Sea Lord between January 1910 and December 1911. Wilson questioned the merits of airships and their naval usefulness; Churchill and Sueter, convinced of their importance, pressed for development to resume.[2] Central to Wilson's assertions was his belief that heavier-than-air development had a greater future. The row led to little except an exacerbation of ill-feeling about the airship. It was one of many unhelpful altercations about the merits of heavier over lighter-than-air and served as an example of the way the services argued over the airships future, purpose and proprietorship.

Change inevitably brought criticism, some aimed at Churchill as the First Lord. Field Marshal Lord Roberts objected to the transfer of airships from the Royal Flying Corps to the Navy, asserting that it would lead to a loss of aviation training and experience in peacetime.[3] He argued that it was 'a retrograde step ... wholly illogical' to merge them into one service. The Navy looked after operations over the sea, the Army over those on land. The military wing of the RFC had an esprit de corps; change, he said, would be 'profoundly discouraging'. But Churchill would not be dissuaded, telling him that the transference of army airships was practically complete. Any problems would be compensated for by 'the avoidance of duplication of organisation and experimental work which the new arrangements will secure'.[4] So, on 1 July 1914, a month before the First World War began, the naval wing was hived off from the Royal Flying Corps. It was renamed the 'Royal Naval Air Service', and its control passed to the Admiralty's Air Department. When war began the RNAS, in cooperation with the Navy, was responsible for bombing naval targets at sea and in port and for the air defence of Britain. But it was a recipe for rivalry between the RFC and the RNAS.

Two committees were established to achieve cohesion between the two competing services and to coordinate supply of aeroplanes, parts and personnel. The first, the Joint War Committee, was set up in 1916. But it lacked teeth and was replaced by the Air Board, which also lacked executive control and was scrapped. A second Air Board in 1917, however, was given executive power for the design and allocation of aeroplanes to the two services. Simultaneously, the Ministry of Munitions was given charge of supplying and inspecting aeroplanes, seaplanes, engines and equipment. On 3 January 1918 control of the RNAS passed to the Air Ministry. On 1 April 1918 the RNAS was merged with the Royal Flying Corps to become the Royal Air Force.

In 1912, when the Royal Flying Corps was established, airships came under the military wing of the Army. In 1914, however, the RFC's No. 1 Airship Squadron passed into the control of the Navy as part of the RNAS. It comprised, at that time, a single airship station at Kingsnorth, on the Medway, with seven small, non-rigid airships, and a complement of 195 personnel. The RFC's future role, for its part, would be to concentrate on aeroplanes, with spherical and kite balloons being used for observation purposes.

In 1915 Victor Goddard, a distinguished aviator and later an Air Marshal, was at the outset of his career as a junior midshipman on the battleship *Britannia* attached to the Third Battle Squadron stationed at Rosyth, Scotland. Goddard recalled leaving his ship at seven bells carrying sealed orders. He had been summoned by the captain of *Britannia* who was in receipt of a letter from Admiral Jellicoe, commander-in-chief of the Grand Fleet. Jellicoe had ordered his Fleet captains to recommend junior officers, midshipmen or subalterns for 'special, temporary service of a secret and hazardous nature.' Unbeknown to Goddard, it was an invitation to join the embryonic airship service that he carried. Goddard and other midshipmen spent a month at Roehampton learning about ballooning and a further month at Kingsnorth being tutored in the art of airships. Goddard said of his first balloon trips: 'I had volunteered for the submarine service. We weren't really great as airmen but we were very hot sailors. I think that could have been one of the chief disadvantages of having Naval officers as aircrew. Otherwise, nobody complained really; we remained Naval officers and took what was coming.'[5]

The Royal Air Force

The Prime Minister, Lloyd George, asked Lieutenant General Sir David Henderson, Director General of Military Aeronautics, and Lieutenant General Jan Smuts[6] to review defences and air policy. Henderson said all aeroplanes, including airships and seaplanes, should be under a unified body; Smuts said the RFC and the RNAS should merge, and that an Air Ministry should be set up with its own Air Minister. Lloyd George's government supported the proposals, and this led to the formation of the Royal Air Force. Major General Sir Hugh Trenchard[7] returned from France as first Chief of Air Staff, and Major General Sir Sefton Brancker became Controller General of Equipment.[8] Though it had been agreed that the RAF would be responsible for all flying and aircraft – civil, military and airships – it still took over a year before the Airship Section of the former RNAS passed from the Admiralty to RAF control.

This was an intensely difficult period for the services, one marked by deep rivalries and dissension. The first Secretary of State for the Air Force was Lord Rothermere,[9] appointed on 3 January 1918. Relations between Rothermere and Trenchard swiftly deteriorated, and both subsequently resigned. Trenchard, the 'Father of the RAF', was to return, becoming Chief of Air Staff from 1919 to 1929.[10]

At last, on 5 May 1919, 6,000 airshipmen were transferred to the Air Ministry, although the 103 airships remained under the control of the Admiralty until 22 October 1919. It was a time of confusion. Airships were built for the Great War which was now at an end. Nobody knew what to do with them. The Admiralty had lost airship personnel to the air force and was determined to hang on to the hardware as long as possible. One suspects, but there is no real historical evidence of this, that the Admiralty were trying to come up with arguments to retain control of the airship service. By this time most men had been demobilised and their ships decommissioned. These were dark days for military airships. Their suitability as reconnaissance and escort vessels had been proven, but scepticism remained in the Admiralty, and they were regarded as less important than aeroplanes by their new masters in the RAF. In the saga of the airship, factors had begun to emerge that would be corrosive to its future: a childish rivalry between the Admiralty and the infant air force, continual sniping from the Army, political meddling and a frustrating degree of vacillation. The airship was a mongrel, a cross-breed, neither fish nor fowl but a sad hybrid. It was not of the sea but of the air; it sailed without water and flew without wings. The airship service comprised members of all three services who bore the loyalties, baggage and prejudice of previous commands. Few were pure-bred airshipmen. And the cross-over of military ranks led to confusion. The airship service comprised people who had held different ranks in the army and navy and fledgling airforce. It was a hybrid in ships and personnel. Who did what? Who answered to whom? A lack of clarity applied in every area, construction, crewing and deployment. According to airship historian Dr. Giles Campion,

> The British airship community ... was plagued from the start by indecision and inconsistency. This confusion in both planning and action continued through the First World War and became almost endemic throughout the chain of command at every level ... this deep-seated lack of trust, and the failure to delegate authority, may have been caused by insecurity that stemmed from a lack of knowledge. It was certainly in total contrast to the confident system practised by the far more knowledgeable and experienced Germans.[11]

Much of the subsequent squabbling over control and proprietorship involved parties who were ill-informed about airships, their purpose and capabilities. Some thought they were merely aerial gasbags. In reality, they were complex behemoths, which could be fickle and sometimes perilous. (See page 13.)

German Passenger Airships

While the military bickered about airships, their utility and money-making possibilities were being convincingly exploited by civilian practitioners. In 1909 DELAG, a commercial airship company, (Deutsche Luftschiffahrts-Aktien Gesellschaft, German Airship Travel Corporation) was set up as a subsidiary of the Zeppelin company. It established an impressive network of internal routes in Germany that demonstrated the feasibility of a passenger-carrying service. In ensuing years the safety record of DELAG, its technical prowess, the design of its ships and the reliability and commercial success of its service would be cited by enthusiasts in Britain and elsewhere as an example of what might be achieved. In a series of 1,600 summer-season Zeppelin pleasure flights before the First World War, the company carried without incident more than 34,000 passengers. It made more flights after the war, but the service was subsequently closed down by the Inter-Allied Commission of Control at the end of the First World War.

The years of conflict added to the pool of knowledge in the Zeppelin company, ensuring it retained its place as the world's foremost airship designer.[12] Count Zeppelin died in 1917, and thereafter the Zeppelin company was run by his protégé, Dr. Hugo Eckener, designer, pilot and businessman. The success of the Zeppelin company attracted worldwide attention and the achievements of DELAG, with Eckener its managing director, were acknowledged by other commercial operators who recognised an opportunity to make money. Set up as a limited stock company with a capital of three million Marks, DELAG had two aims: to provide a regular airship service on key German routes and to ensure a stream of construction orders for Zeppelin. The task of designing and building engines for airships went to Karl Maybach, the son of Daimler's chief engineer, Wilhelm Maybach, who had supplied Zeppelin with its earliest engines.[13]

In November 1917 there occurred a feat that further encouraged commercial interest: the German army used the Imperial German Navy Zeppelin *L59*, piloted by its designer, the skilful Eckener, on an extensive and tropical voyage.[14] It sailed non-stop for 95 hours, covering 4,230 miles from Bulgaria to the Sudan. The voyage proved that an airship could sail on long routes over tropical terrain – there had been alarming prophecies that in extreme climates envelopes would shrink in the sun, gas would expand, lift would be diminished, and petrol engines would explode. Even so, though much had been learned about the alchemy of the airship, much remained unknown.

Airship terminology evolved with a distinctly maritime quality. It became the convention that airships 'sailed on voyages' or 'made passages'; passengers had tickets to 'sail', to 'take a cruise', to 'go cruising'. They embarked from 'port'. Why they 'sailed' is to be found in their mongrelised heritage: they were, for a time, of the navy, with naval crews that included coxswain, boatswain and sailmakers to stitch torn envelopes or sew ruptured gas bags. Airships had hulls, keels, a ship's wheel and rudders. They did not 'land', they 'moored'; they docked not in 'hangars', but in 'sheds'. If an airship was wide amidships it was 'beamy,' as with the midships of a boat. Engines were mounted 'port' and 'starboard', passengers enjoying panoramic views through 'port holes' in 'saloons', or rested on bunks in 'cabins'. Engines and controls were in gondolas fore and aft. Sailors strode 'decks', slept in hammocks or bunks, conducted their duties in 'bow' and 'stern', visited the skipper on the 'bridge', and, if nature called while floating through the skies, they visited the 'heads'.

British Passenger Airships

In Britain, between 1909 and 1928, at least 14 companies registered themselves with the Board of Trade as airship construction or passenger businesses.[15] There was a rush to form companies just before the First World War. Encouraged by the activities of DELAG, perhaps they also felt that if airships were deployed in war it would be a profitable business in which to be immersed.

One such was the White Star Airship Construction Company, registered on 1 October 1913. Although there is no evidence that it ever actually traded (or that it had any connection to the White Star Shipping Line), it provides a good example of the thinking behind the people who started such companies.[16] It had a nominal capital of £1,000 divided into shares of one pound each and was registered through its solicitors, Braby & Waller, with offices in the Strand, London. There being speculation at the end of the war that money could be made by starting a service to the Dominions, the principals of White Star, two Frenchmen from Paris, (one described as an *aeronaute constructeur*) selected their lawyers with careful prescience, for Braby & Waller had offices in Canada, Australia and India. The Parisians, however, dissolved their business three years after its formation, on October 24 1916, a decision too premature to take advantage of any Imperial traffic.

The different Memoranda of Association for these airship companies show the drafting of the shell businesses to be wide-ranging, framed so that companies could exploit opportunities as they revealed themselves. Under its Memorandum, White Star, for example, could acquire patents on new devices, sell its inventions to any government, build airships, operate passenger or mail services, construct buildings, lay roads, uproot forests, and cart drums of hydrogen across Britain. It could also raise cattle for goldbeaters' skin, made from the intestine of young oxen. Skins were sewn together to make gasbags; airtight, they weighed little and were thin enough to stitch easily. There were, though, serious drawbacks: skins were about 18 inches square; hundreds had to be stitched to make one big gas bag, of which there were a multiplicity in large ships. And after a time goldbeaters' skin became dry and brittle, making it vulnerable to cracks and leaks.[17]

More powerful groups emerged at the end of the war, however, and on 6 April 1919 the representatives of senior British companies met officers of the new Air Ministry to examine the feasibility of an international mail and passenger service. Those at the meeting included Brigadier General Edward Maitland, Director of Airships at the Air Ministry and previously in charge of the RFC's Balloon Command. The Admiralty was represented by the Third Sea Lord, Rear Admiral C. M. de Bartolome, while others present included Sir William Beardmore of the ship and airship construction company that bore his name, Sir Alfred Booth of Cunard and Sir Percy Girovard of Armstrong Whitworth, the defence contractor that built airships.

Girovard said the Air Ministry should order two new big rigid airships, one to be built by his company, the other by Beardmore. They would be used on a new service to America and India. Girovard postulated that the growth of the Empire had outpaced conventional communication. The airship was the only way of covering long distances in a sensible time. Other countries were building airships, so Britain needed to catch up. He would visit the United States to ensure, as he said, that 'the Americans fall into line'. Bringing the Dominions closer to the mother country would be good politically and for business. The industry could help unemployment. Cunard were the best people to manage the service. There remained only one stumbling block – money. The service would need to be 'spoon-fed' with government subsidies, which could be reviewed once the service was established. By then five ships would be needed. The government would have to release its only two rigids, R33 and R34. These could be converted from military to civilian ships by his

Above left: In 1852 Frenchman Henri Giffard sailed the first powered aircraft in the history of flight: he covered 17 miles in a non-rigid airship with a 3-horsepower steam engine and an 11-foot propeller. (Library of Congress)

Above: The father of the rigid airship, the ebullient former cavalry officer Count Ferdinand von Zeppelin. His company survived calamities and financial setbacks in the early days. (Cody Images)

Left: In 1883, the French Tissandier brothers were the first to power a dirigible by electricity. Albert Tissandier (left), Gaston Tissandier (right) and an unidentified man in the basket demonstrate an electric navigational system featuring a propeller. (Library of Congress)

Top: One of the airships built by Ernest Willows, the first person in Britain to be awarded an airship pilot's certificate from the Royal Aero Club. He is regarded by some as the true originator of the British non-rigid airship.

Above: The British Admiralty's ill-fated first attempt at building a rigid airship, *Mayfly*.

Below far right: Drawn by artist Frank Brangwyn (1867–1956) for *The Daily Chronicle* in 1915, this 'vow of vengeance' claimed '*Daily Chronicle* readers are covered against the risks of bombardment by zeppelin or aeroplane'. To have bombs dropped on its populace was an entirely new experience for Great Britain. (Library of Congress)

Near right: Zeppelin bombers were depicted as monsters killing families and slaughtering babies. (Library of Congress)

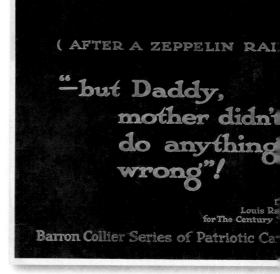

(AFTER A ZEPPELIN RAI

"—but Daddy, mother didn't do anything wrong"!

Louis Ra
for The Century

Barron Collier Series of Patriotic Ca

Left: A wonder of the age. When Count Zeppelin's airships first sailed their scale and lightness caused astonishment. This is believed to be *Zeppelin No. 3*. (Library of Congress)

THE ZEPPELIN RAIDS : THE VOW OF VENGEANCE
Drawn for 'The Daily Chronicle' by Frank Brangwyn ARA

'DAILY CHRONICLE' READERS ARE COVERED AGAINST THE RISKS OF BOMBARDMENT BY ZEPPELIN OR AEROPLANE

Above: The Royal Naval Air Service used North Sea class airships as submarine spotters and convoy escorts. The first was built in 1917. They had two Rolls-Royce engines, could reach 60 knots and stay aloft for 24 hours. Armed with five machine-guns and six small bombs, they carried a 'double-crew' of 10. (Library of Congress)

Left: A First World War recruiting poster believed to feature William Leefe Robinson, who shot down a a predator Zeppelin and was awarded Britain's highest military honour, the Victoria Cross. (Library of Congress)

Above: The Magellan of the Skies, Dr. Hugo Eckener, Count Zeppelin's protégé. A former journalist, he was polished, sophisticated and charismatic, the most gifted sky sailor of the era, who voyaged round the globe by airship. (Library of Congress)

Left: The popular George Herbert Scott was an intrepid British airship pilot. A famous celebrity, he invented the mooring mast, which transformed airship utility. (Library of Congress)

Above and below: One of the world's most capable and elegant rigid airships, the Barnes Wallis and H. B. Pratt designed *R80*. She was built by Vickers at Barrow, on England's northwest coast. Launched on 19 July 1920, she was shapely and streamlined. Some American airshipmen who trained on her died in the *R38* disaster over Hull in 1921.

The stern of a Zeppelin. From bow, stern or side, airships were leviathans of the heavens. (Library of Congress)

R34, which made t[he]
first return crossing
the Atlantic in 191[9]
proving that sizeab[le]
numbers of
passengers could b[e]
carried over great
distances in comfor[t]
and safety.

Building and
operating an airshi[p]
was labour-intensiv[e]
The tool shop at
Pulham was a hive [of]
industry, large
numbers of women [as]
well as men being
employed. Moorin[g a]
ship could entail 40[0]
people.

Giant airships carri[ed]
thousands of gallon[s]
of fuel and millions
of cubic feet of
hydrogen. *R100* ha[d]
petrol engines, but
the *R101* used diese[l]
engines, which wer[e]
so heavy that the sh[ip]
needed a new gas b[ay]
inserted to increase
capacity and lift.

company and by Beardmore. He envisaged his company and Beardmore each eventually building three airships a year.

Perhaps, he suggested, since the war had proved so costly, and with money in the country being so tight, an accommodation might be reached that would be of satisfaction to both the representatives of private enterprise and to the government. The Navy wanted new light cruisers for reconnaissance but could not afford them; so would it not be judicious to develop commercial airships, backed by subsidies, and give the Admiralty first call on them in the event of a military crisis? It would cost the government only half a million pounds plus £100,000 for contingencies and insurance. He made it sound something of a bargain.

Maitland, always enthusiastic in advancing the cause of the airship, took up Girovard's theme: 'In other words,' said Maitland, 'for some £600,000 the government in case of war would have a call on a fleet of five airships, airship stations, crews, personnel and all the equipment for operating the ships.'[18] However, not everybody was as convinced. De Bartolome said the R33 and R34 had been built in the war to a light specification designed to sail to great altitudes and match the Zeppelin 'height-climbers'. It would be as ambitious and costly to convert them into passenger vessels – as it would to turn passenger vessels into fighting craft. Booth of Cunard disagreed: an experienced shipbuilder could easily handle the conversions, he thought.

Beardmore and Girovard thought the new invention of aerograms, which were lighter than conventional letters, made an airship postal service more practical.

As with numerous airship meetings over the coming years, the discussion ended as 'hot air'. The need for government subsidies, in one guise or another, was to become a familiar refrain. Girovard's financial calculations were optimistic: the cost of just the R34, albeit to a specialist naval specification, was in excess of £350,000.[19]

A plethora of airship passenger schemes were mooted at the conclusion of the war. Major General Seely, Under Secretary of State for Air, received a letter from a Major Holden, another contender. Writing from his office in

Throgmorton Street, in the City of London, Holden informed Seely about his company, Anglo-American Airships. Under Holden's plan for a long-distance service, his company would be capitalised to the tune of £6 million, divided into three million 6 per cent preference shares of £1 each, and three million £1 ordinary shares.[20] The service would carry five tons of mail each way at 1/6d an ounce, yielding £1,403,760 a year. Operating costs would be £591,000, covering 24 pilots at £750 each a year, and 1,500 men at between £125,000 and £150,000. Holden calculated he could make £312,760 net profit. It was unclear how the government would contribute, or what form its reimbursement might take.[21]

R80

In October 1919 Vickers, the defence and airship company, examined the idea of its *R80* being used on a London–Paris–Rome passenger service.

Construction of the *R80* had been commissioned by the Navy in 1917 as a reconnaissance airship. Vickers had only their Walney Island shed, at Barrow-in-Furness, where it had built Britain's first rigid, *No. 9*, and where *R27* and *R29* were built. But design had moved on, ships were now bigger and more ambitious, and Vickers would need to build a new shed for the larger airship required. However, in late 1916 and early 1917, while Armstrongs, Shorts and Beardmore received allocations of steel – which was in short supply – to construct large sheds, Vickers were refused steel, no explanation being given.*

The stellar aeronautical engineer Barnes Wallis, famous later for his bombers and bouncing bomb during the Second World War, was the designer

---

* This created a deep bitterness in the company, which felt, with some justification, that it had given good service to the government and was now being snubbed by it.[22] Vickers, not wishing to lose the contract, though still smarting from what it interpreted as government neglect, suggested it build a smaller ship to fit its only shed. The Admiralty agreed. The result, *R80*, though constrained in size, was a triumph. Steel was in short supply, and it has been suggested that Vickers felt snubbed and that other companies were being favoured. This is speculation, and there is little in the way of real documentary proof. A feeling persisted for years on the part of government that Vickers was too strong. With Armstrong-Whitworth, another engineering company, producing cars, ships, airships and aeroplanes, it wanted to break the duopoly. Politicians were keen to encourage alternative defence suppliers. This ambition had resulted in the establishment in 1905 of Coventry Ordnance Works

of the *R80*. He had recognised that the pencil-contour of previous rigid airships was inefficient. The frame, too, was configured differently, giving it a unique 21-sided appearance. Commenced in November 1917 to a design by Wallis and H. B. Pratt, the building of the *R80* was hampered by labour shortages and subject to changes of specification by the Admiralty and the Air Ministry, who bickered continually about what would be her eventual role. In the summer of 1919 building stopped; the Air Ministry had concluded that the ship had neither a military nor a commercial future.

R80 made her test sailing in July 1920. Vickers had fitted her out for commercial sailing, an ambition envisaged by Pratt, who planned a regular service to Rome, carrying passengers and mail. Vickers estimated it would take the *R80* 16 hours to sail 970 miles to Rome, sailing at a maximum height of 2,000 feet. Alternatively, she could moor in Paris, Lyon, Marseilles, Toulon or Nice. She would sail at 60 mph with 30 passengers and mail. Three mooring docks of 30 acres each would be required, each dock needing a 120-foot-high mooring mast. Vickers' patent rotating mooring gear would be used, a refined version of that pioneered by George Herbert Scott; ships rotated moored head-to-wind, 'locked-in-irons' as sailors would say, free of wind buffeting. The mast needed only six ground crew instead of the several hundred sometimes summoned to help moor the bigger ships.[23]

Passengers would pay £64 for a one-way ticket to Rome. 400 pounds of mail could be carried at 6*d* per ounce. As with any shipping company, the report stressed the importance of maintaining regular sailings if a proper service was to be established. Vickers estimated it would cost £600,000 to set up the service.

(COW) fostered by the government. It comprised a consortium of leading private shipbuilders, who were supposed to give Vickers and Armstrong-Whitworth a run for their money. The managing director of COW from 1910 to 1914 was Reginald Bacon (later an admiral and knighted). Bacon was an erudite protégé of Fisher. In previous roles he had been the first Inspecting Captain of Submarines and later the first commander of Fisher's favourite creation, the revolutionary Dreadnought. Bacon had played an instrumental role in military airships by suggesting to Fisher on 21 July 1908 that a Naval Air Assistant be appointed to the Admiralty Staff and that an order be placed with Vickers for the building of a large rigid airship to serve as an experimental prototype (popularly known as the *Mayfly*). It was hoped this would lead to the building of long-range aerial reconnaissance scouts to be used while the Fleet was at sea.

The *R80* was elegant though small in comparison to the ensuing behemoths. With a maximum speed of 70 mph, from four Wolseley-Maybach engines each producing 230 horsepower, her volume of gas was 1,260,000 cubic feet. She was 535 feet long, with a disposable lift of 13.5 tonnes. *R80* was the first airship in which Wallis used his colour-coded wiring system. Wiring in airships was a labyrinth. The solution was typically Wallis, elegant, seemingly simple yet highly ingenious, a breakthrough that seemed obvious once somebody had thought of it and done it.

The *R80* was in some ways a flying-model for the design concepts Wallis would exploit later in his much bigger and vastly more ambitious *R100*. *R80* provided her designers and crew with alarming moments during her initial testing, which resulted in severe buckling of the ship's frame. Years later, in a letter to his friend the airshipman Victor Goddard, Barnes Wallis recalled that test flight: 'One should never allow a lighter than air ship to become seriously out of trim, either plus or minus. I shall never forget when Ivor Little ballasted *R80* on her first trial ... [she was] far too light and we shot vertically up to some 9,000 ft. before he got control. Now that I come to think of it, you and I were both up in the keel and I remember trying to hold a sticky emergency relief valve open in a gasbag that looked as if it were about to burst; while a stream of ice-cold hydrogen poured over my head, and I wondered how long I could hold out before being gassed and falling out through the outer cover! You, I think, were doing the same thing a bay ahead of me, on the port side of the ship, while I was on the starboard side. Our relative positions were important, as we had to climb up part of the keel structure to reach the valves. Those were the days! After the *R101* tragedy I suppose we are fortunate to be still alive! Can it be that we owe our continued existence to our nerve in dealing with unforeseen emergencies?'[24]

Hartley Pratt featured the *R80* in his influential and vividly imagined treatise, *Commercial Airships,* in which luxurious leviathans voyaged lazily through the heavens while criss-crossing continents. But the commercial

Detailed drawings of the *R80*, from the pages of *The Engineer.*

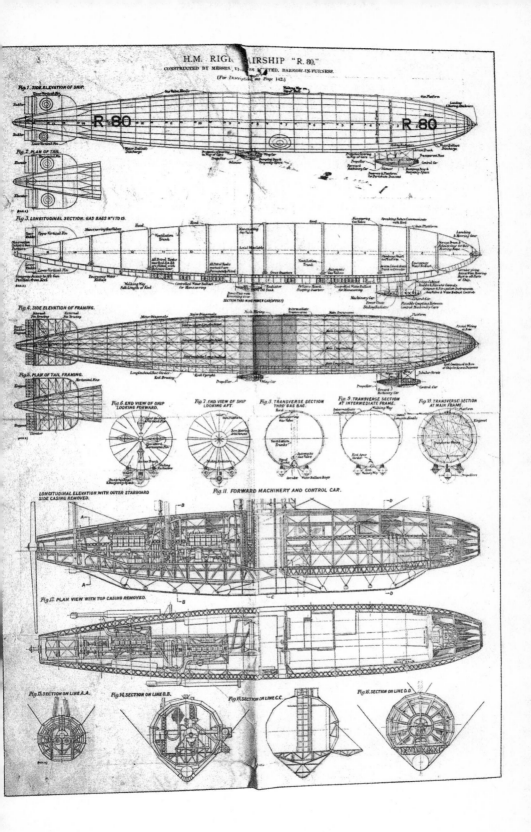

H.M. RIGID AIRSHIP "R. 80."
CONSTRUCTED BY MESSRS. VICKERS LIMITED, BARROW-IN-FURNESS.
(For Description see Page 142.)

Fig. 1. SIDE ELEVATION OF SHIP.

Fig. 2. PLAN OF TAIL.

Fig. 3. LONGITUDINAL SECTION. GAS BAGS Nº 1 TO 15.

Fig. 4. SIDE ELEVATION OF FRAMING.

Fig. 5. PLAN OF TAIL FRAMING.

Fig. 6. END VIEW OF SHIP LOOKING FORWARD.

Fig. 7. END VIEW OF SHIP LOOKING AFT.

Fig. 8. TRANSVERSE SECTION THRO GAS BAG.

Fig. 9. TRANSVERSE SECTION AT INTERMEDIATE FRAME.

Fig. 10. TRANSVERSE SECTION AT MAIN FRAME.

Fig. 11. FORWARD MACHINERY AND CONTROL CAR.

LONGITUDINAL ELEVATION WITH OUTER STARBOARD SIDE CASING REMOVED.

Fig. 12. PLAN VIEW WITH TOP CASING REMOVED.

Fig. 13. SECTION ON LINE A.A.

Fig. 14. SECTION ON LINE B.B.

Fig. 15. SECTION ON LINE C.C.

Fig. 16. SECTION ON LINE D.D.

scenario vaporised, and the *R80* was eventually commissioned by the RAF, though not until January 1921, after which she was caught up in the run-down of airships. The ship was kept in a serviceable state for the training of US Navy personnel (many of who were destined to be killed later that year, on 24 August 1921 in the *R38* calamity). The US Navy made four flights in *R80* totalling 8 hours and 45 minutes between 26 March and 1 June.

The ramifications and repercussions of the *R38* tragedy (see page 81) were immense and, again, confidence in airship technology evaporated. After only 73 hours sailing, the *R80*, the finest airship in Britain to date, made her last flight on 20 September 1921 from Howden in east Yorkshire to Pulham in south Norfolk, where she was laid up in her shed. Her components were subjected to a series of destructive tests before she was finally dismantled, four years later.[25]

4

TRIUMPH, CATASTROPHE
AND COVER-UP

R34's Crossing of the Atlantic

Commercial interest quickened with the epic voyage of the *R34*, which made the first return crossing of the Atlantic in 1919. Built by Beardmore at Inchinnan on the Clyde, her design was inspired by the German super-Zeppelin, *L33*, which had been forced down near Little Wigborough in Essex after a raid on London on 23 September 1916. The Admiralty despatched a team from the Royal Corps of Naval Constructors to copy every detail, led by Constructor Commander C. I. R. Campbell.[1] The German ship, with six engines instead of the usual four, was technically far ahead of anything in Britain. (A problem with copying Zeppelins, however, was that Britain would consistently lag behind Germany; by the time Britain had built her clones, German designers had moved yet further ahead with more technological advances.)

The *R34* was laid down on 8 December 1917 and took a year to construct. The length of two football pitches, she was built originally for long-range naval reconnaissance; by the time of her launch, though, the war had ended. With money corset-tight, and the coming of peace, there was no urgency to get her into service. Administrative change had swept through the services, the Admiralty was still responsible for the *R34* and other airships, but airship personnel had been transferred to the RAF. In short, the *R34* had become a somewhat embarrassing, giant 'white elephant'.

An invitation to sail the Atlantic from Britain's Royal Aero Club and the Aero Club of America, gave the *R34* purpose: the demonstration was to encourage commercial operators. Maitland, resolve matched by enthusiasm, threw his energies behind the scheme.

The Atlantic had been crossed in May 1919 by an American Navy seaplane via the Azores. Royal Air Force officers John Alcock and Arthur Whitten Brown had also made their non-stop flight from Newfoundland to Ireland on 14–15 June 1919, averaging 120mph and flying for just under 16 hours in a converted Vimy bomber. Two weeks later, in the early hours of 2 July 1919, a ground handling crew of 550 eased *R34* from her shed at the start of her first round trip, from East Fortune in Scotland, to Mineola, Long Island, USA, nearly twice the distance of Alcock and Brown's flight. The outward voyage took 108 hours. She stayed three days, during which time she was wildly fêted. Helped by friendly winds, the return journey, which ended at Pulham, took just 75 hours.

Her voyage proved that sizeable numbers of passengers could be carried over great distances in comfort and safety. With more than 20 on the *R34*, within the decade airships grew to carry 50 and 100 people. But the voyage was not free of incident. The ship was buffeted by severe storms, which caused her to pitch and roll; the engines proved to be under-powered; the cover had flapped, had lost its waterproofing qualities and absorbed moisture. She had sailed for most of the time at an uncomfortable bows-up-or-down angle. Gasbags had dangerously overheated, and a stowaway plus a kitten had been discovered to be on board. Even with extra petrol – 6,000 gallons weighing nearly 16 tons – there was alarm towards the end of her outward voyage that she would run out of fuel. There were no gauges on the tanks and when she docked the dipstick indicated that a mere two hours' worth of fuel remained. Fearing the ship might have to ditch, the American destroyer USS *Bancroft* set sail from Boston, but in the event the *R34* managed to moor safely without need for assistance.

Maitland was in charge, and at the helm was the intrepid Scott. Sailing high over the Atlantic, Maitland described 'an excellent lunch of beef stew, potatoes and chocolate'. And as the great ship voyaged the skies at a steady 60 knots afternoon tea (bread, butter, greengage jam, and hot tea boiled over an exhaust pipe) was accompanied by the 'pleasant tones of Miss Lee White on the gramophone ... we would one and all give anything for a smoke ... and the First Officer is vainly trying to discover the culprit who used his toothbrush for stirring the mustard at lunch'. Spotting below them the steamer *Ballygally Head*, out of Belfast and bound for Montreal, Maitland noted: 'They picked up our wireless on their Marconi spark set which has a range of thirty miles only. They were very surprised. She didn't see us ... we were above them, completely hidden by clouds.' After speaking to SS *Canada* on the wireless, there was an occurrence that Maitland called 'slight trouble' – the starboard amidships engine began to play up due to a cracked cylinder: 'Shotter (the chief engineer) is always equal to the occasion and made a quick and safe repair with a piece of copper sheeting and the entire supply of ship's chewing gum, which had to be chewed by himself and two engineers before being applied.'[2]

To those outside its ranks the world of Maitland and Scott appeared esoteric. Within its confines lay fierce competition and, also, a touching camaraderie. Maitland had frequently risked his life as a balloonist, parachutist and airshipman. Scott's career had been equally intrepid. They were seen as outsiders by the military establishment. Though the First World War had wreaked carnage, there persisted an implacable core of early twentieth-century army and navy commanders for whom conflict would remain a game for gentlemen, with rules and proprieties to be observed by either side. To them the airship service was a squalling infant, an upstart too young to have acquired the trappings of tradition. Its members were met with the incomprehension with which submariners had been greeted and from whose ranks some airshipmen had sprung. To sceptics in the senior services, bound by aeons of class and rank, submariners were ungentlemanly; *perishers* in tin fish who behaved as if *in trade*.[3] After the war reservations lingered among generals and admirals who had held proprietorship over the theatres of conflict. Submariners and airshipman were classed together: the first unsporting, the second, flighty and coquettish. They were outsiders, oddballs.

When docking an airship, Maitland would sometimes parachute down in order to galvanise inexperienced handling parties waiting anxiously on the ground. On this occasion he declined, sensitive that as the senior officer it could look 'showy'. Instead, when the great ship arrived over Minneola, Flight Lieutenant J. E. M. Pritchard parachuted to earth, becoming the first man to land in America. Pritchard arrived in full uniform, carrying his 'swagger-stick', and before his descent he had shaved in hot water from one of the ship's radiators. Accounts of his touch-down vary – some claimed his landing was calamitous, others said it was pristine, conducted with aplomb. Whatever the truth, his descent was marked by applause and cheering from the watching throng. Celebrations were held across America.

A stowaway, William Ballantyne, was a young man who had been part of the crew due to make the voyage but had been 'bumped off' at the last minute, the maximum number on board being limited to 30. Ballantyne hid in the darkness between the girders and gasbags until he was eventually forced to give himself up, nauseous from the smell of gas. He would become a world-wide celebrity, the talk of every household, telling reporters in America of his disappointment at being left off the crew list as he had worked hard preparing the ship, and how he had been looking forward to visiting the United States. On being discovered, Ballantyne had been hauled up in front of Scott and Maitland in the control car. They had agreed that little could be done about him; had they been overland he might have been put out by parachute. Their primary concern was in having another mouth (and Whoopsie, the kitten) to feed from their limited rations. And it was pointed out to Ballantyne that his weight in petrol would have been worth another twenty minutes' flying time.[4] Scott and Maitland's options were limited and, remembering their own youthful adventures, he was let off lightly. For the rest of his passage he peeled potatoes as an assistant cook, the 'just dessert' of the stowaway. He had to return to England, however, by liner, where he continued his career in aviation, flying in the Second World War, becoming a pilot and achieving the rank of Flight Lieutenant. Meanwhile, the kitten Whoopsie, a tabby, became as famous as Ballantyne and remained a source of entertainment for the crew.

When the *R34* returned to Pulham in Norfolk – she could not get into East Fortune because of bad weather – 'the shrill cry of a bugle rent the air and there was a rush of khaki-clad and civilian spectators into the broad, open space facing the sheds. The excitement mounted as the blob grew larger, mounting high above the hangar. A small band of musicians struck up *See the Conquering Hero Comes*.'[5] But the ship's arrival proved soggy for the ground handling crew at Pulham; they were drenched in a huge cascade of water ballast from the ship as it came to its mooring. '"A much better journey back," said General Maitland, who was as immaculate as if he had walked out of Bond Street ... among the passengers were the mascot tabby cat and the official pigeon, both in the charge of a mechanic who was promptly collared by cinematographers. The cat escaped from the string, disliking the bioscope, but the pigeon enjoyed the camera. The cat afterwards went in search of a monkey chained to a pylon, the monkey being the aerodrome mascot.'[6]

The *New York Times* reporter covering the ship's arrival at Pulham wrote that as soon as the crew could escape friends and well-wishers they went off for breakfast and baths and to reply to congratulatory telegrams. 'Major Scott, the only member who had not bothered to clean up, sat down nonchalantly at a small table, with an open collar and white muffler round his neck and half an inch of beard on his chin. "I calculated that the return trip would take between seventy and eighty hours," he said. "It took seventy-five hours three minutes." Scott also commented: "The most striking point was the manner in which we completed the journey under adverse weather conditions. Outward bound at one time we registered 73 knots an hour. It was just after midnight when we were over Broadway, where thousands had assembled, but the noise of the engines drowned the cheering. Yesterday (on the return leg) one engine broke down altogether. The connecting rod was bent through the axle case and two bolts broke. One fifth of our power was thus lost. We had plenty of lift and had to let out water ballast and gas on landing. I'm sorry I gave so many of our ground helpers a ducking."'[7]

The first officer, Captain Greenland, said Scott deserved the laurels more than anybody: 'You might search the world ... and never find a quieter and more modest maker of history. Can you wonder that the men love him?'[8] Maitland said: 'Airships will undoubtedly be utilized commercially in the future over long journeys over sea and land without conflicting with the use of airplanes or seaplanes.' The planes, he thought, would offer a radial service for swift, short-distance flights from airship terminals. 'Big airships have a wonderful future for mail and passenger carrying. Airship travel is extremely comfortable and there is no sickness. On the return journey we passed through weather which would have caused extreme sickness on surface ships but there was no sickness on board the *R34*.'

Maitland was generous in praise of his American hosts. He pointed out that, as well as demonstrating the commercial viability of big airships, the flight was to further seal the friendship between the US and England: 'The American reception was extraordinarily good. The Americans were kindness itself. The American Naval Department and service gave every possible facility. The Americans were greatly impressed by the airship voyage and fully realised the future possibilities.' The American government was represented on the return journey by Lieutenant Colonel William Hensley, an American army observer. He was reported as saying: 'We had no particular thrills and we even lived on bacon, eggs, sausages, bread and butter, jam and cheese.' Second Lieutenant Durrant, the radio officer, said his equipment 'answered perfectly throughout'. Scott said: 'Durrant kept us in touch all the way till we sighted land again, the first at Clifden wireless station in Ireland.' The meteorologist, Lieutenant Guy Harris, said: 'Coming home we had fair weather. Picture us in a vast vault of blue of a truly wonderful colour for twenty-four hours. High above us a few wisps of feathery cirrus and below, looking from the gondola, a great, tumbling ocean of cotton wool, upon the white billows of which the sun threw our shadow. That was what it was like for a long period on the homeward trip. Our greatest height was 5,000 feet. I've learned more about weather on this trip than in all my life before.'[9]

After the initial celebrations, Scott and Maitland would conduct a more sober inquest into problems the voyage had revealed. Scott complained that the crew had been cold in the unheated ship: 'The provision of warm silk underclothing covered by woollen sweaters and submarine drawers was adequate ... but much warmer beds should be supplied for winter flying.' The

Sunbeam engines were inefficient, clutches seized, oil leaked at five gallons an hour, gearboxes blew their glands. The ship lacked proper weather reports, and Scott recommended that meteorological officers should always be part of the crew of airships that were about to embark on long sailings.[10] The *R34* was broken up in January 1921, damaged beyond repair by violent winds while trying to moor.[11]

Meanwhile, the airship service was caught between its old masters in the Admiralty, resentful at losing control, and its new chiefs in the Air Force, smug about assuming Admiralty responsibilities but more taken with aeroplanes than airships and suspicious that airshipmen were sailors at heart. 'For some time airship personnel has been controlled by a department almost completely out of touch with airship requirements,' wrote Scott. 'They have had few precedents, and the technical requirements laid down for their guidance are meagre. The airship service has naturally suffered.' Scott was also insistent that long-standing naval traditions should be maintained. 'A small rum ration should be allowed for future extended flights, more from the point of view of assisting the crew off-watch to sleep and promoting general cheerfulness, than from any scientific or calorific value. When the rum ration was disallowed by the medical department they did not realise many of the crew ... were accustomed to drinking a more or less reasonable amount of alcohol daily ... the sudden cessation of all alcohol was definitely not in the best interests of efficiency'.[12]

R38

Britain was becoming affectionate towards its airships and their valiant sky-sailors. Scott and Maitland and the rest of the 'outsiders' on the *R34* became celebrities. After this triumph, more ambitious vessels were in the pipeline. But the Great War had staggered to a close, bankrupting its participants, and, though civilian utility of the airship still held promise, the exigencies of conflict had lessened. The *R38* was the last attempt by the Admiralty to build an airship bigger, faster, and with a greater range and climbing ability than any ship the Germans might possess. Constructor-Commander C. I. R. Campbell, of the Royal Corps of Naval Constructors, who led the team that had copied the Zeppelin when it crashed in Essex, was in charge. Naval staff wanted the ship to be able to patrol the North Sea for six days non-stop, operating up to 300 miles from its base. She was known as the Admiralty A Class and was ordered from Short Brothers, Cardington, in 1918. The following year the company and its base was nationalised and named the Royal Airship Works.[13]

R38 was to be heavily armed: she would carry 12 bombs, four of them of 520 pounds, and her crew was to include 12 machine-gunners. However, money was short, the Admiralty kept changing its mind about what it wanted from her, and as a consequence her construction did not commence until February 1919. In the straitened circumstances that prevailed – the war had been ruinous – it was of no surprise that the Treasury's beady eye settled on her. A number of other airship projects were cancelled, but the Admiralty argued that because of her design – she would be the world's biggest and most advanced ship – the *R38* should be reprieved. Then, to the delight of the British government, desperate for money, the United States Navy decided that it wanted to buy the *R38*, and she was sold for £300,000. She was completed in 1921, three years after being ordered.

During her trials over the Humber river, near Hull in east Yorkshire, at 17.37 p.m. on 24 August 1921, she broke in two 'like a cracked egg'.[14] She had been engaged in tight manoeuvres at low altitude with the rudders being flicked to port and starboard. The inquiry found the disaster had been caused by the ship being insufficiently strong and by stresses that had built up at low altitude through the severity of the turns. Eyewitnesses on the ground said a crease had suddenly emerged, which ran diagonally across the hull of the ship towards its after end; one said a 'great wrinkle, like a twisted and rolled newspaper in her outer cover' had appeared. Others witnesses recalled a cloud of vapour – water ballast being discharged or petrol spilling from her ruptured tanks – which turned the ship from silver to dark grey. From the 'cracked egg' crew and artefacts fell into the blazing waters of the Humber, while some airmen in parachutes descended into the fire. There were two huge explosions.

Tom Jamison, whose home is close to the river Humber, is the author of *Icarus Over the Humber*, the definitive story of the *R38*. He told the author:

The screams which had accompanied the disaster – both from the crowd and from the stricken airship – now gave way to complete silence as the last few minutes of the tragedy were played out. With the shattered forward section already in the water and surrounded by flames and smoke, the stunned crowd watched the comparatively gentle descent of the rear section as it drifted towards the city and came to rest on a sandbank ...

It was truly shocking. The ship was flying at a very low altitude and was only a couple of hundred yards offshore. It was a very public disaster. She was just off the pier. There were crowds of people who saw her break up. It was a very busy time of the day. When the news spread people rushed to have a look, mothers pushing babies in prams. Hundreds of people were watching. There was an observation pier crowded with people.

People in the neighbourhood were used to seeing big rigids cruising about. The ship had been built as a copy of the German height-climbers built to a light template. Every economy in weight had been taken. But given that the density of air is so much greater when you are as low as the *R38* there was no way she could cope with the manoeuvres asked of her. She was a copy, a very bad copy, and she was misused. She should never have been flown and asked to do such things at that very low level.

One of the Zeppelins the *R38* was copied from was the Zeppelin height-climber that had come down at Little Wigborough in Essex. When they were trying to scuttle her the crew had burned off the fabric but the skeleton remained and was copied by Campbell and the British in great detail. But copying is not as good as basic designing. The builders of the *R38* did very little calculating themselves. The British were always about two or three years behind in airship designing; they didn't always understand the reasons the Germans were making changes or the implications of designing something in a different way and how the newer designs had to be flown and treated differently. This very light template was not properly understood.

Campbell was under pressure from all sorts of people when the *R38* was being built, each asking that the ship should be capable of doing different things. During its construction it had been subject to many changes in design and specification. The construction programme was always being interrupted. It would stop for about four months and the people would go home and then it would start up again. After the ship was sold its specification was modified yet again for the Americans and their needs.

The Americans lost a number of ships because they flew too close to the Fleet. They weren't using them for long range reconnaissance for which they were designed. They flew them in conjunction with the Navy as service ships; that's how disasters happened. They flew too low to the sea and too close to the ships they were escorting.

The trials of the *R38* were cut from 150 to 50 hours; it was another major factor in the crash. Originally the tests were to have been conducted at the proper height. But they had to come down low to finish the tests. People involved with her said: 'Well, the hours are being cut back, we haven't got time for all the tests we're supposed to do at a great altitude ... so we'll do them at sea-level.' It was crazy. That's when they started throwing her around at a very low level. Campbell and his people hadn't done any calculations about aerodynamic stress and load factors. It was terribly sad.[15]

Mr. Jamison, a retired college lecturer, who had spent part of his career in the RAF following his father who had served in the Royal Flying Corps, showed the author his archive of photographs. Two pictures show a group of young fresh-faced Americans, laughing, minutes before they boarded the ship. Some had married local girls.[16]

Of 49 people aboard, 44 died. They included the cream of American airshipmen, excited to get their hands on the ship and keen to sail her back to the USA. The dead included the much-loved Maitland; Campbell, the *R38*'s designer and superintendent of the Royal Airship Works at Cardington; Flight Lieutenant J. E. M. Pritchard – the officer in charge of the *R38*'s trial flights, whose experience had included the *R34*'s triumphant transatlantic crossing, from which he had parachuted into America; and John Robert Pannell, an observer from the National Physical Laboratory. Maitland 'was found in the control car, still clutching the ballast toggles in death, and so was at his post to the very last. His memory was revered amongst British airshipmen.'[17] An outcome of the accident was the establishment of an Airship Stressing Panel to ensure designers built a higher level of safety into ships. Gordon Kinsey comments: 'It was ironic that the voice which had pleaded for more rigid rules in the design and stressing of large airships was stilled when Campbell perished.'[18]

At the *R38* inquiry of 27 August to 5 September 1921, held at Howden airship station, Campbell was blamed for fundamental errors in failing to calculate stress and load factors. And the findings exacerbated animosity between the Navy and the Air Force. Nevil Shute records:

> At the enquiry ... it came out that the officials responsible had made no calculations whatsoever of the aerodynamic forces acting on the ship in flight; it was not therefore very surprising that she broke when doing turns at full helm and full speed ... it was inexpressibly shocking to me to find that before building the vast and costly structure of *R38* the civil servants had made no attempt to calculate the aerodynamic forces acting on the ship ... [19]

The destruction of the *R38* was a cataclysmic blow to the already low morale in the airship service. Douglas Robinson comments: '*R38* stands condemned to this day – a bad airship badly designed ... the deaths of so many brave men from both sides of the Atlantic brought an outcry against the rigid airship ... the *R38* disaster seemed to put paid to a costly experiment ...' [20]

Soon after the tragedy, Barnes Wallis, the designer of the acclaimed *R80*, sent a letter of condolence to his friend the respected airshipman Edward Masterman, who five years earlier had been in command of Britain's first successful ship, *HM Naval Airship No. 9* when it flew for the first time on 27 November 1916.[21] The author is not in receipt of the condolences Wallis sent to Masterman, but Wallis's daughter, Mary Stopes-Roe[22] showed him the handwritten letter of reply from Masterman dated 3 September 1921. Masterman sent it from the Aeronautical Commission, c/o the British Army on the Rhine, in Cologne, where he was stationed.[23] Its pathos hints at a growing despair in the service:

Dear Wallis,

My very best thanks for your letter and sympathy which we all need in this saddest of all hours. The blow does seem at the moment to be almost overwhelming, but, like you, I try to think that airships will go on, somewhere, somehow. To me so much seems to depend on what the Court of Enquiry find. Did anyone have fears for the strength of the ship before the fatal flight? Had any weaknesses shown themselves previously? Who checked the constructors' calculations? ... and so on. I only hope that all these points may be brought to light as it is unexplained disasters that do such damage to a cause like ours. If the principle of L than A* are sound, it must go on, whatever the calamities may be, and I have always felt since mooring out proved successful, that they are sound. Without the fellows who are gone, it will never seem quite the same again, whatever happens. Since I have been out in this country my two best friends in the Air Force have gone, R. M. Groves** who was killed at Cairo, and now Maitland.

I hope to be back in England before very long – with very best thanks.

Yours v. sincerely

E. A. Masterman

* Lighter-than-air. ** Captain R. M. Groves died in January 1917.

The Inquiry heard that the *R38* had been designed in August 1918 in the Admiralty Department of Airship Production. Its design incorporated so many new features that it was well in advance of any previous airship, but, the Inquiry found, its designers should have gone back to first principles instead of merely scaling-up earlier calculations, which had applied to previous smaller and less ambitious vessels. The conclusions were damning: the Inquiry had found that the structure was insufficiently strong for the extensive modifications; outside experts should have checked the design before building had commenced; both the construction and inspection were conducted at Cardington, whereas inspection, in the opinion of the Inquiry, should have been carried out by impartial, external examiners.

The Admiralty was incensed. It refuted the allegation that it was responsible for all the sins or that these had been committed in the early months of construction before the RAF assumed responsibility from the Navy. The influential Tennyson d'Eyncourt, Director of Naval Construction, was among the strongest of Naval objectors. He refused to accept the ship had broken into two sections because of 'failure of the structure in the rear and aft engine cars', as the inquiry had found. He did not think it unsound that Cardington built and inspected its own ships, and he insisted that the report of the Inquiry should not be published. As well as specific objections, the Admiralty was aggrieved about the tenor of the proceedings and what it perceived as an implicit bias – the Inquiry had been held at an RAF station, and the court had been constituted with a majority of Air Force personnel. A scribbled note by an unknown author (it appears to be an internal Admiralty note, dated 10 September 1921, five days after the inquiry reached its findings) was explicit in wishing to put the blame on the Air Force, which was demanding full publication. The author of the note wrote of the RAF's demand: 'this required consideration ... I have a feeling that from the wording adopted the man in the street will put the whole of the blame on the Admiralty. The function of airship production ... was transferred to the Air Ministry in October 1919. By that time the design was settled and in that month the first frames were completed.'

Another unsigned handwritten Admiralty note read: 'I agree that the natural assumption on reading the finding is that the blame rests almost entirely on the Admiralty ... it is certainly not desirable to publish the findings as a whole; but if we object it will appear as if the Admiralty were afraid to meet criticism – an unfortunate position if the US government is in possession of the complete report.' The Admiralty informed the Air Ministry on 15 September 1921 that the findings should not be published in full, and requested a meeting. The Air Ministry agreed to the meeting but commented: 'The US Naval authorities have semi-officially expressed views in favour of publication.' The two sides met and, after several drafts and revisions, agreed to put out a 'watered-down' statement. It would omit any mention about the iniquity of Cardington building and inspecting its own ships. Nor would it make mention of the structural failure that had so exercised d'Eyncourt. The phrase 'novel design', after debate, was somehow judged by both parties to sound less contentious in the public domain than the original 'new features and modifications'.

On 3 October 1921, however, Frederick Guest,[24] the Secretary of State for Air, dashed the Admiralty attempts at a cover-up. He wrote to Arthur Lee, First Lord of the Admiralty, saying the findings had to be published in their totality because the Americans had the report in full and he did not want to 'create the slightest suspicion that we are endeavouring to hold anything back'. He warned Lee of the pressure for full disclosure that was certain to emanate from the Press and from Parliament. Three days later Lee replied that if Guest insisted on publishing the complete report, 'I think it would be desirable that the Admiralty should not be actually associated with its issue.' Lee said the Admiralty would conduct its own investigation; it would look at the period up to 1919 when responsibility for airship design and construction passed to the Air Ministry, and it would subsequently issue a statement to that effect. Lee also thought it appropriate that Admiralty and Air Ministry statements be issued at the same time, 'so that any suggestion of friction between the two departments may be eliminated'. Accordingly, the next day, the two communiqués were released simultaneously.[25]

While the cockamamie cover-up betrays the Admiralty in a poor light, doubtless the Air Force would have behaved similarly had it been faced with such censure; nor is there reason to imagine that Guest did not find satisfaction in Lee's discomfiture. To tilt the Inquiry with an RAF majority had been deliberate and provocative; the Navy conducted the airship's initial development and should therefore have been properly represented.

Given its scale and international consequences, today it seems ingenuous in the extreme to suppose that blame for the accident could be quietly buried; eighty years ago, however, the Admiralty felt no obligation to respond to public clamour. While, in private, relations between the Navy and Air Force were bleak, a show of harmony in public was judged as being vital. The attitudes reeked of hypocrisy and arrogance by both parties; had their energies been wholly directed into discovering the cause of the tragedy, rather than shifting the blame, there would doubtless have been benefits to airship development. The *R38* personified much that would happen to the airship in the ensuing years. When airships and their technology were in desperate need of rigorous and forensic investigation they would become caught in the middle of two squabbling parties, neither of which really wanted them but who were both determined to claim them as a prize with which to taunt the other. 'As a result [of the *R38* calamity] the RAF airship organisation was closed down and future British airship efforts were limited to large airships for long-distance passenger services.'[26] History records that the *R38* was an Admiralty, not an Air Ministry, tragedy. '*R38* at the time was the largest airship in the world. It had been designed by naval architects and investigation after its failure indicated that inadequate attention had been paid to the aerodynamic loads in flight ...'[27] Such a partial verdict is a calumny. Those who died deserve a more accurate memorial. Even the most cursory glance at the background and the subsequent proceedings, so swathed in cynicism and squalid politics, shows the Air Ministry to have been as culpable as the Admiralty.

5

AN AERIAL NAVY

The premise that private airships could be utilised by the Navy was beguiling: the Admiralty had no money to build and run light cruisers for reconnaissance, and by the end of the First World War airships had proved themselves useful in that task. On 4 December 1918 the Admiralty recommended the development of airships be continued 'until commercial enterprise is capable of independent development'.

Long before *R38* there had existed robust scepticism about the airships' vulnerability to the weather.[1] Sir Oswyn Murray, Secretary to the Admiralty Board, said airships had to be treated with extreme care. There was no way of 'estimating the limits of their weathering properties'. The issue could be reviewed in 1920, he said, when the 'extent of commercial development has disclosed itself.'[2] His assertions had veracity, although one would not choose to sail on violent seas any more than one would wish to sail in an airship through a storm. Adverse winds also slowed progress, or, as with shipping, made mooring hazardous. Murray's remarks smacked of prejudice: the shock of the new customarily encountered antipathy, especially in the Navy.

Perhaps, too, there was a realisation that power was shifting from sea to sky: the aerial leviathans, history would show, were the intermediate heralds of a new dawn, one dominated by flight. This was still a time, however, in which imperial might was measured by the number of capital ships Britain possessed – airships would remain forever flimsy and flighty to those raised in the unassailable belief that national invincibility could be gauged only by the thickness of steel in hull or deck.

For navy leaders, too, there remained concern about the control and command of airships: whether they would be under naval command or that of the 'upstart', embryo Air Force. There were now new factors to fret about: if airships were funded by private means, would their proprietors agree to recognise naval authority? In reality, would it ever be possible to tally military demands with commercial obligations? The Admiralty accepted, grudgingly, that airships might be commercially developed but remained implacable over an array of fundamental issues: 'The design and production of naval airships should be in the hands of the Admiralty. Airship crews should be selected and trained by the Admiralty. They should be selected from Naval officers.'[3] Admiralty thinking did not allow for much discussion or leeway.

By September 1919 the Air Ministry was at a loss to know what to do with its airships. The end of the war had shifted attention from conflict, and financing the military from the public purse made threadbare by war was not popular. Peace lent emphasis to the resuscitation of the economy, to building up Britain's factories, refreshing old trading links, forging new ones. The importance of empire, especially India, the jewel in the crown, assumed a loftier, beguiling stance in the public psyche.

The Air Ministry advanced a scheme in which airships, under RAF governance, would be used on a service to India. The acclaimed *R80* would be used, the ship at this juncture devoid of purpose. The Ministry was being ingenuous, or devious, in failing to explain that it would have been formidably expensive, if not utterly impossible, to convert it from relatively small naval craft to intercontinental carrier. Vickers could have converted it into a compact civil ship sailing, perhaps, to Rome, but it would have had far too small a range to contemplate ever voyaging to India.

The proposal was to fund the service jointly with government and private monies to the tune of £900,000 over two years. But money was impossibly tight, and it came as no surprise that in June 1920 the Treasury rejected the plan.[4] Worse was to come. Faced with dire economic circumstances and painful memories of the *R38*, a month after rejecting the scheme the government instructed the Air Ministry to cease – in its entirety – all lighter-than-air activities. Trenchard at the RAF was wrestling with slim appropriations, and airship funding placed too great a burden on meagre resources.[5]

During this period of organisational tumult decisions were never enacted swiftly; it took over a year for the run-down of the airship service to even begin. Faced with public apathy towards the service, the parlous state of Britain's economy, the shock of the *R38* calamity and the findings of the Inquiry, which had badly stung the Admiralty, it was to be a testing time for believers. The intrepid George Herbert Scott, however, was never one to waver: ardent disciple of the airship cause, the skipper of the *R34* on its celebrated voyage to America and back, the pioneer of the mooring mast, husband of the daughter of Archie Campbell, the managing director of Beardmore, the ship and airship builder, Scott's canvassing carried weight. He wrote to Leo Amery[6] the Parliamentary and Financial Secretary at the Admiralty, from his station at Pulham. He emphasised that it was crucial the Navy 'took up the airship again even if it is allowed to lapse temporarily'. A commercial operation serving the empire was possible, he said, with 'only a small amount of government assistance'. The benefits would 'be so far reaching,' he enthused, ' that I feel confident the Naval Staff would forego a Light Cruiser provided a [commercial] company is formed.'[7] Scott maintained that mooring facilities, which would be necessary throughout the empire, could be built 'within one or two years and would be of great tactical value to the Navy'. A service could start on the main trade routes of the Empire with moorings in Egypt, India, Singapore and Australia. 'The bases would be immediately available with airships and trained crews to carry out aerial reconnaissance in any part of the empire. Armaments and protective aeroplanes could be stored at these points ready at a moment's notice to convert the commercial airships into a Fleet Auxiliary.' The cost, said Scott, would be borne mainly by the private sector. He estimated that a figure of £1.4 million would have to be found by the Home or Dominion governments, which could be spread over a period of seven years, the equivalent to the running cost of a single torpedo boat or light cruiser. Naval staff had to decide between the value of a small surface unit 'and the enormous potential reserve available for aerial reconnaissance at a moment's notice'. The service, Scott argued, would also employ those made redundant by the rundown of the airship service. Scott said he knew of an American company that was about to sign contracts with German designers for a fleet of rigids; it would be tragic if Britain missed out on such an opportunity. It is unknown which US company Scott referred to, though it is likely it was the Goodyear Tire & Rubber Company. The builder was Zeppelin. Scott warned that the US Navy would soon have 30 airships as Fleet Auxiliaries, saying they 'would be in a commanding position both in the Atlantic and the Pacific Oceans'.

The Air Ministry had instructed that British airships be sold, handed to the Disposals Board, or scrapped. 'Urgent action must be taken if a colossal blunder is to be averted,' said Scott. 'The taxpayer will have cause to regret the decision before long.' He enclosed a ten-page memorandum detailing various airship virtues. Airships were more than reconnaissance craft: successful experiments had been conducted using airships as aeroplane carriers. In 1918 the experiments at Pulham station with a Sopwith Camel fighter 'proved conclusively that an aeroplane could be carried underneath an airship and flown off without difficulty'.[8] Fighters were limited by their shortness of range; the airship could transport vast cargos and convey fighters over great distances to engage the enemy. An airship of 2.5 million cubic feet capacity could lift 38 tons of fuel, armaments and aeroplanes. It had a range of 3,000 nautical miles cruising at 45 knots. As such it was far faster than surface vessels. It could hover, stay aloft for days, and six aeroplanes could be carried by a single airship.[9] Scott envisaged a future in which fleets of airships carried squadrons of aeroplanes to every corner of the globe. When aeroplanes unhooked themselves from the belly of an airship they commenced their flights from altitude, affording savings in both fuel and time. Airships carrying aeroplanes fitted with torpedoes could provide 'the only means of long-distance aerial attack'. Airships were cheaper to build and to run than cruisers, and expensive sheds were obsolete because airships left their masts 'in perfect safety in winds of 40mph'.[10]

His missive was well-timed, if flamboyant in its claims and imaginative in its calculations. Few shared his view of airships embarking in 'perfect safety' in 40mph winds. Though aeroplanes had flown on and off airships, it was a hair-raising business, as other nations had also discovered.[11] How many commercial operators would have risked their capital in a scheme patently biased towards the Navy was unknown. Conversion from civil to military ships was more costly and laborious than claimed. Comparative costs of surface vessels and airships were unproven and made no mention of airship depreciation such as the need for new covers approximately every two years because of their tendency to stretch, sag and rot.

Scott's word, though, was of sufficient authority for his imprecations to be taken seriously by the Admiralty, where they struck a chord, seductive in a manner Scott perhaps only partly appreciated: they provided the Admiralty with more ammunition to continue its skirmishings with the Air Force.[12] Amery at the Admiralty was responsive to the notion of airships carrying aeroplanes. He did not think the Admiralty could scrap a light cruiser 'to subsidise a commercial aeroplane service'. His memo to Admiralty colleagues, though, struck a wistful note: 'I am not sure that even that would not be worth our doing on the basis of having a lien on airships in time of war ...' With airships about to be broken up or sold off, he knew bargains were to be had and toyed with the idea that the Admiralty could buy 'one of the existing airships cheap in order to experiment with her as an aeroplane carrier ...'

Criticising the Air Ministry, Amery wrote: 'As aeroplane carriers are our department, and if the Air Ministry cannot provide us with airships for that purpose, I do not see how they can object to our providing ourselves with our own. Nor can they object if we man them with naval men, enlisting men like Scott, and the other discarded airship personnel, most of whom were, I believe, at one time in the navy.' Outlining how the Admiralty could make political capital from Scott's suggestions, Amery observed: 'Apart from the actual merits, this might prove a useful strategical approach; once we are responsible for the carriers, whether floating or flying, our case for being responsible for the aeroplanes is all the stronger. It might be worth getting Churchill to agree to this principle: he does not take airships seriously, and we may be able to spring quite a nice little surprise on the Air Ministry ... I do not suppose we should have to pay hardly anything for the airships. The difficulty would be to squeeze enough money out of our depleted Votes for even the smallest crew, fuel, hydrogen etc. We should probably be able to get the lease of Pulham for a very trifling figure.'[13] There runs a contaminant throughout the history of airships – a level of government, political and inter-service cynicism that can be breathtaking. It is sometimes so pronounced that it has not been lessened by the passing of the years.

The response to Scott's ideas from the Assistant Chief of Naval Staff was less favourable. Flying aeroplanes from airships had to be treated with 'the greatest scepticism'. Airships carrying torpedo-aeroplanes was beyond the pale – 'What is the torpedo-plane to attack? Surely not merchantmen, for that would be the equivalent of the worst form of submarine warfare.' If any money at all were available, 'let us assist this projected commercial adventure ... such as by a small subsidy ... but this subsidy must not be at the expense in development of the far more valuable naval unit, the heavier-than-air craft.' Roger Keyes wrote: 'It will take us all our time to find sufficient money out of Naval Votes to develop our heavier-than-air service when we gain control of the Naval Air Service, which cannot be long delayed. It is out of the question to commit ourselves to providing a subsidy for civil airships for commercial purposes at present.'[14]

The Burney Scheme

The most determined proponent of a commercial airship service to the Dominions was the former naval officer, Commander Sir Charles Dennistoun Burney. The only son of Admiral Sir Cecil Burney, second in command of the Grand Fleet under Jellicoe at the Battle of Jutland in 1916, he had invented the paravane, a device towed by surface ships to destroy mines. He was a consultant attached to Vickers, a company that had helped him in the past in the successful and highly lucrative development of this ingenious torpedo-shaped device, which was towed from the bow of a surface ship with cables that would cut the anchors of moored mines.

Burney's efforts to set up a commercial airship service were so significant that it is appropriate to provide an insight into his career. He had been drawn at an early age to devices that would eventually wreak havoc on conventional naval thinking, and which the navy of the late nineteenth and early twentieth century viewed with deep distrust. As a promoter of submarines, aeroplanes, seaplanes, mines, torpedos and airships, Burney was another of the outsiders, an 'odd-ball', as were Fisher, Bacon, Sueter, Masterman, Maitland and Scott. Energetic, inventive, entrepreneurial, Burney had received a conventional naval education, training on *Britannia*, before joining the battleship *Exmouth* as a midshipman in 1905. He joined *Afridi* in 1909, and soon after, *Crusader*, which was being used at the time for anti-submarine research. (His father was the first president of the Anti-Submarine Committee.) He also served on the battleship *Venerable* and the cruiser *Black Prince*, but his real passion lay in anti-submarine research and seaplane development. Early in his career Burney had recognised the potential of the aeroplane and had begun to develop a life-long interest in aeronautics. The airship, being a hybrid of sea and air, appealed both to Burney's naval instincts and to his passion for aeronautics.

In 1912 Burney made the far-reaching suggestion that aeroplanes with wireless for hunting down submarines could be carried by ships. At the start of the First World War he was given command of the destroyer *Velox* but soon afterwards joined *Vernon*, the Torpedo School in Portsmouth, where he invented the paravane. He received no official payment, but patents earned him the then fabulous sum of £350,000. For his work on the paravane, which saved hundreds of lives, Burney was appointed a CMG in 1917, an honour rarely bestowed on a lieutenant. Aged 40, he retired in 1920 with the rank of lieutenant commander, being promoted to commander on the retired list. He entered Parliament as the Unionist member for Uxbridge in 1922 and held the seat until 1929, in which year he succeeded his father to the baronetcy.[15]

On 28 March 1922, Burney wrote to Air Marshal Sir Hugh Trenchard proposing a bi-weekly airship service to India with a weekly extension to Australia.[16] Burney believed strongly in Empire and in the importance of binding it with improved forms of communication. He also sent his proposals to Amery who recognised another opportunity for the Admiralty to steal a march on the RAF. Amery, with the silken cunning that marks out the successful bureaucrat and politician, suggested to Lee, the First Lord, that he should write to Lloyd George's Cabinet giving Admiralty endorsement to the Burney Scheme 'as a tactical move to show we are alive to future developments in the air'. Amery suggested that 'a small contribution ... say £25000, or even £50000 ... may be made in the future'. It would only be given on the understanding that 'officers and crews are enlisted as RNR and the airships themselves are put at our disposal in time of war'. It was a good ploy, and Amery, one of the wiliest of the armchair admirals, knew the strategic value of making the initial strike. 'If we get in first and collar the men as RNR we shall have really secured the principle that airships belong to the Navy. The next step may be to attach a few young officers to these things to gain experience; after that we may borrow or hire a spare ship for experiments. Later we may buy one, and if justified, own our own fleet of airships.'[17]

Meanwhile Burney had begun negotiating with Vickers and Shell Oil, corporations of international clout with strong government links. Shell scientist Sir Robert Waley-Cohen was designing a lightweight airship engine fired by kerosene or hydrogen;[18] had it been a success it would have represented a major breakthrough, but after considerable expenditure of time and money the research was eventually shelved.

Britain's cessation of airship development had been greeted with consternation. The Burney Scheme offered a compromise: private enterprise would pay, the Dominions would be knitted together more closely, and the Services could have airships in a war. DELAG had shown the way, and *R34*'s successful voyage to the USA and back was testament to the range and durability of the transatlantic airship. Supporters argued that the *R38* calamity was a consequence of vaulting Admiralty and Air Force ambitions and basic errors of calculation – the constructors of new commercial ships had learned the lessons of *R38*. The ships would operate within their capabilities. Engineering fundamentals about strength and stress would be properly observed.

Amery was of the view: 'In any future war a considerable number of these craft would certainly be of importance to the empire ... development of airships for commercial purposes would be welcomed by the Admiralty.'[19] Captain Roger Bellairs, the Naval Assistant to Lee, the First Lord, told Lee the Scheme might herald an 'aerial navy'. Like Amery, he recognised an opportunity for the Admiralty to regain lost ground. But it would need to move swiftly to steal a march on the RAF: 'The quicker a decision can be given, the better, as there are other forces in the field; unless the Admiralty acts quickly the opportunity may be gone.'

A diversity of proposals were put to the Admiralty. Some were wildly ambitious, failing to recognise financial constraints. Others were blatantly commercial, mooted by operators with vested interests devoid of all appreciation of military prerogatives.

As a former naval officer Burney was seen by the Admiralty as 'one of us' rather than 'one of them' (the Air Force). With his insight into military needs and his commercial abilities. he had 'bottom'. The Burney Scheme, said Bellairs, did not represent the mad-cap proposals of a 'flyaway'; they came from a distinguished Naval officer 'of great business capacity, who by his invention and development of the paravane ... has given proof of inventive genius combined with practical application'.[20]

Burney proposed to establish a subsidiary of Vickers to build and operate six airships making twice weekly voyages to India and later to Australia. At its outset the service would be supported by subsidies, which would be reviewed later. In war the airships and crews would be turned over to the Admiralty. The company would have a capital of £4 million with Vickers and Shell each providing £100,000; the remainder of the money would be raised by debentures paying six per cent a year and guaranteed by the government for ten years. Existing airships would be given to the company that would lease, at a peppercorn rent, Air Ministry stations at Cardington and Pulham.[21]

A large rigid airship would be built, which Burney reckoned would be able to fly for 3,000 miles at 80mph. It would carry 200 passengers and ten tons of mail. In war, passenger accommodation would be torn out and replaced with extra wireless equipment and fuel, giving the ship a greater range. In its Navy guise it would carry so much fuel and provisions that at 40 knots it would have a non-stop range of 24,000 miles and be able to stay aloft for three weeks. With 5 million cubic feet of hydrogen, Burney was confident it could far exceed its role as a reconnaissance vessel; if needed, it could be converted into carrying three torpedo-bearing aeroplanes and two fighters. Where Burney found evidence for all this is a mystery. No airship had a performance that could come anywhere near his figures. It would be a calumny to suggest he intended to deceive, more accurate to suggest that salesmen must always believe in their product, and reality can sometimes become blurred by enthusiasm and belief. Whatever else he was, Burney was a good salesman. There had been experiments with aeroplanes using hooks or a trapeze to attach themselves to airships. But they were still perilous. He said the India route would generate £1,830,000 a year based on a £45 second class and £70 first class fare. He estimated costs at £880,000, giving the company almost a £1 million annual profit. He thought this attainable after three years and claimed ten tons of mail and 400 passengers would sail to India each week.

Being formerly of the Navy it was natural that Burney should turn to the Admiralty for support. But for the plan to stand a chance it had to have the backing of the Air Ministry. In some ways Burney's timing was opportune, in another it was poor. The RAF had already been given the go-ahead to convert Cardington airship station, which Burney envisaged as his main airship base, into a home for two fighter squadrons, a concession the Air Force would not relinquish lightly. Also the Treasury, unsurprisingly, was not enamoured with the Scheme: Britain was in a financial crisis, and there was no money for risky ventures dependent for success on government subsidy or largesse.[22]

Another idea ill-received by the government and military was a suggestion by Burney that the Imperial Scheme might operate with German-built Zeppelins. With anti-German feeling still running high, it was a controversial notion. Burney, however, had no doubts: 'The size of the (Zeppelin) is so far in advance of what could be designed in this country, that the increased performance rendered possible by such a ship ... appears to merit further consideration.' Burney was in regular contact with Dr. Eckener, the boss of Zeppelin, a shrewd businessman and an airshipman of outstanding skill, who was always keen to find new business.[23]

The advancement of the Burney Scheme increased tensions between the Air Ministry and the Admiralty. The animosity, detrimental to airships and their future, could be detected in Admiralty and Air Ministry memos. An internal Admiralty memo by Leo Amery, Parliamentary and Financial Secretary at the Admiralty, dated 5 May 1922, read: ' I see from this morning's paper the Treasury are turning down Burney's Scheme as unacceptable on financial grounds. From what I hear from other sources [not Burney] they have been put up to this by the Air Ministry, who want to kill the project while at the same time wishing to be able to safeguard themselves against a possible charge of having turned down the Scheme on technical grounds.'

Five months later Amery was appointed First Lord of the Admiralty, on 25 October 1922, two days after Andrew Bonar Law became Prime Minister.[24] The period in which Burney was promoting his Scheme was one of political turmoil – there were three general elections in less than two years between 1922 and 1925. Labour became the main party of the Left with the Liberals clinging on. Historian A. J .P. Taylor wrote: 'There was no profound cleavage between the parties, despite much synthetic business. Labour stood for social reform, the Liberals had their last years of free trade, and the Conservatives represented Protectionism.'[25]

Burney regularly visited the Admiralty where he had numerous friends and contacts. He had a meeting on 11 May 1922 with officials and Roger Keyes, Deputy Chief of Naval Staff. Like Sueter and Bacon, Keyes had been involved in submarines. Early in his career, in 1912, he had been appointed commodore in charge of the submarine service. For the first six months of the First World War he had been responsible for the operation of submarines in the North Sea.[26] Keyes said he was impressed with Burney's ideas: 'As a result of the meeting I am in favour of the Admiralty backing the Scheme strongly.' Keyes said the proposal should be endorsed and sent to the Cabinet as an official Naval Staff memorandum.

An argument repeatedly advanced by Burney concerned the importance of light cruisers and their high cost compared to airships. From his work on submarines he knew the importance of reconnaissance. The Navy found the argument persuasive, and Burney presented it with conviction.[27] Lee, the First Sea Lord, shared a widely held view: 'In no naval war that this country has ever waged have we had anything approaching a sufficiency of scouting craft – and in the lean years before us the provision of the necessary numbers of this class of vessel will be beyond our powers.' The airship was a feasible alternative to a light cruiser, and the Fleet would be able to make up its shortfall if airships were produced commercially. 'For these reasons ... the Board of the Admiralty consider it would be justifiable to contribute from Naval Funds towards the cost of the proposed [Burney] Scheme.'[28] One can speculate about whether Lee and others believed in airships, or *really* saw them as a way of continuing to battle with the Air Force. Most in the Admiralty would have preferred a new fleet of traditional, light surface cruisers. But they faced an overwhelming argument: state coffers were bare. Controlling airships would enhance Admiralty standing and their presence held the spice of further irritating the RAF.

Whatever the Admiralty motives, the Treasury remained implacable. Sir Robert Stevenson Horne, Chancellor of the Exchequer, had 'the most profound objection to the government taking an interest in ... any company working for profit'. Horne said previous ventures in which government had taken a stake were 'uniformly unsuccessful; the private investor is never backward in subscribing money to a speculative venture if there is a reasonable chance of profit. The government is never invited to intervene except where the chances of success are so remote as to render it impossible to raise funds in the market.' Indeed, government investments in private ventures in the past represented a 'melancholy record of loss'. He said the Burney Scheme was one in which the government could not win: if it failed, the government would reap opprobrium for squandering public monies; if the Scheme required the rapid injection of more capital the government could not act with the speed and the independence of a private capitalist, since fresh funding required parliamentary assent and disclosure of facts that from a commercial viewpoint should be withheld. Alternatively, if the project were successful, the government would be criticised by rival undertakings who were certain to be incensed that 'the bottomless purse of the taxpayer is used to finance competition to their detriment'. Horne was 'unconvinced that until airships can pay their way – when they will come without government assistance – that the advantages outweigh the cost of the subsidy'. The government could not 'adventure upon plans of a speculative character which involved additional national expenditure'.[29]

Winston Churchill, in 1922 Secretary of State for the Colonies, and by then an airship critic, weighed in: 'The government are to assume a very heavy capital expenditure with [Burney] ... the government cannot hope that the money will ever be repaid.' And Britain lagged too far behind Germany. Britain would never have the requisite knowledge of aerodynamic stress and strains that were involved in advanced airship design. That alone, said Churchill, would make it impossible for any company in England ever to compete properly with the German Zeppelins.[30] In the immediate post-war period Germany was impoverished, and the Zeppelin company went through a difficult period. The Versailles Treaty forbade construction of military aircraft in Germany, and the London Protocol of 1921 limited the cubic capacity of airships, making them too small to sail the Atlantic. To save itself the company had to make aluminium cooking utensils, but gradually it began to reassert itself. Its iconic chief Hugo Eckener secured a contract to build a new airship, *LZ 126*, for the US Navy, which saved the company. It was achieved in the face of continuing hostility towards Germany and especially towards those companies in armaments. The order was won through the considerable charm and sophistication of Eckener. He was always an excellent salesman, added to which his product and the reputation of his company, even though it had taken a financial battering, were unparalleled. Other ships followed, and in

France and Germany internal airship routes were being established. Zeppelin began rebuilding itself as the world's foremost airship builder, and its later craft would include the indisputably successful *Graf Zeppelin* launched in 1928.

Confronted by powerful adversaries, in a period which was politically quixotic, Burney refused to give in, doggedly continuing to promote his idea. Money was short and other important industries were competing for government help. The aeroplane industry was in disarray, bereft of military or civil orders. When taxed about it, Frederick Guest, Secretary of State for Air, agreed that many aeroplane companies and engine makers faced bankruptcy through a shortage of orders.[31] The influential former naval commander Viscount Curzon talked of the 'grave position of the aircraft industry ... it is in immediate danger of collapse, all development and research is virtually at a standstill. The industry would take years to recover.'[32] The powerful Committee of Imperial Defence (CID) was hostile. Guest wanted the government rid of Pulham and Cardington – Cardington might be used for aeroplane research, Pulham could be sold off by the Disposals Board. The stations lay idle and cost £20,000 a year to maintain. In Guest's view they were a total waste of money.

The Earl of Balfour, former Prime Minister, said it was folly to compete in airship construction because the US had a monopoly on helium. Sir George Barstow, Treasury controller of supply services, said costs had been seriously underestimated.

The Committee concluded that no money should be given to developing Imperial airships or communications.[33] The Prime Minister endorsed the view of the CID in the Commons in July 1922: quite simply, he said, there was not enough money. However, to some surprise, he announced he was setting up a new parliamentary airship committee which would look again at the Burney plan. Curzon complained that the Scheme had already been too delayed by different people and committees.[34]

Leo Amery chaired the new committee. It found in Burney's favour, to the astonishment and chagrin of airship critics.[35] But when it seemed the Scheme had gained momentum there came another four-month delay caused by a General Election. On 22 October 1922, Lloyd George, Britain's Prime Minister for six years, resigned,[36] and the election on 15 November 1922 returned Bonar Law and the Conservatives to power. The Amery Airship Committee was recast with a new chairman, the Secretary of State for Air, Sir Samuel Hoare; Amery, First Lord, became a member, which represented a setback for the Admiralty. At the same time another committee came into being: the Air Advisory Panel, chaired by Sir Geoffrey Salmond, the Air Member for Supply and Research, a sub-committee of Hoare's Airship Committee, which was itself a sub-committee of the CID. Salmond's committee examined technical aspects of the Burney proposals, while Hoare's committee investigated its financial implications.[37] Salmond's committee included Burney and Brigadier General Christopher Birdwood Thomson, a former soldier with a passion for aviation. Thomson was a socialist with friends across the political divide.[38] His presence and convictions would be a balance for Burney, with his energetic demeanour and Conservative opinions.[39]

As the weeks dragged into months, there was criticism about the time it was taking for Britain to hammer out a workable airship policy. The *Pall Mall Gazette* said: 'Procrastination, the continued refusal to come to a decision, prolongs the period of idleness and renders impossible the experimental work that could be done.' The *Gazette* said that if the government were to stop dithering and arrive at a positive decision 200 passengers would one day sail the sky in sublime comfort. Cardington would prove a great terminus. The service would cost £4 million in subsidies. The *Gazette* proclaimed: 'It [subsidy] would only be needed in the event of the venture being an absolute failure and a dead loss – an absolute impossibility, of course.'[40]

After another five months, an exasperated Burney warned the Admiralty that a Spanish–South American service was being established and that its operators wanted its ships to be constructed in Britain. From his dealings with the Norwegian Ministry of Defence, he claimed, he had learned that it too wanted to develop a new service. If the committees could move with more haste there might be a possibility of getting in on the Norwegians' overseas bases, which would be of strategic worth to Britain. Or would the government *prefer* that the *German* Zeppelin company pick up the business? While his chivvying was understandable, it might have been kite-flying; Burney was noted for his drive and salesmanship rather than his patience,[41] which after all the lengthy bureaucratic and political shenanigans had been sorely tested.

The Committee of Imperial Defence was informed by Amery that the Navy had 46 light cruisers, 55 less than in the war: 'Forty six is entirely insufficient to exercise control over the Empire's sea communications and ocean reconnaissance.' The Admiralty recommended commercial development of the airship as 'the only possible economic procedure at present'.[42]

Other airship businesses began setting up in competition. Major Harold Hemming of the Aircraft Operating Company wrote to the Admiralty saying he was establishing an Indian service with former airshipman Commander F. L. M. Boothby, and they were thinking of using Zeppelins.[43] Boothby kept revising his plans, becoming ever more ambitious; once, he suggested 12 ships and 30 mooring masts at a cost of £6 million, with the government guaranteeing 10 per cent of the capital for ten years. Boothby tried to get Sir Allen Anderson of the Orient Shipping company involved. Anderson told him he should forget India and learn the business with one airship on an easy European route. As for investing: 'It is essential to have more definite knowledge ... before any commercial man with credit to lose, make themselves responsible for bringing a large number of private investors into an airship Scheme.' Anderson claimed that he was unconcerned about competition: 'We do not look upon a new form of transport as an enemy and competitor of steam navigation companies, but as a new means of communication which ought to enlarge their business.' The owners of Britain's great shipping lines were canny and powerful. In public they refused to acknowledge their fear of competition from airships or aeroplanes. In private they were vexed and flummoxed about how to compete. Having been rebuffed by the wily Anderson, Boothby turned to the Zeppelin company, inquiring if it would be interested in joining his consortium, but Eckener felt 'there was too little change in the political and economic situation to justify optimistic expectations'. On 1 May 1923 the Committee of Imperial Defence decided in its wisdom that Boothby's suggestions were unworthy of further consideration.[44]

While Burney's Scheme seemed lost in committee, behind the scenes the battle for airship control remained bitter. The Admiralty made it plain it might be prepared to forego light cruisers to pay for airships but not if it meant it was going to help the RAF. Amery, the First Lord, reacted vigorously to a suggestion by Hoare, Secretary of State for Air, that France had 64 squadrons of aeroplanes and a large number of airships, and Britain urgently needed more herself. Amery wrote: 'This [request for more airships] is obviously put in to justify expenditure to obtain control.' He was adamant the Admiralty would not cut its quota of light cruisers to pay for airships 'unless the full use and control of airships was guaranteed ... all military control must be in the hands of the Admiralty; in war time airships will be engaged in purely sea operations and there is no justification for military control by the Air Ministry.'

Amery felt the Burney Scheme had 'great advantages over a government Scheme ... because it was easier to retain military control. The Admiralty should resist financial provision being made by the Air Ministry, as military control will obviously go with it. The Air Ministry's proposal really means the money saved by the Admiralty on light cruiser construction should be given to the Air Ministry to develop airships.'[45] Amery told the CID: 'It should be clearly understood ... in a war against a naval power the whole of the airship fleet will be required for naval purposes. All military control must be in the hands of the Admiralty. The company crews [those employed by Burney] must be RNR and not Air Force Reserve personnel. As in war time it will be necessary to augment the company crews by ... Naval ranks and ratings.' Burney's commercial airships, Amery said, which would be taken over in times of conflict and deployed in wartime scenarios, would need a military crew – 'A Captain for military command, whilst leaving the company captain as master of the ship. This will be analogous to the procedure in war in the case of armed escort ships. A navigating officer; the company navigating officer would only be accustomed to working over one route, mostly over land. A Coding officer, Naval W/T and Signal Ratings. These will be required as the airships will form an integral part of the Fleet, and reconnaissance is useless unless information can be rapidly transmitted in a secret form.'[46] Once again, Amery had bluntly highlighted fundamental problems that would have tested to destruction a commercial-cum-military airship operation.

There were constant leaks about the Scheme to the newspapers. Some were intentional and politically motivated. Anything to do with the Empire had become newsworthy, and the Scheme was being promoted at a time when Britain's financial position was bleak. The leaks and rumours generated international interest. Captain C. L. Hussey, of the American Embassy in London, asked Sir Oswyn Murray, the Secretary to the Admiralty, to furnish him with more details – America was conducting its own airship developments and Hussey said he found newspaper reports 'not so authentic as I should like to have'. Murray gave him short shrift, telling him plainly that he could not help him as the matter was being discussed in government.[47]

On 20 April 1923, a month before Stanley Baldwin replaced the terminally ill Bonar Law as Prime Minister, Burney wrote to the Committee of Imperial Defence with yet more detailed revisions, one of several altered specifications he had been requested to submit. Each change of administration, every shift in the secretariat, each demand for changes and alterations would further hamper Burney's progress.[48] And in the background financiers scurried around. They saw the much-discussed Scheme as being a possible money-spinner. Gambling on a positive response from Hoare's Committee, Hemming switched his allegiance from Boothby, whose plan had been ditched, to Burney. He told the CID he would invest £75,000 in Burney's Scheme.[49]

Sir Trevor Dawson, RN, a future chairman of Vickers, asked Hartley Pratt and Barnes Wallis to begin drawing up plans for a giant airship to serve Australia and India. It would sail at up to 80 knots with a crew of 28 men and six officers.[50] While the politicians and the civil servants vacillated, the money-men had kept a beady eye, anticipating that an airship service, in whatever form was finally approved, would spell handsome rewards for both constructors and operators.

At last, on 10 July 1923, almost a year after Amery's Airship Committee had reported favourably, Hoare announced his committee's findings. An airship service should be set up between England and India. The government should negotiate with Burney and Vickers about building and operating new airships. A subsidy should be limited to £250,000 a year on the condition that Burney would operate a bi-weekly service with six airships. Burney's Airship Guarantee Company would have to repay the government half of any profit it earned in excess of 10 per cent after seven years. The Airship Guarantee Company would be granted a lien on existing airships, and it would be permitted to lease the Pulham and Cardington airship stations.[51]

At first glance it appeared that Burney had achieved virtually everything for which he had fought. There remained, though, opposition from Salmond's committee, which judged Burney's claims to be unproven and far-fetched. Though it backed airship development and supported the principle of an Imperial service, it thought that Burney and his Scheme was not the best way forward. Of one specific aspect the Salmond committee remained deeply suspicious, namely that of over-riding Admiralty authority. Salmond's reservations aside, the Duke of Devonshire, the Secretary of State for the Colonies, was in no doubt that Burney's Scheme had been given the go-ahead. He sent an optimistic telegram to the governors general of Canada, New Zealand, South Africa and Newfoundland: 'The Government has decided to proceed ... by means of a commercial service rather than by a direct state operation.' His telegram said its administration would be under the Air Ministry.[52]

Burney's persistence, his networking as an MP and naval commander, his contacts in the Admiralty, the Lords and Commons, where he could bank on people such as Bellairs and Curzon, and the credibility of support from companies of international repute, namely Vickers and Shell, had resulted, against all the odds, in success. Yet the back-biting and inter-service politics would swirl unabated. Naval intransigence over such crucial questions as crewing remained unresolved. A scenario of military and commercial interests working in unity was untested. It was fine for Devonshire to pledge that the Air Force would be in control, but that had not been agreed – and never would be – as far as the Admiralty was concerned.

To support such a grandiose project, whose success rested on unproven technology, and faced with the financial constraints of the time and a demand for subsidies from established industries, it was an audacious decision by Hoare and his committee. Some thought it mad. The antipathy of Salmond's committee had been underestimated, however, and especially the reservations of its most influential member, Christopher Birdwood Thomson.

6

GLUED TO THE EARTH

Civil flying in Britain in 1923 lagged behind that being experienced in France and Germany, a situation *The Times* thought deplorable – it felt Burney's Scheme was a step in the right direction. While most people in Britain were 'glued to the surface of the earth', the French and Germans enjoyed regular routes between one town and another. 'In England', reported *The Times*, 'only a handful of firms cater for private hire and joyrides.'[1]

While commentators hailed the coming service, Burney and the government began their negotiations. The Admiralty insisted that Burney operate from bases in easily defensible locations, paying little heed to their commercial suitability or proximity to the whereabouts of likely passengers. But how could Burney make a profit if terminals were in locations chosen primarily for reasons of military strategy? Pulham and Howden, as examples, were in sparsely populated areas, with inadequate transport links or infrastructure for the handling of large numbers of passengers. There were other considerations to be resolved: 'The company will want their permanent base where there is cheap housing for workmen, good landing facilities, where land is cheap and where women can get work.' The Admiralty had faced difficulties in 1916 when it took over Shorts at Cardington: 'We had to choose between Luton, where women get employment in making straw hats, or Bedford, where there are pickle and biscuit factories.' Three hundred women would be employed stitching gas bags.[2]

Boothby wrote once more to the Admiralty. He suggested German *Parsevals* would be better for the Fleet than Burney's big airships. *Parsevals* were small airships which could be towed behind surface ships before being dismantled and stowed. His overtures had the smack of desperation; he would submit *any* design to *any* specification the Admiralty wished. The Admiralty told him that if he wished to progress his plans he should stop troubling them and contact Burney.[3]

If Burney had ever for one moment imagined that the government wanted the Scheme for its own virtues, the Admiralty thought differently: 'The principal reason the government approved the Burney Scheme was that the airship would prove to be suitable for use instead of Light Cruisers in naval warfare; it would allow for fewer cruisers to be maintained by the navy so they [airships] must have good radio communications and their designers will have to be asked to incorporate guns'.[4] The *R38* and *Mayfly* problems could be traced back to the excessive ambitions of the Admiralty; either the Admiralty lacked basic understanding or it refused to accept the fundamental limitations of airships such as weight. Airships were not surface ships to be loaded with hardware because it was thought vaguely useful. Burney was exercised (as, equally, were Pratt and Wallis) that if the Admiralty and Air Ministry had their way the airships would be compromised before they left the drawing board: radio equipment, for example, was crucial, but the type the Admiralty wanted was ludicrously heavy. Admiralty attitudes also suggested a scant appreciation of business and commercial imperatives.

While lawyers tried to draw up the Heads of Agreement, the Admiralty made clear it would not relent on manning. Crews had to be members of the Royal Fleet Reserve or Royal Naval Reserve. They had to agree to serve in an emergency when the Navy called on them. They had to be trained in the Fleet in the same manner as Naval Reserve Officers. The captains of Burney's ships would have to carry out Admiralty experimental work when and where the Admiralty instructed. How any of this would have squared with the demands of private operators and their various commercial obligations nobody knew. Diesel rather than petrol engines had to be used, even though diesels were too big and heavy. The Air Ministry said the Admiralty's stand 'raised questions of considerable importance and in particular the relative responsibility of the Air Ministry and the Admiralty for military use of airships and control of design'.[5]

Lawyers drafting the agreement sought a compromise in which both parties would enjoy a degree of control. But the RAF's Hugh Trenchard could be as intransigent as the Admiralty: 'I had understood that the Agreement would be between the Airship Company and the Treasury, or in some other form which would entirely avoid the issue of Admiralty control. I do not think this intention is met by making the Admiralty and the Air Ministry equal parties to the Agreement. At present the Air Ministry is the department responsible for airships, and to make the Admiralty a party to the agreement in itself brings into doubt the present allocation of responsibility; it admits that the Admiralty has a *locus standi* which the Air Ministry does not admit.'[6] The airship personified the struggle for an independent air force that would be vested with absolute control over sea and land. The Liberal MP Sir Archibald Sinclair[7] said: 'The unconscious tendency of naval and military officers must inevitably be to cramp the development of a service [air] which threatens the supremacy of their own, in their own element. You might as well entrust the development of tanks to cavalry officers. No longer are aeroplanes the handmaiden of the older services. No longer can the Air Force be treated as an ancillary service.'[8]

Burney was an active MP and always keen to contribute to the annual debate on Navy and Air Estimates. 'Aerial machines would eventually fulfil the political object of the Navy,' he said. 'The aeroplane was comparatively useless for Imperial purposes, because of its limited range. But a combination of aeroplane ... and airship ... could fulfil the political object of the Navy: namely, the protection of trade routes.'[9] The protection of trade routes was a potent argument; it rang bells with naval officers who understood better than most the importance of surface convoys. To add spies in the sky to their armoury – long-range reconnaissance airships – struck a seductive note.

Burney met vitriolic criticism from Labour MP Frank Rose, who mocked grandiose ideas which he asserted benefited only the rich.[10] Fanciful schemes were a short-lived 'air- stunt', he said. Burney's giant airships with an anticipated 800 passengers would need 200 crew. Burney and his ilk were 'megalomaniacs painting glorious visions ... the life of an airship is not worth talking about, and certainly not worth spending money on. I do not believe civil aviation has more than very limited potentialities.'[11]

Burney registered his Airship Guarantee Company (AGC) on 28 November 1923 with a nominal capital of £5,000 divided into £1 shares. Its Memorandum of Association allowed it 'to carry on business as bankers, capitalists and financiers'. It could conduct exploration work, sink wells and pipes, build, buy or sell airships, and carry out a diversity of other activities that seemed to have little bearing on airships. The exploration clause is odd: perhaps Burney thought he might strike helium.[12] The AGC had five directors, including two from Vickers, Sir Trevor Dawson and Sir Vincent Henry Penalver Caillard.[13] Later Vickers increased the capital to £100,000 and tightened its grip, having four of the five directors. The AGC office was listed as Broadway, Westminster; it was Vickers' address, where Burney had kept an office since his paravane days.[14]

A week after registering his company, Burney entered into a draft agreement with the Treasury. It was drawn-up as a catch-all agreement, as neither party knew what demands the military services would make or how such requirements would affect the commercial viability of the service. When the first ship had sailed from England to India in an anticipated seven days, it was intended that the AGC would raise another £150,000 and commit to spending £600,000 on an ambitious construction programme. The government would then provide a further £1,200,000, which would be paid in twelve instalments of £100,000 each. The Treasury wanted three airships, which it was intended would make eight passages a month to India.[15]

Zeppelin in the Post-War World

Following the war and restrictions the victorious Allies imposed upon Germany and its weapons industry, the Zeppelin company suffered. The Versailles Treaty forbade the building of any type of military aircraft in

Germany. Once a jewel of innovation, Zeppelin lost some of its dazzle. The company was also at war with itself, subject to internal wrangling about its leadership: 'Unable to foresee the political and economic chaos that would prevail in Germany for at least five years, or the harsh terms of the Versailles *Diktat,* its directors naively expected to do business as usual.'[16]

The ensuing power play took its toll. Protagonists included the haughty Alfred Colsman, associated with Zeppelin from its earliest days; the chairman, Baron von Gemmingen, Count Zeppelin's uncle; and Captain Ernst Lehmann, respected airshipman and pilot. Count Zeppelin had died in 1917, never to see the fulfilment of his ambition to create passenger lines over the continent and to America. In the event, it was the charismatic Eckener, Zeppelin's operational manager, who would emerge victorious, succeeding the ailing Gemmingen as chairman. Colsman's unbending manner alienated two putative allies of the weakened company – the Goodyear Tire & Rubber company of America, a powerful entrant into airships, and Henry Ford, the car maker. Dynasties such as the Morgans, the Vanderbildts, the Rockefellers and Ford had built America – any entrepreneur who wished to make serious headway in the vast but immensely treacherous US market crossed such families at their peril.

Under the rules of the London Protocol of 5 May 1921, Germany was only allowed to build relatively small airships, and the volume of commercial ships was restricted to 1,000,000 cubic feet – too small to fly the Atlantic. The crisis became so severe for the Zeppelin company that at one point it was reduced to making a range of pots and pans marketed under the name 'Ellzett'.[17] But Zeppelin found a way round the restriction – there was nothing to stop it building ships *outside* Germany. Several countries were keen to do business with it, to tap into its fount of wisdom accumulated over decades. The company held the lead in design, and overseas companies in countries such as Spain (which had retained a neutral stance during the years of conflict) were keen to benefit from Zeppelin's prowess. The value of Zeppelin's experience was priceless: 'German Zeppelin ships had flown tens of thousands of miles during the war in conjunction with the fleet, in patrol, reconnaissance, mine-sweeping and bombing operations. During the war period, Luftschiffbau-Zeppelin designed and built 88 airships at its four construction docks, making a total of 115 built from 1900 through to 1918.'[18]

Despite the damage wrought by internal dispute and external economic distress, after the war the Zeppelin company built a small, innovative airship, the *Bodensee,* named after the lake at Friedrichshafen, Zeppelin's home. She was more efficient and could travel at twice the top speed of pre-war commercial ships, achieving 82.4mph even without opening her four 245-horsepower engines to full throttle. (Historian Douglas Robinson explains that this was because her wartime 'altitude' engines could not be run at full throttle below 6000 feet.) A comparison with one of her forerunners, the *Sachsen,* built before the war in 1913, shows the strides the Zeppelin company had achieved. The *Sachsen* was no mean ship – with a respectable lift of 16,300 pounds, while the *Bodensee* with a volume of gas similar to that of the *Sachsen,* slightly less than 800,000 cubic feet, had a lift of 22,000 pounds, thus increasing her usefulness by more than 30 per cent.

The *Bodensee* was designed by Zeppelin's aerodynamicist, Dr. Paul Jaray. Streamlined, with a passenger cabin situated well forward instead of in the conventional midships position, she featured a long gondola with five compartments, each seating four people. The control car was also in a novel position, set integrally into the fore of the passenger cabin. With sufficient lift, six more passengers could be carried in wicker chairs in the central aisle. A forward cabin accommodated a single VIP passenger, who would be obliged to pay double fare for the privilege. Aft of the gondola were washrooms and a buffet.[19] The *Bodensee* made her first flight on 20 August 1919 and was subsequently used on a successful commercial passenger service from Friedrichshafen to Berlin. The service carried almost 2,400 passengers on 103 flights in 98 days.

But at the point at which the company was putting the finishing touches to a new ship, the *Nordstern,* the Inter-Allied Commission intervened, commandeering the ships, assigning the *Bodensee* to Italy and the *Nordstern* (marginally bigger with room for 30 passengers, but built primarily to the same plans as the *Bodensee*) to France. 'It was due to this circumstance that the Zeppelin company's accumulated experience in building and flying airships became available to America in 1924.'[20]

Eckener saved the Zeppelin company by securing an order from the US Navy for *LZ-126*. In October 1924, under the command of Eckener, *LZ 126* voyaged triumphantly from Friedrichshafen to Lakehurst in the USA and was renamed the ZR-3 *Los Angeles*. Its delivery signalled that Zeppelin, despite internal wrangling and external Allied restrictions, had retained its position as the world's most potent force in airships.

Burney and the Germans

On Friday 25 May 1923, Burney journeyed to the Zeppelin works at Friedrichshafen in Germany – with some discretion, for 'tension in Europe was high. Early in the year French and Belgian troops had occupied the industrial areas of the Ruhr valley in an attempt to force payment of repatriation for war damage laid down in the Treaty of Versailles in 1919'. (21) With him went Barnes Wallis. A shrewd businessman, Burney had ensured that Vickers would allow him the services of its promising young designer, whose *R80* had been hailed as perhaps the finest airship to have been built in Britain.[22] Though Burney had made enemies, and he would make more as his Scheme inched ahead, his determination never wavered, nor his ability to spot winners: in Wallis he had recognised a formidable talent.

Given the social and economic atmosphere of the time Burney's mission to Germany was both sensitive and provocative. The war had impoverished Britain as well as Germany. In Britain, socialism and pacifism were in the air. The climate in which Vickers, the world's most powerful armaments producer, operated had grown hostile. Burney was not, however, the type to allow political niceties to hamper his ambitions. He had not abandoned the idea of using German-built airships on Imperial routes. Indeed, he had his eye on a bigger prize – with typical chutzpah, he and his shell company might, perhaps, acquire the mighty Zeppelin corporation, dominant since the ebullient Count had stumped across Germany raising money two decades before. At the least, he might engineer a merger. The trip he made with Wallis was not the first Burney had made to the Luftschiffbau-Zeppelin works. He had visited the plant several times and had held lengthy and detailed discussions with its iconic chief Hugo Eckener.

Burney was well aware of the difficulties faced by the German airship industry, and the report of the Burney-Wallis visit to the Zeppelin company refers to the building of the *LZ 126*: 'Under the terms imposed by the Peace Treaty all German Airships sheds have been destroyed excepting the constructional shed at Friedrichshafen which has been left standing during the completion of a rigid airship for the USA. On the delivery of this ship this shed also will be pulled down.'[23] However: 'Zeppelin is not anticipating any period of inactivity as they have been approached from several directions with a view to possible design and operation of airships. In every case it would be necessary for the ships to be built outside Germany.'[24]

Burney was also aware that Goodyear was in advanced talks with Zeppelin about a takeover or merger, and that it represented major competition. He remained glint-eyed, determined that his company, still a minnow, would not miss out on any profits generated by the construction and deployment of airships. And there were incentives beyond profit: Wallis and Burney both believed in the Empire and saw in airships an elegant way of drawing together its disparate threads, especially India, the jewel in the crown.

A paragraph of the memorandum by Wallis that chronicled the trip to Friedrichshafen is explicit about its purpose: 'The object of the visit was to negotiate an agreement between the Zeppelin Company and the proposed British Airship Company.'[25] Shortly before his trip Wallis wrote to his future wife, Molly Bloxam: 'Oh Molly, such exciting times. Yesterday, at a moment's notice I had to attend a conference on Commander Burney's financial scheme for starting a great Imperial Transport Company. He didn't know who I was, but during the night he must have found out, for the first thing this morning he rang me up, and asked me to go and talk to him. And then and there he asked me to join in with him in the new company.' Wallis had reservations about Burney's offer. The uncertain progress of airship development had affected Wallis's career – 'My present post in the Vickers company – the biggest engineering firm in the world I think – is an exceptionally good one, with very good prospects of advancement.'[26] He writes of his concern about the uncertainties of trying to build a career in airships, whose progress had been scarred by mishap and volatility: 'Airships have twice stopped altogether, once at the beginning of the war, and then in 1921 ... now however I want to settle down – suppose I join Burney, and in another few years Airships once more break down? ... which shall it be ... adventure again, or safety?'[27]

Wallis wrote that his boss at Vickers might be 'willing to lend me to Burney for three months ... I've been having interviews all day, and there are more tomorrow. I simply hate some of these interviews, when I feel I am being "inspected". I always have my oldest suit on, and feel sure there's a smudge over one eye, or my hair isn't tidy.'[28] Wallis added: 'I'm feeling rather heartbroken Molly. It's been one long conference all day. And now I fear I am out of airships – for none of the reasons that I thought – but because under the very complex circumstances the only decent thing I could do was to stand aside and let Pratt, who has been my colleague for many years, step into the place that Burney offered me. What an illogical idiot I am. When the thing was undecided, I could see many arguments against joining Burney – tho' even as I wrote to you I said to myself – "You are pretending to be very judicial and cautious, but really in your heart you know there is only one thing to do, and that is to join him." And now that it is all over, I feel perfectly miserable!'[29] Hartley Pratt and Wallis were close friends for many years. They had sailed dinghies together as young men when training as boat-builders on the south coast in the early days of their careers. Wallis had high moral principles and felt that he had to reject offers being made to him by Burney and let Pratt take his place, a decision which grieved him in that, as well as worrying about his friend, he was a consummate engineer aware of his gifts and keen for advancement – but not to the detriment of friend or colleague.

Molly replied: 'I am so sorry about the airships, Barnes. When I first read about it, I thought how lovely it was for you to have a chance of going back to them; and it must have been so disappointing when you decided that Pratt and not you must join Commander Burney. I can just imagine how, all the time you were thinking it would be wiser and safer not to join him, you knew that because it was Airships you must join him. I should think you did hate those interviews, with people inspecting and criticising you ... perhaps there will be another chance for you with Airships again soon; I do hope there is.'[30]

Molly's hopes were quickly granted, and Wallis would not be disappointed for long. The thrusting Burney had insisted Wallis was the man for him. He was not the type to be thwarted in his choice of candidate. Wallis wrote to Molly: 'I am awfully sorry I have not been able to finish off the enclosed, but am leaving at a moment's notice for Germany, where I expect to remain about a week. I am going with Commander Burney to Friedrichshafen to advise him on the purchase of the Zeppelin Airship Works. Fearfully secret!!'[31] Whether Wallis was being loose in his choice of words, or if Burney had simply intimated hopes of a coming together of his fledgling company and Zeppelin one can only speculate, though Wallis's vocabulary was usually as precise as his technical calculations. The notion of a David consuming the mighty Zeppelin Goliath might seem preposterous, but it would be in character for Burney, his confidence only ever matched by his boundless ambition.

Outcome of Burney's Visit

The report on the Burney-Wallis visit to the Zeppelin works states:

> The scheme put before the Germans was Commander Burney's scheme for a bi-weekly service of airships to India, involving the formation of a state-subsidised operating company working in conjunction with an airship building company ... the French government have been negotiating [with the Zeppelin company] for the design of three rigid airships to be built in France ... the Spanish–South American airship service is a combined operating and construction contract, for which it is proposed to build the necessary ships in Spain.[32]

Of the Goodyear corporation the report mentions 'the formation of a combined operating and construction company in America', and states that Goodyear representatives were due at Friedrichshafen 'three or four weeks after the date of our visit and these negotiations appear to have reached a very advanced stage. We were given to understand that in return for their technical services the Germans were to receive a third share in the American companies. A ship ... is at present under construction for the USA government.' The report observes that 'in general Zeppelin ... appeared to be in a fairly prosperous condition, and still employs over 1,000 hands not counting those in the subsidiary companies'.[33] Subsidiary Zeppelin companies included the prodigious Maybach motor division, which made the engines for German airships, but which at the time of the Burney-Wallis visit was occupied in producing car and boat engines. Other subsidiaries included a fabric and textile producer, a maker of sheds, a gear-cutting company and the producer of the noted Zeppelin Dornier flying boats, which were to achieve success on their own account. Zeppelin's management, in the battle to keep the company going, had shown versatility in using airship assets for different purposes. The report noted: 'All these subsidiaries are now occupied with other commercial work and the airship interest forms only a small proportion of their total output.'[34]

The substance of the proposed Anglo-German agreement is outlined in the report:

In order to ensure mutual co-operation and support the German company shall exchange some 40 per cent of its shares against 25 per cent of the shares of the British company, in consideration for which each company would place at the disposal of the other its full technical knowledge [and] use of patents and licences without payment; and in all future enterprises both companies would share.

But it appeared that Burney had been pipped to the post by Goodyear. It was not his fault. For a man of his urgency and temperament, his slowness in being able to make overtures to Zeppelin would have chafed; vacillation by the British government and the Services had forced him to stay his hand. It rankled with him that negotiations between Goodyear and the Germans had 'reached so advanced a stage that the Germans no longer consider themselves wholly free to enter into other alliances of the type we proposed to them. The Goodyear combination if closed would definitely exclude the British company from either operational or constructional activities in the USA.'

However, cautiously optimistic, the report adds: 'It was thought possible some three-cornered arrangement might be arrived at whereby the British interest would participate in the Zeppelin-Goodyear combination. It was stipulated that the 40–25 [per cent] share proportion would only be agreed to by the British on this understanding, otherwise the figures would be 40–23.5%.'[35]

Wallis's letter to Molly, from Friedrichshafen on 26 May 1923, hints at the hyper-inflation that gripped Germany and which had helped humble Zeppelin, making it vulnerable to predators:

> I cannot resist writing a line to send you one penny [underlined] in the form of a thousand Mark note. One wanders about with one's pockets simply bulging with sheaves of these things running up to one hundred thousand (8/4*d*) notes. Our dinner at the hotel, if the Mark had its proper value, cost us £13,000. As Commander Burney said, even Rockfeller [sic] couldn't keep it up long at that rate.[36]

Wallis gives an insight into the way Burney worked: fast, unremitting and with a manic energy; this was the Burney way. When he invented the paravane years before as a serving naval officer,

> He [Burney] was now plunged neck-deep into a task big enough to occupy a whole government department. There were experimental trials to be conducted at sea, improvements in design to devise, drawings to be made, specifications to be written, business with private firms to be transacted, official reports to be written, and his inventions to be

patented. He had, in fact, to start and to conduct a vast technical and industrial enterprise, which was eventually to cost millions, in a cabin in the *Vernon* [the ship to which Burney was attached] destitute of modern business appliances, and with such scant clerical assistance as the *Vernon* could provide. Moreover, the urgency of the affair, at least in Burney's view, was extreme ... [37]

The description fits Burney as an airship entrepreneur. In his letter from Friedrichshafen on 26 May 1923, Wallis, famous for working round-the-clock and demanding the same of colleagues, said:

We got here at 5 o'clock on Thursday afternoon after travelling continuously since Wednesday morning. Very tiring, as being in such a rush we could get no sleeping accommodation on the trains, and so got no sleep for 40 hours ... nevertheless we went straight to the Zeppelin Works and started negotiations and got no tea! Friday we conferenced from 10 in the morning till 11 at night, and yesterday from 10 am till after midnight, and today we were at it again till about half an hour before Burney was due to leave at 1.40. He has to be in London for a Cabinet Committee meeting ... and so he has had to leave me in charge to draw up the draft agreement between the English and the German companies. As the whole affair involves capital to the extent of over eight million pounds [English] it is no small affair, and the inter-related companies are very complex. I hope to goodness I do not make a mess of it, but do not feel much worried.[38]

Burney rushing to another engagement leaving the inexperienced Wallis to pick up the pieces sounds in character: his detractors say Burney always passed the buck and left the dangerous, or tedious, minutiae to his subordinates; his admirers, however, would claim that he was never afraid to delegate and that he was a past-master of the difficult art of keeping many balls in the air at the same time.

Wallis wrote of his burgeoning optimism:

There is now, in my mind, not the least doubt that in 2 or 3 years from now, we shall have the most wonderful series of air lines running from England to India, twice every week and back, in two and a half days! Carrying 200 passengers each, and mails and parcels. I don't care if I die after that. It will only be the start of the course, and the line will subsequently be extended to Australia and New Zealand, and then there will be other lines.[39]

Apart from 'drawn out and weary meals' (he also mentions 'delicious, tastefully served food') and describing some citizens as 'the most disgusting men I have seen in my life, huge rolls of fat hanging over their collars, and their tummies!' – Wallis relished his stay in Germany. 'This is a most luxurious hotel, for Friedrichshafen is only a little townlet of 12,000 inhabitants ... picturesque and quaint. It was only a small village before Count Zeppelin chose it to build his first airship. We went thro' their airship museum ... fascinating ... relics of the earliest ships, dating back to 1900. He was a very wonderful old man.'[40] Mary Stopes-Roe, Wallis's daughter said:

My father made some comments about Burney and the food in Friedrichshafen ... *gluttony* is how he might have described it. He was quite glad when Burney went because they had to eat ten-course meals and my father would have declined some courses, while Burney would have been only too happy to help. So I think being left in Germany was not entirely a disaster for BNW [Barnes Neville Wallis]. He might have thought: 'O Lord, the businessman is going and leaving me in the lurch.' But somehow I don't think so.[41]

Wallis recalled an excursion with the directors of the Zeppelin company on a yacht once owned by the late King of Württemberg, a supporter of airships who in the past had bailed out Count Zeppelin. 'There was Dr. Eckener and Frau

Eckener, and Herr Lehmann and Frau Lehmann and Herr Fricker, a banker, who used to live in London and rowed in [the] Henley Regatta. He went back to Germany on the outbreak of war, and was gassed.' Wallis wrote of the party having an elaborate picnic: sausages, white wine, cigars, the Lehmanns with a servant carrying two large baskets of food; the Eckeners with an even larger basket. 'We had enough food for a regiment. Lehmann had also brought an enormous accordion, on which at intervals during the cruise he would play slow and very harmonious German airs, while the old Doctor stumped up and down on the deck, humming the words. They are funny people, just like great children. Somehow I felt absolutely at home among them.'[42]

When Wallis returned to London from Germany, 'he was elated, entirely confident ... certain that he had done a good job.' But soon afterwards the Zeppelin scheme was jettisoned: 'the collapse of the dealings with Zeppelin was no fault of the novice negotiator'. Wallis's relationship with Burney at this point seemed good. 'He [Wallis] was once more entirely certain that Burney was a man with whom he could work. Wallis was beginning to allow his mind to wander more freely than had ever before been possible to him as a practising and practical engineer.'[43]

In addition to political upheaval, there was another airship catastrophe. On 21 December 1923, two days before Labour resumed office, the French airship L.72 *Dixmude* was lost. Given this calamity and circumstances prevailing at the time, it seems extraordinary that the Imperial airship scheme survived at all: squabbling in the services; a vociferous lobby demanding that heavier-than-air development take precedent; Britain's financial plight, its economy hampered by collapsing trade and rising unemployment; the national psyche still scarred by the years of war. That it did (albeit in a wholly changed form) was largely because of Brigadier Christopher Birdwood Thomson, later Lord Thomson of Cardington, the intimate and political ally of Ramsay MacDonald and the new and determined Secretary of State for Air following the General Election of 6 December 1923, which ushered in Britain's first Labour government.

French and Spanish Airships

In the Cimetière du Père-Lachaise, Paris, is the tomb of Joseph Spiess, marked by a bronze airship set into the headstone. Spiess was an Alsatian engineer who in 1873 produced a design for a rigid airship. It was a flimsy affair compared with a patent he took out three decades later for a craft that sailed in 1913 and which caused a sensation when it voyaged over Paris in the opening weeks of 1914. Thought to have been broken up at the outbreak of the war, it is known the ship had been extended, that more gas cells had been inserted and that its engine power had been increased. Joseph Spiess never achieved due recognition for his work in lighter-than-air technology.

Nor did the Spaniard Leonardo Torres y Quevedo. It is true Torres was held in esteem as a mathematician and engineer but largely through many other endeavours rather than as the creator of the Astra-Torres airship. Torres was born on the feast of the Holy Innocents, 28 December 1852, in Cantabria. At the turn of the twentieth century he conducted scientific research in Madrid and in 1902 produced a paper that would result in the construction of the Astra-Torres in which du Plessis honed his airship skills. A French company, Astra, acquired the patent rights from the Spaniard and built Astra-Torres airships in France and Britain; more were sold to the Japanese and American navies and to the army in pre-Revolution Russia.

A former officer in the French navy, Lieutenant de Vaisseau Jean du Plessis de Grenédan was as enamoured with big rigid airships as Peter Strasser in Germany (if less fanatical about his national cause). There were parallels: when Strasser died, German ambitions for the Zeppelin as a raider ceased; when du Plessis was killed, French determination to lead in rigids faded, for the commitment of du Plessis had been pivotal to French ambitions.

During the war, France, like Britain, deployed airships for submarine reconnaissance and as escorts for naval convoys. French involvement with big rigids began with the Treaty of Versailles of 28 June 1919, when Germany handed over the spoils of war to the Allies, and France received three airships, the best being the ill-fated *Dixmude*, which had been constructed as the wartime Zeppelin *LZ 114* for the German Navy.

After du Plessis had served in the French navy, following his training aboard an Astra-Torres airship, he emerged as an accomplished commander and administrator in French airship affairs. He quickly recognised that the *Dixmude* was one of Zeppelin's most advanced craft. A persuasive advocate, he overcame reluctance (albeit to a limited degree) in the French military and the problem of politicians grappling with an economy ravaged by the war. In *Dixmude* he made passages of note, setting duration records and adding to the meagre knowledge of the time about handling and behavioural patterns: ships made light in hot climes or heavy in cold, with gases expanding or contracting. He pursued a rigorous testing programme, sometimes over the Tunisian desert, modifying his ship accordingly.

Then, on 21 December 1923, as she was completing a record voyage of 118 hours from Toulon to North Africa via Paris, tragedy struck. In worsening weather the big ship was seen in driving snow sailing low, and slow, across Tunisia. The last message from du Plessis was that he was winding in his radio antennae because of a storm. Suddenly the *Dixmude* exploded – it was thought she had been struck by lightning. All 50 people on board perished in the worst air accident up to 1930. The premature death of du Plessis removed a talented commander who would have harvested more scientific wisdoms of great value in the construction and operation of ensuing craft.

Spiess, Torres, du Plessis are names that have disappeared from the public memory but are still revered in airship circles.

7

THE NEW ORDER

Burney and the Airship Guarantee Company

In structuring his Airship Guarantee Company, Burney showed himself a cunning fox by splitting the business into two halves: the first would build airships, the other would operate the ships and exploit the patent rights. Burney appreciated the worth of patents, having made a £350,000 fortune from them on the paravane. The dual structure of the company irritated some government functionaries; in fact, however, the somewhat complicated business structure which Burney had instituted was only one aspect with which Thomson was uncomfortable. At a cabinet meeting on 11 February 1924, Thomson summarised the Burney proposals:

1 A guarantee and construction company was to be formed with a capital of £500,000 to acquire all necessary patents and secret processes to procure the formation of an airship operating company with a subscribed capital of £200,000.
2 All the airships were to be given free to the operating company.
3 Cardington and Pulham, the only remaining airship stations, would be leased to the company at a peppercorn rent with an option to purchase for £500,000.
4 Cardington village would be leased to the company at a cost rental of £3,000 per annum with an option to purchase for a cash payment of £60,000.

5 In the first stage the company would receive a subsidy of £400,000 and through the agency of the guarantee and construction company for the construction of a 5-million-cubic-foot airship and necessary mooring mast.

6 When the Company had flown from England to India in less than seven days, the second stage was to be entered upon – and a further sum of £150,000 was to be raised by the Company, while the government would provide a further subsidy of £1.2 million, being £400,000 per annum payable over three years in return for a weekly service to India.

7 When it had run the weekly service for three months the third stage would be entered into and a further £150,000 raised by the Company, while the government would provide a further sum of £1.2 million (as in paragraph six) in return for a bi-weekly service to and from India.

8 The total subsidies of £2.8 million payable over seven years were to be secured by debentures carrying no interest and only repayable out of profits; one half of the net profits in each year, after providing for reserves, was to be applied to the cancellation of the debentures.

9 On completion of the third stage, an annual fee payment of £41,666, 13s 4d was to be made for each airship maintained in commission, not exceeding six (making £250,000 for a fleet of six ships) for a period of eight years.

10 The whole currency of the Agreement was thus 15 years.

Thomson attacked every aspect of the Burney proposals. Central to his criticism was a demand for a far greater degree of government control. He argued that a monopoly was being given to the Airship Guarantee Company. His officials would have to deal with two inter-locking companies that were 'subsidiaries of one of the oil companies, and a powerful armaments firm, whose businesses have world wide ramifications in foreign countries; the development of airships and airship research is virtually handed over in total to these companies for the 15 years' currency of the agreement'. Burney, Thomson insisted, was not independent – he was a paid consultant to Vickers.

Development and experiments would be paid for out of the public purse, but the fruits of research could then be sold to foreign powers. Repayment of subsidies would be 'distinctly dubious'. It would take 56 years to complete repayment. If the Scheme failed, no airships would be available for defence and, again, development 'would be thrown back into the melting pot'. Bases would be leased to Burney at a peppercorn rent, but if the government ever wanted them back it would prove to be costly.

Thomson produced an alternative plan. The Air Ministry would recondition two service airships for experimental work. But the Ministry would also build a new ship at Cardington big enough to go to India. The government would install mooring facilities in Egypt and India. An advisory board would be set up, which in its constitution would be all-inclusive with every interest represented: development of the airship, Thomson observed, had been retarded by a lack of consensus. The board would formulate the specification of the new airship and have as its watchwords 'safety' and 'consensus' – after the *R38* and *Dixmude* calamities, safety would be paramount. The government would not be 'unduly rushed'. Experiments advocated by the Aeronautical Research Committee after the *R38* disaster would be conducted before the building of the government ship began. 'We shall be proceeding more slowly than under the Burney Scheme', recorded Thomson, 'but more surely.'

Thomson's plan had a crucial attraction – it was cheaper. His proposals were based on a four-year programme. They would mean spending £1.4 million not £4.8 million. Of the £1.4million, £200,000 would be needed in 1924–5, as against £400,000, while £200,000 could be found in the 1924–5 Air Estimates. In essence, Thomson's plan would 'entail the rejection of the Burney Scheme in its present form'. He was adamant that 'no undesirable monopoly is created and lighter-than-air research remains under government supervision and control'. Circumstances, he believed, had changed in the three years since airships had been closed down. America and France were developing craft. Since 1920 in Britain a heavier-than-air Home Defence Force had been formed, and aeroplane squadrons were available for cooperation with the Royal Navy. Imperial communication was 'of the first importance; the beneficial effects of bringing India within five days, and Australia within fourteen days, would be far reaching'. Airships, he felt, were of the 'utmost utility' and would enhance mobility of the aeroplane squadrons; squadrons and stores could be moved from one theatre of conflict to another on a scale beyond the capacity of aeroplanes. He offered a glimmer of hope to the Admiralty: 'The Air Staff share the view of the Naval Staff that airships may have great potential as a medium of naval reconnaissance.'[1]

After the cabinet meeting, Thomson sought more anti-Burney ammunition from his civil servants. One wrote to him: 'I understand you have asked for some notes on the possibility of screwing up the Burney agreements.' The official complained about the Airship Guarantee Company structure and said it was impossible for the government to procure satisfactory technical terms. The two-tier structure Burney had established had to be abolished if the government wanted 'full control'. The entire Burney Scheme, the functionary advised, needed to be recast. The two-company arrangement had resulted in 'utmost confusion in the technical clauses; whereas we desire control of design and research in construction, we find all our government money is being given to the operating company which does not construct'.[2]

Though Thomson had torpedoed Burney's original intentions he did not intend to entirely eradicate him from the plan; at a private meeting with Burney he confirmed that he wanted the AGC to build a second ship.[3] This would be a private ship built by Vickers and the AGC and designed by Barnes Wallis. It would be eventually designated the *R100* and would be designed by the rising young Vickers star Barnes Wallis. The subsequent rejection of the original Burney Scheme was endorsed by Prime Minister Ramsay MacDonald in the House of Commons on 14 May 1924. As well as the government building its own ship, to be named the *R101*, Burney would be contracted to build a second ship, the *R100*. On completion, Burney would then be able to buy it from the Air Ministry at a reduced price if it was used on an approved service and if it was made available to the State as required.[4]

ve: The *R100* building shed at Howden, east Yorkshire. (Courtesy Mary Stopes-Roe)

ow: Barnes Wallis in his office some thirty years later, with a model of his creation, the *R100*. (Courtesy
ry Stopes-Roe)

The *R100* had five million cubic feet of hydrogen and was fitted with reconditioned Rolls Royce Condor petrol engines. She made her maiden voyage December 1929 from Howden to Cardington, from where she sailed to Canada July 1930. (Cody Images)

ove: Members of Parliament and worthies seeking joy-rides descended on *R100* and *R101* during their lding. Self-important and ill-informed, they irritated ships' officers (Appendix A). This was a grandees' lunch a gondola mock-up in a building shed.

ow: A bewildering plethora of instruments in a control in. Note the crewman at the large ship's wheel miniscent of marine vessels.

R100 over York 16/12/29

With booing good wishes from
Molly & Barnes
Christmas 1929

ft: In his long and distinguished career, Barnes allis designed everything from airships to aircraft and uncing bombs that destroyed wartime German ms. (Courtesy Mary Stopes-Roe)

ght: Barnes Wallis spent five years at Howden ilding the *R100*. He and his wife Molly celebrated e airship's voyages on Christmas cards sent to ends and colleagues.

t and above: Some of the finest engineering and scientific brains in the ld brought the *R101* into being. Critics said it was over-engineered. ore its ill-fated voyage Michael Rope raised serious questions about the ability of its immense cover.

t right: Michael Rope. Deeply religious, prodigiously gifted, he played a cial role in the design of the *R101*. He moved his family away to avoid the nking culture at Cardington. (Courtesy Crispin Rope)

ow: An illustration from the promotional brochure for the *R101*.

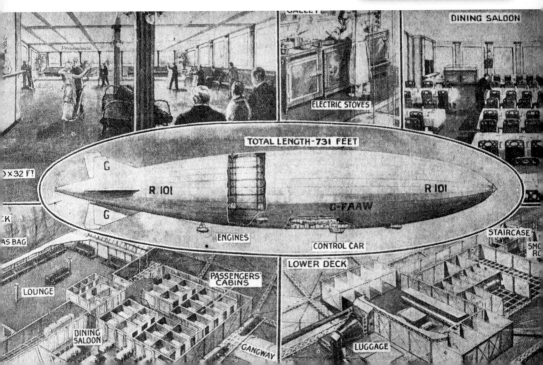

SURVIVORS' VIVID STORIES OF AIRSHIP DISASTER

DAILY SKETCH

INCORPORATING THE DAILY GRAPHIC

No. 6,699. (Registered as a newspaper.)   MONDAY, OCTOBER 6, 1930.   ONE PENNY.

R101 MEMORIAL NUMBER

THE LAST OF THE GIANT R101:
WONDERFUL AIR PICTURE

MEN WHO FOUGHT FOR EMPIRE AIRSHIPS.

FATE OF THE PIONEERS.

THOMSON, SCOTT AND COLMORE.

FAITH IN AIRSHIP SAFETY.

By CAPT. PAUL BEWSHER, D.S.C.

ALL that brave little group of men who fought fearlessly for years to make the dream of an Empire airship line come true have died in its realisation. All save one or two, who in their grief must almost feel sorry that they were not with them. Thomson, Colmore, Richmond, Scott, Johnston, and Irwin all gone! It is difficult to write of them—remembering their almost boyish enthusiasm—their optimism maintained unfading in spite of overwhelming difficulties—in face of the heavy, depressing opposition of many air experts, of politicians, and of a large mass of the general public.

"Unwieldy gas-bags!" sneered their opponents.

"Liners of the air linking the Empire!" they answered, and worked day and night in an unfaltering belief.

ITS PROUD OFFICERS.

I was shown all over the R101 by its proud officers when it was finished. I saw it creep out of its vast hangar at dawn for the first time. I saw it leave Cardington on its first flight.

The last picture of four of the dead in the R101 disaster. It was taken by a *Daily Mail* photographer at Cardington just before the flight began. Left to right: Squadron Leader E. L. Johnston (navigator), Sir Sefton Brancker (Director of Civil Aviation), Lord Thomson (Secretary for Air), Lt.-Col. V. C. Richmond designer of R 101).

and served under Lord (then Sir Douglas) Haig. He gained the D.S.O. and was twice mentioned in despatches.

Air Vice-Marshal Sir Sefton Brancker, who was 53, leaves a widow and a son. Educated at Bedford Grammar School. He was Director of Civil Aviation. War and mentioned in despatches. As one of the first Army officers to take up flying he had his first flight in India in 1910. When in 1911 he was appointed Deputy Director of Military Aeronautics he took a great share in building up the Royal Flying Corps. In 1930 he was appointed

LORD THOMSON.
INTREPID SPIRIT.
MAN WHO LOVED RISKS.

By COMMANDER OLIVER LOCKER-

AN EXPERT'S PROPHECY.

"Forty Men Will Lose Their Lives."

THREE years ago, when the proposals of the Govern-

ove: North Pole airship explorers. Seated, left to right, are Roald Amundsen, Lincoln Ellsworth and Umberto bile. (Pacific & Atlantic/NY Daily News Archive via Getty Images)

ow: The crew of the *Norge* hauling Umberto Nobile's airship during her North Pole expedition. (Library of ngress)

Roma was the last hydrogen craft bought by the United States. Built by Italian engineers who included Umberto Nobile, it crashed in Virginia in 1922. Among its casualties was its captain, Dale Mabry. Afterward, American airships sailed on retarded helium. (Library of Congress)

Milan, Italy, April 1928. Umberto Nobile, in uniform, left foreground, with the semi-rigid N-class airship *Italia*, which a second North Pole sailing was attempted. *Italia* crashed on drifting pack ice on 25 May. (Pictorial Parade/Getty Images)

In the House of Lords, Thomson said the government would spend £1.2 million, while the budget for Burney's ship would be a modest £350,000. The government bill, he said, would be higher because of the research involved and because of having to pay for the overseas mooring masts. Information gleaned from the experiments would be shared with Burney's team. Initially, the government ship, the *R101*, would be for military use; Burney's *R100* would be primarily for civil purposes.

Thomson announcedt that he wanted two airships to be constructed to 'enlist the co-operation of private enterprise ... not so much in competition with the Air Ministry, but rather in a spirit of emulation'. Warmed by his own rhetoric, he launched into an eloquent, if somewhat romantic flight of fancy, telling the House of Lords of his vision for Britain. He imagined 'this island as a great airport, as it has been the greatest sea port in the past'; a future in which 'noble Lords will leave this House ... on gliders with light engines ... and in order to take a rest, or to greet a friend, they may call in at some great flying caravanserai, one of these giant airships, floating serene and safe, high up and far removed from terrestrial dirt and noise'. This was greeted by his fellow peers with prolonged and raucous laughter – the Duke of Atholl was among those critics who felt that Thomson was 'a great schemer or a great dreamer; he may hereafter be numbered among the saints, but the noble Lord will not be remembered among the prophets'.[5]

The MacDonald government lasted nine months. Stanley Baldwin took over and Hoare went back to his old job as Air Minister, replacing Thomson. There was surprise that Hoare decided to continue with Thomson's plan. Hoare felt that a 'double experiment is much safer than a single experiment'; for defence experiments the government had 'full control rather than being dependent on the use of a commercial ship for a few weeks in the year'. Having already spent money, Hoare said, it was 'better to proceed rather than once again throwing development into the melting pot'. The airship saga was one of 'a long history of continuous inquiries and reversals of policy ... it would be better to go with an experiment that is actually going to produce two airships within a not unreasonably far distant time'. His government would be less 'hands-on': 'We have no wish to smother what may be a great development ... by any act of bureaucratic interference.'[6] But the idea of the construction process being one of cooperation not competition, with the government and the Burney team sharing information in a programme free of bureaucracy proved to be nonsense.

Wallis and R80

'My father [Barnes Wallis] would have called himself an engineer and proud of it. He would not have described himself as a scientist or a mathematician or anything like that. An engineer doesn't put in extra bits and pieces. Well, really, what would be the point? An extra fancy bit doesn't make something safer or more functional.'[7]

Others describe Wallis differently. Historian Robin Higham: 'Designers such as H. B. Pratt and later Barnes Wallis were artistic scientists and this made it much more difficult for the Admiralty to handle them than to deal with the production engineers of other firms.'[8] Of Wallis designing *R80*: 'Wallis was freed from all the former restrictions ... [and was] able to design an airship ... with a beautiful shape, in which he still has an artist's pride.'[9]

Douglas Robinson, the airship historian, wrote of the Admiralty's acceptance of the proposal in 1917 by Vickers to build the *R80*: 'The result was a free hand for Barnes Wallis, the engineering genius who in 1916 had become Vickers Chief Airship Designer, and who had numerous original ideas on the subject of airship design. Convinced that the pencil-form *Zahm-*shape*[10] of previous British designs was in error, Wallis as early as 1916 conceived the perfect streamlined shape of the rigid airship destined to become *R80*. 'Here at last we see a home grown ship equal to the Germans' best, created by a designer sure of himself, and producing a rigid airship which reflected credit both on himself and on his country.'[11]

With the notable exception of the bags and valves, which were German, Wallis could claim he had designed each part of *R100* and that he had

---

* Professor Albert Francis Zahm was a gifted early American aerodynamicist who claimed – erroneously as it was proved by Wallis and others – that the thin, pencil-shape of his airship hulls produced just 40 per cent of the aerodynamic drag of the German Zeppelins.

constructed and designed previous rigids. Richmond, the *R101* designer, could not make such claims. But Richmond's defenders (and there are many) have no doubt about his commitment.

'Unlike ... Barnes Wallis he [Richmond] was wholly devoted to the cause of airships. Wallis was a scientist and engineer first and foremost and he held next to no sentimentality or romance to his role as airship designer. He was very much the reluctant airship traveller as a direct result of an experience at Barrow in 1915.'[12] This refers to an incident in a small ship piloted by the redoubtable, if sometimes accident-prone, George Herbert Scott. Sailing low in thick fog, he and Wallis were trying to locate the shed at Barrow-in-Furness. Suddenly, below them, they spotted to their consternation an enormous bonfire, lit as a beacon to assist them in finding their bearings. Alarmed that a stray spark might trigger an airborne conflagration, Scott shot skywards in his craft, clouting the shed roof in the process.[13] 'The experience deeply unnerved Wallis who for many years would swear blind he would never fly in an airship again. He was, however, on board for *R100*'s first flight when it left Howden for Cardington on the 16th December 1929.'[14]

Would Wallis have liked to have been involved in building the *R101*? Mary Stopes-Roe is adamant that he would not. 'Good heavens no! It would have driven him mad unless he'd been given a free hand. Fancy trying to work with that lot! While the *R101* lot were working on their ship they never consulted him. He was never asked to comment on it or to go (to Cardington). There wasn't much doubt what he thought of it. He preserved his silence. If anybody had bothered to ask him he knew they wouldn't have paid any attention anyway to anything that he might have said.'[15]

Was Wallis difficult? 'When you come up against an idiot you speak your mind. He wasn't downright rude. He could be didactic. He would never say: "Well I think", or "maybe", or "perhaps we could try." He would say: "This", "that", or the other, leaving out "I think so", or "possibly". That was the difference in his approach and work.'[16]

Design of the R100

The elegance of Wallis's *R100* design lay in its simplicity. Constructed from only 51 standard components of varying size, Wallis said that if the different thicknesses of material, the varying diameters of tubing and so on were discounted, the number of actual engineering components boiled down to an astonishing eleven parts.[17] Standardisation of parts was crucial. Wallis had to adhere to a fixed budget smaller than that allocated to the *R101*. Burney had planned a fleet of ships. Standardisation would be paramount if margins were to be maintained. *R100* was a template for future designs. The simpler, cheaper, quicker it was to build huge intercontinental ships, the greater the guarantee that Burney would achieve his anticipated levels of profit.

When built, the *R100* had five million rivets, eleven miles of tubing and 400,000 minor bracing pieces, 'and due to metallurgical advances since *R100* was commenced ... Dr. Wallis reckoned that a subsequent ship of the same design would weigh 15 per cent less, which would mean a consequent increase in disposable lift'.[18] Though expected to imitate more closely the design templates of previously successful Zeppelin airships, Wallis's *R100* was not devoid of innovation. The *R101* had a gully atop its envelope as a rainwater entrapment system for ballast tanks to be topped-up while the vessel sailed; Wallis adapted the system for the *R100*. There were more fundamental differences between the vessels. *R100* had only 16 sides, fewer than in previous ships. Here it is difficult not to momentarily venture into the technical:

> *R100* was intended to be based on more-or-less conventional 'Zeppelin' principles. Zeppelins had 13 main longitudinals bolted to the apices of 13-sided transverse frames, braced with radial wires like a bicycle's 'tension-wheel'; each of the 13 sides was a shallow triangle, apex inwards, braced with a kingpost which extended beyond the base of the triangle and carried a light 'intermediate longitudinal', thus producing a 26-sided hull. Further, between each pair of transverse

frames were two 'intermediate frames' which were unbraced on account of the gas cells between them, but helping to stiffen the longitudinals. Wallis decided that all these 'intermediates' added to the weight whilst contributing negligibly to the overall strength. Instead he used stouter (though still braced) 16-sided transverse frames carrying 16 longitudinals. The vastly greater area of canvas between them he supported by an ingenious system of tapes and wires which pulled the fabric in, creating slightly concave 'slices' which, he correctly deduced, added little to the drag-factor, although it detracted from the appearance of the ship. This system led to problems with flapping and chafing of the fabric, and intermediate girders had to be added in some places to mitigate this effect.[19]

Roxbee Cox of the *R101* team wrote of the *R100*:

> He [Wallis] made one quite serious error. With only 16 sides [on the *R100*] the fabric panels formed by the longitudinal and transverse members were shown by flight trials to be inadequately supported. To prevent them flapping in flight a system of wiring attaching them more firmly to the structure was introduced so that the basic panels of the envelope became concave, giving the ship a rather unfortunate appearance and undoubtedly increasing the aerodynamic drag.[20]

The airship historian Norman Peake ran for years an antiquarian book shop in Norwich; it was an eccentric cornucopia of scientific texts and manuscripts and, sometimes, airship memorabilia. The author once haunted the shop, a fusty warren that drew bibliophiles from across the land. In 1940 Peake, who had a BSc and was by profession a chemist, found employment with Britain's largest maker of aircraft dopes. With his knowledge of airships, he makes an interesting point about Wallis doping the cover of *R100* *before* tautening it around the frame, the technique pioneered by 'Dopey' Richmond, who had employed it on the *R101*. Why they did so is odd: both knew doping prior to installation led to problems with covers becoming dry and brittle. Under a microscope, Peake was among those who had observed that hairline-cracks could appear, rendering the covers fragile and permeable. '[Richmond] was nicknamed "Dopey" from his wartime experience with doping non-rigids but on non-rigids the tension of the envelope was negligible. The error was quickly realised on the *R100*, and two further coats of dope were applied in situ, but without fully correcting the problem.'[21]

Nigel Caley raises other considerations: 'The real problem with the *R100* cover and the quality of its gas bags was that they were too old. They were made a long time before the ship was ready for them. The ship had been subject to delays and the items had become unserviceable through age.'[22]

Airship designers took a pride in aesthetics as well as function; there was a sense of the artist as much as the engineer. In Mary Stopes-Roe's home rests a graceful relic: a duralumin cylindrical tube. To further reduce its weight holes were punched along its length in a regular pattern, adding to its elegant symmetry. Designed for the *R100* by Wallis, her father, it is a helical spar, functional but so tactile that visitors touch and stroke it as they would sculpture. A metre long, it is feather-light, a reminder, glinting in the morning sun, of the élan with which Wallis and others invested their designs. Prior to Wallis's ship,

> The 'open' triangular girders of Zeppelins were formed from three duralumin 'channel sections' (pressed out from flat strip) linked by diagonal stiffened duralumin strips. Wallis recognised that tubes would be better than channels and, since such things were unavailable, fabricated them by winding duralumin strip helically and close-riveting the spiral overlap. Three of these were then formed into triangular girders by linking them diagonally with duralumin box-sections. Joints between longitudinals and transverse frames used a cleverly-designed 'spider' which ensured forces always met at its 'centroid' for ease of calculation. One single pattern was flexible enough to be used for every joint in the entire hull.[23]

The *R100* was built on the light, robust, lattice-style geodetic principles of Wallis's *R80*, later utilised in his acclaimed Wellesley and Wellington bombers. By building lightness as well as strength into aircraft design, following the principles of geodetic construction, Wallis was able to greatly increase the aircraft's range.[24] In the Second World War bomber crews would express a preference for Wallis's aircraft, saying geodetic-framed aircraft could better withstand aerial attacks and ground flak.

The *R100* was as big as an ocean liner – 709 feet long, just 50 feet shorter than the ocean liner *Mauretania*. 'She fitted her shed in Howden like a cork in a bottle. When loaded ... she was as light as a feather and as capable of being swayed by the least puff of wind.' Wallis ignored government urgings to use diesel engines and instead gained permission from the Air Ministry to power his ship with six Rolls Royce Condors, second-hand refurbished petrol engines.[25]

The choice of petrol instead of diesel is not as simple as it seems. There is a persuasive lobby that insists Wallis and Burney wanted petrol because they knew the Ministry, alarmed about the use of petrol in the tropics, would have no choice but to send them across the Atlantic rather than to India, precisely as Burney had intended throughout. Peter Davison, an aviation writer and leading authority on airships said: 'As soon as Wallis made the decision [to use petrol engines] he had to go across the Atlantic. Whereas the *R101* with diesels could have done the Montreal journey, *R100* could not have done a tropical journey safely.'[26] Crispin Rope, son of Michael Rope, an axial member of the *R101* team (see Appendix E), commented: 'I think that the reason [for petrol engines] was quite clear. Burney wanted to make money. There was no money in going to India. He wanted the Atlantic run. India was of no interest to Burney.'[27] 'It always seemed to me that Burney was very much a businessman with an eye on profit.'[28]

The testing of *R100*'s engines in the snugness of her shed caused alarm. The engines bellowed as the great ship, suspended from the roof, surged and swayed, trapped by her confinement, the tips of her propellers dangerously close to floor and walls. Early in the trials it was apparent that *R100* was faster than her heavier rival, clocking 81mph with a cruising speed of around 70mph.

The trials revealed a worrying ripple-effect on her cover. Neither ship had a strong cover. Each craft had been designed with fewer longitudinal girders, leaving larger sections of cover unsupported. On a trial sailing the tail of the *R100* collapsed and had to be redesigned. The new rounded shape, instead of the original pointed design, detracted from her looks. More intermediate girders were introduced to give extra support to the cover.

In *Slide Rule* Shute mentioned accidentally sticking his hand through the *R100* cover, a reference to its tenderness. He wrote of constructors at the top of the Howden shed urinating on it, citing workers' bladders as a possible reason for its weakness; given that they worked at a dizzying 150 feet, and that relief entailed navigating an onerous spider's web of stairs and ladders to the ground floor lavatory, the story has credence.

At Howden the chain of command could be fretful but was short; a fixed budget ensured a lean operation. Compared with Cardington, it was fleet of foot. The Airship Guarantee Company made changes swiftly, largely as Wallis saw fit – even if he clashed with Burney – rarely needing sanction of committee or bureaucrat. If the AGC needed cash, Vickers temporarily bailed it out, keeping an eagle eye on the bills.

Building the R100

Wallis headed the Burney team at the airship station at Howden, in Yorkshire. He employed Nevil Shute Norway as Chief Calculator, a critical role that included checking load and stress factors, the neglect of which had been fundamental to the *R38* disaster. Shute wrote:

> I joined ... in the capacity of Chief Calculator, which should not be misinterpreted. I knew nothing of airships at that time and the Airship Guarantee Company, a subsidiary of Vickers Ltd., employed three consultants who were to teach me the fundamentals of my job and carry out research into the methods. Professor Bairstow was our

authority on aerodynamics, Professor Pippard on structures, and Mr. J. E. Temple was the most practical and useful of them all because he had been Chief Calculator for Wallis on the design of a former ship, *R80*, built by Vickers at the conclusion of the war. My job was to get together a staff of calculators to do the work on *R100*, translating the theories of the consultants into forces and stresses in each member of the ship and so providing the draughtsmen with the sizes for each girder and each wire.[29]

Shute was being modest. He had trained at the de Havilland aeroplane company and would later establish with others his own successful aircraft company, Airspeed. He would also achieve global recognition as the writer Nevil Shute. Much of Shute's semi-biographical novel, *Slide Rule*, is a withering attack on government meddling during the five years it took to build the two ships – 'In the five years ... neither designer visited the other's works, nor did they correspond on the urgent problems each had to solve. Each took his thorny road alone, harassed and overworked. If the Gods wanted competition they had got it with a vengeance, but one would not say it was healthy'. Much has been said about Shute subsequently withdrawing his more caustic observations; play has been made of him being a novelist, not a technologist, and thus ill-equipped to give an authoritative technical commentary. The allegation is unfair given his background in aviation and his success after *R100* with Airspeed.[30] Wallis did not tolerate incompetents. Though they were friends, Wallis would have dismissed Shute from the *R100* project had he thought he was not up to it: 'My father [Barnes Wallis] respected Shute's mathematical abilities as a calculator,' said Mary Stopes-Roe.[31] Was there any relationship between Cardington and Howden? 'No ... not really. I think there was snooping. But that was about it." By who? By Scott? He was frequently at Howden. 'Oh no, I don't think so. Scottie just wasn't the sort.'[32]

Britain was in economic difficulties all through the 1920s; burdened with unemployment, its economy was fragile from the pyres of war. Marxism and

Pacifism were fashionable. In the midst of a near-collapse in the economy, the British government had pledged nearly £3 million to building two giant airships. It was a daring commitment, which many thought lunatic. The newspapers dubbed the *R100* the 'Capitalist' ship, progeny of Vickers, the armaments empire; to some the craft and its parent personified the evils of capitalism, while others hailed it as a brilliant prodigy of free enterprise. *R101* was the ship of 'Socialism', the spawn of Britain's first Labour government. Detractors saw it as the demon offspring of Red planning; admirers said it heralded a new harmony in which the people and science would work in blissful unity.

Barnes Wallis and Molly Bloxam married on St. George's Day, 23 April 1925, and moved to Howden airship station a year later. When they arrived at Howden station it had fallen into desuetude, a forlorn survivor of the rundown of airships in 1921. Wallis was aged 38; Molly, an inveterate letter writer, was 21. From Howden she maintained a stream of correspondence with a school friend, Mary Turner, who lived at Princes Risborough, near High Wycombe, in Buckinghamshire. Her letters, archived by her daughter, Mary Stopes-Roe, offer a unique and poignant perspective on life at the Howden airship station during her husband's construction of the *R100*:

> It [Howden] is such a queer place. There are many little red brick bungalows and one white – ours. At present we are all very bare and untidy; but when our gardens begin to grow we shall improve. We have rabbits running around in the grass outside our back and front doors, and cows can come and poke their heads in at your bedroom windows! But the nicest thing of all are the larks; they sing and sing all day long ... Barnes and I went over to the airship shed the other day. It is the most unimaginably huge thing ... St. Paul's would look silly inside it, only the dome would stick out. I was too tired to walk all around it, so Barnes wheeled me round on a trolley the workmen had left. We went careering over the concrete floor at a tremendous rate; it was fun. It is empty at

present, but machines and things are beginning to come. When Barnes shouted there were fifteen echoes and more ... it is an awe-inspiring place.[33]

With Britain engulfed by unemployment and financial chaos, Molly wrote about the General Strike of 1926:

> I don't know if you'll ever get this letter. We have no posts out or in and no newspapers, so we are indeed isolated ... This strike is awful. Of course I only mean in the way it affects our little world. We don't know what's happening anywhere. If it goes on long we shall completely run out of food as Howden has no reserves. If our workmen go out we shall have no water, no light, no sewage system, as it is all worked by one power house ... [34]

In the five years it took to build the *R100* the relationship between the Wallises and the Burneys became strained. In 1926 the young Molly had to cope with giving her first dinner party: 'Commander Burney came to dinner ... we had a very superior five course dinner, with mats, and no table cloth and all the silver we had ...' ([35]). Mary Stopes-Roe remembers Burney's passion for cars: 'Burney used to come roaring up in this great big car ... he drove it around the station at Howden. It used to scare the living daylights out of poor Barnes [Barnes Wallis Junior, her late brother]. It had a scary front view. It looked like a dragon.' Did her brother go for a ride in it? 'No! Good heavens, he would have been petrified. He was only two or three. Anyway, my parents would never have dreamed of letting him go ... not with Burney.'[36] From her 'dragon' description it sounds as if the machine that frightened her baby brother was a prototype of Burney's venture into automobiles: in 1929 as the *R100* was nearing completion, he created the Burney Streamline, a bizarre-looking car. The prototype was built at Howden of scrap aluminium and wrinkled balloon fabric taken from the airship station. Burney wanted it as streamlined as an airship, more efficient and less 'brick-like' than most cars of the time. His car went into production as the Crossley Streamline, one of which exists in the National Motor Museum in Beaulieu.*

Molly was held in affection at Howden:

> This place is full of the darlingest men you can possibly imagine – all ready and willing to do anything on earth for you. Jimmy Newson, Barnes's rigger ... took me out onto the roof of the shed the other day ... he kept on saying 'mind your little head Mrs. Wallis', when we came to cross pieces; and when we got home again he produced a grubby old bit of tissue paper from his pocket and said: 'I brought this for you to wipe your little hands on Mrs. Wallis'... I suppose it's a great help to your husband to have an elegant, silken-dressed, high-heeled wife, who talks intelligently and looks sweet, but it's a fearful sweat.[37]

Shute's recollections were harsh:

> The labour difficulty was always grave. We were three miles from the little town of Howden and twenty-five from civilisation in the form of Hull. It was difficult to get skilled aircraft hands to work upon the ship however high the wages that were offered; accommodation for workmen of good class was almost non-existent. In Howden fourteen of our men slept in three rooms of a small pub. We employed a large percentage of our labour in the form of local lads and girls straight off the farms as unskilled labour, training them to do simple riveting and mass production work. The lads were what one would expect, straight from the plough, but the girls were an eye-opener. They were brutish and uncouth, filthy in appearance and in habits ... [those] straight off the farms were the lowest types that I have ever seen in England, and incredibly foul-mouthed. We very soon found that we had to employ

---

* The author is grateful to Howden Civic Society, and Dr. Bernard J. Nield, who wrote a book about the vehicle.

a welfare worker to look after them because promiscuous intercourse was going on merrily in every dark corner ... as the job approached completion the need for unskilled female labour was reduced and we were able to get rid of the most jungly types.[38]

Nigel Caley, the airship historian, commented: 'Shute was talented in so many ways. But he could be a terrible snob. His comments caused ill-feeling down the years in airship circles. In later years he retracted some of his more outrageous statements and told Masefield [Sir Peter, author of *To Ride the Storm*] he regretted making them.'[39]

Though *Slide Rule* divides the airship coterie, it is highly readable. Mary Stopes-Roe: 'Very readable ... and some of Shute's comments are very sound.' Did Wallis and Shute like each other? 'Oh yes. Shute was very gifted.' Of Shute subsequently retracting his more trenchant remarks she said: 'He possibly said them in haste and repented at leisure. Some of the men working on the ship were riggers from Hull. I dare say their language was a bit fruity. The people who followed my father down from Barrow-in-Furness were certainly of a different quality. They were good solid draughtsmen. They weren't the riggers, the chaps who clambered around the shed like monkeys. I can see they were a roughish lot who chatted up the girls. But so what? My mother didn't find any roughness. She said they were charming.'[40]

Wallis had to contend with technical, budgetary and political pressure:

Building an airship is the most harassing occupation. Barnes didn't get home to his supper till 9.45 ... things kept going wrong. Our nerves are very frayed and if we – or he – doesn't get a holiday soon, I fear he'll break down. It's the responsibility that's so awful; it all comes back to him; if anything does happen ever, it's his fault; so that every last detail has to be seen to with the utmost care and meticulous attention by himself. I sometimes wish he were a bank clerk – not really of course. And – I suppose it's the same in every big works –

there is internal strife and unfaithful workers – all of which Barnes has to see to.[41]

The construction of the *R100* ensured a stream of visitors keen to see its progress. Molly became an adroit hostess, giving dinner parties for eminent visitors who would sometimes arrive unexpectedly at the Wallis's modest whitewashed bungalow:

> We have had seven here this week. Burney MP; Professor Bairstow, member of the Airworthiness Panel, a very eminent mathematician; Dr. Pippard, ditto; Mr. Douglas Vickers, president of the whole of Vickers, and a great financier; Dr. Rudolf, a German chemist who has come to look at our outer cover; Sir Trevor Dawson, chairman of the Airship Guarantee Company; Commander Craven, chairman of the Vickers works at Barrow and a very clever engineer, and Philip we always have with us. And they are all old and wise (more or less) and you have to talk to them and you learn valuable things.*[42]

Mary Stopes-Roe: 'Before she married my mother went to a cookery school. It amazed all the family because she absolutely hated cooking. Yet here she was looking after all these people. And of course she was terribly young. I think Burney and his wife used to stay in a hostel in the village. It was off the station. I know Uncle Philip (Teed) did. Shute had digs in the village. In times of desperation my parents would take guests to eat in the hostel rather than trying to entertain them in the bungalow which was very small and modest.'[43]

A fascination with aeroplanes was meanwhile growing in Wallis:

---

* Professor Leonard Bairstow, of London University and Imperial College of Science and Technology, and A. J. Sutton Pippard (1891–1969) became the Air Ministry's independent consultants on airworthiness. Commander Charles Craven, RN, was chairman of Vickers shipbuilding, Barrow in Furness. Major Philip Teed was Wallis's metallurgist. Teed had rooms at Howden and was a lifelong friend of the Wallis family. To the Wallis children, Teed was 'Uncle Philip', who spoke at the wedding of Wallis's daughter, Mary, to Harry Stopes-Roe. Mary remembers Teed as 'a wonderfully dear sweet man'. The author is unable to identify Dr. Rudolph in detail.

Today Barnes and I got up at five and drove to Brough to see the '*Iris*' – the largest all-metal hull sea-plane in the world – go off on her trial flight. She was a most wonderful and graceful sight, though she looked very small after our ship. I climbed up into her and looked over the inside – a thing Major Rennie [her designer] said no other woman had ever done. It was lovely [being] out at five in the morning.[44]

Wallis's biographer, Jack Morpurgo, writes:

Close to Howden is Brough and there Jack Rennie was designing for the Blackburn Aeroplane Company the largest all-metal seaplane in the world ... soon Wallis was a frequent and insatiably curious visitor ... as he studied Rennie's '*Iris*' he came to be obsessed by the crudeness that hampered aeroplane design. Rennie he liked but his work he despised. He decided on an essay in designing a seaplane wing. He could bring to it his unique experience in the use of light alloys, and this, at first, was the sum of his novel contribution to aeroplane construction.[45]

By September 1927, Molly was seven-months pregnant, and tensions with Burney and his wife were increasing: 'I am having another visitation from Mrs Burney today. Commander B. is here and she came up yesterday. They are both off to Scotland for shooting this afternoon. She's up at the shed now, but will be down any moment. Poor Barnes has a bad cold on his chest ... still I think he's on the mend and it has spared him two days of Burney.[46]

As 1927 drew to a close, Wallis showed his young wife round the *R100* slowly taking shape in its giant shed: 'The passengers' quarters are too wonderful for words. The worst of it is when they are all painted and done, nobody will be able to see or realise the beauty of them. The little cabins, and the dining saloon, and the deck and the balcony – all made out of about three different parts, like a Meccano set ...' [47] Molly Wallis wrote an article for the magazine of her old school, Wycombe High School:

At her fattest breadth she [*R100*] would be higher than the Nelson Column; if you stood her up on end she would reach twice as high as St. Paul's Cathedral ... Such fun it will be going on journeys in her! It will be like living in a hotel with a great dining-room to hold sixty people. There will be little bedrooms; a lounge and promenade where you can walk, and through the windows of which you can see what is happening in the ordinary work-a-day world below you... The only sad part is that it will take such a short time to get anywhere – seven days to Australia, which now takes five weeks, and four to India, a journey of three weeks. She will be able to carry a hundred passengers and forty-five crew and to go 2,500 miles without stopping. She need never come to the ground, for there will be mooring masts 200 feet high, to the top of which the ship's nose will be attached. When you want to travel by her, you will go up, up, up in a lift in the centre of the mast, through a covered gangway and on to the ship. This huge, wonderful thing is being built here in our Shed which is 750 feet long – room for ten tennis courts ... 370 feet wide and 170 feet high. You can walk along a little gangway in the roof and see the men working 170 feet below you, looking like little beetles crawling around on the concrete floor. Or you can go outside and see seven acres of corrugated iron roof ... [48]

Burney scurried around raising money and promoting the *R100* and the transatlantic service. He made fund-raising and promotional trips to the United States, creating headlines from east coast to west. Never averse to stretching the truth about the ship's capabilities, his gallivanting drummed up interest, but some thought him pushy. In Britain he organised publicity stunts, including a trip by 80 Members of Parliament to Howden on 5 July 1928. They were given a booklet explaining the *R100*. Knowing some of the visitors were querulous, it asked: 'Why should this country pay any attention at all to airships; far more, why should it spend any money on them? The answer lies very largely in one word: range. *Over long distances, the airship is safer, more economical, and more comfortable than the aeroplane.*[49] Members of Parliament – many with vehement opinions but usually ignoramuses lacking even a basic knowledge of airships – added to Molly's concerns about her husband's health and the need for a holiday: 'We have 80 MPs coming here next Thursday to look over the ship and have her explained to them with a view to interesting Parliament, so we can't get off till Friday at least. If I ever do manage to get the man off this beastly station I do want to keep him off it for a fortnight plus two extra days for driving home.'[50]

Such was the publicity surrounding *R100* that manufacturers used it to build advertising for their own products.

Mary Stopes-Roe: 'During construction the *R100* team wanted publicity photographs of the airship's saloon with people in it. To furnish it they borrowed two items from my mother and father's bungalow, wedding presents from my grandmother and grandfather. They were delicate pieces in wicker, a table and tea-trolley. They looked splendid in the photograph but were not *R100* furnishings as such.'[51] They were made by Lloyd Loom in the Lincolnshire town of Spalding with its acres of daffodils, the region being Britain's Little Holland. In the past the fields of yellow fell under the shadow of passing airships, Howden being not far distant. 'There's the story of Scott flying an airship over Spalding and the fields of yellow. He asked an aerodrome for a wireless fix to ascertain his position. The message came back saying he was over the North Sea. He laughed and scoffed and said in that case a lighthouse must have been shining with an unimagined intensity.'[52] In 1922, Lloyd Loom furniture came to Britain. It had been invented in 1917 by the American, Marshall Burns Lloyd. It looked like traditional hand-crafted wicker and was said to be impervious to damp and dirt; it did not warp and was unaffected by heat. Produced from paper, transformed by a new weaving process, it was chic, robust and, crucially for the airship, light. In a biography of the company, two passengers are photographed *c*.1929 in the *R100* observation lounge: one watches at a window, the other scans his newspaper in a Lloyd Loom chair. It is convincing but likely to have been a mock-up for publicity, composed while the ship was on the ground.[53]

In America, Burney offered seats on the first passenger voyages to the US at a colossal $5,000 dollars a time. He talked of the postal service being revolutionised by airships carrying vast quantities of mail. Energetic, resourceful, pressing and aggressive, Burney was a one-man band competing with Cardington's hyperactive press-office; sometimes it caused him to be overly shrill.

Shute expressed Howden's frustration at being in Cardington's shadow:

We knew in our hearts that the work that we were doing was good and that we were building a fine ship, but there is no denying that the incessant publicity of the competing staff had its effect upon our spirits. At times it seemed that every newspaper we picked up had a column describing the wonders of the *R101*, ending up with a brief sentence that *R100* was being built at Howden. Our puny efforts at a counterblast could not compete with the Air Ministry press department ... [54]

Mary Stopes-Roe said: 'Even today [2009] whenever the subject of airships is broached all that people ever mention is the *R101* and what happened to her. It's as if they don't know anything about the *R100* and the success she achieved. The *R101* is still the only one they talk about. It's been very frustrating over the years.'[55] However:

Monday, two young men came to lunch – one of them being Queen Mary's nephew. Aren't we coming up in the world! I had precisely half an hours notice so you can imagine me careering wildly around and fetching up at one o'clock all neat and clean with my elegant new dress on. In the evening we had to have dinner with a Captain Heinin (one of the chief Zeppelin pilots and a bomber of us during the War) and a Colonel O'Brien, who were representing some of the rich American people out of whom Burney hopes to get his money. The two at lunch I liked, the two at dinner no.[56]

During the building of the ships there was endless controversy. Sceptics questioned their safety, the competence of their designers, an alleged lack of lift, their flimsy vulnerability in coping with the weather; the wisdom of gambling with public money in grandiose and untested schemes at a time when the nation faced bankruptcy. For some people, airships were a symbol of Britain's class system, toys for spoiled children financed by the poor who would never sail in them. Splenetic technical attacks came from naval architect E. F. Spanner, a retired member of the Royal Corps of Naval Constructors. He castigated airships in general and the *R100* and *R101* in particular.[57] Burney would get others to research his responses to Spanner and the other critics. 'I have seen nothing of your friend C. D. B. [Burney] during the last month or so,' ran a note to Wallis. 'The last occasion was when "stick-in-the-mud" read his paper attacking airships. I had a scare letter, followed by wire and sundry telephone messages, imploring me to write him an outline to base his reply on. I spent all the Sunday obliging him and had a letter of thanks in due course. I don't suppose he'll acknowledge the assistance however.'[58]

The critics annoyed Molly Wallis:

There's a much worse book just come out – *This Airship Business* – by E. Spanner. Barnes is busy writing squashing replies for the Air Ministry. Of course you might say that nothing in the way of research and making new things should be done till there are no longer any slums or cancer. Why build ships apart from those for war? After all has not the airship great possibilities before it? This first one will probably not do much but carry rich Americans and what not about. But think what we may be able to do in the way of bringing corn and grain and foodstuffs etc. from the Dominions. I don't see how anyone can refuse to give us a chance to try. Anyway, it's no earthly good arguing about it with people who disagree. We can but wait till she's finished.[59]

It was a theme echoed in letters that focused on the meagre resources at Howden compared with those at Cardington:

I do think people are mean ... the airship is almost finished now – they might as well let us finish it in comparative peace, because it would be perfectly senseless to stop in the middle. It isn't as if we weren't worried enough as it is. Barnes is working up at the shed till 7 and 7.30 every night and then has to go on writing answers to idiotic people who don't know one end of an airship from the other. Often he doesn't get to bed till after 11. It would be different if they concentrated on Cardington where they have five men to equal our one Barnes, and no end of works managers, men to see to progress and propaganda, secretaries etc etc. Whereas here, our poor little works can only afford one Barnes, one works manager and one secretary and everything else combined.[60]

The Wallises' privacy was being continually invaded by the Burneys: 'Mrs. Burney is staying here and she's been sitting in here all morning telling me how to bring up my children ...'[61] Barnes Wallis's disenchantment with Burney, the approaching completion of the *R100* and his wish to be involved in the rapid progress in fixed-wing developments, saw him putting out feelers for a different job. Vickers knew his worth – though sometimes his relationship with the company had been difficult – and found him a post in which his new ambitions could be realised. It offered some respite to Molly to know what the future held and where they would be based. There was also the bonus that for the first time in five years they would be free of Burney and his wife.

> We have got a new and settled job at Weybridge with Vickers Aeroplane Works. You can't think what a relief it is to have something certain at last. Of course it will be sad leaving Howden and airships; but anyway there will be nothing doing with the latter for a year or two and we shall be in Vickers firms. We are more Burney ridden than ever ... We have had a busy week entertaining the Director of Airship Development; Major Scott, our future pilot, and Air Commodore Masterman [who is] little Barnes's godfather ...[62]
>
> We shall be house-hunting in Weybridge and everybody tells us cheerfully that it is very expensive and practically impossible to get a house there. The ship won't be ready till March or April. Vickers wants us to go as soon as possible and Barnes has an idea that we could go after inflation and he [would] come up here as and when necessary.[63]

Molly would miss aspects of life in Howden. In the bleak winters she had learned to skate '... at Bubwith where the river has overflowed there are miles and miles of ice ... it's perfectly lovely.' Other considerations were less attractive. The whitewashed bungalow had no insulation and could be bitterly cold; it was just one brick thick with only a layer of hardboard between the Wallises and the corrugated iron roof: 'We are pretty nearly frozen; one tap alone runs in the bathroom and we nurse that tenderly with an oil stove permanently going beside it ... everything is frozen from the beer to the water in the glass by your bed.'[64]

Airships were a small industry in which everybody knew each other. In March 1929, Molly organised a tea party for the heads of department employed at Vickers in Barrow-in-Furness. They included Hartley Pratt, Wallis's old confederate, with whom he had worked at the outset of his career in the drawing office of John Samuel White, a yacht-building company at Cowes on Britain's south coast. Pratt had previously worked for Vickers, making his mark with his prophesy that the removal of the keel from Britain's first rigid airship would break its back. In 1913 the Admiralty had been prompted into action by learning that the German government had ordered ten new Zeppelins. Consequently the Navy had turned to Vickers, as it so often did, the intention being to resuscitate the virtually defunct airship industry, albeit on a modest scale. Sir Trevor Dawson, managing director of Vickers, had discovered to his chagrin that the redoubtable Pratt had left his employ and so ordered that he should be found and returned to the Vickers' fold. He subsequently appointed him his chief draughtsman on airship projects. After his installation, Pratt had quickly found a place for Wallis as his assistant. Of her dinner party years later Molly Wallis wrote:

Mr. Pratt stayed the night, he is the head of the submarine mines department [at Vickers]. I was having an argument with him, saying that he and his works were a menace to society and were going directly against the League of Nations. He said firstly it was his bread and butter and he'd do it anyhow (which, whatever a Pacifist says, is true enough) and secondly that one of the ways to prevent another war, is to make offensive and destructive things so terrible that nations don't want to fight.[65]

The sourness between the Wallises and the Burneys became farcical:

> I am writing this in the kitchen in the evening. I've turned off all the lights except this one, locked the front door, dismantled the bell so it won't ring and entrenched myself in here to write letters. That's all to keep Burney out. Yesterday Nan and I were in the kitchen drying up after dinner – we had Scottie (the airship pilot George Herbert Scott) and another man from Cardington – and the three of them were talking none too tenderly or quietly about Burney when Nan suddenly said 'there he is,' and lo there was Burney oozing into the drawing room. You should have seen their faces. Barnes thought I'd locked the door, and I thought he had. It's rather the limit though to come walking in without knocking or anything.[66]

Mary Stopes-Roe said: 'My mother and father were at Howden from 1926–30. They were very happy there. They loved everything about it: Howden Minster, the town, the people, the workforce, the airship station and, of course, the ship itself.' And what of Burney? 'Well, it must be admitted. He brought a certain extra excitement. They used to have a lot of fun playing hide and seek!'[67] The strain Molly Barnes felt in entertaining the Burneys can be gleaned in the gently amusing sarcasm of the following entry:

> This is Saturday afternoon ... about 70 members of the Leeds branch of the R.Ae.S. and Inst. Of Civil Engineers have come over and are being shown round by Barnes. After which he brings three of them to tea. And, my dear Commander B., Mrs. B., and Cecil B. (the boy) and the nurse are all up here for the weekend! This morning it rained and the precious Cecil had to come and play indoors here. This afternoon the Nanny (who, I must say, is a darling) is taking Barnes and Mary [her children] to tea with Cecil. I only hope they behave themselves, and Mary isn't wet and doesn't cry. And Mrs. is coming to tea here and the Commander. Mrs. has been in and out all day

giving me 'mental red flannel petticoats' for self and children as Barnes says.[68]

What were mental red flannel petticoats? 'Charity, patronising, doing one a favour; Lady Bountiful hand-me-downs. My father was a Victorian. Both my mother and father loved Victorian literature. Red petticoats? It's a sort of dishing out soup for the boys at the soup kitchen. Mrs. Burney was obviously just an old bossy boots.'[69] Mary Stopes-Roe:

> Burney may have been totally unlikeable but he didn't stop him [Wallis] doing anything. I think when my father left airships ... he just moved on. He was always on to new things before he had finished the current ones. He had realised heavier-than-air aircraft were becoming able to carry more pay load, and large quantities of fuel, and to go further. It was the next step. I don't think he ever regretted his time at Cowes, the early years, or in airships, or thought any of it a waste. He would have been a shipbuilder ... that's what he would have done ... had it not been for Hartley Pratt; it was pure coincidence.
>
> A lot of his thoughts were concerned with trying to keep the Empire together. It was part of his belief in airships; it seems out of kilter now. But it was that type of thinking which drove him on; some of his last work which was on swing-wing developments would be able to get you to Australia and back in time for supper. I don't feel he thought of anything which only benefited businessmen. By the standards of today he was a Victorian, very Christian; he held firm to what are regarded today as old-fashioned values which now are not quite the thing.[70]

After building was complete, excitement swept through Howden:

> We have actually started inflating! and mighty little do I see of Barnes. Up at the shed at 8 after I have given him his breakfast at 7.15; 40 minutes for lunch; home at 8.30 or 9 dead tired. Thank goodness it doesn't go on for long. Poor Barnes. They started on Tuesday and have

partially inflated four bags without any serious mishap, which, I gather, is quite good ... [71]

Inflation goes on marvellously ... Herr Strobl (the German from whose firm we got the gasbags, and who has been here over the inflating of the first few) says he has never seen an inflation so efficiently organised and so well done as it has been by Mr. Wallis; and he has had some experience. Last Sunday afternoon Barnes and Philip [Teed] had to do 'purity tests' [testing the purity of the hydrogen] up at the shed. I went too, and since no one was about (because it is strictly forbidden that anyone not working there should go into the shed) I climbed up into the roof to watch the tests. Then I climbed down a ladder on to the ship, and walked all the way along on top of it on the little narrow plank they use as a walking-way when it is necessary to go outside her. It was fun. And every evening at about ten o'clock, Barnes has to go to the shed to see that all is well. Of course there are two night watchmen. And I often go with him; it's most awfully eerie climbing about the shed in the dark with just a little safety lamp.[72]

We have finished the first inflation, thank heaven. Barnes has finished up with violent lumbago. The ship is not actually floating, but you can see her swaying very gently. It looks so funny."[73]

Barnes and I go up to the shed at 10 o'clock in the evening. It's such an eerie process all in the dark save for the two watchmen's lights. Barnes is now a positive monkey as regards climbing. It sends my heart into my tummy to see him climbing a wire ladder with a lantern in one hand to see how this and that are getting on. Oh dear I shall be sorry to leave this darling place; it is a most romantic existence. We have been extraordinarily fortunate to have had four such very happy years."[74]

Barnes has been happily designing (he's never so happy as when he's inventing) some new sort of fuselage for aeroplane and flying boat wings, and he went to Mr. Brewer to get it patented, as Mr. B. is an expert on aeronautical patents).[75]

> We have now got the final inflation of *R100*. So we can't be long
> now ... [76]

> *R100* is all but finished. But we now have to wait for *R101* to finish
> her trials [so] that we may have the mooring mast and crew. When that
> will be, I know not.[77]

R100 was manhandled out of her shed. She took to the air on 16 December 1929. Molly Wallis wrote a letter to the editor of her school magazine describing the ship's maiden flight. She wrote of her husband making his will the night before the first voyage, and that they had slept little because of cars and lorries full of soldiers from York arriving throughout the night in readiness for lift-off.

> At 4.30 a.m. we arose. We didn't wake the babies. After breakfast we
> put on many clothes, and in the brilliant, moonlit frosty morning at 6
> o'clock we went up to the shed. It *was* cold. Then my husband climbed
> on board. He had a privileged place in the control car, and we kept up
> a foolish conversation through the little window. At 6.45 she started
> to move. No engines, of course – just the soldiers holding on to the
> handling rails on the control and handling cars and others on the guy-
> lines. I walked along by the control car all the way, save for a little when
> I dashed out on to the aerodrome to see what she looked like coming
> out; perfectly beautiful, the moon turning her silver as she emerged,
> tail first, from the shed, then off she went at 7.45 to a great cheer, just
> as the sun came up, and she turned to a pale pink ... [78]

Molly's letters show how the ship was the creation of one man: Barnes Wallis. He had designed nearly every component, nursed the craft day and night from drawing-board to sailing, afforded her the unique affection only a father can give his progeny. By contrast, the *R101* was of multiple parentage, the sibling of a collective – politicians, service chiefs, fliers and technologists. It is impossible to calculate how much the absence of a sole 'father figure', who would famously refuse to answer to anything or anybody that lay beyond his own conscience, contributed to *R101*'s fate.

The *R100* flew to Cardington to await the start of her transatlantic voyage.

R100's Transatlantic Crossing

Each ship had to make an intercontinental voyage before being accepted by the Ministry. It was agreed that *R100* would sail to Canada. With 44 people aboard, including Burney and Shute, she sailed on 29 June 1929, five years after her construction had been given the go-ahead, and the same year in which Ramsay Macdonald was returned to power, with Thomson back in his old job as the Labour government's air minister.

Wallis was not on board for the Canadian voyage, his passage forbidden by Sir Robert McLean of Vickers. In *Airships: Cardington*, Geoffrey Chamberlain comments:

> It surely says much for the wisdom of Sir Robert that as far back as that date he was not prepared to have Wallis take the risk of becoming a casualty; with the Howden work finished, what better course was there than to put him alongside that other genius at the Supermarine Works at Southampton, R. J. Mitchell [designer of the *Spitfire* fighter]. Wallis had been keen to go on the Canadian flight but shrewdly accepted the force of McLean's logic; thus he made his exit from the airship world for good.[79]

By the time *R100* had taken to the skies, Wallis was employed at Weybridge, the main Vickers aircraft plant, and Shute had been promoted to Deputy Chief Engineer.[80]

Laden with 2,000 pounds of food, 500 gallons of drinking water and more than 10,000 gallons of petrol, the *R100* slipped her moorings at Cardington in the early hours of 29 July 1930 and set sail for Canada. Towards the conclusion of the voyage, while sailing above the St. Lawrence estuary, she was hit by a brief but violent summer storm, which ripped a 15-foot hole in the cover and was repaired by a team who fixed mid-air patches.

In Canada the ship and her crew were fêted on celebratory voyages to Ottawa, Toronto, Niagara Falls and New York state. On her return to Britain, rain leaked through the cover, but her rain-collecting system had worked satisfactorily, garnering seven tons of water, which had served to reballast her tanks. The ship's outward voyage to Canada had taken 78 hours. She had sailed 3,364 nautical miles. She made the return passage on 13–16 August 1930 in 57 hours, aided by kind winds. She had taken a battering and serious problems were discovered on her return to England. While at her mooring, two of the fuel tanks fell out of her.

Though Roxbee Cox was cardinal to the construction of the *R101*, he wrote with frankness and in praise of the *R100*: 'Of the two airships, although it had numerous fabric and gasbag troubles, *R100* was undoubtedly the more successful. It was designed by a brilliant man who nevertheless stuck pretty closely to established practice, and had the advantage of proven aircraft engines.'[81]

Wallis answered to Burney and enjoyed more latitude than *R101*'s Richmond. There were natural demarcation lines: Wallis knew Burney was an entrepreneur and left the business side to him. Wallis never wished to be a businessman. His daughter Mary said her father was disdainful of those whose sole drive was profit. Burney would sometimes try and tell Wallis how to do his job; he told most people how to do their job. On occasion it drove Wallis to despair. But Burney was shrewd. He knew he had in his employ a rare talent and on design and technical questions he would generally defer to Wallis. The relationship was not easy but the two of them made a formidable team: Burney the deal-maker, Wallis the paramount designer.

Burney had a plethora of detractors. But without his drive and doggedness the Imperial Airship Scheme would not have come about. He was frustrated that the concept he had nursed came to fruition in such a watered-down form. His idea had been flagged by the Conservatives when he saw a chance to build six ships and reap big rewards, but thanks to Thomson's intervention his Klondyke had vaporised. Thomson had snubbed him. A former navy officer from a distinguished family, Burney had known success, his business acumen being proved with the paravane; Thomson was ex-army and in love with flight, pro-RAF rather than Navy. Burney was a toff; his right-wing views were anathema to Thomson and the Labour government. Thomson supporters, however, maintain he was too high-minded to let prejudice affect policy and that spite would never colour his judgement. For somebody of Burney's make-up, dealing with dithering politicians and Ministry functionaries, who in the main were neither Navy nor entrepreneurial, would not have been easy.

It was clear early on that the government's real hopes lay not with *R100* but the *R101*. The *R101* would be the prestige ship, backed by the finest minds, built to a big budget. It would lead in design and bristle with fresh technology. Thomson had hijacked Burney's plan and moulded it in his own image. But it remained Burney's, one he had sustained through the years of indecision and politicking.

8

DESIGN AND BUILDING OF THE *R101*

When Thompson gave the go-ahead to the Imperial Airship Scheme, a design committee was set up at Cardington, which had been home to Short Brothers. After the war, in 1919, it had been nationalised, becoming the Royal Airship Works. Most of its engineers had quit. There was no design team left but for those who had lingered on from the Naval Constructors Office versed in building small non-rigids as wartime reconnaissance craft. The Naval Constructors' experience of building big rigids was limited. Their previous attempt had been the ill-fated *R38*, the operation led by Charles Ivor Campbell, chief naval architect to the Admiralty airship division.

The *R101* project was led by the RAF's Squadron Leader (later Wing Commander) Reginald Blayney Basteel Colmore, the Director of Airship Development from January 1930. During the drawn-out building programme, Colmore showed himself an accomplished administrator, displaying the deft political touch and *nous* that his position demanded. Calming a sometimes charged atmosphere over which statesmen, bureaucrats, military chiefs, engineers and scientists lent a ceaseless scrutiny, or less euphemistically stuck their oar in, was not easy; on most occasions he handled the turbulent politics with a high degree of dexterity. Colmore had a reputation as one to be trusted. He was also a stout champion of airships though realistic enough to recognise their dangers. Whether he was robust enough in mentioning his misgivings to his superiors, passing them on to Thomson, politicians and civil servants, ensuring that those to whom he answered were fully informed about Cardington, the ship, its construction and trials, is questionable; many think he was not as effective in that role.

Lieutenant Colonel Vincent Crane Richmond's designation as 'Assistant Director of Airship Development Technical' was Ministry-speak for chief designer. An acknowledged expert on dope and its utilisation in the waterproofing and strengthening of airship covers, Richmond was a strong character, modest, reliable, solid. He lacked practical hands-on experience but was receptive to innovative ideas and steeped in the science and theory of airships and their construction. Being an expert in the doping of covers his nickname was inevitable – Dopey – which was not a comment on his intellectual prowess, nor as Dr. Robin Higham notes, the seventh dwarf.[1] At the end of the war Richmond had led an investigation into brittle covers. Trying to quicken production for the *R101*, he pre-doped them before they were stretched around the skeleton, but this led to problems on the nose and tail areas of the *R101* cover which ruptured, resulting in some pre-doped sections having to be replaced. Nigel Caley comments:

> Richmond had his 'Road to Damascus' moment on seeing the Zeppelin *'Bodensee'* which was then operating a scheduled [commercial] service between Friedrichshafen and Berlin. He became wholly converted to the cause of rigid airships for long distance travel and grew to be quite obsessed by them. He was a structural engineer by training and a graduate of the Royal College of Science. He was most certainly not the brilliant engineer that Wallis was, although he did have an exceptional grasp of the methodology of airship design, and was a first rate administrator and team leader. He delegated detail design work to a team specially picked by himself, and he came to rely on his highly talented assistant Michael Rope. Richmond was an open-minded embracer of innovation at Cardington.[2]

Richmond was an 'inspiring' lecturer at Imperial College on airships; among various accomplishments he had built an experimental glider constructed largely of airship cloth; but he was modest enough 'to admit that he did not know it all ...'[3] Roxbee Cox described Richmond as a man he liked and who he considered a good physicist: 'He was not, however, an engineer. He had been associated with the design of non-rigid airships but had no experience of rigid airship design. Very few people had. In my view he was a good picker and recruited some very splendid people. To balance the gaps in his engineering knowledge and experience he had as his chief assistant a person of great brilliance and extraordinary charm ... Rope.'[4]

Masefield had no doubts about the gifted and deeply religious Michael Rope – 'a design engineer of genius.'[5] Others lauded Rope: 'exceptional technical ability and able to appreciate the possible causes of troubles which arose ... he did, however, lack the aggressive determination necessary to achieve major alterations of design against the opinion of the Assistant Director [Richmond] whose technical knowledge was far less advanced and whose experience of airship design and development was far smaller than his own ... [he was] greatly handicapped by his natural diffidence and shyness.'[6]

The big four at Cardington – Colmore, Richmond, Rope (see Appendix E) and Scott – were different personalities, but all were able and charming. Diffident Rope and daring Scott were especially well-liked. Practical engineering came from Rope, rather than the theoretical Richmond. Rope had established his reputation with the *SS-Zero* ships and was, in all but name, the chief designer; seventy of the competent little *SS Zero* ships had been built, a figure that exceeded production of all other classes. The very early *SS*, meaning 'Sea Scout' or 'Submarine Scout', airships were small, cheap and very quick and easy to build. They cost in the region of £2,500 each to construct, their envelopes held 70,000 cubic feet of gas and they were 140 feet in length. A wingless aeroplane fuselage (usually that of a BE2C aeroplane) was slung beneath the envelope. They were used as submarine spotters and did sterling service as coastal patrols in the First World War. They could be turned out in a matter of weeks – accounts vary from three to five weeks – and their success led to the building of bigger ships such as the

Coastal class. The first trials on the *SS* class were held in March 1915. Various *S*-type classes were built. A total of 77 *SS-Zero* vessels were constructed. They were not used solely for observation. The *SS-Zero* models were also fitted with a machine-gun and would sometimes drop bombs on submarines or marker flares for surface ships in the vicinity, which could then decide to make pell-mell for the predator in the hope of ramming it and chopping it half, or turn and run from it as fast as possible, whichever seemed at the time the most sensible option for the surface commander. The final types were the *SS Twins* which could stay aloft for two days and had a top speed of more than 50 miles an hour. It is a common fallacy that only 70 or so in the *SS* class were built; this is wrong. In all, an astonishing total of 158 *SS*-type airships were constructed.

There was no shortage of brains assembled at Cardington to oversee the *R101* project. Sir Richard Vynne Southwell had one of the finest minds of his generation. After taking a First in both the mathematical and mechanical science tripos at Trinity College, Cambridge, in 1912, he served in the Royal Naval Air Service during the war and afterwards became head of Aerodynamics and Structures at the Royal Aircraft Establishment at Farnborough. By 1929 Southwell was Professor of Engineering Science and a Fellow of Brasenose College, Oxford, where he developed a school of research that grew into an eminent foundation. A consultant to the *R101* design team, he took the critic E. F. Spanner to task. At a meeting in which Richmond presented a paper about *R101*, Spanner launched one of a number of vituperative onslaughts. Southwell rounded on him, accusing him of knowing nothing about the ship's design and telling him it was useless to argue with a man who believed non-rigids to be more stable than rigids. Southwell said that after *R38* a fresh start with new men had been warranted. He asked Spanner (who many thought irrational) if the new men were right in attempting new methods. Should they try to make improvements by research? Or would Spanner prefer they clung to Zeppelin methods, of which they had little experience? At the meeting Scott said he was confident *R101* was strong and sound. He was 'perfectly satisfied' that she was safe. To Spanner's chagrin,

Richmond described Rope's gas bag wiring as 'the most beautiful feature of the design'.[7]

Other important Cardington members included the chief calculator, Roxbee Cox. At 16, Cox had left Kings Norton Grammar School in Birmingham and found work at the Austin motor company at Longbridge, where light aircraft were being built. He later took a First in engineering by external degree at London University and a PhD at Imperial College. On graduation he joined the *R101* team. He would subsequently enjoy a stellar career in aeronautics, being elevated in 1965 as Baron Kings Norton. Nigel Caley:

> At Cardington Cox was aghast at finding engineers using what can only be described as flexible rulers to assess the profile of an airship hull. He explained that by using mathematical formulae he could give them a perfectly curved hull of far greater accuracy than they had known. He was a tremendous innovator and from then on in airship design mathematics ruled.[8]

Cox wrote that he reported for duty at Cardington in July 1924. He was told by Richmond that his position was that of a temporary civil servant graded as a 'calculator'. He was in the charge of T. S. D. Collins, whom he described as extraordinarily kind:

> Collins [was] a naval architect who had been concerned with the design of the ill-fated *R38* [which brought forth derision among the Wallis *R100* team at Howden]. For quite a long time afterwards the calculating department staff was two in number. I was technically responsible to [Collins] for the whole of my time at the Royal Airship Works, though the organisation was rather loose, and Richmond who had not recruited Collins but had so-to-speak inherited him via the Air Ministry, was apt occasionally to by-pass him.

Cox recalled how he introduced the *R101* designers to mathematics:

One day Collins took me into a long room in which men were kneeling on a smooth floor bending long flexible wooden laths into curved shapes. I asked Collins what on Earth they were doing and he said that they were developing the shape of the airship. This I gathered was ship design practice, conducted in what was known as the moulding loft. I remarked that however practical this might be in ship design it was quite unnecessary for the profile of an airship. In its place I proposed that we should adopt as the profile a mathematical curve of streamline form, the ordinates of which could be calculated and used to design the ship's structure.[9]

Cox offered Richmond different shapes. Of the innovative design of *R101*'s skeleton Cox wrote:

It was decided at the outset that there should be heavy transverse frames which were, in effect, toruses needing no additional transverse bracing, and relatively light longitudinals. This was a novel departure from current practice. It had the advantage of permitting much more accurate calculations of the loads in the framework than was possible with the 'standard' geometry, and loads such as fuel tanks and water ballast containers could be carried within the torus-like structures.

The *R38* disaster had emphasised the importance of calculating precise levels of stress and load:

Another departure from standard practice [in *R101*] was the choice of only 15 sides to the ship, rather than the 20 or more of earlier airships ... I pleaded with Richmond to have at least 16 sides [like the *R100*] otherwise we should have serious difficulty in achieving a symmetrical arrangement of members in the region of the fins at the tail. He foresaw no difficulty but the outcome completely justified my fear ... to design twisted longitudinals in a tapering bay was an appalling geometrical prospect, but the job was brilliantly done by one of J. D. North's staff called Adkin ... [10]

John Dudley North at the Boulton & Paul engineering company in Norwich, Norfolk, was described by Cox as 'an engineer and mathematician of tremendous ability ... while Cardington specified the strength required in the longitudinal and transverse members, the design of those girders was the work of North and his staff'.[11] The engineer Cox referred to was A. H. Adkins, a gifted mathematician and another unrecognised talent in the airship story. Alec Brew, the aviation author, wrote:

> His [Adkins'] task was made more difficult because of the shape of the *R101*. Every transverse ring frame was of a different diameter, so that they all had to be separately designed, unlike previous airships of regular cross section, whose transverse frames could be virtually mass produced. The triangular shape of the girders was also useful in that it provided a handy place within them to install fuel and ballast tanks, and other equipment. The intermediate reefing girders were fitted to telescopic kingposts and screw jacks, so that they could push the fabric cover to the required taut cross-section. The rival *R100* had a simpler and more conventional way of keeping the outer cover taut, by pulling it in with wires.[12]

Wing Commander Thomas Reginald Cave-Brown-Cave was in charge of engine development and drew up the original specifications for both *R100* and *R101* with Colmore, Richmond and Sir Geoffrey Salmond, who had been a senior commander in the Royal Flying Corps and in 1919 had been awarded a permanent commission in the RAF with the rank of air vice marshal.[13] Nigel Caley again:

> Cave-Brown-Cave could well have been a candidate for Richmond's job, such was his experience, talent and complete professionalism ... he may well have proved to be a more effective leader for the rarefied

intellectuals on the *R101* staff such as John Fleetwood Baker[14] and Michael Rope. Cave-Brown-Cave was a kindly, though morose man whom Scott on occasion referred to as 'Home-Sweet-Home'.[15]

John Fleetwood Baker was a prominent figure in civil engineering. After a theoretical design difference with Southwell, he would quit *R101* and later read for a PhD at Bristol University, where Professor Alfred Pippard, whose role was to analyse the design methods of *R100* and *R101*, was starting his academic career. Sir Alfred Pugsley was another Cardington contributor who would later become head of Structural and Mechanical Engineering at the Royal Aircraft Establishment, Farnborough, from 1941 to 1945. After the Second World War, Pugsley became Professor of Civil Engineering at Bristol University.

In view of the result, were the Cardington *R101* intellectuals too clever for their own good? Dr. Giles Camplin, the editor of *Dirigible*, the authoritative journal of the Airship Heritage Trust, said: 'Or not clever enough ... to see that introducing several unproven interacting systems into any prototype is asking for trouble; when something goes wrong you don't know which bit to change first.'[16] 'I think perhaps not enough is made of the excellence of the Cardington team ... in some moods I just wonder whether they were too clever,' comments Crispin Rope. 'Certainly Richmond cannot be criticised for recruiting 'dumb-heads.'[17]

Richmond's authority was constantly undermined. If the Air Ministry wished for change then memos would fly and changes would be wrought. Wallis was adamant he would not use diesels on *R100*. Richmond had no choice on *R101*. Consequently it was powered by inappropriate engines and the ship made so catastrophically heavy her designers had to slice her in half to insert a huge new bay to increase the volume of gas. It was the type of compromise the Wallis–Burney–Shute triumvirate, backed by Vickers, had been determined to resist. (Vickers' role should not be underestimated in the Howden operation. Its influence was global. It was experienced in coping with 'wheeler-dealers' like Burney. Nobody knew better the 'back-doubles' of government. Its relationship with successive administrations had been cordial if sometimes tense, the latter being the lot of any military manufacturer working for government. It was a conglomerate with well-placed friends in politics and in the rarefied upper echelons of capitalism.)

The press office at the Royal Airship Works in Cardington produced an unending stream of *R101* success stories. The ship was painted by its supporters as a triumph for the people and by newspapers of a Conservative persuasion as a giant white elephant that would fly the flag of Socialism, with the hard-pressed taxpayer footing the bill. Either way, it made good copy on pages that were grey and dense with stories of rising unemployment, the flagging economy and international political uncertainty. In constantly promoting the astounding (though quite untried) virtues of the *R101* the busy bees in the press office managed to boost the morale at Cardington while simultaneously sapping that at Howden. However, stories that promised so much about the *R101* and its breathtaking capabilities stoked expectation to a pitch that could never be satisfied.

From the start there had been confusion about what either ship was for. Would they bring faraway continents within easy grasp? Were they liners of the heavens, which would serve a vital role in cementing together the crumbling remnants of Empire? Or were they really colossal test beds to plug gaps in aerodynamic knowledge? *R101* was described as a carrier for aeroplanes to be launched over distant targets; a mammoth mother-ship for little fixed-wing raiders inhibited by lack of range. Perhaps they would ferry battalions of warriors and their equipment across oceans? Or be reconnaissance craft patrolling alien lands, hovering over distant waters? In reality,

In the *R101* programme there appeared to be considerable vacillation where the objective was concerned. Was this a scheme of Imperial communications, or a scientific programme to provide accurate data for future airship building? Was the end result to be a military or a commercial ship? The answers were not always consistent.[18]

For every defender of *R101* there are those who condemn it as a disaster from the outset. The allegation that it was over-engineered is a familiar one.

Where *R100*'s skeleton was of duralumin, *R101* was principally of high-tensile rolled steel strip: 'Duralumin was used for bracing pieces, but the wire bracing, and gas-bag support wiring was also of steel. The structure required 27 miles of steel tubing in total, plus eleven miles of bracing wires …' [19] The choice of steel over duralumin suggested a lack of confidence; after the *R38* calamity, if steel was considered even marginally safer, then steel it had to be.

The engines, too, had to be British – there would have been a furore if Maybachs from Zeppelin had been bought. The engine units came from the marine ship builders Beardmore. Crucially, as it transpired, they also had to be diesels, for the *R38* petrol fires and explosions had alarmed the Ministry. Diesels had a lower flash point and were thought safer especially in the tropics (though there was no real evidence to support that theory). Diesel engines were also cheaper to run. But they were ludicrously heavy. In striving for that which was ultra-safe the Ministry unwittingly contributed to the ship's demise: while achieving safety margins in excess of anything before, it was almost inevitable that the *R101* would be seriously heavy and lacking in lift. Cox was damning: 'The Cardington officer concerned with the airship's engine problem was … Cave … his undoubted qualities did not prevent Beardmore, a firm with mainly naval experience, producing engines of such great weight that, despite their economical fuel performance, they affected the weight of the airship and handicapped its performance.'[20] The engines were 'an appalling handicap'.[21]

R101 had balanced rudders and servo-motors, which also added to her weight. They were eventually removed. The airship author and historian Alex Brew wrote:

> The four cantilever tail fins were triangular in shape … they had been designed after extensive wind tunnel research, and the rudders and elevators were fitted with specially designed servos operated by hydraulics driven by a small electric motor. Revealingly Barnes Wallis saw no need to install servos on *R100*. Rather extravagantly a complete bay of the

structure was ordered from Boulton & Paul solely for test purposes. This
money-no-object approach was to be a feature of *R101*'s construction.[22]

Rope created 'parachute wiring' to hold and suspend the ship's gasbags (see
Appendix E). The bags were 'encased in a network of longitudinal and
circumferential wires, and attached to the lower hull framework by a system
of bridles ... the gas bags so restrained that they could not touch or chafe on
the girders in the upper part of the hull'. Rope's 'parachute wiring' was
designed to stop the gas bags surging and to prevent them chafing on the
structure, which could lead to ruptures and leaks. In simple terms, they were
suspended in the envelope as if on a parachute, the idea being that as the ship
moved the bags remained stable. Like much airship technology, it sounds
straightforward but was innovative. Dr. Higham: 'Instead of holding the gas
bags sandwiched between two rigid rings, the bags were suspended from
independent wire nets that could "slosh" from side to side and longitudinally.'[23]
Critics said the wiring was heavy and consumed space. Wallis was
unimpressed. His biographer Morpurgo wrote: 'Of Rope, whom some have
described as "close to genius" and whose parachute wiring innovation was at
the time highly regarded by the experts "as one of the most brilliant and
progressive features of the design of R101", Wallis complained later that the
enormous harnessing system ... resulted in a large loss of internal space "which
since natures abhors a vacuum, was filled with air".'[24]

Rope veered from conventional design in another way. In place of
conventional manually vented gasbags, he designed automatic valves. Valves
were used to vent gas if pressure in the bag rose to the point at which the bag
would rupture and also to change the degree of lift in a ship. In conventional
guise they were relatively simple, usually positioned at the foot of the bag so
that hydrogen, with its low density, opposed the outflow and limited the
amount of gas being released.

Praised by some, the valves on *R101* have their critics: 'So sensitive was the
valve that it would open automatically if tilted more than three degrees; later
experience showed that *R101* often rolled further than this, causing a constant

loss of gas which contributed to her chronic heaviness when flying.'[25] Rope's valves were halfway up the bags, opening and releasing gas into the central space if the ship rolled: the degree an airship rolled in normal sailing conditions was negligible, so the gas released should have been marginal. But Richmond was sufficiently concerned to log his worries about the amount of gas being lost. The valves were ingenious. But some maintain they personified the charge that *R101*'s engineering was too fussy and clever; that fundamentals of simplicity and versatility had been lost to mathematical formulae and scientific novelty.

The main airframe of the *R101* was unstressed, a major deviation from previous designs. The airframe comprised only struts, girders and rigid tubes, whereas previous airships had used tensioning wires. The departure from accepted practice was inventive but caused problems: the ship needed giant reinforcing rings positioned deep into the envelope. The rings consumed valuable space and limited the size of the gasbags that could be carried: partly in consequence, the ship lacked half a million cubic feet of gas, which meant, inevitably, that she was in dire need of greater lift. In a desperate bid to cure the problem, major surgery was undertaken: she was sliced in two and another massive section of hull inserted so that the amount of hydrogen could be increased. As a further 'solution' the gasbags already installed were 'let out', their holding-wires loosened, which allowed them to be filled with more hydrogen.

Chopping her in half looked like a quick-fix. The effectiveness of Rope's wiring depended on the firmness with which the bags were buckled. Loosening them to fill them with more gas severely compromised his initial design. Given the solicitude invested in the ship's build, such fundamental alterations had the smack of panic. They epitomised the pressure on the *R101* team to get her up and away, no matter the cost. Nigel Caley:

> The parachute wiring worked perfectly throughout early *R101* trial flights. It depended for its success upon clasping each bag in place very tightly ... it was decided to let the gasbag wiring out to maximise the volumetric capacity of each gasbag ... leading to a number of serious problems hitherto unseen. Chief amongst these was the chafing of the

bags against parts of the *R101*'s structure, leading to holes being worn in the bags and possibly catastrophic losses of gas, as well as surging problems that caused instability problems with the airships' flight path. The disastrous lack of lift lay at the root of the problems. Cutting a ship in two had been done before. Zeppelin did it successfully with the *L59* to give it greater range and with two smaller ships the *LZ120* and *LZ121*. But the *R101* was enormous. There had been nothing like it ...

The aerodynamic hull created by Roxbee Cox was superb. In its original form it was beautiful. But the calculations and mathematical detail were all bunged out of the window when this huge new section was dropped in. They needed more practical testing time. The parachute wiring worked well but really it had been designed for another ship; the ship which flew was nothing like the original. The valves would have worked well. But again there was a need for more testing on other big ships. A tragedy is that the period was one of penny-pinching and belt-tightening. There was no money or time to carry out testing on what had become really a new vessel.[26]

Masefield wrote:

> Thomson's hope of collaboration – or, at least, co-operation – between Cardington and the AGC [Airship Guarantee Company] teams was largely stultified by Wallis, who rebuffed Richmond's overtures – Richmond, the kindly autocrat who did not believe that 'he knew it all' and was ready to delegate to design collaborators of competence such as J. D. North and F. M. Rope.[27]

Note the unpleasant 'knew it all' jab at Wallis. Wallis was as far from today's faceless corporatism as can be imagined. He refused to 'cosy-up' to bureaucrats, was dismissive of politicians, suspicious of businessmen and intolerant of 'jobsworths'. A designer with few peers, he was not, and nor did he ever wish to be, versed in the black arts of spin or public relations. He did not regard being silver-tongued, or bothered about the advancement of his career, as a credential for building an airship.

The academic Dr. Robin Higham said: 'I knew Barnes Wallis personally. I found him to be very mild-mannered and a bit naïve. But he started first with principles and thought the whole project through. He could point out logically the realities.'[28] Throughout his life Wallis felt that nothing of excellence sprang from that designed by committee; *R101* sceptics say it was doomed from the start by a surfeit of cooks. The distinguished military historian John Sweetman said:

> I only knew Sir Barnes Wallis during the last years of his life, but his energy and commitment even then remained striking. When, well into his eighth decade, addressing the massed ranks of the Officer Cadets at the Royal Military Academy Sandhurst in the imposing Churchill Hall with an account of his post-war work, he suddenly advanced towards the edge of the platform and spoke to the Commandant in the front row: 'Am I being too simple?' The audience roared with laughter. His exposition, delivered with enormous enthusiasm and utter clarity, was a masterpiece of scientific explanation.
>
> This was characteristic of his insistence on close attention to detail and sound scientific justification for designs, which he had portrayed during his whole life. A critical subordinate, who dismissed Wallis's innovations, 'if it looked right, it was right', had never seen the mass of diagrams and formulae with which Wallis covered endless sheets of paper, when developing an idea ... Norbert Rowe, a senior scientist at the Ministry of Aircraft Production during the Second World War, described Wallis as 'a genius, no doubt about it'. In the well-known definition of that quality perspiration far outweighs inspiration, and Wallis most certainly illustrated this. He was immensely hard-working, his contemporary diary entries bearing silent witness to the length and intensity of his working days.
>
> Inevitably, like other driven men, he had scant patience with those whom he believed professionally incompetent and, above all, in his

view indolent. Intellectually and physically Wallis exuded a powerful presence, and he lived in an age when work forces were organised on a strictly hierarchical basis. Superiors were not questioned, ventures did not evolve from group planning sessions. So, in retrospect, to criticise Wallis for not being a team player is to misunderstand the environment in which he existed, to apply later practices to a bygone age.[29]

Barnes Wallis's talent is indisputable; it was his way of working that can divide opinion. In the way of such things, his élan was so pronounced it was always certain to trigger resentment. Detractors allege he was truculent and impossible to work with. Yet it should be of minor surprise that somebody so gifted might fail to fit the mould as snugly as those of a more mundane turn; history is peppered with creative people whose star flared so brightly it could scorch those around them. The notion that everybody *must* be a good team-player is mildly faddish; while appreciating its obvious virtues, it can mask inadequacy in a crowd and offer sanctuary to the pedestrian. Wallis was an excellent leader of those who answered to him: though always demanding, which was to be expected, he inspired and stood up for his people, fending off criticism and shouldering blame on their behalf with a lusty energy.

'Wallis was an engineering genius whose career suffered as a result of his uncontrollable ability to make certain sections of the British government feel inadequate in the presence of a man of his intellect.'[30] Such opinion is commonly held. But it is not universal. The author Sir Peter Masefield took a critical view. Of Wallis as the designer of the celebrated *R80* airship, he wrote that Wallis 'had shown technical competence combined with an imaginative flair and a mental arrogance – and gained a reputation for both erudition and as being difficult to get on with – as he was unwilling to delegate'.

Wallis was corruscating about the work of John North, the mathematician at Boulton & Paul responsible for the *R101* girders. Morpurgo wrote:

[Wallis] explained severely how [North] had evolved a system of transverse frames triangular in section, in order to avoid the necessity for transverse bulkhead wiring, thus losing 500,000 cubic feet that might otherwise have been available for gas. Further, according to Wallis, North, relying presumably on the clearance between gasbags and structure, so designed his girders that bolts, nuts and even the points of taper-pins protruded into this space, with the consequence that if any movement of the gasbags brought them into contact with the structure, small holes would soon be made by their chafing.

Morpurgo quotes from a letter Wallis sent him: 'It is the crudest piece of design which I have ever seen. It is, in fact, inferior to the framework of the Naval Ship No. 1, the girders of which were designed by the Works Manager who was not a technologist in any sense of the word.'[31] Morpurgo added: 'It is clear from the patents that for Rope's system there was a third claim: that it held the bags away from "touching the longitudinal girders and any other sharp projections", so that if Wallis was right here was a case of two designers on one ship cancelling each other – of Rope cancelling North.'[32]

But Masefield presents a different picture based on statements from Richmond:

> Early in 1925, a further important decision had been taken to contract-out to Boulton and Paul ... the detail design and manufacture of the structural components of the hull. John D. North of B&P was acknowledged to be the leading authority in Britain on metal aircraft construction and he had collaborated fully, in a happy relationship, in the task of making R101's structure the most advanced of its type yet designed anywhere in the world and – unlike R100 – an almost complete departure from Zeppelin practice.[33]

Masefield notes that North was chief engineer at the Grahame White Aviation Company before joining Boulton & Paul Aircraft in 1917 as chief engineer and designer, and that he was a pioneer of metal aircraft construction.[34] In other words, it is inconceivable North would have lent his name to engineering as abject as that described by Wallis. Nigel Caley said:

Wallis had a revisionist view. Even Shute, so critical of the *R101*, says how beautifully built and polished she was. The quality of her build was amazingly high. Everybody was exceedingly careful about trying to get it right. Safety was paramount after the tragedy of the *R38*. Wallis was not the most objective of people. One wonders if his memories were somewhat coloured? Rope and North both had very specific areas of the *R101* to concern themselves with; they were localised areas of responsibility. Rope said he was very unhappy about the outer covers on both ships. There's no doubt that he would have fired off a memo about the girders if he had thought they were not right. Wallis strikes me at times as very mercurial. He was odd in many ways. He could, for instance, be quite snobby if people didn't have letters after their name, strings of academic qualifications, that sort of thing.[35]

Wallis's daughter, Dr. Mary Stopes-Roe, bridles at Caley's criticisms.

They are wrong and unfair. My father was a great respecter of position and rank. He was of the old school which believed things are achieved through merit or sometimes by chicanery. Paper qualifications should indicate that at least some level of competence has been reached. But he wasn't snobby about anything like that. He was never snobby about anything or anybody. That was just *not* him. Outside the family people don't understand how kind and *warm* he was. He took his own first degree later in life; subsequently he was awarded every degree and commendation imaginable from universities across the world. There was an early period when he had to tell people what to do and he would say it was embarrassing that they had more paper qualifications than him but that he happened to be in charge of them.[36]

Caley has strong views about Shute.

Shute too could be very snobbish. He had learned to fly and on one occasion flew to Cardington and landed there. The *R101* was at its mast. There was a well-known rule that for safety nobody was allowed to land a plane within three miles of an airship when it was at its mast. Shute blithely ignored the rule and strolled in. He must have put a Hell of a lot of noses out of joint in the officers' mess. They would have thought: 'Who the blazes does this fellow think he is … ?' As for Wallis, one wonders how much envy and jealousy coloured his thinking about Cardington having so much money and attention paid to it. Wallis could be divisive. He was very much against airships later on. He gave short shrift to people who talked to him years later about a possible airship revival. I wonder if he regarded his time with airships as an irrelevant or insignificant part of his career? He was odd in many ways. It was strange how he turned on people. He had been very close to Scott. But he turned on him after the *R101* went down and Scottie was killed. Yet Wallis said he found Shute's subsequent criticisms of *R101* somewhat embarrassing and that it wasn't cricket to damn people after they were dead, though that was precisely what he did with Scottie.[37]

Mary Stopes-Roe said:

My father and Scottie were at one time very close. He always admired Scottie as a pilot but he did not necessarily admire his lifestyle. Over the years Scottie had changed a great deal. There was a marked deterioration. There was a lot of – what shall we say? – quaffing. It was a quaffing, drinking culture at Cardington. You didn't want to go flying with anybody if they were sozzled. I'm not saying for a moment Scottie ever was. But there's no doubt he liked a drink.[38]

My father never disliked Scottie's character. But he [Scottie] did drink too much and BNW [Wallis] would not have liked that. My father was not tee-total. But he was never over-indulgent, in any way. It was not his style. If we had somebody in the house it was a family joke that he would say to one of us: 'Would you mind getting Mr. Brown or Mr. Green half a glass of beer or something.' Half a glass! He wasn't mean. It was just his way. Within the family he was a very private man. He had an authoritarian rule and a hot temper. I doubt he was ever downright rude but he could certainly be determined and didactic.' [Dogmatic?] 'Yes, I think you could say that.' [Was he opinionated?] 'No, not opinionated .. that means you would never consider anybody else having a point of view. That wasn't true of him.'[39]

What of Barnes Wallis's relationship with Scott?

Well, I gather it was Scottie who said to my father the reason your ship is going to be numbered the *R100* is that it's the last of a line. There won't be anything new in it. Whereas the *R101* is going to be exciting with all new ideas. Perhaps he was saying it in jest. In whatever context it was a terribly hurtful and unfair thing to come out with, especially from an old friend who had known Daddy and my mother for years, they were always in each others pockets. The Scotts had enjoyed so much hospitality at Howden over the years.[40]

A letter that Barnes Wallis's wife, Molly, sent from Howden in March 1929, shortly before the *R100* sailed, gives a slant on Scott and the drinking culture:

We went into York on Tuesday evening to dine with the Scotts. Periodically *R101* officers come up from Cardington to see how she's progressing. We have two here at the moment feeding with us. I think they jolly well ought to give us a maintenance allowance for all the food and drink we provide for H.M. officers. Scott brought up his Mrs and to get away from Burney, who was here, we all went to York. Well she and he drank two whiskeys and soda and three cocktails before the meal, a stiff whisky at the meal, a liqueur after it, and another whisky after the pictures. She drank all that as well as he. They cost us a small fortune in drinks when they come.[41]

In 1923 Barnes Wallis had written of his affection for the Scotts. His letter hints at the friendship the two men had shared. Wallis had been staying with Scott and his family at Pulham, where Scott was based. Molly, Wallis's future wife, had sent him a letter which had gone astray. On finding it he had replied to her saying he had been 'dancing a mental can-can of impatience', recalling how Scott had teased the love-struck Wallis: 'That's alright Wally ... you're not in any hurry for it are you?' Wallis wrote to Molly: 'Scottie and his wife are the most delightful people. Scott is the pilot who flew *R34* across the Atlantic to New York and back. I made my first flight with him when I was in the Air Service in 1915, and had my first accident with him too. They've been married nearly five years, but seem just as much in love as ever – I quite felt in the way sometimes. He's the same age as me, and she was married when she was nineteen or twenty and they have two ripping children ...' [42] But years later Wallis would write: 'Scott ... was lazy, fond of a drink and too mentally inert to trouble to think complex technological matters out for himself.'[43]

Nigel Caley:

People involved in airships were a highly-strung, volatile lot. The main players were an extraordinary mix. Thomson the air minister was wine women and song on the one hand – and on the other, in a position of immense power and authority. Sefton Brancker was the same. Brancker had great responsibilities but was conducting a very public, and to some quite shocking affair with a leading actress [see Appendix D]. The carousing and heavy drinking culture at Cardington became notorious. Rope moved some distance away because he didn't want himself or his family caught up in it. As an aside ... it was rather funny when Rope said he was going to get married and Richmond said it would be bigamy as he was already married to the ship.* It's a small insight into how dedicated people were to the *R101*. Airships attracted people of polarised opinions. There was something deeply romantic about them. Consequently they seemed to draw people who were romantically inclined themselves.[44]

Scott's peers were saddened by what they considered a deterioration in him. Popular and heroic, his loyalty to the service has never been questioned, nor his courage and skill. For someone of his vast energies there were long intervals of boredom. The *R101* took five years to build – primarily a task for designers and constructors rather than fliers. Carousing was a way of escape. He had much to forget and ghosts to lay – many friends and contemporaries had died in the war and in airship accidents.

The building programme had taken five years, the ship subject to every scientific and aeronautical test. The cleverest brains had debated the inclusion of each nut and bolt. The National Physical Laboratory had lent its expertise. After the *R38* catastrophe there had been an unshakeable determination to ensure that the strength of the *R101* was unmatched. Public money had been poured into her. The credibility of Thomson, the air ministry and the government rode on her success. But Thomson has been condemned as overbearing. Richmond had limited first-hand knowledge of airship construction. North's work was damned by Wallis, while Rope's inventions were praised as elegant by some and dismissed by others as being overly novel. Conceived and nurtured in a blaze of publicity, the world had seen her grow from embryo to behemoth. Failure was not an option.

---

* The occasion is in *To Ride the Storm*. Thomson was lunching at Cardington with officers including Rope and Noël Atherstone, *R101*'s First Officer, a romantic figure with an exotic background. He kept a telling record during the building of the *R101* (see Appendix A).

9

TRAGEDY AT BEAUVAIS: THE *R101* DISASTER

On 4 October 1930 the *R101* slipped her moorings at Cardington en route for India. She was under the command (although there was still confusion about Scott's role) of Flight Lieutenant Herbert Carmichael Irwin, the tall, quietly spoken Irishman known as 'Bird'. He immediately had to jettison four tonnes of water ballast because the ship was too heavy at the bow. She was overloaded and weighed down by the five Beardmore diesel engines imposed on her by the Air Ministry; they had originally been designed as railway engines and weighed 17 tons – six tons above the original specification.

There were 54 people aboard including Sir Sefton Brancker, the ebullient, monocle-sporting Director of Civil Aviation, who had made his first ascent in a balloon 30 years before; Scott, whose belief in airships and protest about the closure of the airship service had helped set in train the building of the two ships; and, accompanied by his erstwhile valet James Buck, Thomson, who was planning a regal entry into India and intended sailing back in time for another grand entrance at the coming Imperial Conference in London.

As the weather closed in, with teeming rain and a strong headwind, officers and crew went about their duties: among them the First Officer, Noël 'Grabby' Atherstone and the diffident Michael Rope, meticulously checking his valves and parachute wiring. Despite *R101* being too heavy in an unloaded state, lacking in lift and performance, silver cutlery, glassware, fine porcelain and a great quantity of luggage had been stowed. In addition, Thomson took a couple of good-luck items: a bulky Axminster carpet and a red slipper that had once belonged to Princess Bibesco, the Romanian aristocrat (see Appendix D). It was important that the fortunate foreign dignitaries invited to the aerial banquet over Ismailia understood that Britain now ruled the skies – just as its navy had for centuries commanded the oceans. A glittering dinner in the sky by the Mother of Empire would show she could do peerless ceremonial in the air as well as on the ground. Adding to the ship's weight, a hefty amount of food, wine and champagne had been loaded aboard. The weight of ego that set sail that night is unknown.

The *R101* had a rich panache. Impeccably finished, in her envelope the passenger accommodation was on two decks. She had 50 passenger cabins. The asbestos-insulated smoking-room accommodated 24. There were washrooms, kitchens, crew accommodation and an extensive passenger lounge. The dining room seated 60. Two promenade decks afforded heavenly views through capacious windows, too large to be port-holes. Her customising had a suggestion of fashionable Art-Deco with a touch of the Arts and Crafts movement, hinting at the elegant styling of the grand steamers that came to dominate the oceans in the 1920s and 1930s.

Eight hours after embarkation she dived slowly, her speed estimated at no more than thirteen miles an hour, into a hillside near Beauvais, in northern France. She had covered little more than 200 miles of her 4,400-mile voyage. Within minutes the vessel that had taken six years to build was consumed by fire. She had been making slow progress in the face of a gusting wind and driving rain. Witnesses said she had been sailing dangerously close to the ground. Of the 54 on board 48 died. Forty six perished immediately including Scott, Brancker, Rope, Atherstone, Irwin, Thomson, Colmore and Richmond. Two of the six survivors died in hospital.

The inquiry into the disaster was chaired by Sir John Simon, an ambitious lawyer and statesman. Political opponents described him as slippery. In his time he was Solicitor General, Attorney General and Home Secretary. He had been briefly in the Royal Flying Corps under Trenchard. In May–July 1912 he had served on the *Titanic* inquiry and immediately prior to *R101* had headed a report into India. He subsequently became Foreign Secretary under MacDonald and Chancellor under Chamberlain.

On the 50th anniversary of the tragedy, Rebecca Atherstone, at the time a TV reporter, made a commemorative film. She interviewed Masefield, the author of *To Ride the Storm*. Even by his standards – as a convinced apologist for Thomson and the *R101* – his remarks were extraordinary and certain to incense Howden's R100 supporters. Masefield said:

There was undoubtedly a bit of jealousy from the Airship Guarantee Company who built the rival *R100* which was a good ship in its way. There was jealousy and therefore the credit that the *R101* team really ought to have had was never given to them and they were not there to hold up their end of the story.

The *R101* when it was wholly completed ... was really a very good, sound, airworthy ship ... deficiencies that were there to begin with had been put right and there is a good deal of evidence now from the inspection of the ship just before the last flight that it was in good order, a sound ship, the best in the world at that date.

Of the inquiry, Masefield said:

It wasn't very well done. It was done by a lot of lawyers ... but they had absolutely no airship knowledge, no knowledge of how to conduct a technical inquiry, so they didn't get at the facts at all ... there was a lot of smokescreen ... the fact is that the *R101* team at Cardington was very competent ... led with great competence, spirit and enthusiasm by Lord Thomson who was a very fine Secretary of State for Air who hasn't been given his due.

The disaster was a tragic train of events. Circumstances which led one to another and finally to this ... which on the day, in the circumstances, and in the prevailing wet weather which had a lot of influence – would have happened to any airship in the same conditions ...' So where did blame lie? 'No blame. It's one of those aeronautical tragedies which comes from a series of incidents building up together.'[1]

R101 supporters insist Nevil Shute's *Slide Rule* muddied the waters. The *R100* lobby could argue with an equal conviction that Masefield's *To Ride the Storm* is less than impartial in its judgement of Thomson, Cardington and *R101*. Masefield's endeavour is admirable; it is his interpretation of facts that is open to question. Nevertheless, for those of the *R101* persuasion, *To Ride the Storm* remains definitive, and supporters of *R101* feel the ship and its designers have been maligned. Giles Camplin: 'Ninety per cent [of it is] down to *Slide Rule* by Nevil Shute.' But was Masefield in love (metaphorically) with Thomson? 'Yes. I think Masefield believed his own propaganda.'[2] Though an admirer of *To Ride the Storm*, Crispin Rope admits: 'I would have to say he [Masefield] was hugely taken by Thomson ... on balance, yes, Sir Peter over-washed Thomson.'[3]

Masefield was active in aviation. Among many appointments, he was the deputy chairman of the Caledonian Aviation Group, holding company of British Caledonian Airways. The author asked Crispin Rope the same question he put to Camplin: was Masefield so enamoured with Thomson he was blind to his failings? 'Yes, I think so. But the whole story of Thomson and Marthe Bibesco going back to about 1900 is fascinating [see Appendix D]. I am sad *Catch the Sunlight* [4] which went through various incarnations never saw the light of day and probably never will. I think Masefield was correct in trying to right the balance of Thomson bearing too much of the blame. Perhaps I have to admit that Masefield has gone overboard. But no one else has taken up the cudgels for Thomson.'[5]

Rope agrees with Masefield about the weather: 'Given the rough conditions any airship would have crashed. Having said that, there were all sorts of things that nobody in their right mind would do now.'[6] Nigel Caley: 'Historically, the *R101* has been maligned; especially so because the *R100* has been over-egged; this is partly to do with the way Wallis was lauded, almost deified. If the *R100* had been in storms as severe as those which hit the *R101* it would not have fared much better.'[7]

While acknowledging the perils of the weather, the critics of the *R101* remain adamant that it was not the sole reason for the calamity. 'While the *R100* was an engineering triumph, and the simplest rigid ever built,' writes the author and historian Douglas Botting, 'the *R101* was the most complicated ever built, containing a plethora of new-fangled, half developed technological innovations. Overweight and underpowered, unable to fly high, fast or level enough.'[8]

Irrespective of R101's technical merits, it is beyond dispute that rain and wind played an essential part in its demise. Crispin Rope:

> My own belief is that no airship that could have been constructed at the time, and the same may be true even today, could fly safely in all weathers ... even an *R101* Mark II could well have suffered disaster ... I essentially agree with my father's view of June 1930 that the risks of long flights by either ship were great and, in retrospect, probably neither of them should have been undertaken. In particular, I think it is quite likely if the *R100* had been at the Beauvais ridge at the same time in the same conditions, it also might well have perished. Looking back, everything seems to have been rather over risky. The idea that one can land an airship safely at intervals of thousands of miles, even over land, is pretty extraordinary. The *R34* crossing in 1919 was in the event accomplished safely but that was a fairly near thing. Of course [the German] *Graf Zeppelin* [9] was very successful ... but the *Hindenburg*[10] succumbed as did virtually all the US rigid airships.'[11].

The *R101* was a heavy ship made more so by the weight of bureaucracy heaped upon her. The use of inappropriate engines had been catastrophic. She had lacked lift and power. Too many changes of specification had been demanded by ministry officials.

Barnes Wallis was not invited to give evidence at the official inquiry. Years later he wrote:

It seems incredible that Richmond in his craze for novelty should have thrown away 15 tons of lift ... by substituting enormous transverse frames for the well-tried diametral wire-bracing. Once more, I am surprised that Professors Bairstow and Sutton-Pippard should have passed such crude design. They must have known that it was all wrong. But no doubt he [Richmond] was very badly advised by Constructor-Commander Campbell [RCNC] who passed it on, I presume, to Bairstow and Sutton-Pippard ... join with me in marvelling that some four men, Richmond, Scott, Nixon and Colmore could, in their supreme ignorance, be appointed to bring about this awful tragedy. And Scott once jeered at me as being old-fashioned and out-of-date. Maybe, but I *am* alive.[12]

Too little time had been allowed for *R101*'s trials, as Crispin Rope points out: 'The shortage of the trials was ridiculous. If you haven't flown a ship in bad weather you've got no business trying to go to India. It was insane.'[13]

There was speculation about the amount of gas vented by the valves. The wiring that held the bags was heavy and had consumed space. Loosening the wiring to allow the bags to take more gas had compromised Rope's design. Did the bags surge? It was estimated 4,000 pads had been installed to stop them chafing on the frame. But had the padding been effective? Or were the bags holed and leaking?

It was madness to further leaden an already heavy ship with grandiose trappings for an aerial banquet and such idiocies as Thomson's carpet: a blue Axminster covering 2,630 square feet and at his request to be laid at the entrance gangway and lounge.[14]

Few dared question air ministry diktats about deadlines. Thomson – being tipped as the future Viceroy – was accused of being so keen on making an entrance in India and to return in triumph for the Imperial Conference in London that he had pressed for a premature departure. Yet there was evidence that he had told Cardington not to run any unnecessary risks; that if the ship was not ready she must not sail.

Years later the distinguished airshipman, Sir Victor Goddard, wrote a letter to Wallis in which he was acerbic about Thomson. He blamed the weight of Thomson's effects into forcing the *R101*'s captain into jettisoning four tons of ballast at the start of the voyage:

As you may know, Lord Thomson was motivated by personal vanity and ambition to be the Viceroy of India and to get back from his flight to India to report to the Commonwealth Conference in order to obtain their support for the England–India air service. Without warning he brought with him a considerable amount of extra personal equipment which was loaded into the ship just before the consignment of Champagne! It was temporarily stored at the forward end of the keel and caused Irwin to release water ballast from the fore-car control to compensate, otherwise the bows would not have lifted from the mooring tower … [15]

It has been suggested that senior Cardington personnel and Thomson's officials failed to inform him or to stand up to him, knowing the ship was insufficiently tested, especially in the weather prevailing on the night of her sailing. Crispin Rope: 'There was quite a move at the time to blame it all on Thomson and that is not fair. Colmore had a big level of responsibility. I think Colmore was a nice man, a little bit aloof. But he just hadn't the guts to stand up for his people. Of course he was overshadowed by Richmond and Scott who were much more decisive characters.'[16] Peter Davison, the author and airship historian: 'I don't think he [Colmore] buried it deliberately. He just wasn't the sort to go to the next person up the ladder.'[17] Crispin Rope:

I do think Colmore must share a portion of the blame. In particular it is quite wrong to entirely blame Thomson and not at all Colmore. I certainly think there were times when Colmore should have been stronger … he should have insisted on *R101* being taken out of service earlier (as indeed he wished to be the case) so that the insertion of the new bay could have happened earlier and there would have been more time for proper trials and so on ... in the same way I think he should have been more forceful in early October. But against all this ... these were men who were used to danger and embarking on trips they knew were dangerous. Apart from the *R38* disaster they largely got away with the risks they took ... undoubtedly Colmore was more worried prior to the *R100* flight than he was on 3rd/4th October 1930. Accordingly, I do not think it was too unreasonable that everyone felt (or at least nearly everyone) that they would support departure on 4th October.[18]

Nigel Caley: 'Let's not forget the *R101* had had two brilliant days of testing – 17 hours in the air – just before the voyage when the ship had behaved perfectly and everybody seemed very confident and certain that all the problems had been ironed out.'[19]

Was Thomson as informed as he should have been? Rope: 'No ... and that's why too much blame on Thomson is unfair.'[20] Was he determined to go? Rope: 'It wasn't just Thomson ... there would have been a lot of pressure from Scott to go. It was Scott's reputation to keep pressing on.'[21] Peter Davison: 'Scott was a national hero ... it's difficult to shoot down such people. It's a bit like Barnes Wallis and Whittle [Frank Whittle, inventor of the jet engine]. They're beyond reproach. It's difficult to say no. The country likes celebrity; people such as Thomson, Brancker and Scott were up there. You can see [Thomson] saying: 'It's my moment of glory. If the Cardington people are going ... I'll be there to share their moment of triumph. I've lived with this. I'll be there with them. Because he wasn't well enough informed about the problems – partly because of Colmore – he didn't see it as such a big deal. He still had people queuing up to go on the flight ... other dignitaries saying: "I want to go, I want to go" ...'[22]

Did Colmore pass problems up the line? Giles Camplin: 'Only when it suited him. Colmore was generally accepted as being a nice guy. He did not want to cause offence. But there is some evidence that he was bullied by Lord Thomson. When the *R101* first came out and bad weather threatened

Colmore ordered that it be put back in the shed and Lord Thomson tore him off a strip. This meant that Colmore would be wary of doing anything in future that would displease Thomson.' Was Thomson kept in the dark or did he plough on obdurately? 'I'm not sure what he knew. Clearly many at Cardington were afraid of him.'[23]

Thomson has been widely blamed for insisting Cardington stick to his deadline for departure. Squadron Leader Ralph Booth, the *R100* commander, told the inquiry that embarkation of *R101* was 'biased by the Imperial Conference coming off, and the psychological moment in airships when they could carry the Secretary of State to India, and bring him back on time. It biased their judgement in agreeing to fly. If the Imperial Conference had not been coming off, I feel confident they would have asked for more trials.' Thomson had his admirers. But others maintain he was lost to hubris. Was it Crispin Rope's view that Thomson was pushy and arrogant? 'Yes, a bit. But aren't most ministers who actually achieve anything? Remember, without him, I really wonder whether the airship programme would have got pushed forward.'[24] Rope:

Looking back ... Roxbee Cox was most keen to go on the last flight. It was a toss up as to whether my father or Cox would go. But my father was insistent. My mother always said she did not feel my father was anymore worried than he would have been about many other flights. It was seen as really just a very big adventure. These people had all been through the war together. It was a different atmosphere. They were used to putting their lives on the line. There's a story that my father was due to go on the *R38*'s fatal trip. But he wanted to get his pilot's licence. He was training at Martlesham next door to here. So he might have been killed on the *R38*.[25]

Crispin Rope has spent years investigating the *R101*; Peter Davison, a former aviation curator at the London Science Museum, has helped him with his research. Rope: 'There are so many myths, so many different stories ...' How many of the stories concern Scott? Was there a drinking culture at Cardington?

'Oh yes ... the drinking was well known. My father moved a distance away to avoid it ... there are all sorts of things ... Mrs. Atherstone (Noël's widow) said Thomson came to Cardington in June or July and had Scott on the mat about his womanising and his drinking and probably said to him, well after all this ... you've just got to go, simple as that. I think all that has the ring of truth about it.'[26] Peter Davison: 'Thomson was known to be somebody who if he did go over the edge ...then he was feared. He didn't suffer fools. It took him a while to find fault. But if he did he could have a sharp tongue. If Thomson had had a spin-doctor, as he would have had today, the spinner would have advised him that it would have been better to have forgotten India for a while – to have kept the ship for the Imperial Conference in London, sailing gloriously over the capital, and to have bought himself another month, even a season [to get the ship ready].'[27]

Crispin Rope said it pained him to be critical of Scott.

I have very mixed feelings about this. For a start Scott and my father had known each other and worked together for very many years. I feel sure that my father would not wish me to be any part of over-criticism of Scott. Nevertheless, I think it is fair to say that his judgement had definitely deteriorated over the years. But look at things another way. The success of the *R34* was to a considerable extent due to Scott being able to persuade everyone to press on with planning the flight – despite all the risks – and in fact he got through. This 'press-on' nature was part of his character at all stages ... [though] I have to agree with Sir Peter [Masefield] that Scott was someone who could have urged more caution once the state of the weather on 4th October was known. But ... well, that was simply not in his nature.[28]

Nigel Caley:

Scott was drinking. There's no doubt about it. Over the years his eyes had become black-ringed, his skin had grown very pale, his judgement had been eroded. He led his wife Jessie a dance. She was the daughter of Archie Campbell of Beardmore, the ship builders. She was well liked, a very nice woman. A lot of people at Cardington felt sorry for her. Scott seemed quite open and public about his affairs. There was a pub everybody avoided because they knew they'd both be there. If people were unhappy about his goings on it's possible they got in touch with the Ministry. That might have resulted in Thomson's visit and the so-called 'carpeting'. As the ship was embarking it was reliably reported that Scott's speech was 'thick', that his words ran into each other. It seems clear he had had a drink.[29]

Is it valid to speculate on Scott's carousing? He had enjoyed a distinguished career. In charge of the flying programme at Cardington he was not, supposedly, in command of the *R101*. That was the job of 'Bird' Irwin, the shy, nervy Irish captain. Scott, in effect, was in the impossible position of being an 'admiral' on his 'flagship', but not in command. He had been sidelined. His alleged decline is pertinent for dissection if his heroic reputation is considered and when his role on previous voyages is examined. Nigel Caley: 'As a ship lifted off people would shout: "Good luck Scottie! Well done Scottie!" He was very popular. A larger than life figure in the nation.'[30] Giles Camplin thinks Scott's presence on the *R101* was the 'most potentially disruptive' and cites his role in the *R100* Canadian voyage: 'On *R100*'s flight to Canada, Booth [*R100*'s captain] was persuaded by Scott to go through a mid-Atlantic squall that he would otherwise have gone around. They only just made it but it shows Scott was prepared to interfere in the running of the ship … Irwin [was] a far more sensitive flower than Booth [and] was Captain of the *R101* in name only. He [Irwin] could not have over-ruled Scott even though it was in writing that Irwin was in command until Colmore issued contrary instructions. It was a ridiculous situation to have got themselves into and Colmore should have resolved it beyond doubt before they set off.'[31]

Whatever else happened on the ship in the hours up to the disaster, it is reasonable to speculate that Scott would have acted in character, boldly urging his fellows to press on. With his long experience he had known first-hand what it was to sail in perilous weather – on occasion opting to sail through thunderstorms rather than skirting round them. In considering the fate of the *R101* and the personality of Scott it is easy to overlook the spirit of the age. When the *R101* departed it did so in a culture that is unrecognisable today; for several on board the prospect of death was not unfamiliar. Scott was a *Boy's Own* hero: his derring-do and lust for life was 'part of the package', and so too his grit and aptitude. As with many clever people, he would become swiftly bored. If something lacked appeal he put it aside; if his imagination was fired he was consumed. With his determination and boundless optimism, he was in the mould of many of the young officers cut down just a dozen years before in the First World War. 'Scottie was a character. He once hurled himself bodily at somebody who was silly enough to start lighting a cigarette close to an airship. He knocked them to the ground shouting: "You damn fool, you could blow us all to kingdom come!" But there was another side to him. He had a reputation for working out complex mathematical problems in his head. He would go to bed, sleep on the problem and in the morning wake up with the answer, a sort of Eureka! moment.'[32]

As for Thomson and the rest, the die was cast. They had enjoyed a fine supper, the wine had flowed. Scottie was in his element: up in the heavens with some of Britain's *crème de la crème*. They had a drink or two and toasted the voyage. They were in high spirits. There was laughter, magic, the frisson of adventure. Perhaps Scottie regaled them with his stories: the fun and perils on his voyage to Canada, the incident in the fog years before when he had scraped the roof of an airship shed and alarmed Barnes Wallis. Maybe Brancker had been persuaded into swallowing his monocle. The last message from the ship said that after the excitements of the day the passengers had retired to their cabins for a good night's sleep. Mercifully, they succumbed quickly to their slumbers, helped by a last cigar and a generous nightcap.

Though R101 had withstood strong winds at her mast, such conditions could not be compared to the incessant pounding of her final voyage. The cover and doping had been of continual concern. The inquiry found that the forward part of the cover had been ripped by the wind and that the forward gas bag, soaked by rain, had deflated. This would have made the ship heavy at the bow – the wind gusting above her and forcing her into the slow dive from which she had been unable to recover. Crispin Rope: 'I think it is particularly significant that the cover was the greatest problem with *R100* on its Canadian flight and it is very probable that it was the cover that was the downfall of *R101*.' Of the memorandum his father had despatched in which he had warned of the abject state of the ships' covers, Rope said that it was 'only written because of a very heavy sense of duty for his colleagues and everyone else. I believe it would have caused him extreme pain and difficulty to write it.'[33]

Gas vented by the automatic valves was swept through and out of the envelope of the ship by a constant stream of fresh air, another revolutionary feature but, again, one untested in bad weather. Air entered through flapped openings cut into the ship's fabric at the nose – ingenious gills – sweeping gas out through vents farther down the envelope. Did the openings cut into the nose weaken the cover? Did the gills work or did rain pour in, drenching the bags, making them sodden and the ship bow-heavy?

Peter Davison: 'Michael Rope would have been walking around. He always did. He was totally conscientious. He was always clambering around, checking on things. He was one of those people who would never have slept.'[34]

Crispin Rope: 'Richmond had suggested to my father that perhaps he should not go on the flight but my father was insistent that he should. One source has it that my father and Irwin had agreed that my father would be up all night on the 4th/5th October.'[35] Davison:

If a gas bag had started to fail, bag one, two, or whatever ... Michael Rope would have immediately appreciated its significance. One has to remember that there was a distance of about three hundred feet from the control car to the nose – after all, the whole thing was 777 feet long. With a failed bag ... subject to degradation ... you've got a recipe for calamity. Bags hanging on, soaked, friable, decayed. Then

... and what could be more catastrophic? ... there's a complete rip of the outer cover, with the wind and the rain pouring in, finally caving in the bags.[36]

Rope: 'The cover at the front giving way ... this was broadly the conclusion at Cardington and then the conclusion of the inquiry. Down the years no one seems to have come up with a convincing alternative that meets all the facts, despite quite a lot of effort.'[37] Most of the cover had been replaced – but *not* the vital front section. During the voyage, with rain beating for hours on the nose, that area of fabric would have been subject to intense stress. 'The outer cover had not been replaced at the nose. That's the whole point. They'd patched it. It was madness not to have replaced it.'[38]

Crash investigators found no major structural failure. But damage was discovered at the rear of *R101*'s skeleton thought to have been caused when the vessel touched the ground, or by the frame cracking in the inferno that had engulfed her in seconds.

At the Hendon air show, alluded to in Atherstone's log, the *R101* had behaved alarmingly, entering a steep dive. Returning to Cardington she had dived again. It was found she had lost a serious amount of gas and that her cover was rotten. It could take minutes after a change of watch for a new incumbent in the control car to get the 'feel' of a ship; the watch had changed shortly before the disaster.

The ship's stability has been questioned. One opinion had it that her fins were of insufficient scale for her size, failing to register in her slipstream. Control through elevators, fins and rudders – whether it was their size, weight, shape or positioning – could make her 'coquettish' to sail.

Just before she touched the ground the officer of the watch rang for her engines to be cut to dead slow, stripping her of forward thrust, bereft of which she could only continue on her slow, downward trajectory. To have increased speed to propel her forward, and upwards, would be to claim wisdom after the event; if disaster loomed, one might instinctively slow down in the hope of lessening the impact. Nobody can know the terror in the control car in the last moments. To imagine rational thought prevailed, that there was a fine balancing of probabilities and consequences, would be ingenuous. Masefield told Rebecca Atherstone things might have been different if her grandfather, 'Grabby', had been at the controls. Well, perhaps; but to believe that is to defame the men who died doing their utmost. What they endured, when five million cubic feet of hydrogen exploded in a roar that ignited a once anonymous hillside in northern France, deserves a more sympathetic epitaph.

What ignited the hydrogen is unexplained. There is a misconception today that airships were always consumed in gaseous infernos. In truth, most calamities were not caused by fire. The belief that they were stems from the *Hindenburg* pyre; most people's knowledge of airships is encapsulated in those hideous scenes and the heart-rending commentary that accompanied them on film. It is not *R101*'s blackened skeleton, like that of a cremated mammoth, which sits in the public mind but the billowing fire of the German vessel as it docked at its tower. Clearly it would have been preferable, had the option been there, for all ships to have sailed on an inert gas; but the dangers of hydrogen were so familiar that stringent safety procedures were observed as a matter of course by both passengers and crew. Camplin:

> Had it [the *R101*] not caught fire everyone would have survived ... those on board knew of many instances in which the German war time Zeppelins had been grounded and everyone on board had walked away ... so, even if the crew thought they would not get to India they had no real reason to suppose they would be killed. Nowadays, if an aircraft crashes, it is going so fast that survival is unlikely but with large airships it was completely different. The Royal Naval Air Service blimps made countless forced landings and no one was hurt. So those on board *R101* who had forebodings for the ship did not necessarily see that their lives were at risk.[39]

Sir Hugh Dowding, later Baron Dowding, in charge of RAF Fighter Command in the years prior to the Second World War and during the Battle of Britain, felt bow elevators would have checked the final dive. Dowding was mentioned in a letter Victor Goddard sent to Barnes Wallis: 'Hugh Dowding ... believed that the reason for the fatal dive was that the elevators were only at the stern and so the whole length of the body of the airship had to get in to the up position before dynamic lift could be restored. Had the *R101* also had elevators at the bow the dive might have been corrected much sooner ... ' [40] In his reply to Goddard, Wallis was dismissive: 'Sir Hugh Dowding was wrong in thinking that bow-elevators would have checked the final dive of *R101*. Pratt and I examined the use of them when we started on the design of the old *R9* in 1913. Moreover, I have inspected the profiles of every class of Rigid that I can to find evidence to bow elevators. Does Dowding (I don't know whether he is still alive?) claim to know better than 100 or more German designers plus the French, the British and the Americans?' He added: 'I am disturbed to think that Dowding should have such a poor grasp of the fundamentals of his profession.'[41] There was always one certainty with Barnes Wallis: he never allowed diplomacy to inhibit his opinion.

Wallis, the most experienced airshipman left in Britain, was not called to give evidence at the inquiry. After thirty years of bickering, which had hampered the airship from birth, there still persisted politics and obfuscation. With his cussedness, candour and authority, it seems likely Wallis would have excoriated design fundamentals, the lack of testing and the meddling by Ministry apparatchiks. But too many reputations were at stake for that to be allowed. The inquiry lacked rigour. Ministry 'hog-wash' was permitted to pass largely unchallenged. Wallis's daughter, Mary Stopes-Roe, said:

He [Wallis] was never asked to give evidence at the Inquiry and during the building of the *R101* he was never asked to comment on it. Had he been asked to do so it would have been very difficult for him because he would have had to tell them the truth. They would have construed whatever he said as sour grapes. Although, of course, there was absolutely no doubt what he thought of it. He preserved his silence throughout. He would have given his opinion to people like Philip

Teed and Masterman, people he knew well – though he couldn't, of course, give it to Scottie because it would have been … 'Well, my dear chap, you're going on your death sentence', simple as that, which would not have been very encouraging.

Did Wallis regret keeping his silence? Mary Stopes-Roe: 'What choice did he have? He knew perfectly well he wouldn't have been listened to. So what would have been the point?'[42]

The divide between supporters of *R101* and *R100* remains stark eighty years after the disaster. Stopes-Roe:

What the Cardington people said in the past upset everybody very much. At one point they referred to BNW [Barnes Wallis] as a murderer because he didn't tell them it [the *R101*] would fall apart. That is such a terrible, cruel and stupid criticism. Had he told them until he was blue in the face they simply wouldn't have listened. As far as Cardington was concerned BNW was the opposition, the other side, and we *don't* listen, we *never* listen to the other side, do we?[43]

John Sweetman, the military historian, wrote:

He [Barnes Wallis] was employed by a commercial firm, The Airship Guarantee Company, at the time of the *R100/R101* controversy. It was neither his place nor his responsibility to advise a professional competitor, especially as he had already expressed grave doubts about the ability of at least some of that organisation's design team of the ill-fated *R101*. Shortly before he formally retired in 1971, Wallis explained to his biographer, Professor Jack Morpurgo: "I have never been able to understand the mentality of Scott, Richmond, Colmore and Nixon [Flight Lieutenant Sidney Nixon, later Squadron Leader, Chief Administrative Officer Royal Airship Works, Cardington]. Not one of them was an engineer; not one of them had ever built or been responsible for the building of a Rigid Airship. It seems as though they had not the faintest notion that no man can perform a great engineering task successfully unless he has started at the very bottom of the ladder of experience." He noted further that, in 1923 "knowing that the four were not competent", he had refused to work with them but "they then persuaded the Government to nominate them to build a rival ship at Cardington". Of their fatal involvement with the *R101*, he added: "The best thing one can say of them is an intense admiration of their courage in starting off on a lengthy trip in a ship which they must have known in their heart of hearts was grossly unairworthy; in other words they must have known that they were risking their lives, and only brave men can act with such resolution." Wallis was particularly critical of the fact that the *R101* "had already been cut in two and an extra gasbag inserted, but had not done her Airworthy Trials when she left for Ismailia". In short, long before the crash at Beauvais in 1930, he had major reservations about the engineering qualifications of the airship's design team. His fundamental unease by no means evolved from convenient hindsight.[44]

There was, some claim, a stronger relationship between Wallis and Cardington than has been previously imagined. Wallis's biographer, Morpurgo, teasingly suggests that Colmore at Cardington was keen to establish a relationship with Wallis and Howden: 'His [Colemore's] eagerness for sensible liason was more advanced than Wallis believed and more genuine in later years than Wallis would admit.' Trying hard to be impartial in his assessment, Morpurgo continues: 'Generally, the failure to co-operate was the fault of organisation and, if one must also put into the scales the arrogance and tactlessness of the Cardington team, it would be unfair to ignore on the other side the weight of Wallis's fierce professional pride.'[45]

In retrospect it is a disgrace that Barnes Wallis's presence was not *demanded* at the inquiry. His absence betrays the peevishness of the time. Masefield suggests that if the inquiry had been more expert the opprobrium attached to

R101 would have been less. Well, possibly. But a more rigorous investigation might as easily have seen a harsher verdict passed on *R101*, Thomson, the Air Ministry and the Cardington hierarchy.

There is no mistaking Wallis's view.

It does not require any mystic prescience[46] for any level-headed and sane person to realise that *R101* was doomed from the start. To begin with Richmond was a dope expert whose only experience of airships (as far as I know) was with small non-rigids, and some purely theoretical articles that he had written; and how misleading they can be. Added to which he was intensely vain, and succeeded in impressing his personality on Scott. Colmore doesn't come into the technical side of the argument at all, and Nixon was, I believe, a stockbroker!![47] Nor really does Scott, who was lazy, fond of the drink and too mentally inert to trouble to think complex technological matters out for himself.[48]

R101 had only a temporary Permit to Fly, which restricted her to domestic sailing. It was the job of Inspector Frederick McWade, in charge of the Inspection Department at Cardington, to grant a full Certificate of Airworthiness. But he refused. More testing was needed to see how stability had been affected by the insertion of the huge new bay. It had increased the vessel's capacity by half a million cubic feet giving her another 15.5 tons of lift. Letting out the gasbags had added a further 130,000 cubic feet. Servos on the elevators and rudder and a heavy reversing engine had been removed; instead, two existing engines had been fitted with a reversing facility. Such changes had fundamentally changed the ship's sailing characteristics. On 3 July 1930, McWade wrote to the Air Ministry expressing his concerns. Loosening the gasbags had meant that they were pressed against longitudinals, rubbed hard on nuts and bolts and fouled on the heads of the taper points. 'This matter ... has become very serious as the points of fouling occur throughout the ship and amount to thousands', he wrote. Padding to stop the gasbags chafing on the skeleton was so extensive it was 'very unsatisfactory because the bags move when the ship is in flight, and the padding becomes loose, and the projection ... is again exposed'. He wrote that when installed the bags had been in good condition but were now full of holes. He was concerned about that which he could not see, hidden beneath the padding, and wrote of unseen corrosion setting in on joints. Fabric pads would be damp in flight; wetting and drying would be 'detrimental to the metal underneath'. He warned that the remedy might be lengthy and necessitate the removal of the pads for inspection. 'Until this matter is seriously taken in hand and remedied I cannot recommend to you the extension of the present permit to fly or the issue of any further permit or certificate.'[49]

There could not have been a starker warning. But the deciding powers ignored it. On receipt of the letter Lieutenant Colonel H. W. S. Outram – McWade's boss – talked to Colmore, who assured him: 'As far as we can trace at present there have been remarkably few nips in the gas bags of *R101*, and the holes which have occurred are due to fouling girders. We have little doubt that padding will be a permanent remedy, and if this is accepted, then it is certainly not a large undertaking to put the matter right.' McWade's 27 years of airship experience had been ignored. At the inquiry Outram admitted he had not passed McWade's opinions on to the Air Member (Sir John Higgins, member of the Air Council responsible for airships) because after talking to Colmore he said he had had no wish to carry the matter further. At the Inquiry the hapless McWade stuck to his guns. He reiterated that he did not think padding was a satisfactory way of curing chafing and had it been left to him the airship would not have received its Certificate of Airworthiness.[50]

The criticisms were so fundamental that, before responding to Outram, Colmore *must* have talked to his two key people: Richmond, the chief designer, and Scott, in charge of the flying programme. But the 'Cardington Three' saw only that *R101* needed more lift and that they had to meet Thomson's deadline, which would probably have been missed if McWade's warnings had been heeded and pads removed for examination. Giles Camplin:

The one unforgivable sin was that of McWade's boss Outram who allowed Colmore to convince him [Outram] not to pass McWade's letter up the chain to Higgins. It is not clear if Lord Thomson was ever aware of this damning letter from the highly experienced inspector who was put into an impossible position by Outram's cowardice and Colmore's persuasion. Other than resign what else could McWade have done? His only channel of complaint against the Director of Airship Development went straight back to the man himself.[51]

With Thomson's death in the disaster, Ramsay Macdonald lost one of his closest friends and was heartbroken. Just before his departure, Thomson had assured him that nothing could go wrong but for the millionth chance.[52] Princess Marthe (Bibesco) visited the crash site and was overcome with a grief from which reputedly she never entirely recovered. Her charred red slipper led to false and sensational reports that a woman stowaway had been aboard. The fire set the hillside ablaze. It was so intense that the diesel (thought safer than petrol) had caught light. In the tangle of blackened steel, a scorched remnant of the RAF pennant that had fluttered from the *R101*'s tail hangs today in Cardington parish church. In the graveyard is a memorial marking the mass grave.

The catastrophe ended British airship development. On government instructions, the *R100* was destroyed and sold for scrap for little more than £400. The lives of those in the now decimated ranks of the airship service had been cast into turmoil. Among those who faced a precarious future was a young engineer called Granville Watts, whose distinguished career had included service aboard the *R100* (see Appendix B). In the following years, Barnes Wallis would build an illustrious career, his designs contributed hugely to Britain's efforts in the Second World War and were of significant importance for almost four decades after the cessation of that conflict. He died in 1979 at the age of 92, as technically energetic and creative as he had been as a young man at the outset of his career with the yacht-building company at Cowes on the Isle of Wight. Shute with others formed the successful aviation company Airspeed and achieved global recognition as an acclaimed and prolific novelist. He died in 1960 aged 61. Shute and Burney worked during the Second World War on the design of novel and innovative weapons in a secret government department which was dubbed 'Wheezers and Dodgers'. Burney's revolutionary car, the Burney Streamline, which had the unmistakeable cigar-shaped lines of an airship, was costly, advanced and moderately successful. In 1968 he died in Bermuda aged 80.

10

ITALY, NORWAY AND RUSSIA

The Exploits of Umberto Nobile

The airship story is as rich with the personalities of sky sailors as it is with incident. The life of the Italian General Umberto Nobile is studded with adventure, achievement and disaster.[1] He will be forever linked with the Norwegian polar explorer Roald Amundsen[2] who in 1925 asked Nobile to sail him by airship to the North Pole. This would be a challenging first in the annals of polar endeavour. Amundsen chose his man well, for Nobile had the spirit and knowledge to bring the voyage to fruition.

Tenacious, diminutive, animated, Nobile had started out on what would become a significant and controversial career by reading two degrees at Naples University, neither of which were directly concerned with aeronautics but which would prove of value in the building of an airship: electrical and industrial engineering.[3] For five years Nobile worked for the Italian state railway before his interest in aviation, a discipline still in its embryo but which had caught the European imagination, asserted itself in 1911 after he had taken a course in aeronautical engineering sponsored by the Italian army. He wanted to participate in the First World War but was rejected as being medically unfit, but he did gain a commission with the infant Italian air force and secured a job involved in the design and construction of airships.[4] During the war, the Italians built and deployed airships as bombers, electing to use semi-rigid ships rather than the rigid craft favoured by other European operators. Semi-rigid vessels, sometimes called pressure-ships (the latter could also embrace non-rigids) had a keel that ran the length of the bag, hung beneath it or faired into the ships belly. Semi-rigid architecture allowed construction of bigger ships than if a craft was built as a non-rigid, devoid of a keel. In semi-rigid and non-rigids the shape was ensured by the pressure of gas, whereas a rigid craft, with a skeleton, kept its shape irrespective of whether or not the envelope was inflated.[5]

At the conclusion of the war the Italians embarked on a programme of testing and development with its ships reconfigured for commercial use. Italy built airships for overseas customers, including Japan, and its fleet was supplemented in 1920 by the addition of two German war-reparation vessels, the streamlined *Bodensee* and the *Ausonia*. The *Bodensee* was based at Ciampino, outside Rome, and was renamed *Esperia*. Powered by four Maybach six-cylinder engines, it had a length in its final form of almost 131 metres, a diameter of nearly 19 metres and a gas capacity of more than 22,000 cubic metres. With a crew of 16, it was capable of 82mph, and its range was 1,700 kilometres. It was used primarily by the Italian military but sailed for a limited time as a passenger vessel. It was scrapped in 1928 after eight years in service. The second ship was an *L30*-class Zeppelin developed by Germany shortly before the end of the war. Renamed *Ausonia* by the Italians, it was larger than the *Esperia* and had six Maybach engines; its length was 198 metres, its diameter nearly 24 metres, and it had a gas capacity of 55,000 cubic metres. With a crew of seventeen and a maximum speed of 64mph, its range was 7,400 kilometres. The *Ausonia* made almost thirty voyages during the year it was in Italian governance and was broken up in 1921.[6]

After the war Nobile spent time in academe, lecturing at his former university, and formed with a coterie of engineers the Aeronautical Construction Factory. Nobile and his colleagues aimed to build the first airship to cross the Atlantic; that prize, however, was claimed by Major George Herbert Scott and Air Commodore Edward Maitland and their crew on 4 July 1919 in the British-built *R34* (see page 71). The ship that Nobile and his compatriots constructed, with its controversial box-tail section, was sold to the United States and christened the *Roma*. It crashed in Virginia in 1922, killing 34 people.[7]

In 1925, Amundsen approached Nobile about the joint arctic venture, a voyage by airship to the North Pole. In the intervening period Nobile had enhanced his knowledge and ideas by working with Goodyear in the US; the corporation, with Paul Litchfield its chief, acted as a magnet in drawing talent. The airship world was small. The limited pool of technologists and flyers remained a handicap throughout the airship narrative, a shortage aggravated by its disciples being habitually extinguished in calamities. Their vocation lay at the cutting-edge, and its nature was perilous. Those attracted to airships (though not all) were risk-takers: Amundsen and Nobile were in that category. They were joined by another explorer, the son of a millionaire financier, Lincoln Ellsworth, a Chicago-born adventurer. Ellsworth and the Aero Club of Norway jointly sponsored the expedition.[8]

Nobile had been building a new airship since his return from America in 1923: a semi-rigid, the *N1* was 106 metres long and 19.5 metres in diameter. A hydrogen ship, it had three Maybach engines each of 240 horsepower. Top speed was 50mph, with a range of 3,300 miles. It was relatively small, its gas capacity a fraction of that carried, for instance, by the *Shenandoah* (see page 212). Nobile adapted his design for the Arctic, reducing weight by minimising the size of the control car, making it uncomfortably small. Other modifications saw strong cruciform tail fins, the stern and bow strengthened by steel frames. At the insistence of Amundsen, the voyage would be under the Norwegian flag, to which Nobile objected, and the ship was named *Norge.*[9] Amundsen had built a reputation as a fearless and successful explorer, credited with several epic feats. Fourteen years earlier, on 14 December 1911, he had become the first to reach the South Pole, beating by one month the tragic British expedition led by Captain Robert Scott who, with his four compatriots, had perished on their homeward journey from cold and malnutrition.[10]

The voyage of the *Norge* began in Rome. It was completed in four stages: the first to Leningrad, which took almost 20 hours; the next to Vadsø, in the north of Norway; the third to King's Bay at Ny-Ålesund, Svalbard, on the west coast of Spitsbergen, the largest of the islands comprising the Svalbard archipelago. *Norge* made its final passage from there on 11 May 1926, crossing the North Pole the next day. It was a hazardous voyage. Though some had thought the *Norge* too puny to withstand the rigours of the Polar region she sailed successfully for more than 80 hours. Thick ice encrusted her, weighing her down and making her handling leaden. Huge splinters of ice cast off by the propellers speared her cover, miraculously failing to puncture the gasbags. The engines were in constant danger of freezing. Heavy with ice, further laden down with 16 people and their equipment, she was bitterly cold and cramped, her occupants imperilled by fog, sleet and snow. The distances across the frozen wastes were colossal. The crew were exhausted. There were moments when one or other fell asleep at the controls, causing Nobile's swift intervention. As she sailed over the Pole, Norwegian, Italian and American flags were dropped to the ice. After the crossing it had been planned to moor at Nome, Alaska. But in deteriorating weather Nobile and his comrades had to make a forced landing at the Inuit settlement of Teller, 600 miles from the Alaskan capital, Anchorage. By radio from Teller an astonished world learned of *Norge's* voyage – during the passage her own radio had malfunctioned. She would be later dismantled and ferried back to Europe by sea.[11]

The author has first-hand experience of the remotest corners of Alaska; sailing across its emptiness in a primitive contraption in the early 20th century would have needed astonishing reserves of fortitude and audacity. Having vanquished such obstacles, it was sad that acrimony marred the voyage. Accounts of their mordacity suggest a corrosive rivalry between Nobile and Amundsen, a churlishness played out with glee in the newspapers. Their personalities were at variance, but each had drive, competitiveness and ego, without which such pinnacles would not have been scaled.

By any conventional standard, *Norge* was small. Its diminutive dimensions and the testing confines on a voyage inherently fraught with tension magnified discordance. Of the three flags that fluttered to the ice, that of Italy was the largest. From this stemmed friction; with nerves stretched, in prolonged circumstances of danger and discomfiture, such trivialities can burgeon into dissent. The red, white and green flag of Italy had been given to Nobile by the Italian dictator Benito Mussolini. As with Hitler and the *Hindenburg* and

Graf Zeppelin, Il Duce muscled in on any venture that held the promise of aggrandisement – the notion of his Fascist state capturing the North Pole was irresistible. But Mussolini's hand was bound to inflame Amundsen, for national pride is as combustible as hydrogen. Proprietorship of the voyage was in dispute from the outset. Who was in charge? Who deserved the laurels? Nobile built and sailed the ship; airships were his bailiwick. Ellsworth financed the expedition. The initiative belonged to Amundsen. The contribution of each was primary; the expedition would not have succeeded had any component been absent. Born in Lauro, educated in Naples, Neapolitan clichés fit Nobile: he was passionate and on occasion discomposed. Historian Fergus Fleming comments: 'Nobile was a small, proud, excitable man ... he was not the best pilot in the world, nor indeed in Italy, but was a skilled airship designer, whose dirigibles were in international demand.'[12] Captious judgements on Nobile's sailing are commonplace, but his handling of his craft on the voyage was adroit. History tends to overlook Nobile's intellect: he wrote well and was an accomplished engineer. He also proved the utility of non-rigid and semi-rigid ships.

Such was the animosity between Nobile and Amundsen that during the following year Nobile, determined to pursue his Arctic explorations, launched a second voyage; it would be without Amundsen and his unparalleled polar knowledge. Nobile had a second airship built, the *Italia,* funded by civic subscription. Virtually a clone of the *Norge* but marginally bigger, it had a gas capacity of 654,000 cubic feet and could reach 70mph. From the outset the expedition was plagued: foul weather, breakdowns, structural damage, a string of delays that amplified nervous expectation. There were 20 people aboard. In addition to the crew, the party included a journalist, scientists and Titina, Nobile's beloved fox terrier. It was planned to make a number of voyages. Almost two million square miles of the Arctic lay unexplored. Each sailing would begin and end at Ny-Ålesund. The first was curtailed by icing on the controls and envelope. In the second, a successful voyage on 15 May 1928, *Italia* was aloft for two and half a days. Newly discovered areas were charted while the scientists collated useful magnetic and meteorological information.

Ten days later, however, in dreadful weather, *Italia* crashed on to an ice flow. The control car was torn apart, and the belly of the ship sustained a gaping wound. Ten people including Nobile were thrown on to the ice; one was dead, another had a broken arm. Nobile broke his right leg and arm. The broken shell of *Italia* lurched back into the sky, swept away into a fog with six aboard who were never seen again. Limited rations, a radio and a tent had been hurled on to the ice with the survivors. Devoid of them, the survivors would have perished; it was their only sliver of good fortune.[13] After two weeks and close to death, their radio distress calls were eventually heeded. An international rescue began with aeroplanes and surface ships from six countries. It took almost another two weeks before Italian aircraft spotted them. A Swedish airman rescued Nobile; he would have saved more but to have overloaded his plane would have imperilled it. Nobile was reluctant to leave, wishing to remain until all could be rescued. Eventually he agreed to be lifted off, but when the Swede returned to pick up more survivors he crashed on landing and had to wait with the others for rescue. A Russian ice-breaker eventually reached them. Amundsen, who had quit polar adventuring and was settling his differences with Nobile after a series of prolonged and public harangues, joined the rescue mission, hiring a seaplane in Norway. He was never seen again. His loss compounded the tragedy.

The calamity remains a mystery. Armchair sky mariners apportioned blame; some said it was the fault of Nobile. Diverse hypotheses were unconvincing. It all came as a profound blow to the Italian national psyche and effectively finished Italian airship production. Nobile was stigmatised as a poltroon by Mussolini's malefactors, his reputation besmirched. His treatment was a foretaste of the darkness that would descend upon Europe. Once lionised, he was now hounded into exile. During the ensuing years he would work in Russia. Though still in revolutionary ferment, the USSR had a programme for the construction of airships. Little is known about Soviet airship work during the 1930s; the author understands, however, that research which is currently being undertaken suggests a greater involvement than had been imagined. During the Second World War, Nobile spent five years in

圖陣化興

early image of the French using tethered balloons in the capture of the fort at Hung Hoa, April 1884, during
French Tonkin campaign (Vietnam), 1883–6. (Cody Images)

SANTOS · DUMONT · Nº 6 ·

GEO · HUM ·

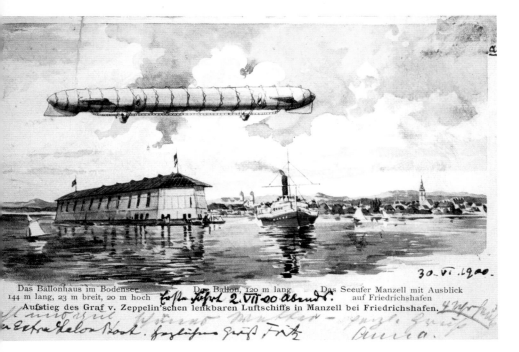

Das Ballonhaus im Bodensee
144 m lang, 23 m breit, 20 m hoch
Der Ballon, 120 m lang
Das Seeufer Manzell mit Ausblick
auf Friedrichshafen
Aufstieg des Graf v. Zeppelin'schen lenkbaren Luftschiffs in Manzell bei Friedrichshafen.

Fabled Brazilian Alberto Santos-Dumont. Chromolithograph of a caricature by George Hum from *Vanity* magazine. He circumnavigated the Eiffel Tower in his airship in 1901. (SSPL/Getty Images)

ve: Colour print of the maiden sailing of Count Ferdinand von Zeppelin's first rigid airship, *Zeppelin No.1*, ne Bodensee (Lake Constance, near Friedrichshafen, Germany), 2 July 1900. (SSPL/Getty Images)

w: Scale model of the Lebaudy airship, France, April 1904. On 12 November 1904 the French Lebaudy hers sailed some 38 miles in an hour and 41 minutes from Moisson to the Champ de Mars in Paris. ²L/Getty Images)

Overleaf: *Left*, Posters extolling the glamour of the airship were used in America to encourage recruitment into the Air Service. This one was published in 1917 a year before the end of the First World War. (Library of Congress) *Right*, a British propaganda poster of 1915. Graphic visuals and text exploited the horror of the German Zeppelin bombers to boost army recruitment. (Library of Congress)

JOIN THE AIR SERVICE

"give'er the gun"

LEARN-EARN

IT IS FAR BETTER
TO FACE THE BULLETS
THAN TO BE KILLED
AT HOME BY A BOMB

JOIN THE ARMY AT ONCE
& HELP TO STOP AN AIR RAID

GOD SAVE THE KING

The cover of a Zeppelin brochure promoting sailings between Hamburg and South America. Zeppelins were used for commercial sailings until the late 1930s. They ceased after the *Hindenburg* disaster on 6 May 1937. (SSPL/Getty Images)

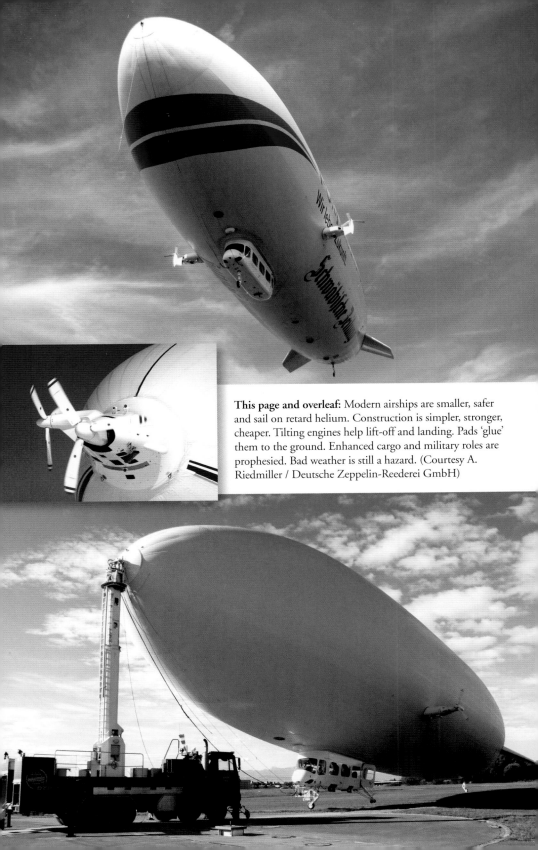

This page and overleaf: Modern airships are smaller, safer and sail on retard helium. Construction is simpler, stronger, cheaper. Tilting engines help lift-off and landing. Pads 'glue' them to the ground. Enhanced cargo and military roles are prophesied. Bad weather is still a hazard. (Courtesy A. Riedmiller / Deutsche Zeppelin-Reederei GmbH)

America, finally being absolved of the calumnies that had been heaped upon him. He later rebuilt his academic career as a distinguished professor of aerodynamics at Naples University, where his career had begun.

Russian Airships

Nobile influenced Russian airship design. He was there for five years and the 'star turn' in an industry that had been in existence from the earliest days and whose use of non-rigid ships lasted longer than in other countries. Airships operated in Imperial Russia; they sailed throughout the First World War; during and after the Russian Revolution; up to, during and beyond the Second World War. As with much Russian, and later Soviet, history the detail is still sketchy if it exists at all, and Soviet 'authorised' versions can differ from reality. At the turn of the 20th century both Germany and France, eminent in the field, sold airships to Russia. In the early 1900s the Russians laid the foundations for what would become an ambitious building programme of their own. By 1914, though, faced with economic meltdown, and caught in the early cross-currents of upheaval, Russia had 17 airships, a remarkable tally, though how many were fit for combat in the war is unknown.

Almost two decades would elapse before Nobile's arrival quickened and improved Soviet development. Joseph Stalin's demands for a squadron of airships in the 1930s built rapidly to a tight budget – in part to demonstrate the superiority of a coordinated workers' effort over profit-driven construction in the West – proved impossible to fulfil, even for a designer of Nobile's sometimes manic drive. Soviet airships lagged far behind those built in the West. Under Nobile's tutelage, strides were made in the construction of non-rigid ships. As with the Nazis in Germany, airships in the Soviet Union were seen as propaganda tools, used to boost empty claims about the superiority of Socialist construction. Romanticised, iconic airship images were depicted in vivid colours on posters pasted on billboards throughout the nation. In fact, the airship was used with some success, but there were also calamities. Given Stalin's relationship with the truth, and the vast wilderness that is Russia, nobody can tell with certainty what level of grief was encountered. Nobile wrote subsequently of his Soviet adventures, but he was not privy to all Stalin's secrets.

One particular catastrophe stands out. Nobile's *V6* was built in 1934 and met its end four years later. A competent vessel of 345 feet with three engines and a crew of 15, it attained various endurance records before it ploughed at full speed into a mountainside south of Murmansk, killing 13 of those aboard. Cruel fate determined that the Arctic would again impose on Nobile's universe – the vessel had been on a mission to rescue a Soviet explorer and his team trapped on a drifting ice floe. At its despatch it was thought that sailing to Murmansk would prove a useful test in Arctic conditions. The official Party version had it that the ship had been saddled with pre-Stalin charts. Others maintained that shortcomings in the ship, inclement weather and decisions by the captain and crew had collectively, or individually, been to blame.

The Soviets were still using airships during and after the Second World War. The Soviets heeded Nobile's preference for non-rigids rather than more costly big rigids; it was a prescient decision, though a dearth of money gave Nobile and his Soviet masters no alternative – grandiose plans for a squadron of ships under a Stalin Five Year Plan were ludicrously ambitious. The enormity of the USSR made the airship ideal for monitoring remote forests and mountains, for logging, mineral and geological surveys. An especially dangerous task involved pumping Soviet airships up to seam-splitting maximum fatness and then using them as hydrogen transporters for the mid-air refuelling of barrage balloons; unwitting citizens on the ground were doubtless unaware of such overhead hazards.

11

AIRCRAFT CARRIERS OF THE SKY: AMERICA'S AIRSHIPS

While exacerbating tensions between the British Admiralty and the Royal Air Force, the *R38* calamity of 1921 also caused inter-continental political and military friction – between the United States and Great Britain. This focused on the notion that Britain was delighted to have found a gullible buyer on which to unburden itself of an expensive 'white elephant' (which is true) and that it had tried to pull a reckless trick in ridding itself of a ship it knew to be fundamentally unsound (which is not true). In the USA, however, such allegations held a raw appeal and played well to the 'buy-American' gallery; the US domestic market gave protectionism a credibility lacking in more meagre economies. But the charge was balderdash. The disaster was a consequence of the ship being built with too few calculations and being sailed in an inappropriate manner. Nevertheless, lingering suspicions encouraged America to concentrate its efforts on home-built vessels, albeit sometimes tapping into ample German know-how.

Roma

In the years after the First World War the United States cast around to find the most cost-effective way to enter the airship market. One of Europe's foremost builders, the Italian General Umberto Nobile, had designed a 410-foot hydrogen-ship the *T34*, later called the *Roma* (see page 204). Though only half the length of the American behemoths that would follow, namely the *Akron* and *Macon*, it represented the world's biggest semi-rigid airship at the time. It was a useful vessel, with a maximum speed of 80mph. America bought it for training purposes from the Italian government for a quarter of a million dollars in 1921. Her commander was Captain Dale Mabry from Tampa, Florida, one of the brightest young stars to come out of the American army's air service. It was to be the last hydrogen ship the US would use: a year after her purchase, *Roma* caught on power lines while sailing over an army supply depot in Norfolk, Virginia. The ship's innovative box-shaped rudder had failed to respond to her helm. In her descent she became entangled with the high-voltage wires, being horribly suspended as fire and explosions tore through her. Thirty-four people perished, including Mabry, who was found with his hands still clutching the wheel. He is today revered as a pioneer of American aviation, his name familiar to users of the Dale Mabry Highway, one of Florida's arterial roads. The calamity mortified America. With the shocking mid-air collapse of the British-built *R38* over the River Humber in Great Britain just a year earlier, and now the loss of the Italian *Roma*, America's experience with foreign-built airships had been scarred by tragedy.

Shenandoah

Over the decades the United States' role in lighter-than-air experimentation would be auspicious. America produced advanced craft and some of the foremost airship personalities. Admiral Charles Emery Rosendahl, USN, was one. Born in Chicago, Illinois, Rosendahl graduated in 1914 from the US Naval Academy. Making his mark as a resourceful officer, he served in a diversity of surface vessels including the battleship *Oregon*. In 1921 he was given command of the destroyer *Claxton*. In 1923 he volunteered for airship service and became the navigator and mooring officer aboard America's first rigid dirigible for the US Navy. The *Shenandoah* (ZR1) made its maiden flight on 4 September 1923, having been built at the Philadelphia Naval Aircraft Factory in 1922 and assembled at Lakehurst airship station, New Jersey, the following year. Sailing on the retard gas, helium, her design was based on the Zeppelin bomber *L-49*, a lightened height-climber, built to a fragile template, which had been downed earlier in France and extensively copied. Two years later, in the dark of the early hours of 2 September 1925,

Shenandoah broke up in mid-air, the victim of a violent thunderstorm over Ohio.

Rosendahl and six crew members were trapped in the *Shenandoah's* wrecked bow section. There was for a short time an eighth survivor, engineering officer Lieutenant E. W. Sheppard, but the damaged structure to which he clung gave way. Before falling off he was heard to shout to a fellow airshipman who was trying to help him: 'Never mind me, look out for yourself.' His body was found in woods a quarter of a mile from the wreckage of the *Shenandoah's* tail. The control car of the ship had been wrenched away. Devoid of weight, the bow section rose high into the sky. Rosendahl and crew members vented gas from the buckled bow and free-ballooned it to earth, landing at Sharon, Ohio, 12 miles from the bulk of the wreckage. The wrist-watches of the dead in the control room were stopped at 4.45 a.m. and 4.47. Rosendahl and the others came to earth at 6.45 a.m. – so their astonishing feat had taken two hours.[1]

It was *Shenandoah's* 57th flight. Fourteen of the 42 people aboard died, including her commanding officer, Lieutenant Commander Zachary Lansdowne, an experienced airshipman from Ohio in the Mid West. Lansdowne had been an observer for the American Navy on the *R34's* east–west transatlantic crossing in 1919. He was of distinguished US navy stock; his uncle was Harry Knox, an Admiral in the American navy. Lansdowne's death, at 36, was not merely another tragedy, one of many that bloodied the airship saga. It also signalled a controversy that echoed down the years during the building and sailing of the British *R101*, in which the design of the gas valves became the subject of scrutiny (see pages 169 and 186). Lansdowne had removed 10 of the 18 automatic valves from *Shenandoah's* gasbags in the belief that too much gas was being lost, and to save weight and helium, which was scarce and costly. Initially blamed for the disaster to the *Shenandoah*, his honour was restored when an inquiry exonerated him from culpability. The destroyer *USS Lansdowne* was named in Zachary Lansdowne's memory.

Los Angeles

Rosendahl built on his reputation, gaining experience in different vessels and roles, and a year after escaping from the *Shenandoah* he was appointed commander of *Los Angeles*. Despite her name, USS *Los Angeles* (ZR3) was not constructed in America. In October 1924, *LZ126*, as she was originally designated by her German builders, embarked on a three-day transatlantic crossing from the Zeppelin works, Friedrichshafen, to Lakehurst naval air station, New Jersey. Completed in August 1924 as a hydrogen ship, on the understanding that she was for 'civil' purposes (in later years a diplomatic elasticity applied to the definition), she was funded in part under the German reparations covenant following the war. With a gas capacity of almost 2.5 million cubic feet, *Los Angeles* was hardly a minnow but relatively small when compared with succeeding leviathans. On docking in the United States, an early modification was to change her lifting gas from hydrogen to helium. Though safer, helium is marginally less buoyant, which reduced her range and payload. And helium was precious, its paucity witnessed when *Los Angeles* was serviced in June 1925 and her helium transferred to the tragic *Shenandoah* (ZR1). The loss of this airship three months later in September 1925 led to a serious helium shortage; the dearth of helium meant *Los Angeles* could not return to service duties with the US naval fleet until March 1926, a costly and militarily wholly unsatisfactory delay of six months.

Los Angeles was an admired craft; used extensively as a trials vessel, her worth was assessed for naval and commercial utility. Over the next three years Rosendahl's ship would make more than a hundred voyages totalling 1,400 hours. He made numerous moorings, dockings and embarkations from a floating airship station built on a converted marine vessel, the *Patoka*, which had been laid down as an oil carrier plying between American and European ports during the war and then converted in 1924 into an airship tender, a mooring mast being fitted at her stern. For five years *Los Angeles* was the American navy's only rigid. In her successful 15-year career she achieved a number of firsts, some intentional, others less so. Her missions included helping to calibrate radio compasses on America's eastern seaboard, and she was a pioneering craft used to explore the practicalities of airships as aircraft carriers – the radically changed features of the *Akron* owed much to experiments undertaken by *Los Angeles*.

In August 1927 there occurred a frightening incident. A wind beneath her tail played havoc when she was moored at the tall mast at Lakehurst. Despite a 2,500-pound ground weight fixed at her stern, the 658-foot ship rose by her tail into a vertical position, standing on her nose on the top of the mast.[2] Her aerial ballet resulted in the use of a stubbier mast by rigids and non-rigids for the next 30 years. In June 1932 she was decommissioned and placed in preservative storage.

Reconditioned in 1934, she was used in non-flying experiments including a study of the effects of long-term open-air mooring. In 1939 *Los Angeles* was finally struck from the Navy list and later reduced to scrap.[3]

Goodyear

The Goodyear Tire & Rubber Corporation was a proud name in the annals of lighter-than-air flight. Over the decades Goodyear built more than 300 airships, making it the world's biggest constructor. Most were built at its headquarters in Akron. Founded in 1898, Goodyear had established a reputation building non-rigid and small pressure-ships. The shape of a 'pressure' airship is maintained by the pressure of gas rather than by a frame or skeleton; a generic, it applies to non-rigid and semi-rigid vessels. A non-rigid airship was devoid of a frame; a semi-rigid had a rigid keel running the length of the bag. The keel was hung beneath the craft or, alternatively, faired into the lower part of its belly; one could attach gondola(s), engine(s) fuel and ballast tanks to it. A rigid keel allowed designers to build craft larger and more ambitious than non-rigid airships. These are fundamental differences to the big rigid vessels, with their massive skeletons, which were developed later and which, though very unusually, are sometimes called 'pressure-less' ships.

Goodyear had gained experience in ballooning during the war; American free balloons were used in training and covered more than 200,000 miles, carrying over 33,000 passengers and being airborne for more than 11,000 hours. Almost a thousand *Caquot R type* observation balloons were built in the US in the war and used by Americans on the Western Front in France. More than 90 feet long and over 30 feet in diameter, they had been designed by a Frenchman, Albert Caquot. Goodyear also built six non-rigids for the American army and two more for commercial use, the first being the *Pony Blimp*, of 35,000 cubic feet capacity, in 1919.

The second, *Pilgrim*, in 1925, was an enclosed passenger cabin ship, described as an 'aerial yacht' and a forerunner of later larger vessels.[4] A semi-rigid, the *RSI*, was another vessel developed by Goodyear. Christopher Sprigg in his treatise *The Airship* said that at the time the *RSI* represented 'almost the extreme limits of development possible with the pressure airship, even when stiffened with a keel. It has a total gas capacity of 719,000 cubic feet, a top speed of 70mph, with four engines developing in all 1,200 h.p. and its cruising radius with a crew of nine is 1,100 miles. It has been successfully modified for carrying and releasing an aeroplane in flight.'[5] *Pilgrim* was a successful promotional craft for Goodyear, one of a fleet of dinky vessels on which it trained its pilots. *Pilgrim*'s voyages in America caused a sensation. Charmingly 'bijou', she accommodated a pilot and two passengers in stylish comfort on velvet and mahogany-veneered seats. *Pilgrim* had an air of well-being; even her name engendered goodwill. With a three-cylinder Lawrence air-cooled engine, she sailed at 40 miles an hour with a range of just over 500 miles. At the end of her life, six years after her birth, the helium-gassed *Pilgrim* had flown almost 3,000 hours, made nearly 5,000 voyages and carried over 5,000 passengers.

On 6 October 1928, Goodyear signed an agreement with the US Navy to build two ships – the *Akron* and *Macon* – at a cost close to eight million dollars, a tidy sum not without its critics: after British, European and American tragedies, politicians were sceptical about the efficacy of continued funding. These vessels would be the US Navy's most ambitious aerial craft. In an echo of the pioneering trials at Pulham in Britain in which airships carried aircraft on a trapeze, the big American rigids were conceived as long-range naval scouts with the far-reaching potential of being deployed as aircraft carriers. In accompanying the fleet, these airships would act as control and command centres. Within the belly of the ships would be a hangar for five Curtiss fighter aircraft. Inboard hangars marked a significant advance. To embark or moor, the ship's small fighters would use a trapeze (though it took an interminable time for the aircraft, and even the trapeze, to be properly installed). The planes would enter or exit the hangar through a T-shaped incision in the ship's belly, the aircraft being heaved aboard by winch. 'The returning aeroplane had to adjust its speed to that of the airship, position itself below the airship's hull, and then fly upwards to hook itself on to a support sticking out from the hull.'[6] But the scale of airships would make them easy prey. However, as with British airships, it was reasoned that on-board fighters would deter predator aircraft and could also be used for reconnaissance. Given the vulnerability of airships, deploying them as motherships in a background role had logic. The airship offered sanctuary to the pilots and a harbour to service the aircraft.

Goodyear and Zeppelin

In a prescient move in 1923, Goodyear teamed up with the Zeppelin company of Germany to forge a alliance that would have sufficient clout to win the US navy contract to build the *Akron* and *Macon*.

The design of Zeppelins had been the responsibility of Ludwig Dürr. He had joined Zeppelin in 1899 aged 21, becoming a pilot as well as a designer. He showed personal loyalty to Count Zeppelin and commitment to the company in its early volatile years: in 1900, when the Count ceased trading and his enterprise suffered a financial crisis, Dürr remained as sole employee. He was to work for Zeppelin until 1945. A technologist of puissance, he was an empirical designer. But Dürr has been ill-served by history: 'Swabian provincial qualities made Dürr congenial to Count Zeppelin, but he was ill at ease in dealing with outsiders ... [and was] described by Americans ... as living almost a hermit's life ... has never travelled and has very narrow views. Believes implicitly in German theory of absolute secrecy about work; also in building just about as he pleases ... is a very difficult man to deal with.'[7] The author thinks this inequitable; it confuses personal traits with professional achievements and pays paltry regard to Dürr's technical gifts. His role deserves proper assessment. It is true he was reserved and close-lipped; some described him as taciturn. This in part is because he was a young man in a position of confidence in a competitive industry; he had to be discreet, especially with Americans keen to know the secrets of Zeppelin's success. Dürr became Zeppelin's design chief in 1906, when he had played a fundamental role in the design of *LZ2*, the second Zeppelin; he had helped with the first, *LZ1*, designed in 1900 by Theodor Kober. After *LZ1* the company went into liquidation. It took five years before the ebullient Count could raise funds to build *LZ2*, after which Dürr designed every Zeppelin. *LZ1* had flaws: its anaemic tubular frame was so flimsy it contorted in the air. Dürr scrapped it in the *LZ2*, installing muscular triangular girders, a courageous choice that gave meaning to 'rigid' in airship design. Dürr's detractors allege his longevity of service instilled staidness; it is more charitable to suggest that he believed in trial and error, drawing on his experience, learning from his mistakes. The author is also of the opinion that given the lengthening list of airship calamities a sensible conservatism was warranted. Dürr was the driving force behind the *Graf Zeppelin*, the paragon that emerged from its shed in 1928 as the acme of design and the star in Dr. Hugo Eckener's universe, the peripatetic master of the Zeppelin corporation.

The astute chief of Goodyear, Paul Litchfield, imported twelve carefully chosen Zeppelin engineers from Friedrichshafen to build the two ships in America. They were led by Karl Arnstein, a talented designer. Born in Prague, Bohemia, he had formerly been Zeppelin's chief stress engineer. Free of Ludwig Dürr's yoke, Dr. Arnstein had his chance: he would bring new thinking to the *Akron* and *Macon*.

The Story of the Airship was an informed series by Hugh Allen, published annually after 1925 by Goodyear as a 'convenient reference book for students, writers and others interested', a confirmation of Goodyear's desire to be central to airship culture.[8] It was an ambition that exceeded the motivations of most companies in merely wishing to enhance the blackness of their bottom line. Allen gives a useful account of the manner in which the Arnstein vessels departed from previous designs – there were numerous minor changes, but some were startlingly different. For example, instead of the conventional single keel, there would be three: 'Some idea of the increase in strength may be realised by the simple illustration of lashing three lead pencils together and trying to break them, as compared to breaking a single pencil.'[9]

Earlier ships had a central keel accommodating a catwalk, which ran bow to stern providing access and space for fuel, ballast, baggage, mail, crew and passenger quarters. The new ships retained the central corridor, but by positioning a new corridor 'at the top of the ship and the other two 45 degrees from the bottom, the accessibility to service facilities and to maintenance is more than tripled'.[10] The configuration meant gas leaks could be detected quickly and remedied more easily. Automatic valves were positioned at the top of gas cells; gas being lighter than air and flowing upwards, the position of these valves ensured gas could be released immediately; and by installing valves along the top corridor they were more easily available for inspection.

There were other innovations. The US Navy and public had been stupefied by the *Shenandoah* disaster; the inquiry had revealed structural weaknesses. Just as the *R38* tragedy had engendered a determination in British designers to build ships that were prodigiously strong, so the *Shenandoah* accident instilled a determination by the US Navy and the Goodyear-Zeppelin coalition to build two peerless vessels of Herculean strength. Their sturdiness would come from the triple keels: one at the top of the hull giving access to gas valves, the other two running port and starboard along the lower hull supporting the eight Maybach engines and providing space for the crew. The hull was built round 36 longitudinal girders and stiff eight-foot deep rings, in reality large triangular structures like the keel: their design augmented both weight and 'muscularity'. The ships were colossal, their scale surpassed only later by the *Hindenburg* in 1936.

The use of helium heralded more innovations: since it was a non-inflammable gas, the engines could be positioned *inside* the ships, sited on the lower keel, making maintenance easier and reducing aerodynamic drag. In previous ships external engine cars were as small as possible to minimise drag. Drag militated against streamlining, reduced performance, increased fuel consumption, which lessened range, and could make handling difficult. If an airship made an impromptu touch-down, exterior engine cars were vulnerable.

For engineers, conventional engine cars were cramped, hot and deafening, with engines so 'shoe-horned' into place that servicing was difficult.

On the American vessels, with their eight larger internal engine rooms, such problems were in part alleviated. But new thinking creates unexpected problems. The engines drove outrigger propellers attached by long shafts. The propellers gave forward and reverse propulsion and could be swivelled to assist in lift-off or docking. 'Pointed downward to exert vertical thrust this will enable a ship to take off "heavy", carrying additional fuel and so increasing the cruising radius. They can be used also to drive the ship downward if it comes in for landing "light" due to atmospheric conditions or other causes.'[11] The Maybach V8 engines were in a line along the twin port and starboard keels that ran in parallel along the bottom of the ship. In previous craft, engines were sited at different heights on the hull, the staggering of their position ensuring each operated in undisturbed air. The new straight-line design meant the forward engines created a wash of air that disturbed engines situated to their rear. And the new layout caused extreme vibration and shuddering. There were stories that it was so bad it could dislodge teeth! Rosendahl held this view, his candour (some said misplaced) being as famous as his exploits. Designers fretted and considered modifications, so that in this respect the design was seriously compromised. But it still represented a sort of progress, being considered by many (though certainly not all) a less costly, lighter, more elegant configuration than had been produced in the past.

It was customary to vent lifting gas to compensate for decreasing weight as petrol or diesel was consumed. The designers of *Graf Zeppelin* experimented with Blau gas as fuel; being close to the same weight as air, the Blau gas used made little difference to the weight of the ship (see page 233). The Americans found another solution, which they used on the *Los Angeles*. Their motive lay in the cost and scarcity of helium, a natural gas not easily acquired. In trying to maintain sailing equilibrium, without having to squander helium by venting it off, engineers devised a ballast-recovery system. It entailed condensing vapour from exhausts into water, which proved to be only marginally heavier than fuel burned. 'This not only conserved the helium but had an operating advantage in that the *Los Angeles* could start on a journey with a minimum quantity of ballast, building up its supplies as it went along, thus increasing its cruising radius by permitting it to start off with more fuel in place of the heavier ballast load formerly carried.'[12] For the *Akron* a condenser system 'was devised composed of small ribbed fins along the side of the ship, something like the louvers in the hood of an automobile, getting a maximum cooling result with minimum resistance'.[13]

Some of *Akron's* gas cells were made of a cheaper and lighter cotton fabric, proofed against leaks by an artificial latex-gelatin compound. It had a different type of tail construction. Previous vessels had a cruciform tail structure, which offered great strength. Arnstein's team abolished the cruciform construction, a resolution that led to criticism.

Another design change also became subject to contention: Charles Rosendahl was among those who insisted that officers should be able to see the lower fin from the control car.; the original fins were more slender than those finally decided upon. He had experienced an alarming incident on the *Graf Zeppelin* while on its round-the-world journey (see page 238). During a lift-off with the ship heavy, the lower fin, not visible from the control car, had come close to catching on power-lines. Had it done so it would have been catastrophic. The resulting modifications on the *Akron* entailed changing Arnstein's original design. Other fins on the ship had to be shortened and deepened to permit visibility of the lower fin. The original fins extended to over a hundred feet. Each had been attached to major frames in the hull. The new fins, the leading edge of which were subject to heavy aerodynamic stress, were attached to intermediate frames that were less strong. The implementation of redesigned fins also necessitated another design change: the control car had to be moved back eight feet towards the stern.

Akron

Akron was a giant. With her mammoth skeleton constructed of duralumin, she could carry 20,000 gallons of gasoline with a range of 10,500 miles. At 785 feet long, with a beam of 137.5 feet, she could cruise at 58mph, with a top speed of 83mph. Her helium capacity was nearly seven million cubic feet. She had seven machine-gun emplacements and a crew of 60 officers and men. She was so big that a new ground handling method had to be devised. As the Germans and British knew, in a wind large airships could be a nightmare for ground handlers. An ingenious mechanical system was created in which the ship's nose was linked to a portable stubby mast, which could be moved on double rails. The ship's lower fin was clamped to a transverse beam, which weighed 133 tons. The airship and mast were shunted out of the shed by a diesel locomotive on rails that ran in a circle allowing the ship to be turned head-to-wind for lift-off. Thus, instead of a squadron of handlers, a relatively small number of people were needed to get the ship in and out of her shed .

Akron was launched by the First Lady, Lou Hoover, and her first commander was Charles Rosendahl. Her maiden voyage was on 23 September 1931 carrying 113 passengers including Litchfield and Arnstein around the vicinity of Cleveland, Ohio. Two more towering figures in US naval aviation were aboard: the first was the revered Admiral William Moffett, Chief of the Bureau of Aeronautics from its foundation in 1921 to his death, a pivotal position. An open-minded defender of naval aviation, Moffett sanctioned the funding of *Akron* and *Macon,* chaperoning his decision through Congress and fending off hostility in the military and media. Many see Moffett as the father of the modern American navy; developments nurtured by him included surface aircraft carriers, flying-boats and lightweight, powerful, air-cooled radial engines. Others acknowledge him as the architect of the sea/air victory of 1945 over Japan.[14] A comparison may be drawn with Britain's Admiral 'Jacky' Fisher. Each was unafraid of fresh thinking and new technology. Fisher had around him bright young officers in his 'fish-tank', disciples of his innovative creed; Moffett too had an admiring coterie attracted by his boldness in backing daring ideas. A persuasive advocate for naval aviation, he fended-off broadsides from the controversial General Billy Mitchell credited by some as being the father of the United States Air Force.

The second consummate lighter-than-air advocate aboard *Akron's* initial flight was Captain Garland Fulton. Graduating from the Naval Academy in

1912, he had studied naval architecture at Massachusetts Institute of Technology, followed by aeronautical engineering under the inspired tutelage of Naval Constructor Lieutenant Commander Dr. Jerome Clarke Hunsaker. There was no better teacher: Hunsaker was an aeronautical engineer, intellectual and writer. He had constructed airships, flying-boats and the first wind tunnel at the MIT. In Europe, Hunsaker had been permitted to inspect the DELAG passenger airship, *Viktoria Luise* in which he had sailed over Berlin.[15] Given the confidentiality in which DELAG cloaked its commercial secrets, this was some achievement. Hunsaker was among those convinced that rigid airships would prove a potent aide to the work of US navy scout cruisers.

Fulton had been sent to Europe in 1922 to help in negotiations for the airship reparations programme. Under the Versailles Treaty, German airships should have been handed over to the Allies, but they were destroyed by their crews before their transfer. Fulton served at Zeppelin in Friedrichshafen while a 'Reparation Ship' was being built: this was the *LZ126*, which in 1924 became the *Los Angeles* (ZR3). Fulton worked until retirement as chief of the lighter-than-air division at the Bureau of Aeronautics in Washington. When *Los Angeles* was complete, it was he who oversaw the design and building of *Akron* and *Macon*. He was among those who lobbied tirelessly to persuade naval and commercial operators to accept rigid airships, while under him the US Navy's non-rigid fleet expanded in the years up to America entering the Second World War.[16]

There were nine trial flights before *Akron* was commissioned into the US Navy on 27 October 1931 at Lakehurst. During her trials she fell slightly short of her contract top speed, and some commentators exploited this marginal failing[17] – the frequently levelled charge that the *Akron* rarely received a good press has validity. Subsequently she made several significant voyages, offering a capacity, range and flexibility in advance of anything at the time. The ship was criticised by some in her role as a naval scout, much of the animus coming from an intransigent and prejudiced lobby. *Akron* had ardent admirers, but there remained enmity among a legion of politicians and the military.

From the outset *Akron* was susceptible to mishaps. In one, watched by rheumy-eyed politicians awaiting a joy flight (US congressmen relished 'freebie' aerial sojourns as much as their British counterparts) the colossus grew wayward: she broke free of her ground handlers and smashed her lower fin into the ground. Repairs took eight weeks; addressing the public relations fall-out took longer – of *all* days, it had to be *this* day, when the press and politicians had gathered in force. *Akron*'s reputation was impugned by naval exercises that were too ambitious for her (but not all: in some she acquitted herself in style). She was not yet in a state of readiness and still devoid of a trapeze and her fighters. Instead of hovering at a judicious distance as a mothership it was demanded she be 'in the thick of it' in the forward manoeuvres, making her a sitting-duck for 'kills' by planes from marine ships. In judging her capability the exercises were a mockery, allowing non-believers an opportunity to recite arguments about airship fragility.

Akron's lacklustre showing came at a difficult time. Progress in heavier-than-air flight had been dramatic, and rivalry between the aircraft lobby and the champions of airships had grown heated. The economy was fragile, money scarce, budgets tight. Seaplanes and others held a novel allure. An aggregation of public, Congress, military commanders and media controversialists held to a common creed: lighter-than-air craft were fragile, their utility superseded by fixed-wing developments. The noble airship, which had once promised so much, was now being judged as unworthy of further patronage. Indeed, from its early days the passage of the airship had been storm-tossed: times had changed from 1913, when the perspicacious US Chief Naval Constructor, Admiral David Taylor urged the US navy to supplement the Fleet with airships. Taylor was a naval architect of acuity, known for test-tank experiments (pioneered in 1871–2 by the stellar British engineer William Froude) in which models were used to evaluate the hydrodynamics of surface vessels.

On 8 May 1932, *Akron* sailed from Lakehurst to the west coast en route to Sunnyvale, California. On 11 May at Camp Kearney, in California, she tried to moor. She had become 'light' by sailing for hours in strong sunshine, from heat generated by her enormous engines and by using 40 tons of fuel. At Camp

Kearney the ground crew drawn from the San Diego Naval Training Station were, in the main, surface-ship sailors, inadequately trained in airship handling. The ensuing tragedy gave sceptics further ammunition. Four sailors, members of the ground crew clutching at their mooring lines, were suddenly hoisted into the heavens when the great ship rose abruptly into the sky. One was carried some 20 feet into the air before he loosed his grasp and fell, enduring a broken arm as he hit the ground. Three others were lifted higher: two fell to their deaths, the third managed to fasten himself to the rope and after an hour of struggle was hauled up into the safety of the ship. The accident was captured on newsreel and flashed across America – another blow to airship morale and to public confidence. In airship history the fates would conspire to ensure that if craft or men faced harrowing adversity there would never be a discreet shroud of dignity, but that such moments would always be played out in public.

Akron's experiments included one in which an object resembling a small aircraft fuselage was suspended from beneath the ship. It recalled the dangerous sky-chariots, or cloud cars, pioneered in the years of conflict by the Zeppelin bombers (see page 43). The Americans wanted 'sky-eyes' while *Akron* sailed high protected by cloud, which was the thinking of German commanders who had sought to enhance bomb-aiming while maintaining height and cloud-cover. The test was abandoned when the gondola cavorted from side to side; thankfully, inside was a sandbag rather than a human observer.

Akron underwent a concentrated period in which fighters were installed and their pilots mastered the trapeze. On 22 June 1932, Alger Dressel replaced Charles Rosendahl as the commander. In a period in which faith in airships and their reputation was tarnished, Rosendahl's drive and persuasiveness remained key to their survival. In 1928 he was on the magisterial *Graf Zeppelin* on its first transatlantic crossing to America and aboard it for its round-the-world voyage in 1929. In 1936 he would be a watch officer on the *Hindenburg* and make four transatlantic crossings between Germany and North and South America. He was to be remembered as the commanding officer at Lakehurst at the time of the *Hindenburg* calamity on 6 May 1937. During the Second

World War he commanded the surface cruiser *USS Minneapolis*, which saw action at Guadalcanal and for which he was decorated. After sustaining injuries he returned to Lakehurst in 1943 as the officer in charge of airship training and experimentation. He died at the age of 84 in 1977.*

On Dressel's watch, plans were laid to have two of the aircraft flank the airship – flying at a distance beyond the vision of the airship. The formation permitted a grand 'sweep' or reconnaissance path a hundred miles wide, which could be searched efficiently and quickly. *Akron's* performance was flawed in that she was devoid of long-range spotter-planes, fighters being more suited to defence than reconnaissance.

Dressel later became commander of *Akron's* sister ship, *Macon*, and Frank C. McCord became *Akron's* third commander on 3 January 1933. McCord was a skilled commander, another who was ill-judged by history. In the US Navy he had enjoyed a distinguished surface career, much of it in aircraft carriers. With 2,000 hours of sailing time in airships, he impressed officers in skippering the vessel on exacting voyages. The worst, a severe storm with gusts of 30 knots, had made mooring at Lakehurst impossible. The ship had already sailed for 40 hours but had been forced to stay aloft for a further 32. McCord found a circuitous route, allowing him to thread his way back to Lakehurst *behind* the storm. *Akron* was a colossus, meteorology was still in its infancy, radio and communications were immature. The great ship had bucked and pitched as lightning dancing on her silver cover and thunder rattled her skeleton. The officers and crew at their stations were weary from struggle. It was an exemplary feat of sailing and navigation.

Frank McCord was no greenhorn. A seasoned naval officer, he knew first-hand the cynicism in the surface fleet towards airships. He had heard all the hoary wardroom jokes about their fragility. He knew it was crucial for *Akron* to put on a convincing show, and he appreciated that overcoming the elements was only half the task: the rest would be in persuading politicians and the Fleet of the airship's usefulness.

* The author is grateful to the excellent endeavours of Rick Zitarosa and the Navy Lakehurst Historical Society.

McCord and his crew sailed their vessel to Cuba and to Panama, their intelligence reports leading to the erection of a mast at Guantanamo. There was a suggestion another might be built in Panama. In helping to survey distant outposts of political and military sensitivity, the airship with its great range, speed in excess of surface vessels, and carrying capacity, had a useful strategic purpose.

A prestige voyage occurred on 4 March 1933 when *Akron* sailed over Washington, DC, where Franklin D. Roosevelt was being sworn in as America's 32nd president. A multitude watched as she cruised the sky above the ceremony – it seemed as if America owned all of heaven and every wonder in it.

But a month later, on 3 April 1933, a new page was turned in airship history. *Akron* embarked on a standard mission to help calibrate radio direction-finder stations along the New England seaboard. Among her company were two especially respected sailors: Rear Admiral Moffett and Fred T. Berry, commanding officer of Lakehurst Naval Air Station. The weather turned hellish – turbulent winds, ground fog and a forbidding cloak of dense cloud. The ship sailed into a tempest, the most violent storm seen in the region for years. McCord took the ship inland, but the storm showed no sign of abating, so he headed back out to sea, intending to ride it out. It had been wrongly calculated that the eye of the storm was elsewhere: in reality, McCord and his ship were at its centre. In the darkness of the night the vessel was hit by a series of violent gusts that pressed it down to the sea. Suddenly it was sucked down nearly 1,000 feet by a massive downdraft. In desperation, McCord jettisoned most of the water ballast and, with the eight huge Maybach engines roaring on full power, the helmsman tried to force the vessel back up into the sky. But it was too late. As the ship began to nose reluctantly upwards, her tail caught in the water, rendering her beyond control – in moments she was drawn inexorably into the freezing Atlantic. There were no lifejackets, no time to launch her one liferaft: 73 of the 76 aboard perished including McCord, Moffett and Berry. It was the largest single aviation tragedy to date. A Navy blimp, *J-3*, joined the search; it also crashed, killing two men.

In the eighteen months since her launch, *Akron* had made 74 flights totalling 1,700 hours. There was a surfeit of conjecture – suspicion about the strength of her build; she was devoid of the strong cruciform tail structure; her configuration had strayed from Arnstein's original concept; the control car had been shifted; different fins had been attached to less 'muscular' frames. But over the decades theorists tended to blame Frank McCord: it was his poor decision-making; he had thought the ship higher than it was; he had been fooled by an altimeter that had malfunctioned due to low pressure in the storm; an experienced commander should have allowed for the fickle tricks of a barometric altimeter. Or, perhaps, in the frenzy of the ship's last moments he had forgotten *Akron*'s extreme length, the way he had pointed her skywards, failing to remember her tail was 800 feet astern and that it would dip into the sea and drag her beneath the waves at such a steep angle of climb. It became a macabre game: pick a hypothesis and make it fit. In truth, the secrets of those last moments will never be known. Two certainties emerged: it is too easy to blame a dead man; and the credibility of rigid airships had suffered a devastating blow.

Macon

Akron's destruction reverberated across America. Her sister, the *Macon*, was almost complete when the calamity occurred. The *Macon* had been named by Rear Admiral Moffett's wife, Jeannette Whitton Moffett, two weeks before her husband's death. *Macon* was similar to *Akron*, but slight improvements had been incorporated. She was lighter, a little faster and with greater lift; there had been a plan by Moffett during construction to make her even bigger, but he knew the chances of getting more money were slim and he was too shrewd to engage in a battle he could not win.

Macon's maiden voyage was on 21 April 1933, three weeks after the *Akron*'s demise. She underwent three test flights before she was commissioned into the US Navy by Moffett's successor as head of the Aeronautics Bureau, Rear Admiral Ernest Joseph King. One wonders if King's elevation would have pleased Moffett; at the Bureau it was King's second coming. He was dogged with a reputation for being rebarbative. He had once been the number two at the Aeronautics Bureau but had quit because of strategy disagreements. He was to rise to high office, emerging as the Navy's number two sailor as Commander-in-Chief of the US Fleet and chief of Naval Operations during the Second World War.[18] Born in Lorain, Ohio, King had served in cruisers, battleships, aircraft carriers and submarines; admirers said he was exceptional and an astute strategist. Detractors said he was cold to the point of rudeness, an Anglophobe with an ingrained suspicion of the British Royal Navy.

In that she achieved only a modest degree of mixed success in Fleet exercises, the *Macon* mirrored the career of the *Akron*. Two more names would enter the airship orbit, neither of which could be regarded as especially staunch friends of the dirigible. Admiral David Foote Sellers was the Commander-in-Chief of the US Fleet. The second was Admiral William H. Standley, the Chief of Naval Operations.[19] Standley and Sellers made it patently clear that *Macon* was on trial.

Macon would be subject to inappropriate use in the same way that the *Akron* had been deployed. Did Stanley and Sellers want to kill off the naval airship? The timing was perhaps ripe for a coup de grâce. *Akron's* terrible end still echoed across America. Her death had shaken the most loyal adherents; there was outrage in Congress, widespread public unease, and the newspapers and radio stations were in full cry. During another round of war games, instead of the *Macon* being sensibly utilised as a reconnaissance mothership – despatching her aeroplanes forward as scouts – she was made to stay close to 'enemy' ships who 'killed' her with anti-aircraft guns or 'shot' her down with their fighters. She was, again, the easiest of targets. The manoeuvres had two consequences: the elegant *Macon*, which had sailed serene above the Fleet, was belittled, and the belief spread like a contagion that airships were vulnerable. Alger Dressel, *Macon's* commander – his caution honed by the death of the *Akron* – triggered opprobrium from naval chiefs by quitting exercises to avoid worsening weather fronts; he also expressed consternation about a dubious frame in his ship's stern, which required remedying and on which work was postponed several times. Sellers despatched a damning critique on *Macon's* allegedly lame performance to the Chief of Naval Operations. 'The Sellers report was obviously intended not so much to criticise *Macon* as to scuttle the airship in the US navy.'[20]

On 11 July 1934, Dressel's place as commander was taken by Lieutenant Commander Herbert V. Wiley, one of the three survivors of the *Akron*. His command included a period in which the *Macon*'s fighter pilots became versed in the use of the trapeze and in their role as scouts. The airship was finally being used in her correct role as a radio relay station, command centre and transporter. During previous exercises her radio and navigation equipment were inadequate (which was not acknowledged in Sellers' lambasting of the ship), but improvements had been made. On earlier exercises, distant scouting operations by the airship's fighters had posed communication problems. The safety of the aeroplanes when they flew far from *Macon* was enhanced by a reliable, low-frequency radio homing device invented by *Macon*'s communications officer, Lieutenant Howard N. Coulter, and a civilian, Dr. Gerhard Fisher. Other fundamental improvements were being made. It was long argued that *Macon*'s aircraft should be modified for their specific role: with aeroplanes hooking on to a trapeze, it was sensible to strip them of landing gear that in their specific role had now become obsolete. The change allowed space for a 30-gallon fuel-tank, and their top speed was improved. They could also stay out for five hours, so the scouting radius they could fly from the airship increased to 250 miles.

During one exercise Wiley planned a novel night-time 'raid' on a surface aircraft carrier using his fighters as dive-bombers. Nocturnal flying by fighters from the airship had become commonplace, but regulations at the time insisted that a surface carrier had to have its aeroplanes stored before dark. However, because of structural problems with *Macon*, Wiley had to forego his attack.

Wiley thought up several ways in which the airship could prove its usefulness to the navy. He knew the importance of good headlines, swaying public opinion and silencing (or at least muffling) the critics in Congress. He pulled off a coup that caught the nation's imagination and brought to his vessel the novelty of good news. President Roosevelt was travelling by ship from

Panama to Hawaii. Wiley calculated the ship's location and despatched two fighters. They found the ship and to the President's delight dropped newspapers and souvenir letters on its deck. Roosevelt was baffled how little planes with no wheels and limited range flew 1,500 miles out to sea – when the *Macon* emerged the mystery was solved and a cheer went up from the President and his entourage. Roosevelt congratulated the airship and its company. But even his plaudits failed to deter a sour response from the Navy. Admiral Joseph Reeves, then Commander-in-Chief of the US Fleet, signalled that Wiley's display was a 'misapplied initiative'.[21] Wiley and his crew must have despaired: what would they have to do to win the approbation of their brethren in the surface fleet?

Macon was damaged when she had to fly across America above the mountains of Arizona. It was a route Sellers insisted upon: Dressel wanted to take an alternative route. An experienced commander, he was aware of the effects of hot air and volatile winds. But Sellers overruled him. The ship's 'pressure height' was less than 3,000 ft. But she had to fly at over 6,000 ft. Pressure height is when falling atmospheric pressure allows the lifting gas to expand. It increases relative pressure in the gasbags causing the automatic valves to activate; the valves open and gas is blown out, thus avoiding an explosion. Up to or below pressure-height a ship could climb or descend as its commander wished without fear that gas would be vented. But *Macon* ascended beyond her pressure-height; accordingly the valves discharged helium and the ship became heavy. Due to her increased weight she was forced to jettison a large quantity of fuel and ballast. To maintain equilibrium she had to sail at cruising speed at a slight nose-up angle. This created additional stress, especially on the fins of the tailplane. When subject to violent winds over Texas, the strain at the point where the port fin was fixed to the hull became too severe: the frame in the hull to which the fin was attached buckled and two girders in the hull broke. The temporary in-flight repairs that were necessary were helped by Karl Arnstein's accessible design. Later a Goodyear-Zeppelin team said all four fins and the ring should be reinforced. Instead of grounding her it was decided to make repairs when they fitted in with operational commitments. By February 1935 work was complete apart from reinforcement of the upper tailplane which was scheduled for March.

There was little warning of the tribulations that would befall her on the afternoon of 12 February 1935, ten months after the *Akron* had perished. Wiley was in command, the ship heading for her base at Sunnyvale, near San Francisco. She had been on exercises with the Pacific Fleet. The weather was stormy with a capricious wind, while rain fell with a sad persistence and fog shrouded the mountains. The ship had followed a passage north along the California coast; Point Sur lay off her starboard bow. Suddenly she was clouted by a vicious cross-current that detached the upper fin from her tail. In the control car the helmsman wrestled with the wheel, which had become dead and heavy, the *Macon* feeling leaden at her stern. Her cover had been ripped, remnants flapping in the wind. Jagged shards from the wrecked tail speared the aft helium cells so that gas rushed out and rain poured in, saturating the cells, adding to her weight. The ballast-toggles were yanked, jettisoning 33,000 pounds of fuel and ballast. Though heavy in the tail, she continued to climb. At almost 3,000 feet, her pressure-height, the automatic valves opened, expelling more helium. Still she climbed, to nearly 5,000 feet, but she was no longer a ship that was lighter-than-air. Her fate was sealed, her descent into the sea inevitable. It was a relatively peaceful end. She fell slowly from the sky and gently touched on the water, settling into the waves, with sailors diving from her, others using knives to slice open the bow cover in which they had been trapped, hacking their way to freedom. Most had lifejackets, and rescue boats were swiftly at the scene. The Pacific was warmer than the icy waters of the Atlantic in which those on the *Akron* had been claimed by hypothermia. Of the 76 aboard, two were killed.

American technologists and sailors had made great strides in progressing the airship. But it was not enough. The public, politicians and swathes of the military had lost faith. There were too many accidents; the cost in lives had been too high. No more rigid airships would be built in the United States.

12

THE MIGHTY *GRAF* AND THE *HINDENBURG* CALAMITY

Graf Zeppelin

In 1928 the Zeppelin company produced the *Graf Zeppelin*. Sailed by Dr. Hugo Eckener, it would girdle the globe, impressing a legion of admirers with feats certain to embellish the Eckener legend. The voyages showed that it was possible for a sky ship to make lengthy passages carrying passengers in safety and style. Safety did not mean its expeditions were devoid of adventure, though there is a suspicion some were self-induced to ensure the ship occupied the headlines: Eckener was a wily operator and a capable publicist; as a former journalist, he knew how to generate attention and understood the commercial importance of maintaining a high-profile for the Zeppelin company and his vessel.

The *Graf* (Count), as it came to be known, bristled with innovation: its lifting gas was the usual hydrogen, but its five 560hp Maybach engines were powered by Blau gas and petrol. While not *identical* a parallel may be drawn between Blau gas and the commonplace propane. As an airship burned through its propellant of petrol or diesel it became lighter. To maintain equilibrium or, put another way, to stop it rising in the sky and exploding, the hydrogen or helium had to be vented off.[1] Blau gas is almost the same weight as air; thus its consumption made little difference to the overall weight of a craft. The idea obviated the need for a vessel to waste gas by its release into the atmosphere, helium at the time being both scarce and costly.[2]

The *Graf*'s illustrious career began in an alarming manner. On its maiden voyage across the Atlantic from Friedrichshaven to Lakehurst it ran into a vicious storm midway across the ocean. Eckener was in command. Other luminaries aboard included the accordion-playing airshipman Ernst Lehmann, whose right-wing political sympathies during the following decade as Europe edged towards the world war tarnished his reputation. The US Navy's Charles Rosendahl, famous for free-ballooning to safety from the *Shenandoah*, was also aboard. So too was the reporter Lady Grace Hay Drummond-Hay. A minor English aristocrat, she was the beguiling widow of Sir Robert Hay Drummond-Hay, a British diplomat. She had been commissioned by Hearst newspapers to produce accessible copy, sometimes with a woman's angle. Her reporting would increase the public's fascination in airships. Her former lover, who was also sailing, was the senior reporter Karl von Wiegand, tapping out his geo-political commentaries.

The *Graf* succeeded in weathering the storm but sustained serious damage. The cover on her port fin, which ordinarily carried a high degree of horizontal load, was ripped off, and the flying shreds of cover could have easily jammed in her elevators.[3] Eckener was so concerned that he instructed his officers to radio ahead requesting that a surface vessel venture out in the event that his airship might have to ditch. In the event, laborious and dangerous mid-air temporary repairs were expedited,[4] and the surface craft's mission was halted. The incident showed Eckener as an instinctive sky sailor, of daring when it was necessary but always of prudence if his vessel or those in his keeping were in jeopardy.[5]

The *Graf* was comfortable, but it most notably personified Teutonic competency.[6] Every inch of space was utilised. The dining room was not large but worked well, doubling up as a sitting room for passengers. Large windows offered panoramic views. The galley was small but sufficient, the crew serving hot food of quality. Passenger cabins had beds that converted into sofas for daytime use. The *Graf* could carry 20 passengers, a relatively modest number compared, say, with the *R101*, which had been designed for a hundred.[7] The bridge, navigation area and radio room were in the bows, with the dining-

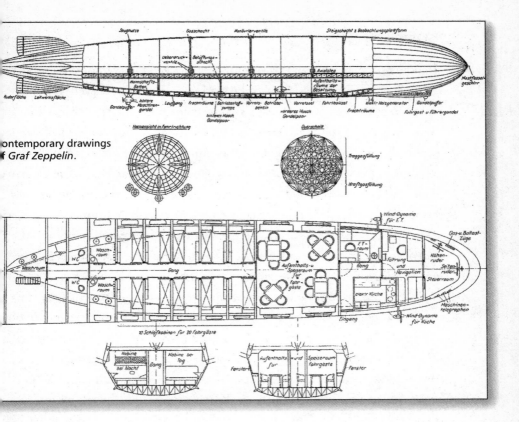

Contemporary drawings of *Graf Zeppelin*.

lounge in the middle where the gondola was at its widest. The key word was *efficiency*. In economic terms it was not so convincing.[8] With fuel, maintenance, a crew of 43 and on occasion as many as a hundred ground handlers, the *Graf* had to impose high ticket charges on its passengers. The Atlantic run has traditionally beguiled air and shipping lines. For some it proved ruinous. Shipping lines forever sought state subsidies or strove to be insulated from commercial uncertainty by postal contracts; so too the Zeppelin corporation, which made useful money carrying mail. However, such funding was insufficient to free it of the caprice inherent in businesses built on international travel.

On reaching America the *Graf* was greeted with euphoria, hailed as a wonder of the age. The 30th President of the United States, the Republican Calvin Coolidge, honoured Eckener and his officers with an audience. Eckener spent time in America trying to raise money to set up a global service. He had an influential circle, but in this ambition he attained only minor success. The climate was difficult. Money was becoming scarce. Only eleven years had passed since the war. Airships were seen by many not as graceful giants but as ominous behemoths that carried a deadly payload; not for nothing had Zeppelins been branded 'baby-killers' in British wartime propaganda. In the decade after the war, antipathy was less pronounced, but airships in the United States and Britain were still viewed as being *German* in their origin which, though immeasurable, could arguably have hindered their advance.

When the *Graf Zeppelin* crossed the Atlantic money coursed through the American economy. Too much of it, though, was of the fast and speculative type. Though Europe was spiralling into bankruptcy, there was a new sense of *fin de siècle*, an interval of naïve complacency with the seductive rhythms of the jazz age to distract from systemic weaknesses. In America the poison of joblessness had begun its inexorable climb, a contagion that already infected two million people. The Wall Street Crash of 1929 heralded financial chaos. American and European economies shimmied into depression and despots began strutting across the world stage. Paul Litchfield of Goodyear was tapped by Eckener but he was too cagey to commit, as were others. Beyond back-slapping and promises, Eckener exited the US as bereft of long-term funding as when he had arrived and been welcomed as a hero.

If he was to remain the Admiral of the Sky, Hugo Eckener would need to conjure up more stunts and find fresh forms of funding. He had planned a round-the-world voyage which was costed initially at half a million dollars. On rehashing the figures it seemed possible that such a passage could be made for half that. Before the ascendency of accountants, newspapers were the impregnable citadels of those whose vanities were matched only by their wealth: the American publishing baron Randolph Hearst would pay half the cost, with German newspapers and enthusiastic philatelists the rest – stamp collectors would prove a novel and intriguing source of money. They would pay handsomely for items that bore stamps from the *Graf*s different ports of call. At her embarkation she carried thousands of postal items, and on her return her stamped mail drove collectors into something of a frenzy.

In 1929 the *Graf* began her round-the-world trip from Friedrichshafen. In reality she had two starts. For the record books she began the voyage from Lakehurst because the pay-master, Hearst, insisted it held more appeal for readers if she started and finished in America. There were twenty passengers aboard. The reporters included Grace Hay Drummond-Hay and von Wiegand, her intimate. Airshipmen included Rosendahl and Lehmann. There was also an Arctic expeditionary, the Australian Sir Hubert Wilkins, who personified the sense of dare-devil with which the trip was imbued. He was a friend of the American explorer Lincoln Ellsworth and of Hearst; the latter financed him in 1931 when he led a North Pole expedition in a submarine. He had won the Military Cross at the Battle of Passchendaele in 1917 and been knighted after an epic 21-hour flight across the Arctic by plane from Alaska to Spitsbergen.

The price for a passenger to voyage round the world on the *Graf* was just under $3,000 a ticket. But for this particular passage few had to pay, the trip being financed before it began. Eckener's concern, beyond getting there and back in one piece, was to generate publicity that would help forge a regular transatlantic service. In this sense it was a glorified public relations exercise, albeit an extremely intrepid and ambitious one.

To a background of German folk songs and rousing Wagner on Lehmann's accordion, there grew among the passengers the unique camaraderie of those confined by extraordinary circumstance: the food and wine and anecdotes flowed as the *Graf* sailed into history, casting her giant shadow across Europe and into Asia. She passed through sun and storm, darkness and light. Rain streamed from her plumpness down across her windows. Along a gusty mountain ridge she sailed, low through a twisting valley, Eckener on the bridge, the wizard of the clouds who knew the weather as well as he knew each murmur of his ship. Beneath the *Graf*'s fat belly the earth unfurled like a patchwork quilt, revealing itself from the air for the first time; from the gondola came the tap of a typewriter, a tinny bell to mark each crafted line.

After four days she lowered herself slowly back to earth, a sea of heads craned to the sky, and a thousand eager hands seized at her lines: Tokyo, Japan, the first stop. A quarter of a million well-wishers greeted her, fêting her occupants as if they were gods from a far planet. Fettled and fuelled, she got under way once more, and for the first time an airship sailed across the Pacific from the Orient to America. Her entrance into America was spectacular. Being a former journalist, Eckener knew what the expectant throng on the ground wanted, and what the headline and caption-writers needed. He knew what made a good story and a strong picture, and he had an innate sense of theatre. Consequently he timed his arrival with precision, knowing his ship would be at its most magical if he sailed across San Francisco's Golden Gate Bridge at sunset, the *Graf*'s silver acres glinting in the light. Later, however, the ship and her passengers would have a narrow escape avoiding power lines. Strong Californian sunshine had expanded her gas, causing the valves to vent hydrogen and thereby increasing her weight. It was only through Eckener's extraordinary adroitness at the controls that calamity was averted. By the time the *Graf* returned to Lakehurst she had crossed two oceans and three continents and covered more than 21,000 miles.[9]

Once the trumpets had faded Eckener still needed money to keep his ship airborne. He could rely to a degree on domestic and European sailings, plus the occasional excursion to Britain and an ever-popular programme of joy-rides. Such receipts were of value, but in the overall cost of the operation relatively trivial. Though such monies kept his craft aloft, they were too menial to offer long-term security. Post-war archives show that over England she photographed two RAF aerodromes and at Brough, near Hull, the Blackburn aircraft company; these were likely to have been spying trips when Eckener's influence was in decline and Hitler's in the ascendency.[10]

Eckener learned commercial lessons from the surface shipping lines who for generations had enjoyed long-haul monopolies. He made deals with the agents of shipping lines through whom Zeppelin passages could be booked.[11] The call of distant destinations began to beckon. Taking his cue from the shipping companies, he thought that South America looked promising. German communities flecked the Latin continent: there were plenty of German nationals in Argentina and Brazil, many of them rich with sprawling haciendas and powerful businesses. A regular service for the wealthy could be a money-spinner – voyaging from Latin America to Europe might take a steamship three weeks, but an airship could do it in three days. Users would pay a premium to be afforded such swiftness. Eckener chose Recife on Brazil's eastern coast, 5,000 miles distant. On 18 May 1930, the *Graf* lifted off from Friedrichshafen at the start of a regular service that would include Rio de Janeiro, then Brazil's exuberant capital. She crossed the south Atlantic 18 times in 1932 and by 1934 was sailing from Germany to Brazil every other week. Passengers could fly on from Brazil to Argentina by connecting aeroplane. The service continued to grow in 1935 and 1936. During the ship's nine-year life she crossed the south Atlantic 136 times.

To conquer the Latin American routes, to overcome obstacles of distance, weather and myriad technical and aeronautical problems was a startling achievement.[12] The *Graf*'s South American run was the world's first scheduled, regular, intercontinental aviation service. Aeroplanes had made progress, but were small and limited by range. Flying boats were leaving their mark and promised much. But for a brief and halcyon spell the airship was the queen of the skies. She offered rapid and luxurious travel over unimagined distances.[13] And as a carrier of cargo and mail she spelt serious competition for shipping lines and cartels.[14]

The forever restless Hugo Eckener – newspapers after his round-the-world foray dubbed him the 'Magellan of the Skies' – always wanted more. If the world is advanced by those who are never satisfied, then Eckener deserved his recognition. Now he would be drawn to the hostile magnet that had lured others of the era, and in which some had perished – the Arctic wastes. His expedition, its cost funded by stamp collectors and newspapers, was another that would attract global attention: it lasted seven days, covered more than 8,000 miles, the ship discovering land masses and mountain ranges previously uncharted. The *Graf* set off in July 1931 and kept an assignation, which sent philatelists into paroxysms, with the Soviet ice-breaker the *Malygin*. Aboard it was the Italian airshipman Umberto Nobile, driven into exile in revolutionary Russia by Mussolini and assisting the Soviets with their airship building programme. The *Graf* carried scientists and academics and assorted polar-watchers and 60,000 postal items to be exchanged for mail carried by the Soviet ice-breaker. Eckener landed his great ship on a drifting ice floe, as softly as a feather, where it was temporarily tethered by sandbags. Because the floe was moving he could only stay for as long as it took to exchange the mail bags, and after a few minutes he was forced to lift off, sailing quietly away into the Arctic sky, leaving Nobile wishing that he could have gone with him.

The *Graf Zeppelin* fell under the control of the Nazis in 1933, twelve weeks after Hitler had wrested the Chancellorship. Its handsome lines were defaced with Nazi insignia, and the ship was commandeered for propaganda sailings. Eckener was a bitter critic of the regime; it is a miracle he was not dispatched to some satanic depository. Perhaps his salvation lay in his global status, though it failed to save others of an equal standing. The *Graf* sailed last on 18 June 1937 from Friedrichshafen to Frankfurt. She was displayed, deflated, and in 1940 broken up on the orders of Hermann Göring (1893–1946) whose level of understanding was too deficient to appreciate her virtues.

Hindenburg

The most majestic of airships, *Hindenburg* took five years to build, from 1931 to 1936, and became the belle of the skies for Eckener and his Zeppelin company. Bigger than anything that had flown, a Titan almost 804 feet long, all that the company had learned from its decades in the airship business was invested in her design. Powered by four Daimler-Benz engines of 1,200-horsepower each, she could carry up to 72 passengers. She had a crew of 61, though 40 was more normal. She floated on seven million cubic feet of hydrogen. It had never been intended that she would fly on hydrogen – she had been designed for helium – but when the time came to inflate her the US, the world's sole supplier of helium, refused its export, in the perspicacious belief that Germany was going to war and that the ship might be deployed against them.[15] This refusal by the Americans necessitated that the vessel be reconfigured; helium being heavier than hydrogen, the changes allowed the designers to make her slightly larger and able to carry more passengers. In the end the switch to hydrogen would have shocking consequences. During her period of gestation her creators were convinced that the United States would yield in their ban on the export of helium, but they failed to understand properly how the political scene had deteriorated and the swiftness with which the Nazi contaminant had spread. The famously astute Eckener found himself cornered: unless the project were abandoned, which was unthinkable, he must renege on his pledge never to sail in another hydrogen ship.

Fractionally shorter than the ocean liner *Titanic*, the *Hindenburg* boasted every refinement with which to satisfy the whims of the discerning who could afford to sail in her. In the golden age of the liner, the well-heeled expected to be as cosseted in the air as they were on their ocean-going excursions. The *Hindenburg's* accoutrements included that which had been novel but which as the years had passed had become *de rigeur*: a smoking room. Another touch of luxury was a baby grand piano of lightweight aluminium covered in pig-skin; Captain Ernst Lehmann would sometimes play.

While it sailed, the passage of the craft was usually so smooth that a pen or pencil could be balanced in the perpendicular. Her interior designers had refined their artistry on the elegant funnel steamers which plied the seas. If the *Graf Zeppelin* and *Hindenburg* had evolved, the steamship monopoly on long-distance routes would have been challenged by international airships prior to their assailment by aircraft. Twenty-five two-berth bunk-bed cabins had sinks, desks and a duralumin ladder with which to scale the upper bunk; the ladder folded away to save precious space. As was the custom in steamships and hotels, passengers at night left their shoes outside their cabin knowing that by dawn the stewards would have them returned polished and buffed. The gracious promenade deck had large, slanting windows that could be opened to afford panoramic vistas; they were so designed that if open when sailing no draught would enter the ship. A comfortable and capacious dining room had tables dressed in white linen and bearing fine china stamped with the ship's crest, and the room was decorated with paintings of the smaller *Graf Zeppelin's* exotic voyages. The scale of the *Graf* had been restricted by the size of the largest shed available at the time of its construction; there were no limitations on the size of the *Hindenburg*, a vast new shed being built for its creation. From the *Hindenburg's* fully-appointed kitchen, with its specialist ovens, refrigerator and ice-maker, chefs produced fine cuisine accompanied by an extensive range of excellent French and German wines.[16]

One of several *Hindenburg* tragedies is that from the outset she was beset with despotic interference. Eckener had discreetly slipped his ship's name into the system. It enraged the malfeasants in power who demanded that she be called *Adolf Hitler*. In a barbarous clime, to christen his vessel after Field Marshal Paul von Hindenburg, President of Germany from 1925 to 1934, was an act of naivety or provocation; given Eckener's wisdom and the vehemence with which he publicly bearded the Nazis, one inclines to the latter. His nervous intimates were convinced that soon the charnel-house would beckon. Instead, he was cast into the abyss, proscribed by Joseph Goebbels, Hitler's propaganda chief, as a 'non-person', his name expunged from newspapers and the airwaves. The ban was ham-fistedly applied, its imposition fitful; but Eckener was almost finished. The Nazis commandeered the Zeppelin operation, partly financing it, dictating construction and policy and sidelining Eckener. The ship made voyages in Germany and Europe, sailed to North and South America and docked in Rio, with the politically more compliant Lehmann sometimes at the helm. The graceful *Hindenburg* was daubed with swastikas and made to perform propaganda leaflet drops. Nazi apparatchiks used megaphones to bawl slogans and blast marching music at the citizenry below.

On the early evening of the 6 May 1937, the *Hindenburg* came in to moor at her mast at Lakehurst, New Jersey. She had lifted off from Frankfurt am Main, in Germany, three days before, now the designated embarkation gate for all her transatlantic passages. The voyage had been delayed, the ship slowed by powerful headwinds, and her docking was further impeded due to stormy weather in the Lakehurst vicinity. Her captain was Max Pruss, with Lehmann aboard as an observer. Lehmann had not joined the Nazi Party, but his behaviour suggested a tolerance towards it that Eckener despised. In a previous incident Eckener had castigated Lehmann for imperilling the *Hindenburg* by sailing her in dangerous weather in order to appease the demands of Goebbels.

The Lakehurst station commander was Charles Rosendahl, free-ballooning hero of the *Shenandoah* catastrophe. As the *Hindenburg* edged towards the mast she was suddenly engulfed in a roaring fire, which appeared to begin at her stern. In seconds she fell to earth, a black and melted shell. Of 97 people aboard, 35 died, plus a member of the ground crew. Pruss and Lehmann were severely burned, and Lehmann died the next day. Just before he succumbed he told Pruss he believed it was sabotage, a conviction Pruss shared. Other theories included lightning, flammable cover-varnish and a short in a circuit causing a spark to ignite a gas cell at her stern. Some speculated that an anti-Nazi saboteur placed a bomb on board wishing her destroyed while moored and absent of people, but the bomb exploded while the ship was full of passengers, its timing mechanism triggered because of her delayed passage. An indisputable certainty is that the presence of hydrogen had been cardinal to her destruction.

There had been tragedies on a greater scale: when in 1912 the *RMS Titanic* of the White Star Line sank on her maiden voyage more than 1,500 souls had perished. Unlike the *Hindenburg*, however, the *Titanic*'s demise was not captured on newsreel. When the world saw the flickering images of the *Hindenburg* inferno and heard the hysterical commentary of the radio reporter Herb Morrison, it was the cruel finale for big rigid airships. Her duralumin skeleton was cut up, returned to the Fatherland and used to build aircraft for Göring's Luftwaffe, soon to release its terror on Britain and Europe.

Hugo Eckener was born in 1868. With millions more, he and his family endured significant privations during the Second World War and its aftermath. He died aged 86 on 14 August, 1954 at home on the shores of Lake Constance, Friedrichshafen, sentinel over decades to the calamity-strewn rise and eventual collapse of the airship dream.

EPILOGUE:
WILL THE AIRSHIP SAIL AGAIN?

Whether as a charred and tangled hulk on a hillside in Beauvais, drowned in the freezing waters of the Atlantic, or torched at its mast in New Jersey, the airship was born in hope and died in tragedy. Ambition outstripped capability. Wretched politics played its part. Sometimes a twist of fate summoned those who dared to dance at the cutting edge of technology. The rush of the aeroplane and the surge to war so soon after its denouement consigned the airship to history with little to show for it but memories singed brown by conflagration. Airship science had made rapid strides but had been brutally truncated. Had its progress continued what might have been achieved? It was all a long time ago in a world of different values and conceits, where much of that which happened would not be permitted today, and those who volunteered for airships might be thought fit only for counselling.

The differences between then and now – with modern day obsessions about health and safety and thickets of gimlet-eyed lawyers at every turn – are evident in an anecdote from 1921 concerning one of Britain's most heroic pioneers, the elegantly insouciant George Herbert Scott. The story was recalled seven decades later by Tommy Elmhirst, the navigator on the *R36* sailing at the time of the incident under Scott's command. Elmhirst went on to a distinguished career, becoming the highly decorated Air Marshall Sir Thomas Elmhirst. *R36* had been intended as a patrol vessel for the Royal Navy. Built by surface-ship builders Beardmore at their Inchinnan works, near Glasgow, Scotland, construction began during the First World War in 1917. She was not completed until 1921, when it was decided to convert her into a passenger-carrying ship. A stretched version of *R33*, the rogue ship that broke away from her mast at Pulham, in Norfolk, the *R36* had a uniquely elongated gondola to accommodate her voyagers. Today it is inconceivable that civilians would be taken aloft as passengers on airships still undergoing test sailings, yet such occurrences were commonplace. Scott had a party of journalists aboard and had been testing rudders and elevators, moving the ship vigorously from port to starboard and back. Satisfied all was well, he left the control car to join the doubtless convivial press lunch in the gondola, instructing the crew to keep the ship at full power, steady on her course, sailing at a comfortable 6,000 feet. 'Some twenty minutes later ... *R36* entered into a steep dive, with the height coxswain reporting he had lost control of the ship ... and the steering coxswain reporting that the steering had gone also.' *R.36* was now in the unwelcome position of being driven downwards at considerable speed, quite out of control and in full dive. Elmhirst managed to reach the engine telegraphs and rang 'immediate stop' to all five engines, and also let go half-a-ton of water ballast in the airship's forward gas bags, in the hope that this would bring the bows up and halt the dive. It was at this point that Scott came trotting into the control car, seemingly quite unconcerned and with a devilish grin playing on his face. In the best traditions of the Senior Service, he took control of the situation with a nod, a wink and his toothy grin; wholly unflappable, exhibiting consummate professionalism and a breathtaking confidence. He inquired of his Navigator [Elmhirst]:

> 'Tommy, what on earth have you been doing to the ship?' and went on to relate how his passengers were not at all happy, and were at present engaged in a hunt for parachutes, of which there were few on board, and presumably allocated for crew only! Elmhirst's actions had stopped the dive and the airship was in effect acting as a giant balloon with no motive power or vertical and directional control. The crew were despatched to check on the damage, reporting back that the vertical and horizontal control surfaces at the stern had failed and partially collapsed. The entire tail section was in a parlous state and in danger of breaking off.

Scott had the crew expedite what mid-air repairs were possible – over the years he had become skilled at instituting what was in nautical terms a jury rig, cobbling together his ship as best he could. It had dropped an alarming 3,000 feet at which he had managed to get it in equilibrium and sailing on an even keel; in the gondola journalists still searched for parachutes and tried to retrieve their stomachs. Elmhirst was ordered to set a course for home. Scott was sailing in difficult winds and told him he could only manage 30 knots; any faster and his tail would have fallen off.

> As there was a wind blowing from the NW, and the ship's course home was NE, Elmhirst had to steer *R36* North and drift NE "crab-wise", which took six hours to reach Pulham and the end of a most taxing day of flight trials for her crew and, without question, her passengers.[1]

There is a further chapter to be written in the airship chronicles. For all the anguish, the dream was never entirely quelled. Sky sailors in celestial ships of the twenty-first century would voyage in vessels swathed in a strong, light membrane. Tilting engines would be small, powerful beyond their size, ultra-efficient; pointing upwards to the sky, or down towards the earth, to help in lift-off or docking, mirroring vertical take-off aircraft. There is research into forms of nuclear propulsion or the harnessing of power from the sun, the envelope incorporating solar panels. Such vessels might not be of the conventional cigar-shape; more oval, perhaps, or saucer-like. With range and lift and their ability to hover for long periods, they could have a multiplicity of functions: as cargo or passenger carriers, as hospital ships stationed above natural or man-made catastrophes, as aerial pack-horses servicing feats of civil engineering in locations inaccessible to more conventional transport. Some still imagine them as liners of the sky, voyaging lazily from one exotic port to the next. Much speculation would be 'pie-in-the-sky'. There are still imponderables: the weather is one, human frailty another. Little can be done about the latter, but for the former long-range forecasting has seen vast improvement. Computers can now warn and divert a sky-ship hours in advance of a storm, though as mariners and aviators appreciate, caprice and the elements will always ride in wilful harmony.

Since the burning of the *Hindenburg*, a plethora of airship companies have emerged, some ghostly spectres, mere will-o'-the-wisps. Others have been brazen frauds, offering little but hot-air. More had financial controls as porous as early gas bags. A handful have achieved lift-off, scaling financial problems and walls of prejudice; drawing-board to sky, their ships sensibly modest compared with those of yesteryear. Their passage-making is becoming more ambitious; if it was anything but the cross-bred airship one might say they were spreading their wings.

Small blimps have been used over many years for corporate flag-waving and as filming platforms. An interesting passenger-airship company that sails today is the Deutsche Zeppelin-Reederei. Its headquarters are at Friedrichshafen, Lake Constance, where the Zeppelin Museum is based and where so much of the airship legend began. The company offers a diversity of passages lasting from 30 minutes to two hours. Hans Paul Strohle is a pilot with the company. As well as sailing commercial airships, he holds a helicopter licence. His dinky Zeppelin craft carries 12 passengers plus two crew. The craft is miniscule if measured against past leviathans. It has no rigid frame. The structure is based on 14 carbon fibre triangle structures linked at each corner by aluminium longitudinals. The envelope is of polyurethane, polyester and Kevlar. The familiar cigar shape is attained by the pressure of helium contained in two internal ballonets, made not of goldbeaters skin but polyurethane and nylon – quite different to the giants of the past with their multiplicity of vast cells and adjustable pressure of gas. The ship has three tilting engines that swivel up or down, allowing it to hover like a helicopter, and used in mooring or lift off. By the use of his swivelling engines Paul Strohle can land his ship and keep it on the ground without the need for a huge ground crew. To maintain its position on the ground an airship keeps its bows 'to wind'; the nautical manoeuvre of keeping the craft 'in irons'. This was an aim of the ground crew when trying to tether the old rigids, and which because of wind and their scale could end in calamity. On the ground Captain

Strohle's ship makes obsolete the strenuous efforts of a ground crew, sometimes several hundred strong, as they wrestled with the wayward rigids, by the use of an after engine and a lateral propeller. Where yesterday's behemoths had extensive on-board crews, each vested with different responsibilities, on today's little Zeppelins the control of engines, rudders and elevators are the sole responsibility of the pilot. Strohle's company sails from March to October, and since 2002 it has carried more than 120,000 passengers without incident.

How safe are today's miniature airships? Strohle: 'Very safe, probably one of the safest aircraft you can find. The only real danger is the pilot and his decisions and an in-flight collision with another aircraft. We have to do a special inspection every 100 hours and a major inspection of the entire aircraft each year. Zeppelin pilots are trained like any other pilots: technical, theoretical, practical. You must be able to *feel* the ship and what it does in different wind and weather environments. You must continually question your decisions and double-check situations. This is due to the extreme dependence of any airship on the weather. It's necessary to be a good team player. Not a hero or a cowboy.' How did he rate Zeppelin's former boss and famed commander Hugo Eckener? 'He had an extremely good understanding of weather and how it changed and developed. He had zero-tolerance when it came to safety. He would not allow any commercial pressure, by whoever or whatever, to compromise safety.' Are today's airships as fragile as those in the past? 'In a sense, yes. The materials, instruments, engines, structure are more thought-through and developed so they have extreme reliability. But any airship is going to be fragile when it comes to weather, and especially wind if compared to heavier-than-air craft. It still has a relatively huge surface exposed to the wind and only a small amount of power available. Any thoughts of getting around this are not realistic. There are dreamers who think we could avoid the dependency on good weather by implementing technology. It's not going to happen. Technology can deliver some better levels of performance, and enhance safety, but any airship will *always* be very dependent on weather, especially winds. Meteorology has improved very much. New satellites, improved speed in computer processors; these have all helped increase the accuracy and the speed in delivering viable forecasts. But anything predicted for more than three days ahead, however, still entails guesswork due to the huge amount of variables involved.'[2]

The airship lives on in the memory as romantic leviathan or sinister behemoth. Across the globe the ancestors of those who were brave or rash or foolhardy enough to clamber aboard the mammoths cling to their memorabilia, the scraps and remnants of a vanished time. A joy in writing this book has been the small part one can play in assisting the airship continuum, talking to people whose pride in their ancestors shines through, who are eager to help, to share their stories, to remember their forebears, sagas passed down through their families over the years. Wendy Pritchard talked touchingly about her grandfather, Flight Lieutenant John Edward Maddock Pritchard, killed with his close friend, Edward Maitland, when the *R38* broke in two over the River Humber at Hull in 1921. 'He was 31 when he died; they never found his body. That was particularly terrible for my grandmother,' she said. Jack Pritchard was half-American – his father had fought in the American Civil War – and his mother was Welsh. Jack took a degree in natural sciences at Cambridge University and studied at the Royal School of Mines. A mining engineer, with a brilliant future at a time when Britain had a booming coal industry, he joined the Royal Naval Air Service at the start of the First World War. Married to Hilda for seven years, they had three children. He was the first man to land in America when he parachuted from the *R34* on its record-making transatlantic voyage, with George Herbert Scott at the helm (see page 74). Ms. Pritchard said: 'It was quite a hard landing. He swung around a lot as he was coming down. Parachuting was still in its infancy. He landed with a bit of a crump. Somebody asked him what he thought of America and he said: "Hard!" We have one or two things left. A wallet ... we're not sure about it ... we think it was his. It looks as if it had been soaked in water.' Wendy Pritchard lives in the hamlet of Burnham Norton on the North Norfolk coast, of marsh and dunes and adventurers; close by is the tiny village of Burnham Thorpe, where Britain's greatest admiral was born, Horatio Nelson. Jack Pritchard would have sailed over the area. In November 2011, Wendy Pritchard went to London to witness the auction of his medals, sold for £16,000 to the Fleet Air Arm Museum in Yeovilton, Devon. 'Somehow it seemed like Jack's last journey and it was simply that I wanted to be with him. When he parachuted out of the *R34* he was in his best uniform, carrying his swagger stick. He was so young, it must have been so exciting for him. He was twenty-nine when he landed in America.'[3] Because of relatives such as Wendy Pritchard, now archiving her grandfather's papers, and hobbyists keen to familiarise themselves with an extraordinary era, plus the intervention of nosy and questioning historians rooting through the minutiae, the airship legend survives.

Though it seems the age of the giant rigid sailing across the Atlantic or the Southern Ocean has passed, there are new and extraordinary developments. The United States army has ordered three British-built hybrid craft to be deployed over theatres of conflict. They will sail high, unmanned, hidden above the clouds; traits reminiscent of the height-climbing Zeppelins of the First World War. They have been made by a company called Hybrid Air Vehicles (HAV) of Cranfield, in Bedfordshire, situated close to the colossal sheds, now rusting into oblivion, where the *R101* was built. For years an internationally known figure in airships was Roger Munk, who died at the age of 62 in 2010. He ran a company called Airship Technologies, which changed its name to the Advanced Technologies Group and subsequently went bust for £8 million. Out of it grew HAV. Munk was instrumental in forging the HAV-US Army deal, worth half a billion dollars, but he died just before it was sealed. His family still hold shares in HAV. Munk qualified as a naval architect but spent his life since the 1960s building and trying to raise finance for airships. In recognition of his endeavours he won the coveted British Silver Medal for Aeronautics. To some he was a visionary. To others he was controversial and financially fleet-footed. Worldwide the dirigible business has been high-risk for investors, some of whom have lost fortunes. Munk's financial reputation took a hammering when his company went under. His long-time colleague Canadian Gordon Taylor, the HAV director of sales and marketing, said: 'He was the most competent dreamer and entrepreneur I ever met. He was very astute and inspiring. Going into administration was terrible. He took it very badly. We all did. I know there was a lot of criticism of Roger but he never did the crook. Every penny was spent legitimately.'[4] There are those who would dispute Taylor's defence. I interviewed Roger Munk in 1998 for my column in the London *Evening Standard*. He was charming and friendly, essential in the uphill business of overcoming prejudice and garnering airship capital. When I met him he was building an airship in a draughty corner of one of the decaying sheds at Cardington, a setting I found melancholic and oppressive with the ghosts of yesteryear. He told me: 'Why keep harking back to the past? It damages today's industry. Nobody's used hydrogen for years. Airship safety far exceeds that of other types of transport. Far safer than helicopters. The big airship will be successful. We have learned so much. Airships are not an easy science. We have overcome huge problems. There is no question ... we will achieve our goal.'[5] The HAV army hybrids embrace much of Munk's thinking. They will bristle with electronics. About 300 feet long, they have a double-hull configuration. They are destined for an important defensive role, being able to hover in situ for weeks at time. But with all dirigibles history suggests it is wise to heed the maxim about slips and lips and cups. Fourteen years after talking to Munk I interviewed Hardy Giesler, the Business Development Director of HAV. Unsurprisingly, given his job, he was as upbeat about the future as Munk had been. The company is designing a range of big, manned, cargo-carrying airships that sail on helium, each propelled by a quartet of powerful engines. These are commercial rather than army craft, though they could be utilised by the military as cargo carriers. Of a triple-hull design they are 380 feet long. Giesler says they will carry loads up to 50 tons. He sees them operating in 'challenging or extreme environments, typically northern Canada'. Mining, oil and gas companies are among potential users. 'Lots of people take a personal interest in airships. But if it's not going to be a commercial success it won't fly. People dream of building one in the back yard to get from A to B. That's great. But it's hobbyist. It's not mainstream. It's not what the industry is about.' He says using a mix of fuel and helium 'should make it cheaper to operate. It can carry a lot of cargo, 50 tons. It requires little or no infrastructure. You can land in three or four hull lengths. You can use it with lesser capacity, about 20 tons, in a vertical take-off mode with a range of 1,200 or 1,300 nautical miles. That degree of range and lift is beyond most vehicles and certainly most helicopters.' There would be no need to build roads, airports or runways, with attendant environmental damage and the spiralling cost, delays and legal and 'green' inquiries geological expeditions incur. On regular routes a mooring mast would be built. What about the weather in climes as harsh as north Canada? I am assailed by thoughts of the beleagured Nobile and his snow and ice disaster. Giesler is forever optimistic: 'It's a lot flatter and wider than a typical airship. With its four engines it'll be able to cruise at about 90 knots with a top speed of 105 knots. With cross-winds on the ground it'll be pretty stable up to 35 knots. You use hover-pads and a bow-thruster to re-position yourself.' Hover pads allow the vehicle to stick to the ground. Gordon Taylor, Geisler's colleague said: 'It has only one-third cross-wind drag compared with an equal volume airship. That's because it's flatter and wider. It has very powerful engines so it can move pretty quickly if needs be. Its propulsion is so much greater. It can drive its way out of trouble. There's far greater directional control. The hover pads can stick you to the ground in winds of up to 50 knots on the nose.' Taylor was central to raising money for the hybrid. He worked with Munk for more than 13 years. Geisler said: 'You can hop from A to B and be on the ground in pretty severe conditions, conditions which any type of fixed-wing aircraft or helicopter would have to contend with.' What happens if one is hit by a violent storm en route from A to B? 'Distance is an issue, there's no doubt. Remoteness of location ... those are some of the difficulties and we recognise them. There are very clear guidelines about the amount of snow and ice, for instance, permitted on working surfaces. No pilot would lift off if these conditions and guidelines weren't entirely met. The rules apply to us just like any other fixed wing aircraft or helicopter. None of this is guesswork. We know what we have to do to make it work. It's totally different to the way things were done in the past. Because of the history of the airship certain events stand out. Shipping didn't stop because of the *Titanic*. If you look at the beginnings of the Comet aircraft there were problems. But it didn't stop aviation developing. Not a lot has happened in the airship industry. If it had developed properly over the years such problems would have been dealt with and we're dealing with them now.' Giesler and Gordon Taylor are as charming as the late Roger Munk. But I remain sceptical, so drenched in the history I have become a doubting Thomas. Airships hold a magic and I *want* to believe. They have a romantic thrall, but with airships it would be imprudent to allow heart to rule head. I returned to the airship nemesis, the weather, and pressed Taylor about coping in circumstances of severe snow and ice: 'Look, nothing's perfect. We certainly don't have all the answers. Obviously thick snow and bad ice can create difficulties. But it's the type of challenge we're properly addressing. The ship will be certificated to minus 50 to plus 55 degrees Centigrade.' This means it should be able to operate from Arctic to desert. Geisler, an economist, talks money – today's airshipmen have to be hard-faced about cash. Ships are high-tech and costly. There's no room for sentiment. 'It comes down to pounds per ton mile', he says. 'It's about pounds, shillings and pence. Is it cheaper to operate on an alternative basis? Or is it slightly more expensive for an operator but provides flexibility and options not offered by other means of transport? Oil and gas companies are reaching their "cliff of despair". Assets [oil or gas fields] which are being developed are so far away they put the range of a helicopter under extreme pressure. So operators are studying alternatives. They've never liked helicopters. Helicopters have a worse record if you look at fatalities. Helicopters are seen as not the best aircraft to use.' Are surface ships of no purpose? 'Too slow. It's just the way it's developed. To switch from helicopter to boat is seen as unacceptable.' The growth of HAV on the back of its defence contract has been remarkable, though it's easy to forget Munk and his disciples spent half a century trying to perfect the technology. 'When we won the army contract we were 19 people in a Portakabin,' Geisler says. 'In weeks we'd grown to over a hundred.' In the HAV office software engineers fret over aerodynamics and avionics, poring over computers. Barnes Wallis would probably have loved such an environment, though he had little patience with any idea of an airship revival. George Herbert Scott might have tired of it; he'd rather have been sailing through the heavens. HAV has two major shareholders; the management has a clutch, and small blocs are held by individuals. If it goes to plan they'll grow rich and the sky will be full of cargo ships. Giesler talks not of tens, but of hundreds being built. He assures me he hasn't been sniffing the helium, a familiar joke in today's airship industry.

Are the cargo designs financed by profits from the military contract? 'It's a useful revenue stream.'[6] One has heard and read so often the silken blandishments of the past. But much has been mastered in 80 years, and it would be churlish not to wish today's pioneers good fortune. They deserve plaudits for overcoming, as mentioned earlier, a depth of hostility that rarely afflicted other industries. If the concept of the cargo airship works and catches on it could become a major industry. It would be a handsome source of revenue and employment, which might help correct the imbalance between the service sector and the long-neglected science-based manufacturing sector. I have maintained that the hand of the military has been as much a hindrance as a help in the history of the airship; it would be mournfully ironic if resuscitation hinged again on military patronage. One trusts the airship of the future will not be subject to the giddy development, inappropriate deployment and political shenanigans that hampered it in the past. There is a contemporary urgency for the airship to be revisited: compared with an aircraft, its ecological footprint is seductively faint. It still seems unlikely, but perhaps one day green giants rather than silver behemoths might roam the skies.

THE GRABOWSKY-ATHERSTONE LOG

he First Officer of the *R101* was Noël Grabowsky-Atherstone, known as 'Grabby'. During the building and test-sailings of the *R101* he maintained a log. Being of emotional and material value, this is kept in the safety of a bank vault in the Suffolk seaside town of Southwold and is the property of Rebecca Atherstone, his granddaughter. She made it available to the author. It offers a unique insight into the troubles that bedevilled the *R101* and to a degree (it was not Atherstone's ship) the *R100*.

At times Atherstone is scathing about poor management at Cardington; of parsimony that impinged upon safety; of technical tests being 'wangled'; of stunts to impress MPs or journalists; of too little cognisance being given to the officers; of *R101* being heavy and bereft of lift; of continuing problems with gas bags and covers; of crews working to a manic timetable with insufficient time for testing. It mentions the running of unacceptable risks and predicts that one day 'murder will out'.

Noël Grabowsky-Atherstone was a Count, descended from Polish aristocracy, born in St. Petersburg, Russia. On 17 January 1918, it was announced in *Flight* magazine that an engagement had been announced between Flight Lieutenant Noël Grabowsky, RN, the eldest son of Carl and Mrs. Grabowsky, and Evelyn Susanna Atherstone Hales, elder daughter of Lieutenant Colonel H. M. A. Hales, of the Gloucestershire Regiment, late Bedfordshire Regiment, and Mrs. Hales.[1] *Flight* later recorded that Captain Noël Grabowsky-Atherstone, AFC, RAF, had married his bride at St. Mary Abbot's, Kensington, London, on 28 April 1919.[2]

'Grabby' desisted from using his family name, shy that his aristocratic lineage would mark him out from his fellow officers. Rebecca Atherstone, his granddaughter, told the author: 'My Nan, Evelyn Atherstone, married Count Noël Grabowsky. When they married there was an agreement that the surname became Grabowsky-

Atherstone. My grandfather never carried on using his title, though it has passed down the family. I'm known as Atherstone. But I'm really Grabowsky-Atherstone.'[3]

Evelyn, Noël's wife, was married for just twenty months before her husband's death. She later married a member of the distinguished Waley-Cohen family; Sir Robert Waley-Cohen was a prominent Shell scientist who had worked on a new airship engine, the slow and troublesome development of which was eventually abandoned.

31 August 1929, 29*

Atherstone writes of the crew poring over the ship and attending to a range of fundamental problems: 'No. 3 bag appears to be losing gas to the extent of about ten per cent in two days, but as there are so many men working on the ship it may be that the valves and controls are accidentally disturbed ... examined the wiring on the bag yesterday ... the bag has not been pulled up far enough at the top. As there has been no provision made in the way of handling patches on the flat ends, it is quite impossible to do this until patches are provided. This question of patches has been raised several times throughout the process of inflation. It would be rather more helpful if the opinions and recommendations of ships' officers were given rather more consideration ... Saturday and Sunday overtime is now being done on the ship in a sort of frantic endeavour to get her ready to do her first trial about the beginning of October. It appears there is a "very special reason" for this panic, which is probably no more than an effort to provide a joy-ride for MPs before Christmas.'[4]

13 September 1929, 35

'By dint of much waiting we got No. 10 bag through its tests and spent the rest of the morning in gassing up No. 11. By noon we had got No. 11 up to 97 per cent and came to the end of the gas. We are now waiting for more gas and in the meantime the crew are now rigging bag 14 for inflation which should take place on Monday. The date for the first flight seems to be unduly optimistic but apparently the "heads" are quite serious about it. There is a mad rush and panic on at present to finish the ship at all costs by the end of the month and she is to do a flight the moment she can fly. I am very much against rushing things like this and I think it is grossly unfair on the officers and crew to expect them to take out a novel vessel of this size the moment it has got the bare necessities for flight on board, without allowing them the time or opportunity to carry out a few very necessary practice drills and to satisfy themselves

*Numbers following the dates indicate the original page numbers of the Log.

that each member of the crew understands his duties. Also it is very necessary to get used to the various controls and their method of operation by trying them several times.'[5]

19 September 1929, 39

'Crew employed in making final adjustments to siphon systems and padding corridor arches etc. An alteration is being carried out on the fin covers ... these alterations are not supposed to officially alter any of the dates given yesterday, but the extra time required for this work and also a number of other items must come from somewhere.'[6]

20 September 1929, 39

'It appears that the ship is to be made airborne tomorrow (in the shed) although there is still a considerable amount of work to be done on the outer cover and especially the fins ... tested our rate of discharge of water main and control cock in the control car. The test was very unsatisfactory and the cock was dismantled for examination. It appears it has been assembled wrong!'[7]

21 September 1929, 39

'It was obvious she is very tail-heavy ... not at all an encouraging result and everyone left the shed looking very glum ...' [8]

30 September 1929, 43

'The fuel supply was not connected up ... there was considerable delay ... the water tank on the shed roof ran dry ... a lot of unnecessary time was wasted over the whole performance and I am very much afraid that the gloom caused by the apparent lack of lift when the ship was airborne on the 21st will be confirmed when the results of todays test have been worked out.'[9]

1 October 1929, 45

'A day of titivation. The reason being the impending visitation of the Press. The passenger accommodation got its face washed and hair brushed, all cabins, lounge, smoke-room, dining-room, frantically furnished. The other piece of work that really matters was the calibration of the bow strain indicator. But owing to various delays this was only half done ... bags on frame one are still pretty bad and will have to be altered. There is much talk of the ship going out on Saturday, but the A.I.D have got to do their bit yet and as matters stand I feel very thankful that there is ... A.I.D!'[10]

2 October 1929, 45

'Up to 1100 hours the frantic furnishing went on … came the Press … 200 of them and they swarmed like earwigs all over everything …' [11]

10 October 1929, 51

'The cheap Press is full of blight and sensational headlines about the ship not coming out and to "help" matters Burney has published a book in which he condemns both *R100* and *R101* as useless and damns the designers, at the same time holding himself up as the proud possessor of the true solution to all these difficulties!' [12]

The publication of Burney's book, *The World, the Air and the Future*, at one of the most sensitive times caused ill-feeling in both camps; among a welter of swingeing criticisms, he claimed neither ship could ever be a commercial success, the mooring tower system was unsound and the speed and lift of the vessels entirely inadequate. Why Burney chose to lambast the craft – especially to scupper his own – is unknown and seems bizarre. Opponents said it confirmed every unpleasant thing that they had suspected about him, though none imagined he would attempt to torpedo his own ship and the Imperial Scheme to which he had devoted so much of his energies. Some thought he wanted headlines to sell his new tome, but this seems a petty reason for an action so extreme. If true, he succeeded. His comments caused a worldwide sensation and deep resentment at Howden and Cardington.

He advanced three ideas: the first concerned the so-called Howden Propulsion system. He claimed it would give an astounding 65 per cent gain in propulsive efficiency without increasing weight. It involved the use of fuel gas and a form of oil or diesel; engines would be transferred from the sides to the rear of the airship to drive screws, as on a surface ship; it would be possible to swing the screws to provide vertical thrust that would counteract the up and down movements of the tail of a ship when it was attempting to moor. His second notion was to create a Mooring and Docking Raft, allowing a ship to be put into its shed in most weather conditions by a mechanical process; a giant clamp would hold the airship in a frame, thus eliminating the need for a docking tower. The third suggestion was that the conventional plump cigar-shape was wrong and should be replaced by an elliptical design enabling an airship to alight, unaided, upon enclosed – or partly enclosed water – such as a lake or estuary and anchor like a surface or marine vessel. The ellipse would have the greater axis in the horizontal plane with two hull-floats on each side of the centre line, the floats allowing it to alight on water in the same manner as a flying-boat.

The ideas were fantasy. To describe them as experimental would be to do science a disservice. His scribblings damaged the already battered morale of the constructors and provided critics with ammunition; if the progenitor had now rejected his own child, things must be even worse than had been alleged. But the *R101* and *R100* teams had no choice but to live with his criticisms and move on.

13 October 1929, 55

'Things are shaping very well and the hands are beginning to shake down very quickly considering only a nucleus have been in the air before. The ship was let up on the wires to about 900 ft this afternoon to test out mooring gear ... the mooring gear works very well and very much according to plan, which is most gratifying.'[13]

The next day the ship was taken on a test flight with fourteen official observers aboard – among them Colmore, Richmond, Rope and Cave-Brown-Cave. Scott was at the controls.

14 October 1929, 57

'I couldn't feel the engines start or hear them from the winch platform. The first thing that impressed me about the ship was the almost complete absence of vibration and no creaking ... the cover is wonderfully good and doesn't move anywhere. The whole ship feels immensely strong and gives one a wonderful feeling of security and confidence. We passed over London ... and created immense interest. I took the wheel and the elevators in turn and found the ship answered very well indeed to both controls and that very little helm and practically no effort was required to keep her steady for direction and height. The air was quite bumpy but we really only felt two bumps that made the ship pitch slowly about three degrees up and down ...'[14]

Atherstone and fellow officers sometimes slept on the vessel. Taking early morning and late night watches, it was a sensible arrangement. On 16 October strong winds gathered while the ship floated at her mooring.

16 October 1929, 57

'Storm routine was started ... the highest gust reached 43 mph ... but the ship appeared quite indifferent to the increasing wind, except that she rolled a little now and then. I am more than ever impressed with the "feel" of the ship and she is behaving *like* a ship and doing the things I would expect a ship on the water to do. She feels confident, strong and alive ...'[15]

During test voyages it was inevitable that hair-raising moments would occur. Docking at the top of the tower was a highly skilled job.

3 November 1929, 71

'The ship charged the tower and the receiving arm hit the ship just under the cone and bent one of the bow tubes. At the same time the port guy took some of the strain and crashed a reefing girder besides tearing a lot of fabric. All this looked very alarming from my window in the bow, and I am told that from the ground it looked horrible. The whole thing was a clear case of too many cooks and rotten handling ...' [16]

The government had to continually persuade the Commons and the public that the ship and its cost was not an indefensible waste of money. The Press office at Cardington stoked up expectations, while a crass public relations campaign ensured a stream of visitors to the ship. On board they were wined and dined and sometimes given joy-sailings. However, amid the 'jollies' time was running short, and the ship's complement were trying to prepare for the India voyage. Atherstone's irritation is clear.

6 November 1929, 73

'Preparations were put in hand for giving lunch on board to a bunch of Dominion delegates to a Conference on Empire Legislation! All these window dressing stunts and joy rides during the ship's trials and before she has got an Airworthiness Certificate are quite wrong, but there is no one in the RAW [Royal Airship Works] executive who has the guts to put their foot down and insist on trials being free of joy riders. The lunch came off very well, all things considered, and the extraordinarily dull and third rate looking delegates seemed to be suitably impressed ...' [17]

After eight years of intensive research, scrutinising myriad documents and absorbing a wide-range of scholarly opinion, the author concurs with Grabowsky. The bosses at Cardington were shy of complaining to Thomson and his ilk if they were unhappy about matters. They were dedicated officers; complaining was not part of their bag. Each had a strong sense of duty and rank. They had been set a task. There was a schedule to be kept and a deadline to be met. There was no argument, no debate; the plan had been hatched and approved and that was that. Few of the leaders of the project had the 'guts' to say no. If it was because of their concerns about career advancement, or being of the military and unused to questioning orders, or that they were simply determined to achieve the objective no matter the cost, is impossible to tell. The climate was far more deferential. The creation of the *R101* was prestigious and expensive; the eyes of the world were upon it. The reputation of the government, of Thomson and the fledgling air force, rested on its success. In yellowing letters musty with age there is still a whiff of the 'gung-ho' spirit that lingered after the war; hostilities had only ceased twelve years before the *R101* set sail, a mere seven before its construction began. There was a camaraderie at the Royal Airship Works. It wouldn't have been 'cricket' to have complained. It would have been judged unmanly, letting the side down, sneaking on ones fellows. Officers and gentlemen didn't do that sort of thing; though times have changed, one suspects that most would still think twice about it. With hindsight, it is blatantly obvious that joy-riding and the like should have been stopped and, crucially, that those engaged in *R101*'s creation should have spoken out about the voyage and capability of the ship. Some did, Rope being one. But in the main the attitude seems to have been a reluctant acceptance of that which was handed down from on high. After five wearisome years spent building their behemoth an air of some resignation had set in at Cardington.

Parties of dignitaries – sanctioned by the Ministry and the top brass at Cardington – tested to the limit the patience of the increasingly fretful *R101* officers.

8 November 1929, 75

'It blew up a bit during the night and it rained steadily with some rather heavy bursts at times. The usual mess occurred on board and things began to look pretty second-hand. Yesterday evening the flight that had been planned for today was cancelled, but today at 0830 we were informed that the flight and party would take place after all! Very helpful and *so* considerate! Of course the fact of the ship being as wet as a scrubber and having no lift is not even considered and the ships officers are completely ignored ... the visitors commenced arriving about 1100 and wanted to go straight on board, but this time we instituted a proper control and only allowed them on board five at a time, and each batch only when the captain said so from the control car. The result was that it took about an hour to get 40 passengers on board ... the ship left the tower ... with only eight tons of water on board, eleven tons of fuel and a pressure height of 500 ft !! We staggered round the vicinity of Bedford for a couple of hours ...' [18]

14 November 1929, 81

'During the flight ... our chief passenger was Sir Sefton Brancker and he spent most of the time in the control car. As we left at the worst time of the day with the ship 100 per cent full of gas owing to superheat she was very heavy all the time and there was not enough time to trim properly with water ballast during the flight. The landing, done by Irwin, was perfectly carried out under very difficult conditions and cost 8 tons of water ballast!! We picked up the wire at 1542 but it was not until 1640 that the ship was secured and the usual mess up with the guys took place, resulting in a hole again being torn in the bow. I was in the control car when the ship was being landed and I had a horrible feeling of nervous tension owing to the shortage of ballast and the inadequacy of the storage ballast system.' [19]

One hundred MPs were due to be taken joy-sailing. But to the officers' relief, with the onset of rain, the barometer falling and the ship heavy, the public relations voyage was cancelled. The decision delighted the officers and crew.

16 November 1929, 81–83
'We are going to live on the MPs food that is a cheerful thought.' [20]

Atherstone makes a bitter entry in his log. It highlights the criminal way in which the Air Ministry was removed from the day-to-day operation and failed to understand the range and complexities of the problems that still confronted *R101*'s crew.

20 November 1929, 87
'This wretched attempt to lunch 100 MPs on board and fly them around for a couple of hours is still seriously being considered, but how on earth it's going to be done I simply don't know. The ship really hasn't got the lift to do this kind of stunt and it's damned unfair of the Air Ministry to [author's note: there is an indecipherable word here, which looks like 'lark'] us in this way. The ship has *not* finished her trials, has *not* got her Certificate of Airworthiness, and has *not* got enough lift to cart 12 tons of humans about with any degree of safety [note: the author has italicised words that Atherstone underlined]. It is only a cheap and vulgar form of eye-wash at the best, and it doesn't say much for the brains up at the Air House if this is the only way they can think of getting Parliamentary support for airships. I hope something will happen to prevent this stupid flight, because it is really stretching things too far and only asking for trouble. I wonder if Reynolds [L. G. S. Reynolds, private secretary to Thomson] realises what Irwin is up against, because if he does then he ought to be publicly shot for putting such almost impossible tasks on to us. The trouble is that *nobody* up at the Air Ministry understands anything at all about flying a ship like this one, and they haven't the decency to ask the men who have to do the job, if it can be done.' [21]

22 November 1929, 87–89

'Found we were some 3.5 tons short of the lift we required to do this 100 MPs flight ... the whole show is an absolute farce and if we fly tomorrow it will be taking an absolutely unjustifiable risk with practically nothing to gain and everything to lose ...' [22]

23 November 1929, 89–91

'Found the ship to be about five tons short of the required lift ... the wind started to get up, the barometer was still falling ... it was commencing to rain ... still no orders for cancellation of the show, although it was obvious that the flight was impossible. Quite a crowd of Lords and Commoners congregated at the foot of the tower ... at 1130 we commenced taking them on board ... the signalling system between the control car and the ground broke down and 30 people arrived in the ship before Irwin knew they were coming. A few well chosen phrases on the telephone restored order ... the lift stuck half-way up the tower! ... so the only alternative was to walk up. When all were on board there were 148 people in the ship and if it hadn't been for the 40–50 mph wind blowing she would not have carried them. A very good lunch was served in two instalments. I told a couple of MPs a few home truths about the shorthanded way this ship is being run and pointed out that there were no spare engines etc. Some of our legislators got very drunk. During the second sitting a line squall passed over the aerodrome with very heavy rain and hail, the wind veered about 30 degrees and the temperature dropped ... the wind reached 56 mph. Our visitors commenced departing shortly after lunch and by 1600 we had got rid of the last of them. The Air Ministry were terribly bucked at having pulled off this stunt, but I fail to see that it can have served any useful purpose. The whole show was merely stupid, a lot of illegal things were done in order to gain enough lift to carry this load, amongst others, taking all the emergency and tinned rations and parachutes out of the ship! Later on ... we heard that the Speaker and a few friends would be coming along tomorrow at 1130 to have a look ...' [23]

In the strong winds the ship had been moving at her mast and after the non-flying visit stories circulated that some of the MPs were so drunk that they thought they actually *had* been flying – they even spoke of how much they had enjoyed their voyage.

24 November 1929, 91

'An invitation had been issued for officers and heads of departments and wives to partake of tea on board at 16.00! As neither Irwin nor I knew anything about this we were rather staggered at the cool audacity with which this had been arranged without even the common politeness of asking the captain of the ship for his permission! Personally I went home to bed where I stayed till 1630 and had a very much needed sleep. Irwin turned up for the morning visitors and found a party of 27 escorted by Scott, Colemore and Richmond!! There was no necessity to drag him out at all, but a complete disregard for the convenience and consideration of others is an outstanding characteristic in a certain quarter.'[24]

On 1 December 1929 a complete refit of the airship was ordered.

1 December 1929, 97

'Neither Irwin nor I have received any information as to what the re-fit is to consist of, that is a very peculiar state of affairs but typical of the manner in that the whole of this place is run. We have not been supplied even with an official lift and trim statement although this has been repeatedly asked for.'[25]

The question of who was in command of the *R101* was never properly finalised. Was it Scott? Or Irwin, who had the title of 'captain'? If Irwin was in command, what was Scott's role? Scott was higher ranked and vastly experienced and would not have cared for being usurped. Such decisions should have been the responsibility of Colmore. It was a thorny question still largely unresolved even after lift-off.

2 December 1929, 97

'Irwin (the *R101* captain) is fed to the teeth about the way promises made to him by Colmore and Scott have not been kept and he is still in the unenviable position of being unofficial captain of the ship, although he was definitely assured that the ship would be officially handed over to him before she came into the shed [for the re-fit]. This has not been done.'[26]

3 December 1929, 99

'I don't know how much extra lift the ship will have by the time she is again ready to take to the air, but unless there is *at least an extra 15 tons* there is no use in talking of flying to India with only one stop for refuelling. I investigated the question of lift in England, Egypt and India about a year ago and gave the result to Colmore, so I don't understand how a flight to India can even be contemplated unless a lot of extra lift is got from somewhere.'[27]

Atherstone's growing frustration is evident from the following entry in which he records some of his most damning criticisms.

6 December 1929, 99–101

'I learnt from Cave this morning that No. 3 engine big-ends are showing signs of failure! It begins to look as if the engines would have let us down properly if we had done any more flying, so it is just as well we didn't. I wonder if the 'Big Three' and the Air Ministry realise how *damned* lucky we are to have got away with it so far? I'm sure they can have very little idea of how very, very close we have been on more than one occasion to wrecking the ship. We have never had any confidence in the machinery and we have not made a single flight on that something or other has not broken down. The way the engines were nursed through their tests before they were passed as airworthy was a bare-faced wangle that barely covered up their imperfections, but murder will out sooner or later and defects, which should have been brought to light during the tests, and would have been had those tests been 100 per cent genuine, are now making themselves felt so much that they cannot be ignored any longer. But it is not only the engine people who have failed to produce the goods, the same sort of thing has happened on the airship design side. The ship has no lift worth talking about, she is very tail-heavy, ballasting arrangements are inadequate in their rates of discharge and filling, gassing is too slow, interior communication for voice-pipes is rotten and there are no telephones. The speed of the ship is nothing wonderful being slightly below the theoretical speed, but the arrangement for getting astern thrust is a joke. Fancy carrying a whole complete power unit weighing 4 tons so as to be able to go astern!! The new things about this ship that have worked really well and are an undoubted success are the pressure controlled outer cover, the inflated covers in way of propeller wash, the gas valves and siphon tubes, the flexible bulkheads and gasbag wiring, the stability and controllability of the ship, the gasbags themselves, and most important of all, the undoubted strength of the hull. The point I want to make is that the unsatisfactory condition of the ship as regards lift, trim and internal arrangements is not due entirely to novelty of design, although that may account for some of it, but to a very large extent it is due to inefficient design owing to lack of experience and a stiff neck!'[28]

A problem in building not one but two ships was the dire shortage of people in Britain with engineering know-how and flying experience. Consequently personnel had to double up. Atherstone was among those who would gain experience with the *R100* as well as his own ship the *R101*. He recalls in his log the day the *R100* flew from her home station at Howden to Cardington prior to her transatlantic voyage.

16 December 1929, 101–103

'She [*R100*] flew over York and then direct to Cardington reaching here at 1I.15. I gather that she handles well and behaves in the air in very much the same way as *R101*. I went on board in the evening ... and had a look round. The officers and crew have been well looked after and their accommodation is roomy and comfortable, there is any amount of room in the control car and it seems quite palatial after the rather cramped quarters in *R101*.'[29]

In the New Year, while the *R100* was being readied for her voyage to Canada, Atherstone sailed on one of her tests flights that lasted for more than 53 hours.

29 December 1930, 111

'I tried the ship [*R100*] on both rudder and elevators and found her to be very sensitive to small angles of helm and quick to respond. She handles better than *R101* and seems much lighter on the controls. This is probably due to a large extent to the fact that the ship is neither tail heavy nor bow heavy but nicely balanced about her centre of buoyancy. The outlook from the passenger coach is very bad, but the control car is roomy, has plenty of windows and there are no draughts even when the windows are open.'[30]

By May 1930, Atherstone was preparing to go to Canada by steamer from Liverpool, a member of the advance party that would greet the arrival of the *R100*. Meanwhile *Graf Zeppelin*, piloted by Eckener, had visited Cardington, docking and embarking with his characteristic precision. He and his ship's company were stylishly attired.

15 May 1930

'As a result of the *Graf Zeppelin's* visit the Air Ministry have at last decided that officers and crews of airships shall wear a uniform! There was tremendous panic about trying to get the stuff in time. There is absolutely no hope of the advance party getting any uniforms ... this is typical of Air Ministry methods. The whole question of uniform was put up to them well over six months ago and was turned down flat!'[31]

Throughout the building and flying of both ships the covers caused problems. At various times they cracked, rotted, sagged, stretched and split. Mid-air patching sounds alarming, with repair teams clambering around the exterior of a vessel while it sailed. But they had to do it so frequently they were well-practised. Mid-air faults could develop in stormy conditions if a ship was buffeted. In normal conditions ships were so stable that with ordinary care in-flight exterior maintenance held few risks.

28 June 1930, 139

'I hear that very serious weakness [on the *R101*] has developed in the pre-doped outer cover ... she hadn't been at the tower very long before the cover split for about 150 ft. along the top. This was repaired by the crew under very difficult conditions, and shortly after the cover split again for about 80 ft. This was also repaired at the tower and some transverse bands doped on inside the cover ... she really is by no means in an airworthy condition.'[32]

The ship was due to make a promotional appearance at the Hendon Air Show. Problems with the gasbags continued, and the crew installed padding to stop the bags chafing on the framework. Various new mechanisms were installed.

30 June 1930, 141

'Some of the oil fuel tanks have been fitted up with an internal gasbag fabric sleeve so that fuel can be dropped from these tanks in an emergency in the same way that water can be released. I feel there is a catch in this idea and I don't think it is as clever as it seems ... riggers employed in padding all bays where bolts and projections are sticking into the gasbags. Instead of using the carefully designed patches supplied by our scientists, and which are quite useless, we are using cotton fabric bandages that take much less time to apply and stay put.'[33]

There is a sense in Atherstone's log of Cardington being bombarded with clever ideas imposed by a scientific hierarchy, some more successful than others. In part it was in the spirit of the project. *R101* was supposed to be a vessel of experiment and innovation. But time was short. Novel solutions were being suggested for design problems that should have been settled long before. The log is a reminder of the continuing determination to outwit German designers and to better their preferences. There was always rivalry between British airship builders and operators and those in Germany, who through the endeavours of Count Ferdinand von Zeppelin and Dr. Hugo Eckener, his protégé, had set the bench-mark.

1 July 1930, 141–143

'The question of these bridle pulleys has been very carefully investigated and it appears that our scientists have again boobed; the diameters of the pulleys should have been 14' whereas they are only 3.5'! New panels of outer cover are being fitted as they are delivered to the shed from the fabric shop. This time it is raw aeroplane linen that will be doped in place, thank God; also all ideas of fancy lacing edges have gone by the board. The new panels have plain straight lacing edges, the same as the Germans use.'[34]

Problems with the cover persisted. Michael Rope had registered his concerns, and other members of the team including Atherstone were in agreement.

2 July 1930, 143

'I examined some of the outer cover which has just been taken off the top of the ship and find it is completely rotten. It can be torn without using any force at all just like paper. I don't understand how any of it stayed on the ship at all. The cover is very much worse than I expected it to be and to have ordered the ship to fly with a cover in such a rotten condition was, in my opinion, a totally unjustifiable risk ... the rest of the old cover is being left on for the present but is having three inch transverse bands doped on the outside, spaced three feet apart. I don't think this scheme is going to add any strength at all to the pre-doped covers, as the adhesive dope that is used for sticking the bands on seems to make the fabric of the pre-doped cover absolutely rotten, so I don't see where the gain in strength comes from.'[35]

While the crew and officers tried to solve problems on *R101*, the Canadian voyage of *R100* to Canada was delayed – *R100*'s tail had collapsed during trials. She had been fitted with a new tail to the consternation of Nevil Shute and Barnes Wallis. Shute was by then in charge, while Wallis had already quit airships and started in his new role at Weybridge. The original lines of the *R100* (about which there would be disparaging remarks by Roxbee Cox years later) were further marred by the scrapping of Wallis's original pointed tail and the imposition of a curved replacement.

3 July 1930, 143

'*R100*'s new stern is now finished and she is ready to come out of the shed for further trials. The last 25ft of her sharp tail has been removed and a hemispherical cap fitted in place. It looks rather odd, but no doubt one will get used to it.'[36]

12 July 1930, 145

'*R100* has had a bit of trouble with her gas bags getting ripped and torn in the radial wires and has consequently swallowed an enormous amount of gas.'[37]

Political pressures to meet deadlines had become intense. The *R101* was heavy and lacking in lift. Ministry and Cardington chiefs dithered about whether to chop her in half and insert the new section. Atherstone mocks the ministerial deadline. Could Thompson sail on *R100* if *R101* was not ready? No, his colours were on the 'Socialist' *R101*; it was inconceivable he could make such an historic voyage in the 'Capitalist' *R100*. How much Thompson knew about unresolved technical problems and the folly of sticking to a deadline so he could arrive in India and be back in time for the Imperial conference has been the subject of speculation. Some say career-minded subordinates kept him in ignorance. Others claim he was informed but determined to push ahead. Cancellation would have meant massive loss of face for him, the Ministry and Ramsay MacDonald. It would also have delighted *R101*'s critics.

19 July 1930, 145

'The powers that be are trying to make up their minds whether to cut *R101* in half right away so that work can be immediately commenced on the erection of the new bay, or to keep *R101* in reserve for the Canadian flight in case *R100* does not come up to scratch. It appears that the S.of S. [Secretary of State, Lord Thompson] has stated that *R101* is to take him out to India towards the end of September, so that the ship will have to be ready by the end of August or the beginning of September! How this miracle is going to be accomplished is entirely beyond me. I suppose it will be another flap and panic like getting the ship ready for Hendon [air show] and I suppose the flying staff will again be called upon to save the faces of the "heads" by taking over the ship in a semi-ready and nearly totally unairworthy condition!'[38]

The *R100* eventually made her successful voyage to Canada and back. It was a spectacular achievement. But on her return to Cardington she was in a fragile state.

16 August 1930, 159–161

'Found a large hole in the outer cover at the bottom of the ship ... with three petrol tanks hanging out of it! Irwin told me that shortly before I arrived, while the engineers were refuelling, there was a loud crash and the three tanks ... appeared through the outer cover! Scott paid a visit to the ship and had a look at the damage. The cause of the failure is not at present understood, but there is obviously something wrong with the design for such a thing to be possible.'[39]

Airship historian Nigel Caley: 'Wallis was a designer of superlative ability. But one forgets in all the glorification that the cover of the *R100* was shot to pieces when it returned from Canada. Two days after getting home, when the *R100* was at its mast, the fuel tanks fell out of her – they were just hanging there. If that had happened over the Atlantic two days earlier the ship would have been lost and there would have been no Shute to tell his story.'[40] The *R100* was in a wretched state. As well as the fuel tanks, the engines needed reconditioning – one had failed totally – a propeller had fallen off, corrosion was in the hull, she needed new gasbags and a complete new cover. It was estimated the cover and bags alone would cost in the region of £100,000.

The stress levels at Cardington were enormous. Everybody was under serious pressure. Atherstone's log shows how tempers were becoming frayed, and the raw manner in the way that justice was sometimes meted out. After *R100*'s return there was an incident in which three members of the relief crew got drunk while aboard her.

17 August 1930, 163

'Several bottles of liquor were missing as well as private articles from officers' cabins ... some of the relief crew had broken open various lockers and had gone on the jag during the night. There is going to be an enquiry ...' [41]

18 August 1930, 163

'The three men concerned have been stood off, one with a very sore face, the result of being knocked down in the shed yesterday by Johnson for insolence. Very merchant service, but rather unnecessary, especially ashore!'[42]

Squadron Leader Ernest L. Johnson was the *R101*'s navigating officer. His son, the late Group Captain Ernest A. 'Johnnie' Johnson, subsequently enjoyed a distinguished RAF career and was godfather to Rebecca Grabowsky-Atherstone's brother, Paul Noël Grabowsky-Atherstone.*

Johnson's behaviour – punching to the floor a member of the crew – was reminiscent of summary justice in the early navy in which insolence was a serious

---

* His book, *Airship Navigator* (Skyline, 1994) is a reflection on his father's life.

The US Navy airship *Shenandoah* sometimes
[moo]red at a mast on USS *Patoka*, a converted
[tanker/c]arrier. (Library of Congress)

Front Section Shenandoah Disaster Sharon Ohio Sept 3

Z R 3 Leaving Shed First Time

U.S. NAVY

Shenandoah broke up over Ohio in 1925. Navigator
les Rosendahl and six others escaped by free-ballooning
amaged bow section. (Library of Congress)

e: The successful ZR3 USS *Los Angeles* entering her
for the first time at the Naval Air Station, Lakehurst,
Jersey. (Library of Congress)

t: USS *Los Angeles* had a spectacular mooring-mast
ent at Lakehurst, New Jersey, in 1927, when wind
her tail. Crew members clambered up her keel into
ern to weigh her down. Damage was slight and she
the next day.
ary of Congress)

Highly advanced and innovative, US Navy airships
as *Macon* and *Akron* were more ambitious than any
had sailed before, new techniques in design,
truction and operation being developed. At 785 feet
Akron could carry four aircraft (see overleaf). She had
machine-guns, eight huge Maybach engines mounted
nally, more than six million cubic feet of helium, a
e of more than 10,000 miles and cruised at 83 mph.
n was lost in 1933. Of 76 aboard 73 died. (Cody
es)

AKRON WORKS
AKRON OHIO

Akron, Ohio, home of the Goodyear
& Rubber Corporation, which became
world's leading airship builder producing
s of craft. Among its output were the
Akron and *Macon*. (Library of Congress)

t: Early experiments with airships
ing planes on a trapeze took place at
am in England. Later the mammoth
rican ships housed planes in hangars in
nvelope. (Library of Congress)

w: *Graf Zeppelin*, the world's most
ssful airship. It girdled the world –
een 1928 and in 1937 it made almost
passages and covered more than a million
s. (Library of Congress)

Meadville, Pa., New York, N. Y.,
Chicago, Ill., London, England.

The Graf Zeppelin's Rendezvous with the Eternal Desert
and the More than 4000 Year-old Pyramids
of Gizeh, Egypt.

Above: October 1928. *Left to right*, Captain Hans Curt Flemming, Dr. Hugo Eckener and Captain Ernst Lehmann in front of the world's most successful airship, the *Graf Zeppelin* (pictured right) at Friedrichshafen, Germany, before a transatlantic sailing to Lakehurst, New Jersey. (Photo Evening Standard/Getty Images)

Above: The *Graf Zeppelin* was well-appointed for its round-the-world voyages. (Cody Images)

Inset left: The German Maybach company made powerful airship engines and had an association that reached back to the earliest days of Count Ferdinand von Zeppelin's company. (Cody Images)

TAYLOR, BRAWN & FLOOD Ltd.,
Chemists,
68 HIGH STREET, 36 ST. PETER'S STREET,
1a MILL STREET, 25 BROMHAM ROAD,
BEDFORD; and at SANDY.

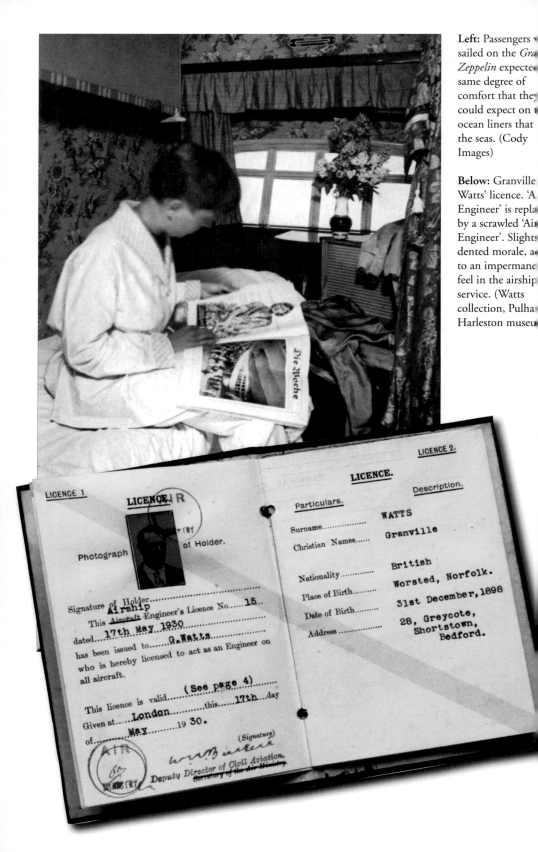

Left: Passengers who sailed on the *Graf Zeppelin* expected the same degree of comfort that they could expect on the ocean liners that sailed the seas. (Cody Images)

Below: Granville Watts' licence. 'Aircraft Engineer' is replaced by a scrawled 'Airship Engineer'. Slightly dented morale, added to an impermanent feel in the airship service. (Watts collection, Pulham & Harleston museum)

LICENCE 1

LICENCE.

Photograph of Holder.

Signature of Holder........

Airship

This Aircraft Engineer's Licence No.....15..
dated....17th May 1930.........
has been issued to........G.Watts...........
who is hereby licensed to act as an Engineer on
all aircraft.

This licence is valid.........(See page 4).......
Given at.....London..........this....17th...day
of..........May.........19 30.

(Signature)

Deputy Director of Civil Aviation.
Secretary of the Air Ministry.

LICENCE 2.

LICENCE.

Particulars.

Description.

Surname................ **WATTS**
Christian Names...... **Granville**

Nationality............. **British**
Place of Birth.......... **Worsted, Norfolk.**
Date of Birth.......... **31st December, 1898**
Address .... **28, Greycote,
Shortstown,
Bedford.**

offence and men could be flogged, shackled and sometimes executed. It highlights how the airship service was in part the bastard child of the navy; it also has the smack of class, a reminder of the social divisions evident in the navy of a previous era. Atherstone's observation that Johnson's action 'was very merchant service' (written by an aristocrat with a sense of humour), might as easily have been: ' ... very lower decks'.

There was a closeness between officers and men of the type found in submarines where rank applied, but life was less starchy than in the surface fleet. There was no room, literally, in airships or submarines to stand on ceremony. Aboard a surface ship there was space, albeit cramped, for a physical divide, and the authority of a ship's officer was backed by four centuries of practice and custom. As with submarines, airships were *new* technology: engineers were important, not 'lower-deck' or necessary nuisances. Most crew were civilian rather than RAF; this made obsolete the notion of a service built on military ranks, but it brought other problems in maintaining discipline.

Dr. Giles Camplin:

The majority of the crew, and nearly all the officers, had been through a war together. This was a war where you did your duty without question and you could be shot for disobeying orders from a higher ranked officer. But there was also a camaraderie and a deep-seated belief in being manly and heroic. All this is quite alien to our modern thinking and it is difficult for us to imagine how we would have reacted in their circumstances. Nowadays we can see that many of them were clearly suffering from stress and that while we would today call much of what went on 'bullying', to them it was perfectly normal and your job was to take it on the chin and be a man. If counselling had been available at the time none of them would have taken it. That said there are many instances of higher ranks dictating their wishes to their underlings on the *R101* team. Lord Thomson tore Colmore off a strip for ordering the *R101* to be put back in the shed ahead of bad weather. Richmond taunted the seniors in the Royal Airship Works drawing office by asking innocently how they had solved some problems on the ill-fated *R38* and then sneering that *R101* would certainly not be done that way. Scott more or less forced Booth [captain of the *R100*] to take *R100* through a mid-Atlantic line squall and Johnston knocked a man down after the *R100*'s return from Canada.'[43]

The shortage of experienced personnel caused continuing problems during the construction of the *R101*. It exercised Atherstone.

26 August 1930, 165

'I have asked the "heads" what steps are going to be taken about obtaining some more officers as some extra ones are very urgently required now, both to take charge of the mooring tower and also as watch keepers in the ships. As things are at present ship's captains are in the very difficult position of having to keep watch in flight, that is really quite wrong. Also there is at present no officer at RAW [Royal Airship Works] in charge of the mooring tower. I am nominally doing this job, but as we are supposed to be taking *R101* out to India in a month's time I can't do two jobs ... this present position has long been foreseen by the flying staff and numerous minutes have been written pointing out the urgency of obtaining more officers, but, as usual, the matter has been shelved time and again presumably on the score of "economy"! This sort of attitude on the part of one's superior officers does not help one to place that degree of confidence in those who are running this show that one should. It is all rather disturbing.'[44]

Giles Camplin:

> 'It is clear to me, certainly among the lower ranks of the *R101* crew, that there was a degree of resignation and the feeling that if the top brass insisted on pressing on and ignoring the test programme then they would ultimately have to take the responsibility when it all unwound. The option of resigning was constrained by the depressed labour market. Most of the serving officers could not refuse to follow an order. It is often said that Irwin [captain of the *R101*] considered stepping down but was dissuaded by the certain knowledge that others would step forward to take his place.'[45]

The ship was due to embark for Karachi in India on 4 October 1930. With little more than a month before its departure, there was still much to do. A programme of frantic testing ensued. The ship's cover was almost entirely replaced – but, crucially, not all of it. It then had to be doped and laced, time-consuming in itself. The officers and crew had to try and familiarise themselves with new equipment such as a Tornado reversing engine, an echo sounder and electrical gas and air thermometers. Atherstone's final entry, the day before the flight to India, has its own poignancy.

3 October 1930, 177

'It was decided this morning that the flight to India would not commence until 1800 hours tomorrow as it would be too much of a rush to get everything ready by this evening. We really did need all yesterday and today to get everything on the top line. A reserve lubricating oil tank was put in today to hold 112 gallons of lubricating oil and a spare air cooler is to be carried! One of the emergency ballast bags was found to be defective and had to be renewed and all the others carefully examined. Also the gas bags with low purities were purged through, and altogether the ship was given a proper look over. The weather conditions appear to be pretty good with not much wind about. I think we should be able to get away with about 28 tons of fuel on board that should give us nearly 100 per cent reserve. Everybody is rather keyed up now, as we all feel that the future of airships very largely depends on what sort of a show we put up. There are very many unknown factors and I feel that that thing called "Luck" will figure rather conspicuously in our flight. Let's hope for good luck and do our best!'[46]

Rebecca Atherstone said: 'My Grandfather was meticulous in his notes. He usually took the diary with him. It's rather telling that his last entry reads "Let's hope for good luck and do our best" and that he left the diary behind. I think perhaps there was an inner feeling on his part ... perhaps he thought ... "Oh well, I'll leave it here".' [47]

A GALLANT YOUNG
ENGLISH GENTLEMAN

G ranville Watts became associated with the British air service in 1916, midway through the First World War. He was an engineer. Early on he was involved in the construction of the successful small *Sea Scout* airships used in reconnaissance work (see pages 39 and 51), known more commonly as submarine spotting. In Great Britain he worked at airship stations at Pulham St. Mary in south Norfolk, Howden in east Yorkshire, and the Royal Airship Works at Cardington, in Bedfordshire. His career saw him engaged with a diversity of vessels. Watts had an adventurous life; he was a member of the *R100* crew when it sailed to Canada, the *R33* when it was torn from its mast and swept backwards out of control over the North Sea, and the *R34* when it hit a hill in Yorkshire and was later wrecked while handlers tried to moor it in strong winds.

The author found part of the Watts' collection of musty photographs, letters and newspaper cuttings in the guardianship of Brian Carr, the chairman of the Pulham Market Society.[1] In the adjacent village of Pulham St. Mary a former historic school has been restored as a community centre in which it is hoped to stage an airship exhibition that will feature the Watts chronicles. Mr. Carr received the records, curled and yellowed, from the late Dr. Patrick Rawlence, the village doctor who with his wife Joscelyn and others in the locality did much to uncover Pulham St. Mary's past, epitomised in the carved wood village sign that features an airship. Dr. Rawlence had been entrusted with the annals by Ida, Granville Watts's sister, who wanted them to be retained for posterity. She donated them for use in an airship exhibition staged in 1989 by Doctor and Mrs. Rawlence. The rest of the Watts collection is in a tiny museum in the little market town of Harleston, Norfolk, close to the former airship station, in the care of curators Judy Alder and Mervyn Hickford.[2]

It was primarily Alice, Granville's mother, and Ida who collated the registers – most of the photographs lacked dates or identity – and the pride in their assembly shines through. It is an important find: military history errs in favour of chronicling the ruling class, it being the custom for officers to maintain journals. Such entries can skew the way the past is viewed, history presented from above looking down. In contrast, these journals are a voice from the 'front line', an echo of the ordinary men and women who made up the service. Apart from the author's minor tidying, the letters are as Watts wrote them; ellipses usually indicate deletion of extraneous material; words in parentheses are the author's. The author acknowledges the courtesy of the Watts family in allowing him to use the letters, documents and photographs.

Granville Watts was a Norfolk man, stationed for a time at the Royal Naval Airship Station at Pulham St. Mary, in south Norfolk. Pulham is on the far side of the county from his home at Worstead, in east Norfolk, on the edge of the Norfolk Broads, a historic and idyllic network of more than 120 miles of inland lagoons linked by waterways that merge into the sea at Great Yarmouth on the eastern seaboard. The north of the county is bounded by the coast. Geographically Norfolk is one of Britain's larger counties, though its population is still relatively sparse.

Early in his career, serving with the airship *R32* at Pulham St. Mary, Watts sent his mother a pencilled note: 'Am still at Pulham as the wind has been a bit too strong for *R32* to get out of her shed. We are going for a 24-hour cruise before we land at Howden; there are 1200 gallons of petrol aboard. The Daily Order will show I am getting 2/– a day more, so it is alright. Have just drawn flying kit that is a lovely set, all leather and fur. Well, I must close. Hoping you are well. I remain, Your loving son, Granville.'[3]

At the end of the war he received the conventional royal 'thank you' issued to those who had served the nation. In a brown envelope stamped: 'Presented by the Rt. Hon. Lord Weir, Secretary of State and President of the Air Council', his copy of *The King's Message to the Royal Air Force*, dated 11 November 1918, sent to members of the embryonic air force, began: 'In this supreme hour of victory I send greetings and heartfelt congratulations to all ranks of the Royal Air Force.' It mentioned 'the birth of the Royal Air Force, with its wonderful expansion and development, will remain one of the most remarkable achievements of the Great War'.[4]

In peacetime Watts maintained his involvement with the airship service, abandoning it temporarily at a point in 1921 when the government jettisoned airship development. At the beginning of 1921, however, he was involved in one of several mishaps. He was sailing aboard the *R34*, sister ship of the runaway *R33*. The *R34* was one of the most famous vessels in the world: two years earlier, in 1919, with the legendary George Herbert Scott at the helm, it had undertaken its epic passage to Canada.

Giving his address as 'Hut 2 B' in Howden, on 28 January 1921 Granville wrote to his mother about a subsequent voyage he made on the *R34*, which after its Canadian passage had returned to more conventional duties. His letter gives a perspective of life on an airship: the primitive engineering, the rascal humour of an airship crew, the serendipity of voyages – with discoveries tending to the alarming rather than the pleasant and the insouciant manner in the way sky-sailors dealt with hair-raising incidents. Watts wrote:

Dear Mother,

Am quite well and getting on alright. I will try and explain what happened during that twenty-nine hour cruise. We had been ordered out to do a ten-hour instructional cruise to train officers in navigation. So a day's rations for thirty-six men was put aboard and after the *R32* was taken out the landing party took us out. After the usual preparations [involving] lift and trim we were released at 12.10 on Thursday. It was a calm day – the first since I had been off leave – so the ship flew for the coast. I was in charge of the for'd [forward] engine gondola that is a continuation of the control car ... when we left the ground all engines were running with the clutches out. But when we rose to 1,000 feet all clutches with the exception of ours were ordered in and then we had to stop-engine because the noise made it impossible for the people in the control car to hear themselves speak.

The *R34* would have been sailing on its three remaining engines, one in the stern and two amidships.

All went well and we were flying at 3,000 feet over Hull down the Humber towards the coast. I then found that the water [in the radiator] had begun to freeze. So I asked if I could start the engine so that the radiator would not burst because of the frozen water. I started the engine and after ten minutes I let the clutch in and the propeller revolved at 1400 revs per minute. The wireless observer came in and told me we had been recalled because a gale was brewing. It began to get dark and my telegraph [an instruction from the control car] showed that I had to increase to 1600 [propeller revolutions per minute] and the ship started to return to the station.

Watts explained he had been working with his mate and that they had shared four-hour shifts, his mate taking the first, Granville the second.

At eight o'clock my mate came in and took over. I returned to the keel for supper and to sleep, if that was possible. I got in to the crew's space and began to eat some bread, butter and jam and bully beef ... the lads were talking [saying] that the navigators did not know where we were. The wind was springing up and the ship was making very little progress with the engines running full out [full power]. I thought this was lively [fun] and jumped into my hammock.

As well as hydrogen, the service always floated on optimism – in fact, the scene was not one of unalloyed joy. The engines roared, the night was black and freezing, the ship making little progress, buffeted by gale-force winds. The crew thought the trainee navigators had got them lost. And what does Watts do? He retires to bed; both sky and surface sailors knew the art of sleeping in inclement conditions. With the *R34* being tossed around, girders groaning, wind clutching at its fabric, he is awoken by a cook who plays a practical joke; even in a storm there is still badinage.

I was dozing when I tasted something stinging my lip. I looked up and found the cook had put some pickles over my face. He then told me it was 11.45 pm and that I had better get up so that I could have some tea before going on watch. This I had before I began to walk to the forward [engine] car. The ship was rolling. One minute I was walking up, the next minute down. It woke me up and I realised that we were in for a rough time. I relieved my mate and took over. He said that an oil pipe from the gearbox had broken and the water pump on the engine was leaking very badly.

Watts now confronted a nightmare:

I started to tighten up the flange on the pump when there was a crash. The gondola shook and rattled. The water from the radiator and tank from above rushed down on me. The accumulators and spare gear fell on the engine and floor. Worst of all, the lights went out. The noise was deafening. In a second I pulled out the clutch, jammed on the propeller brake and switched off the engine. The girders were breaking. Men began to shout. I could not see or move. The windows were shuttered up to keep out the wind. The door leading to the control car was my only way to get out. This I did and bumped into someone. After a minute or so they got an Aldis lamp [portable lamp to transmit morse code] to light the control car. They shone it in my car to see what had happened. It was a hopeless mess. Then they put it [the Aldis lamp] out of the control car windows but its light could not penetrate the clouds or mist.

The men of the *R34* were in peril. They had suffered a calamity that had almost crippled the ship and could have ended in tragedy. 'We had struck a hill at 1200 feet, possibly higher. It had broken my propeller and that of the aft car. As luck would have it, the cars amidships escaped undamaged.' A hint of unvarnished terror momentarily replaced the Watts' insouciance that characterised so much of the airship service: 'No one can realise what it was like to be in a place like that not knowing our fate.'

He adopted a more buoyant tone, aware perhaps of causing his mother undue alarm: 'Our skipper kept his head and ordered the ship to be put to a higher, safer altitude. Well, I was out of work. I could do nothing more in the car. So I went into the keel and having had a chat with my mates I turned into my hammock. After waiting for what seemed days it began to get light. We were [by now] again over the North Sea. Then the struggle for home began, running on the two engines we had that were undamaged. My mate was ordered to relieve them [other engineers] in the port wing [engine] car and I had to write down all the damage done to the ship.' The danger failed to diminish his capacity for sleep, nor did it quell his appetite: 'I felt hungry but found there was no food aboard.'

The skipper ordered that the ship sail lower in search of gentler airs. 'An hour or so passed and we could just see the coast[line]. We were only moving at four to six miles an hour so the captain ordered the ship down to 500 feet to get into lighter winds. At 9am we crossed the coast at Hornsea. Above the Humber we made for home so slowly that we did not seem to be moving. As we were crawling along people on the ground waved and cheered not realising that we were in trouble; and, of course, being happy and enjoying the trip we waved back. I don't think we could have slung the dud engines at them.'

Unless the wind lessened *R34*'s crew faced a second night trying to coax it to safety. Sailing on two engines instead of four provided negligible propulsion. 'It meant being out all night without any food, very little flying kit and only two engines to rely on. The engines had been running twenty-six hours without stopping. One of them had a hole in the crank case that meant that it could break down at any minute.'

Though the ship's fortunes improved, respite would be short-lived:

The gale eased up and allowed us to move at sixteen miles an hour. This put new life into the crew. At 4.20 we were over the shed and my mate and I went into our car and saw that the landing party were ready. Will, our captain, handled the ship well and with some difficulty made a beautiful landing. The landing party held all the guys [ropes] and started to take us to the sheds. But the wind caught us and crashed the ship to the ground smashing the forward car and breaking all the rigid struts so the gondolas were only held then by eight suspension wires. They began to walk the ship again and the same thing happened, this time causing serious damage to the controls and breaking girders. One bump followed another. They found it impossible to get us into the shed. So they walked us to the mooring posts. But the wind hit us so hard it separated my engine car from the control car. It made it dangerous for us because the floor was so slippery with oil ... the wind crashed into us again and dragged us almost on our side along the ground breaking more girders in the keel and making a terrible noise. The wind bumped and pulled us about until the ship was absolutely out of control. One minute we were a hundred feet up in the air and the next we would crash on to the ground like a steam hammer. Then General Maitland [at the time in command at Howden] ordered us to leave the ship. The crew did not hesitate, only waiting for an opportunity to make the shortest leap possible. Lieutenant Drew [Captain H. Drew, in command of *R34* at the time] was the last to leave. After a struggle the ship was moored on the three-line mooring system. But the strain was so much it pulled out the mooring wire that goes round the hull at the bows. It tore a great hole in the bows and deflated three gas bags in the nose ... the ship collapsed and started to break up in the wind. It was wonderful to think that no one was injured. Well I must close, hoping all at home are well. I remain Your Loving Son, Granville.[5]

Damage to the famed ship was so great it had to be written off, a sad end for an illustrious vessel. *The Yorkshire Evening Post* headlined its story on 29 January 1921: '*R34* bumped to pieces in the night by high wind. Four hundred men not enough to house her.'[6]

The ship's propellers were buckled. Tufts of heather clung to her underbelly where she had hit the hillside. To assist in the mooring, Maitland had mustered every man on the station, some four hundred. Officers were cagey in admitting that the ship had sailed into a hill. Their coyness lacked logic: the local press was supportive of the service; the local populace held 'their' airships in affection, proud of the crews and sympathetic that the night had been fog-bound. From early days in the service it had become the habit to claim that airships and crews were infallible; to admit to less would be judged almost unpatriotic. The defensiveness was rooted in the suspicion of airships by politicians and military chiefs prevalent since the start. Maitland and his officers were determined that nothing that could denigrate ships or the service would leak out. While understandable, a lack of candour made inquiry and criticism by the Fourth Estate that much more vigorous.

Watts served also on the *R34*'s sister ship, the *R33*. Aged 26, he was aboard the truant vessel when in 1925 she broke away from her moorings; with his comrades he was later honoured by the King and awarded an inscribed gold watch to commemorate the crippled craft's return after its alarming voyage.[7] The presentation was at Pulham station by Sir Samuel Hoare, the Air Minister, who said: 'If the crew had failed to navigate the airship ... it is my firm conviction that airship development would have been stopped for a generation in this country.'[8]

In his papers Watts kept a list of the congratulatory telegrams sent to Pulham station to mark *R33*'s return. They were wired to Flight Lieutenant Ralph Booth, the most senior officer on the *R33* at the time it broke free. Booth was destined for an illustrious career, being later captain of the Atlantic-conquering *R100*. As a boost to morale, and not wishing to hog the glory, Booth circulated the telegrams around the station. They had been sent from across the country and the world, from the crew of the American rigid *Shenandoah* to unexpected well-wishers such as traders on the Liverpool Cotton Market. 'The directors and staff of the Airship Guarantee Company [Dennistoun Burney's operation that with Vickers was building the Barnes Wallis *R100* at Howden in Yorkshire] send their heartiest congratulations ...' 'Delighted to hear of your successful return after so trying an experience,' wrote Philip Sassoon, Under Secretary of State for Air. 'Well done ... you have proved everything we have said about the safety of the mooring mast,' wrote Sefton Brancker, director of civil aviation. The Bishop of Norwich wired from his Palace, 'May I motor over today soon after 4.30 to congratulate you on your safety and gallantry.' Another was addressed directly to the *R33* as if it was human, which to some it seemed: 'Many congratulations to all the brave boys who have brought you back so well,' signed, 'A British Woman'.[9]

On 22 July 1924, an official letter caused excitement at The Laburnams, Worstead, Norfolk, Watts's home. Bearing the royal crest, it was addressed to Granville from the Royal Airship Works at Cardington and sent by George Herbert Scott, in command of the flying programme at Cardington. It was headed: Civilian Personnel – Airship Crew – Engineer. It read:

Dear Sir,

In view of H.M. Government's decision to inaugurate an Airship Development Programme, I am directed to inform you that I can offer you employment for Flying Duties as Airship Crew – Engineer ... @ £4.7.6 per week. These rates are fixed to cover all time worked, but a minimum average of 50 hours per week must be maintained over consecutive periods of four weeks except for weeks in which a public holiday occurs, when the minimum will be reduced by the period of the holiday. If you are prepared to accept these terms you should inform me immediately, stating the date when you can report for duty. Yours faithfully, G. Herbert Scott, O/C Flying.[10]

Watts was quick to accept. Six days later he moved in with his kit to a single man's quarters at the RAW. Three months afterwards he was informed by the secretary and accountant at the RAW, in a note dated 10 October 1924: 'With reference to your tenancy of the above quarters, arrangements have been made for the deduction of the rent due, from your wages each week, the deductions to commence on Friday October 17th, with the rent for the week commencing Oct. 13th. The arrears from 28-7.24 to 6-10.24 amounting to £2. 4. 0 will be cleared by 5 deductions of 8/– and 1 of 4/– per week in addition to the current rent, a total deduction for 5 weeks of 12/– & for 1 week of 8/– reverting to the normal 4/– per week when the arrears are cleared.'[11] Eking out his wages, he paid sixpence each month for *Airways* magazine. The edition of September 1925 bore a photograph captioned *The Skyscraper* showing engineers, perhaps Granville among them, replacing the *R33*'s huge smashed nose after its return from its dash for freedom, 'an operation that was completed in 50 minutes'.[12] In May *Airways* Zeppelin chief Hugo Eckener, the former journalist and totemic airshipman, had a three-page spread with photographs of American airships, in which he extolled the virtues of mammoth, long-range dirigibles. Two further pages bore an entreaty by the *R100* sponsor, the ambitious and publicity-conscious Dennistoun Burney. Entitled 'Airships and Empire', its subheading was characteristically rich with chutzpah: 'Highways of the Air will be the Imperial Roads of the Future.'[13] Watts's edition of *The Engineer*, for March 1927, an authoritative and compulsory read for those in his trade, had five pages with pictures and a diagrammatic breakdown on the mechanical intricacies of the Cardington shed, the mooring tower and telescopic arm. In engineering innovation, airships and equipment set the pace. A tower of the type depicted in the article, a description officially dropped and replaced by the description 'mast', would cost, said the journal, around £50,000.[14]

From Cardington, Watts wrote to his parents about Flight Lieutenant Booth's wedding. In its ranks the airship service was highly social, while beyond its confines its members were seen as celebrities. Aviation was in its infancy; its 'cachet' embraced those at either end of the spectrum: from British, American and continental flyers, the daring pioneers establishing international records, to members of the services, or civilians alongside, especially those in the exotic world of transatlantic ships. From his note comes a sense that Watts felt privileged to be invited to Booth's wedding. Booth was an officer and heading for an eminent career. Though the war had decimated the officer class and put a match to many social mores and divisions, the post-conflict period was still more deferential than the following decade and markedly complaisant if compared with the re-ordered Britain that emerged after the Second World War. It was not uncommon for civilians and lower ranks in the service to be invited to an officer's wedding, in Booth's case, a full-blown society affair in Central London. Such invites were attestation of the camaraderie in the airship cosmos that cut through ordinary boundaries of rank and caste; whatever else, the solicitation was a mark of Watts' popularity and the esteem in which he was held by senior officers.

The Booth matrimonials had éclat. When Granville wrote to his mother he was full of it:

We left by bus at 10 am and arrived in London at 12.30 after a nice ride. Then we went to St. Georges Church in Hanover Square near Marble Arch – it was a nice service and very impressive. We went to the Langham Hotel not very far away where we were announced and met the Bride's mother and the Bride and Groom and mixed with the crowd. Several people introduced themselves to us and they were pleased to meet and talk to us as we were with him [Booth] on the ship etc. I was surprised that we were made such a fuss of as most of the other people were in morning coats and top hats ... but they knew who we were and soon got us talking. We had champagne and drank the toast of bride and groom and more champagne and ices and cakes and more champagne and I woke up on Tuesday ready for work, perhaps, with a fat head and sorry that I went to the wedding. I did not go to Captain Meager's on Saturday [Meager was to be *R101*'s First Officer: Granville's social life was becoming something of whirl] I was going but I had not forgotten Major Booth's. My uni [uniform] fits alright and looks nice. Well, I will close now. Hoping you and Dad are well. I remain, your loving son, Granville.[15]

Watts came from a close family in Worstead, isolated between the Broads in the east of the county and the north Norfolk coast. Worstead prospered in the middle ages as a centre of textile weaving, giving its name to Worsted cloth. Weaving lasted there for more than five centuries; its last weaver, John Cubitt, died in 1882. The village succumbed to pastoral slumbers when the Industrial Revolution passed it by, forcing hand-weavers out of business and shifting the cloth trade to West Yorkshire. A clue to its monied past can still be seen in its fine houses and church, proudly majestic in a county with more churches than any other. Granville's family were proud of his achievements. His father, Christmas Henry Watts (he had a brother called Henry Christmas Watts) was a tailor to the local gentry. He ran a shop attached to The Laburnams, his home, and owned other properties in the locality. There were six children: Granville's brothers, Alec and Stanley, and his sisters, Ida, Eva and Cissy. Ida and Eva were schoolteachers. The Watts family, in which Granville was known as Mike, were industrious. On 14 July 1989, at the age of 81, Ida wrote to Mrs. Joscelyn Rawlence in Pulham: 'Granville loathed his name; it embarrassed him. He was also known as Willy.' She mentions how as a young woman she had taught at Hempnall village school, in south Norfolk, cycling the 26 miles home to Worstead on Fridays and back to school in Hempnall on Monday mornings.[16]

Granville attended Paston Grammar School, in the nearest small town of North Walsham. His Air Ministry exercise books, when he was learning his trade, are crammed with unfathomable formulae and hand-drawn mechanical diagrams, testimony to him wrestling with the fundamentals of science, engineering and mathematics, the disciplines of the senior charge-hand engineer he would become.[17] In a 1930 copy of the school magazine, *The Old Pastonian No.3*, Watts is described as the 'flying Pastonian'; the article recalls his participation in dangerous trials at Pulham station which involved airships being tested as aircraft carriers. He was 'engaged to carry out a number of experiments such as releasing and re-hooking aeroplanes to the airship ... he has found himself in very queer positions.'[18]

On 26 September 1924, with the crew of HMA *R33*, he was invited to a reunion dinner at the Silver Grill, in the High Street, Bedford, its proprietors among those who had sent a telegram marking the ship's return. The invitation had an *R33* cartoon depicting its hapless crew aboard a bizarre hybrid: a galleon with sails, rigging and anchor flying through the heavens, a propeller at its bow. It bore the motto 'All adrift again'. With toasts to the King, crew, ship – a dinner of steak and kidney pudding and baked apples and custard – it was a high-spirited evening with 'conveyances' leaving Shortstown at 6.45 p.m. and returning to the Royal Airship Works after midnight. Granville had his invitation signed as a souvenir by guests who represented the *crème de la crème* of British airshipmen, from 'Sky' Hunt (coxwain of *R33*) to Rope, Richmond and Scott.[19]

Granville enjoyed a supper given by burghers at the Swan Hotel, Bedford, on Saturday, 25 April 1925 to celebrate the gallantry of Lieutenant Booth and the crew of the *R33*. The Mayor of Bedford, Alderman G. H. Barford, was in the chair. The invitation bore a photograph of the errant *R33* with its stoved-in nose. Conveyances returned celebrants to Cardington as the night's delights, including a dinner of fillets of sole and roast haunch of mutton, drew to a close. Once more, airship lights pencilled their signatures on Watts's invitation.[20] The author is familiar with the Swan. Of mellow stone, it nestles by the town bridge that crosses the River Ouse. It was an escape from the RAW at Cardington; of ribaldry and romance, politics and intrigue, its private quarters offered a sanctuary for more discreet affairs. The Swan and the Bridge Hotel provided a respite from Cardington. They became the country Mess. Bedford's reputation grew as the airship capital of Britain. Not since the Baptist preacher John Bunyan, author of *Pilgrim's Progress* and born in a cottage in the nearby village of Elstow, had it known such fame. The RAW was of such celebrity telegrams only needed to be addressed 'Airships Bedford'. Chauffeured cars swept a procession of politicians,

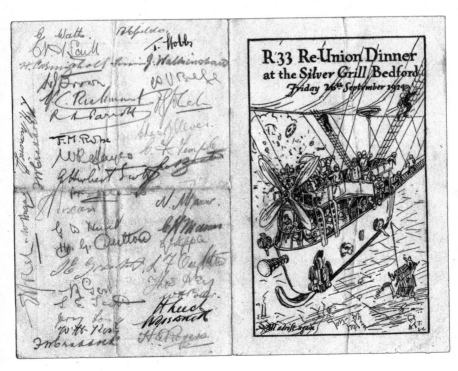

military chiefs, journalists, foreign dignitaries and ministry apparatchiks from the town's railway halt to its airship hub.

The twenty-fifth of September 1925 marked the *R33* annual dinner at Pulham, Norfolk: *consommé Julienne*, boiled turbot, *bouchées à la Reine*, roast beef, trifle Chantilly and praline cream ice. The convivial Major Scott was in the chair. Guests signed Granville's invite. If Brancker had been present he would have swallowed his monocle. Though budgets were tight, there always seemed to be enough money for a celebration.[21]

In Britain the *R33*'s adventures had caught the nation's imagination. In the archive glued to the back of a Mother's Day card is a *Daily Express* cartoon of 18 April 1925. The *R33* is portrayed as a likeable rogue, a portly reveller returned to its mooring after a night on the tiles, a partygoer who had imbibed too generously, with a bulbous drinker's nose, crushed top hat, dishevelled evening wear. The caption is forgiving: 'Boys will be Boys.' The ship is being welcomed home by Mother Britannia, clutching at a mooring line, Mrs. Pulham inscribed on her pinafore. As if scolding a cherished, mischievous child, she inquires: 'Now where have you been to all night?'[22]

Watts's airship engineer's licence was a reconstituted aircraft engineer's licence. Twice the word 'aircraft' is scrawled out and 'airship' inserted in its place. It was disappointing the Air Ministry could not run to a purpose-made licence. Was this a snub or sensible parsimony? Whatever the motive, it had the smack of airshipmen being made to feel of a secondary importance to aircraftmen. But with budgets that were corset-tight it would have been profligate to issue a purpose-made licence if airship development slowed or ceased as it had in the past. In its small, hurtful way, a licence intended for a different category of engineer personified the uncomfortable transience that had become ingrained in the service. Watts's address is given as number 28, Greycote, Shortstown, his lodgings near the Royal Airship Works, home before nationalisation to the Short Brothers aviation company. On 29 October 1929, after a medical, Watts was declared 'fit,' his licence stamped accordingly.[23]

On 21 May 1929, Watts received in the RAW internal mail a small brown envelope marked 'On His Majesty's Service'. The note was from Booth, Director of Airship Development: 'Dear Sir, I am instructed to inform you that you have been selected as Crew Engineer for *R100*, and that you will be required to proceed to Howden as soon as inflation starts, when crew pay will commence.' He was excited about his new posting and the prospect of going on the *R100* to Canada.[24]

A fragment of torn telegram paper in the Watts collection is headed the 'Royal Canadian Signals Radiotelegraph Service'. It has suffered from damp or a ravenous mouse. A handwritten pencil message looks hastily scrawled: 'Watts. Charge Room

Engineer. Canteen. Airship requires non return valves out of spare starter also 3 [there is an unrecognisable word that looks like 'olives'].' There it concludes. Or does it? Perhaps the rest was discarded? Whether sent or received by Watts the author cannot establish; perhaps it was a request for *R100* spares while the ship was in or on its Canadian voyage. What the canteen or olives had to do with it must remain a minor mystery. The fragment offers no clue to date, time, sender or recipient.[25]

R100 personnel sent elegant Christmas cards that saluted the ship's transatlantic success: an embossed gold crown and wings, 'H.M.A. *R-100*' written beneath. Inside was a photograph of the ship at its mast at Saint-Hubert, Montreal, in August 1930.[26] Envelopes in air force blue, embossed with a dark blue crown and wings and stamped 'H.M.A. *R-100*' had a significant panache.[27] To those in its ranks the airship service may have felt transient and uncertain: ships could be dangerous, the science at the leading edge; funding was tight and elements in the military establishment viewed it with a corrosive resentment. But there was an indisputable certainty – it had *style*. In 1924, when development of the *R100* and *R101* was sanctioned, the Royal Airship Works produced a finely drawn Christmas card of an airship girdling the globe.[28]

In Watts's collection is a child's school notebook headed *Happy Days, Vol. No. 10.* Dated Christmas 1929, it contains a poem, *The Airship*, by a certain Marjory Augur:

> *The R101 is huge and big*
> > *It looks like an overgrown pig*
> *It hasn't a tail or ears or legs*
> > *They hold it down with great big pegs*

> *The R100 its sister ship*
> > *Hasn't yet done its maiden trip*
> *They'll get it out as soon as they can*
> > *Don't you think Major Scott is a lucky man.*

Miss Augur illustrated her poem with a sketch of an airship from which two parachutes are descending. Her drawing bears the motto: 'New stunt for MPs when they go up'. Even school children had a low opinion of politicians and their vulgar clamour to joy-ride on the *R100* and *R101*, the newest sensations of the Empire.[29]

The arrival in Canada of the *R100* caused intense excitement. Newspapers carried special supplements. Magazines devoted editions to its voyage and the celebrations that marked its stay. The Department of National Defence for Canada produced a commemorative booklet of nearly 100 pages, priced at 50 cents. The Honourable J. L.

Ralston, Canada's Minister of National Defence, wrote the forward: 'This flight is an historical event. It marks another advance in air transport worthy of note even in this age of scientific and engineering marvels.' Granville had been given or bought a copy. The booklet contained a detailed history of airships; it bore full-page pictures of Scott and Booth. Pages of advertisements from American and Canadian businesses extolled the ship's coming: oil and petrol companies, banks, insurance houses, travel agents, hotels, textile conglomerates, businesses offering postal services. *R100*'s passage seemed to signal a new commercial dawn: every business in Canada and beyond saw a chance to make money. The silver liner of the heavens promised a glorious future for those of a capitalist bent. It would put Canada and its new airship facilities in Montreal on the world business map. If Burney had any reservations about the commercial viability of a transatlantic airship service, the welter of advertisements in the blue booklet should have allayed his fears.[30]

While in Canada Watts received a letter from a Brother Hubert, of Mount Saint Louis Institute, Sherbrooke Street, East Montreal. Sent on 12 August 1930, it was addressed to Mr. G. Watts, Chargehand Engineer, The *R100*, St.-Hubert Airport. It began: 'Majestically your floating monument to the 20th century science development flew over "my" college, between its two extremities, yesterday afternoon ... I am the Brother Hubert of the Christian Schools who had the privilege, with two "confreres" of mine, to visit the *R100*, Saturday morning ... I was dressed in a long black gown ... I came to say goodbye, Mr. Watts, and to wish all your mates, a perfect home-ward trip. I would highly appreciate a short visit of yours to this college, whose cadets are renowned all over Quebec and Ontario'. The letter was signed: 'Yours very friendly, Brother Hubert'. It is not known if Watts accepted the invitation. Inside his letter Brother Hubert included a postcard depicting his college.[31]

In an undated letter Watts told his mother about his Canadian adventure. The envelope has a picture of the imposing St. James Hotel, at 1010 St. James Street, Montreal, with the name of the manager, J. B. Fafard; there is no evidence he stayed there; his notepaper does not bear the hotel's name. His wages would not have run to it, and the Ministry would not have paid his bill. He stayed on the ship at its mast, giving his address as Saint-Hubert Airport. He says he is 'quite alright though a bit tired as I have been on the ship all night. I am writing this while at the mast but will be relieved at 8 o'clock. This is a lovely place but very hot. As soon as the sun rises at about 3.30 am it's off [with my] coat'. In a passage that must have worried his mother he recounts: 'We had a good trip across the Atlantic but it was very rough over the St. Lawrence river and was delayed 24 hours by torn fabric on one of the elevator fins.'

Watts and the crew were privileged. It was exciting to experience the wonders of Canada first-hand, rather than through the schoolbooks of Paston Grammar.

This place is like a French town. Nearly everybody speaks French and the adverts are in French. It all seems funny that they should be in an English province ... I like the place; it's very busy and everything is fast. I am having a bit of a struggle finding out what the money is ... it's all strange, wrong money. Hoping you and Dad are well, I remain, your loving son, Granville. PS. Don't take any notice of the address on the envelope but write to the address above.[32]

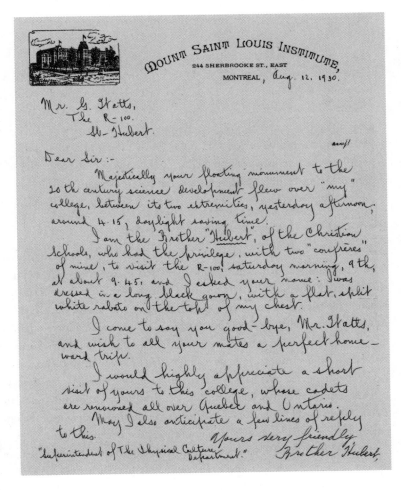

Brother Hubert's letter to Watts.

As with any tourist, he bought a set of souvenir coloured postcards for 25 cents showing Saint-Hubert Airport. He enjoyed showing them to his mother and father on his return to England.[33]

There are two stories about Granville Watts and the *R101*. One is that he was asked to join the airship on its fateful sailing to the tropics. He declined, saying it was fairer to let another engineer savour the experience he had enjoyed as a member of the *R100* crew on its Canadian passage. The other story is that he turned the offer down because he had reservations about the *R101*'s safety. Whatever his motive, he was not aboard when it crashed near Beauvais on 4 October 1930, killing many of his friends. Instead, he joined hundreds of mourners for the mass funeral at Cardington church.

A family friend wrote to Watts 13 days after the disaster:

Dear Mike [as he was known to family and friends]
Lucy and I would like to tell you how very sorry we are about the loss of your comrades and of the ship. We were very relieved to hear that you were not on board – I thought it unlikely as you are a member of the *R100*, but we were not sure if they had two complete crews or not. [The correspondent adds later:] Bearing in mind what you told me about Mr. Spanner [the acerbic airship critic whose dire pre-crash predictions were now seen as prophetic] it is very annoying to see all his writings quoted in the newspapers during the past two weeks. Signed: Thomas G. Hicks, Brading Road, Mitcham Road, Croydon, London.[34]

Eleven weeks after the catastrophe, on Christmas Eve, 1930, Watts rode his motorbike from Cardington, which had become a sad and ghostly place, to spend Christmas with his family in Norfolk. The future of British airships and the *R100* hung in the balance. He felt displaced, unsure about his future and that of the service as a whole. At about 7 that evening he was involved in a collision with a lorry on a dark stretch of the London to Norwich road near a spot called Roudham Heath. He died immediately, his motorcycle wrecked.[35] *The Eastern Daily Press*, the regional newspaper, reported that he was 'shortly to have been married to a Worstead young lady in business at North Walsham. The last time he was at home coincided with the *R101* tragedy and he mentioned that he had been offered a place in the crew of that airship but declined because he was doubtful about her capabilities.'[36]

On 29 December 1930 he was buried at Worstead church, where as man and boy he had sung in the choir. Only weeks before his funeral he had helped organise an

R101 service at the church, one of hundreds held in parishes across Britain. It had been eleven years since his attendance at a 'Recognition dinner and entertainment' to honour those who had served in the war, organised by Worstead Parish Council and held in the village school.[37] His young adult life had been spent entirely in the service of his nation.

At his funeral the Reverend C. W. Kershaw told the large congregation in the magnificent Worstead church that the comment made to him about Granville was that 'he was such a nice chap', he was more than popular, he was loved and liked for what he was and he was as loyal to his work as he was to his friends. Kershaw described him as 'a gallant young English gentleman'. Commander Booth and Captain Meager of the *R100*, and 16 members of the crew immediately followed the bier, four of them pushing it.[38] The large church was packed to capacity – there would have been more had not so many of his friends died in the *R101*. Granville's father, Christmas Henry, was too ill and too overcome by grief to attend.

Arthur Watts, 93, was proud to show the author round the church and cemetery where his uncle Granville is buried. 'I was only thirteen but everybody remembered him as a strapping young man. He would do anything for anybody, kindness itself. He loved his Norton motor bike. After the accident it was in Ida's shed for years, smashed to pieces.'[39] Three years after Granville's death, Arthur, then aged 16, joined the Royal Navy for four years, serving in HMS *Orion* and HMS *Crescent*. Mr. Watts served in the army medical corps during the Second World War. Granville's grave has his name and age in lead lettering that has peeled from the stone as the decades have slipped by. It is next to that of Alice, his mother, and Christmas Henry, his father. Without Mr. Watts's help and memory it would have been impossible for the author to identify the photographs in the Watts archive.

Four decades after Granville's death, on 26 October 1971, Captain George Meager, the First Officer of the *R100*, wrote to Eva, Granville's sister. In 1915 Meager joined the Airships Section of the Royal Naval Air Service and enjoyed a distinguished career. In 1918, after being in command of different types of airship, including the early *Sea Scouts* and *Coastal* classes, he was made captain of an Italian semi-rigid, the *SR1*, flying from Rome to England. He was appointed second officer of *R33*, being involved in experimental work, the results of which were utilised in *R100* and *R101*. Kenneth Deacon, author of *The Men and Women Who Built and Flew the R100*, notes that the Italian government awarded Meager the *Croce di Guerra* and the Cross of the Order of the Crown of Italy for his services to Italy. Meager's duties included, in 1917, being second-in-command of an airship flight sent to Italy for Adriatic patrol duties. Meager led crew members on the examination of the rips in the *R100* cover when the ship encountered violent turbulence over the St. Lawrence valley on its Canadian voyage, the incident recalled by Granville in one of the letters to his mother. Meager and Booth were among those of the view that the *R101* was a bad ship.[40] They had both sailed in her, once on the occasion when she had dived alarmingly at the Hendon air show; they both stated that they were determined never to repeat the experience again unless specifically ordered to do so.

In his letter to Eva, Captain Meager wrote: 'I was terribly shocked when we heard of the untimely tragic accident to your brother whom I always looked on as a very brave man besides being a very efficient and conscientious engineer ...' From his letter it is apparent that it was he who took a photograph of Granville leaning over the edge of an airship engine car while the *R100* was on its Canada passage. He says he took it while Watts was 'repairing one of the engines in freezing cold over the Atlantic. It even affects me today to think of him on his way home on Christmas Eve to spend Christmas with his family in Norfolk. What a shock it must have been to you ... it gave me great pleasure to hear that the snap of your brother slung over the side of one of the engine cars that I sent to your parents gave your Mother some easement in her great loss. What a time ago it all happened!'[41]

Meager's letter suggests a small enigma. Two days after he attended Granville Watts's funeral he sent a black-edged letter of condolence to Granville's mother, Alice. It bore the *R100* crest, was sent from the Royal Airship Works and was dated 30 December 1930. He enclosed the photograph of Watts. Unlike the letter that he sent to Eva decades after the tragedy, he states that he took the photograph over London, not the Atlantic:

Dear Mrs Watts,

I am sending you with this letter a snapshot of your son as he was in the act of making a repair to one of the engines during our long flight last January 28th. I took the photo at a height of 3,200 feet. We were over London at the time (10.15am). The photo shows your son fixing up a broken exhaust pipe. He was slung by ropes over the side of the engine car. It is typical of his fearlessness carrying out his work. If the old ship does recommission we shall miss your son very much as he was the most conscientious man we had at his work. Only this morning Squadron Leader Booth said to me: 'We shall find Watts hard to replace if the ship goes out again.' This must be a very hard time for you and yours. I cannot hope to emulate the vicar's beautiful address but I must tell you how very deeply we feel for you and your sorrow.
Believe me. Yours sincerely, George F. Meager.'[42]

Did he take the photograph while *R100* was on its trials over London? Or was it taken on its Canadian voyage? His first letter, sent in 1930, is so detailed and despatched in the immediate aftermath of the tragedy that it seems likely to be the more accurate of the two.

Mr. Watts is the last of his family in Worstead. The shop and post office have closed, and Christmas Henry's tailoring business ceased long ago. Arthur Watts looked up from Granville's weed-strewn grave at the vast uninterrupted Norfolk sky, his cap shielded his eyes from the sun; painters know it as the *Norfolk Glare*. Pointing his stick at the flint steeple of Worstead church he said: 'In the past you'd have seen airships going over. It was a different Britain. Attitudes, manners, the way we feel about the country. It's all changed. If Granville were ever to come back, he wouldn't know it.'[43]

CYRIL BROUGHTON AND HENRY ADDINELL

D uring his research the author encountered many lives and families touched by the airship years. They included those of Cyril Broughton and Henry Addinell.

Cyril Broughton (1901–1966)

Like others in airships, Cyril Broughton had spent time in the merchant marine, in his case as a Hull trawlerman on Britain's east coast. It was a harsh life, poorly paid and dangerous. Fishermen and others in the merchant fleet were disciplined and tough and had a diversity of esoteric skills; useful characteristics in the building, servicing and sailing of airships. A life at sea was a good apprenticeship for the rigours of Howden, in east Yorkshire, where Barnes Wallis and Commander Burney ran a tight outfit and working conditions were basic: in the winter the site and construction shed were icy.

Mr. Broughton joined the airship service as a rigger and riveter. He worked at Howden building the *R100*, having served on Hull trawlers for twelve years. He was on the *R100* transatlantic voyage. In America the crew became known as The *R100* Boys, fêted by the wealthy and influential. Souvenirs were popular among members of the crew. Some were made from the wood of the dismantled Cardington mooring mast. Cyril had a cigarette box, used today to hold Susan Sampson's (his daughter) husband's cufflinks. Cyril and his wife lived at Hailgate, in Howden. Nevil Shute had digs in Hailgate Street. When Mr. Broughton returned to Cardington on *R100* from Canada a telegram was sent to the Broughton family in Hailgate saying '*R100* arrived Bedford quite safe'. It was signed 'Spencer,' thought to be S. T. Keeley, the *R100* wireless operator. The Broughton family also lived at Shortstown, in Cardington, where as a treat workers' children were given rides in the basket of a tethered 'humpty-dumpty' barrage balloon allowed to float up to the high roof of the giant hangars. Mrs.

Sampson, Cyril's daughter, was born at Shortstown in 1945. She can remember riding in the basket. The 'humpty-dumpty' balloon could only be used in the summer months: it was too cold in winter when the huge hangar doors froze on their hinges. After the *R101* calamity and the deliberate destruction of the *R100*, Mr. Broughton continued working at Cardington in an Air Ministry unit that built barrage balloons. He eventually rose through the ranks to become a warrant officer.

Henry Addinell (1898–1977)

Self-taught, meticulous, gifted at languages and adroit at mathematics, Henry Addinell, known as Harry, was born at Cargo, in Cumberland. An apprentice in Hull shipyards, as a young soldier he spent the final year of the First World War in northern Russia as a member of the expeditionary Syren Force. In 1927 he began work on the *R100*, being issued on 21 October 1929 with his coveted Airship Engineers Licence, No. 11. On 14 February 1933 he was issued with his Ground Engineers Aircraft Licence. A member of the *R100* advance party that went to Canada ahead of the airship to await its arrival and assist the ground crew in its mooring, he travelled by sea on the SS *Duchess of Richmond*, returning later aboard the *R100*. He is one of those thought to have helped Burney build his extraordinary-looking 'dragon' car. Fluent in German (an important asset at the time that would have been of interest to British Intelligence) on 28 February 1933 he was formally thanked by the Admiralty for translating the technical handbook of an aero engine developed by a foremost German designer, Helmuth Hirth. During the Second World War Mr. Addinell had a confidential government job. It could have been with the Intelligence services; his daughter Christine Addinell, born in 1938, said her father often travelled to Manchester and Northern Ireland with a locked briefcase bearing a crest and the initials GR. Subsequently, with a Cyril Huckle, who worked on *R100*, he established a workshop and patented inventions including a digital car lock. In 1952 his family watched the Coronation on his homemade TV; the picture was green as he had utilised an old radar screen. Other creations included an automated radiogram made of Meccano parts. He died at his home in Little Weighton, east Yorkshire, in April 1977.

Appendix D
A GLAMOROUS QUARTET

The Air Minister Lord Thomson was a debonair former soldier. Known as 'Kit', he was middle-class, cultured, a citizen of the world with friends across the political divide. He was passionate about aviation and airships; his critics said that was his problem – he was a dreamer, a romantic, his head too much in the air. Although deeply committed to aviation and convinced of its future, Thomson was not a technologist. His introduction to the airship was unusual. As a soldier in Bucharest he was taking a bath when a bomb from a Zeppelin destroyed his home and blew him, literally, out of his bathroom.[1]

Why Thomson joined the Labour Party is a mystery: his background and *milieu* made him a more obvious candidate for the political right. He twice failed to be elected as a Socialist Member of Parliament, so Ramsay MacDonald, recognising his flair and keen to make use of his considerable administrative skills, created him a peer.

Critics found Thomson suspiciously self-assured; perhaps pragmatism was the reason he had signed up to Britain's first Labour government. Whatever his motives – and admirers always insisted his sympathies lay sincerely with the underdog and the lower ranks – he and MacDonald forged a bond so close that it far exceeded the parameters of politics, becoming a deep friendship that seemed to personify the attraction of opposites.

The MacDonald government was a *real* Labour administration comprising the tribunes of the disenfranchised; it was ingenuous, though, and collectively untutored in the nuances of administration and the devious ways of State. Thomson bore MacDonald rare gifts: a former army officer, he wore authority lightly; he was familiar with command; of an urbane charm, he was versed in the social niceties; he mixed easily and could bridge the pronounced social and class divides of the inter-war years. His diplomacy would help the government cope with the entrenched banking, shipping and aviation lobbies; his finesse would calm the partisan claims of service chiefs and assuage the alarm of fellow politicians convinced dirigibles were a parlous waste of money and the Imperial airship scheme a *folie de grandeur*. Thomson would keep the rambunctious Burney in place and remind Vickers, which over the decades had become an empire in itself, that the climate had changed; under a Socialist government its role as the supreme Imperial arms supplier would be under surveillance.

Beyond aviation and politics there was another major influence in Thomson's life. As well as being smitten with flight he was head over heels in love. The woman who captivated his heart – and that of several others – was an exotic, and her admirers said exceedingly beautiful, Romanian countess, the Princess Marthe Bibesco. She and Thomson met in 1909 in Paris, where Thomson was attached to the British Embassy. Their romance blossomed during his later posting to Bucharest. But Marthe was already married. Her husband, Prince Georges-Valentin Bibesco, was her cousin, the eldest grandson of the last reigning Prince of Wallachia. The marriage was not a success. For some years her husband paid her little attention, reserving his passion for cars, sport and (with a certain irony) aviation. Marthe was a devout Roman Catholic, so, for her, divorce was never an option. An intoxicating mix of the cerebral and the coquettish, Bibesco wrote more than 40 books and was fluent in several languages. Ramsay MacDonald would also become enamoured: after Thomson's death he and Marthe remained devoted friends, indulging in lengthy and regular correspondence. The toast of Europe, she adored powerful men: Thomson fitted the bill. Tipped as a future Viceroy to India, he was tall, of an aristocratic bearing, well-connected and of an easy manner. For Marthe, with physical as well as intellectual appetites, Thomson represented the perfect *beau*.

Other principal figures in the political, economic, military and civil aviation 'loop' included the ebullient Sir Sefton Brancker, the determined and energetic Director of Civil Aviation. Brancker was a colourful and popular personality who had long preached the gospel of flying. An enthusiastic pilot, he was famed for flying around Britain opening flying clubs and encouraging civic groups to organise neighbourhood aerodromes and aviation facilities.

He was also a diminutive bundle of fun. Brancker's favourite trick, guaranteed to bring the house down at aviation dinners, was to swallow his monocle with a glass of water; he carried several spare monocles in the event of being obliged to perform this famous feat. He also kept an eye out for the ladies. Brancker and Thomson would sometimes 'paint the town red' – tall, suave, greying Thomson with the vivacious Marthe; Brancker, shorter but dapper, laughing, arm-in-arm with the raven-haired actress Auriol Lee (later to die in a car accident in Kansas). British born Lee, regularly on stage, made only two films, both directed by Alfred Hitchcock: *A Royal Divorce* (1938) in which she played Napoleon's mother, and *Suspicion* (1941), starring Cary Grant.

Aviation was still daring. Airships were the ocean liners of the heavens. The world of flight was exclusive, accessible only to the wealthy and to the privileged. Thomson and Brancker were powerful figures with beguiling companions. Their presence brought a touch of star-dust to the gossip columns of the day.

Crispin Rope, the son of Michael Rope, a prominent member of the *R101* design team, said: 'Thomson was a real phenomenon ... in the 1920s very few of his social class openly sided with the underdog. To me Thomson was a great man. Thomson was quite friendly with Tony Benn's father ... I personally do find Thomson extremely fascinating and in many ways a very attractive figure.'[2]

NOT FORGOTTEN: MICHAEL ROPE

Some of the people involved in airships went on to famously illustrious careers, notably Barnes Wallis and Nevil Shute. Others would die prematurely or be destined to remain largely unrecognised outside the airship domain. One such is Squadron Leader Michael Rope, the Assistant Chief Designer of the *R101*, whose abilities most believe surpassed those of Vincent 'Dopey' Richmond to whom he answered.

Rope was tall, lean and handsome. An inveterate pipe-smoker, devoutly religious, modest and diffident. He and his inventions played a crucial role in the *R101*. Educated at Shrewsbury School, he graduated in engineering from Birmingham University. His first jobs included a stint in locomotive engineering with the London, Brighton and South Coast Railway. In 1915–18 he was an engineer in the Royal Naval Air Service, responsible with Wing Commander Tom Cave-Browne-Cave for the design of *SS Zero* non-rigid airships which operated as submarine patrols and reconnaissance craft towards the end of the war. Rope transferred to the RAF on its formation, and from 1921–4 he was stationed at Hinaidi, Baghdad, as a technical staff officer in the Royal Air Force Middle East Command on heavier-than-air aircraft. During this period he gained his pilot's licence. He returned to airship work in 1924 as assistant designer of the *R101*.[1]

He was well-liked and highly regarded, but some have commented on his unassuming nature and have suggested that he was not strong enough to stand up to his boss, 'Dopey' Richmond, Lieutenant Colonel Vincent Crane Richmond, chief designer of *R101*. This can only be for conjecture; despite his modesty and diffidence there is evidence that he was unafraid of raising strong objections and committing his concerns to paper (brave, given the politics). His innovations included 'parachute wiring' for gasbags and automatic valves. He sent his superiors an explosive memo on

2 June 1930 as the building of *R101* drew to a close. Rope had carried out tests on the cover. He was exercised that it was not strong enough to withstand the expected levels of stress.

R100's cover had also caused concern. Rope's tests on the *R101* fabric showed that it tore and stretched more easily than at first thought. 'Laboratory experience cannot account for the deterioration,' he wrote in his memo. 'The only explanation that suggests itself is that, throughout the history of these covers, permanent extension has taken place locally rather than uniformly along the weft. Calculations and small scale laboratory experiments may be liable to large errors – but what scant information is available from these and other observations in the shed suggest that there is no margin of safety for flight in rough atmosphere.'[2] From a designer of authority it was a devastating note given the urgency to get the voyage to India underway. Despite his diffidence, he was not afraid to 'stick his head above the parapet'. His mettle was evident in the second part of the memo. 'It is for consideration as to whether the risk involved in sending either ship on a long overseas flight is – or is not – greater than is justified by the need to fulfil public expectation.'

Hopes for the ship were indeed at fever pitch. His memo fell like a shell on the desks of Richmond and Wing Commander R. B. B. (Reginald) Colmore, who led the *R101* project. Rope concluded: 'Is it not conceivable that a public statement could be made that would satisfy the people who matter – to the effect that overseas flights have been postponed for, say, six months on account of improvements that have been shown by test flights to be desirable before long flights could be undertaken with the reliability required of convincing demonstrations – etc – etc?'[3] His memo should have galvanised his superiors into telling the 'people who matter' that the Great Adventure would have to be postponed. It is clear from the note that Rope would not permit politics, rank or considerations of career to impede him in warning of possible calamity. His sense of duty and diffidence stemmed in part from his Roman Catholicism. It was Rope's way to solicit people's opinions and sometimes to stand aside for them; this was not weakness but indicative of an open-minded and attentive listener. Eve Atherstone, widow of the *R101*'s First Officer, remembers a 'good Catholic and a truly saintly man. Without exception everybody loved him. He was extremely modest and thoroughly sound at his job. There's no doubt that most of the good features of the ship derived from Rope's genius.'[4]

Rope's background indicates the depth of his convictions and the extent to which Roman Catholicism ran through his life. He had two brothers, one a Catholic priest, the other a doctor; and three sisters, a Carmelite nun, a Sister of Charity, and the third the first WRNS officer to command a unit outside Britain. Rope's wife, Lucy, had two sisters and two brothers: Katharine, a Sister of Charity, Margaret, a Carmelite nun; and her brothers were William Thory Fairfax, a priest of the Diocese of East Anglia, and Philip Oliver, a farmer, who carved the altar for the church at Kesgrave, in Suffolk, built in 1931 in memory of Michael Rope and in which, before the Chancel Arch, hangs a scale-model of the *R101* made by personnel at the Royal Airship Works in Cardington.

Michael's widow, Lucy, was 23 and seven months pregnant when her husband died; they had been married for 15 months. Insurance on his life and other inheritances enabled her to establish a charitable foundation, which she ran with her son, Crispin, born weeks after Michael's death. She became patron of the Airship Heritage Trust and built the church. Through the foundation she and Crispin supported a hospital for treating lepers at Jorochito in Bolivia, and St. Stephen's Hospital in Kampala, Uganda, which helps families impoverished by the scourge of aids. The foundation funds the Science and Human Dimension Project at Jesus College, Cambridge.

Lucy was born in 1907. She died at the age of 96 in 2003.[5] After a long and successful City career Crispin Rope now runs the foundation and has spent much of his life researching his father's ship, the *R101*, and its eventual fate. At 2.10 a.m. on Sunday 5 October 1930, Squadron Leader Michael Rope, the father Crispin never knew, died with his colleagues in northern France when his craft came down at Beauvais. At the time Lucy, Michael's young and heavily pregnant wife, was staying with her parents at Kesgrave, in Suffolk.

Lucy was woken by her father relatively early that Sunday. RAF stations had been notified by telephone of the disaster and the local telephone operator, kindly but against all the regulations, had rung her father William Oliver Jolly to tell him. The message was that there were just a few survivors but their names were not yet known. Later in the day Lucy learnt that Michael was not among the survivors. No later than Wednesday, much encouraged by her mother Alice, Lucy had decided to build a small chapel at Kesgrave in memory of Michael and his colleagues with the proceeds of Michael's life insurance. With his usual effectiveness, her father organised the necessary permissions, the design of the church and the choice of the builder, Reade of Aldeburgh, in Suffolk. Five family members made items for the church, in particular one of Michael's sisters, a Carmelite nun and noted stained glass artist, who designed and made windows. Lucy's brother, Philip, made the altar and some of the wooden furniture. The church formally opened on 8th December 1931, exactly 14 months after Lucy's decision.[6]

Initially the church was built to accommodate 40 people but after two major extensions the number has been increased to about 150, and the weekly congregation is some 300.

NOTES

1. The Birth of the Airship

1 Giffard, Henri (1825–82). Giffard's machine had a 3-horsepower engine and an 11-foot propeller fixed to a balloon with a rudder. In 1858 he patented a steam injector, which was used in locomotives and made him a fortune. Left estate to the State for humanitarian and scientific purposes. *Chambers Biographical Dictionary* (W.R. Chambers, 1990), 586.

2 *The Story of Flight*, ed. Bill Gunston (Sundial, 1973), 22–3.

3 Otto, Nikolaus August (1832–91), German inventor. Invented 4-stroke internal combustion engine 1876, its sequence named the Otto cycle. *Chambers Biog.*, 112.

4 *Giants in the Sky*, Douglas H. Robinson (University of Washington Press, 1973), 3.

5 Santos-Dumont, Alberto (1873–1932) Built the world's first airship station at Neuilly, France, 1903. Experimented with heaver-than-air machines flying 715 feet in a plane built on the principles of a box-kite. In 1909 he built a light monoplane, a forerunner of modern light aircraft. *Chambers Biog.*, 1295.

6 *Story* of *Flight*, Gunston, 23; *Giants*, Robinson, 3–5; *Shadow in the Clouds*, Douglas Botting (Kestrel, 1975), 4–9; *Flight*, R. G. Grant (DK, 2004), 13; *The World of Wings and Things*, Sir Alliott Verdon-Roe (Hurst & Blackhurst, 1938–9) 154–5; *Wings of Madness*, Paul H. Hoffman (Fourth Estate, 2003); *Man Flies*, Nancy Winters (Ecco Press,1997).

7 *Giants*, Robinson, 3–5; *An Encyclopaedia of the History of Technology*, Ian McNeil

(Routledge, 1989), 614–15.

8 Zeppelin, Count Ferdinand von (1838–1917). Served American Civil War in Union Army and Franco-German War. Began first rigid airship in 1897.

9 Schütte, Professor Johann. Conducted exhaustive testing into stress, aerodynamics, lightweight materials. Zeppelin was organised, popular, an energetic businessman, while Schütte was innovative, scientific, the factory dominated by academic theory and inefficient; *Giants*, 69, quoting Schütte in *Der Luftschiffbau Schutte-Lanz,1909–25* (Munich and Berlin: Druck u.Verlag von R. Oldenbourg, 1926), 2.

10 *A Manual of Naval Architecture*, W. H. White (Murray, 1894), 366; S. G. William Froude (1810–79). English engineer, naval architect, assistant I. K. Brunel 1837 overseeing railway construction. Used scale models in pioneer test-tank to assess effects on ships. Calculations on stress, hull, profile; the longitudinal gravity field and the mechanical properties of fluids and liquids permeated both submarine and airship design.

11 Schütte used plywood girders of glued aspen that he said were light and flexible; he tried to waterproof them with lacquer and paraffin wax; *Giants*, Robinson,70.

12 In 1906 Prussian Government asked German metallurgist Dr. Alfred Wilm (1869–1937) for alternative to metal used in cartridge cases. Created duralumin: 3–4% copper, 0.5–1% manganese, 0.5% magnesium, and in some formulae, silicon. *Biographical*

Dictionary of the History of Technology, Ian McNeil/Lance Dark (Routledge Reference, 1990), 482.

13 *Up Ship*, Douglas Robinson and Charles Keller (Naval Institute Press, 1982), 5

14 PRO ADM 131/64 Airships and balloons 1914–18; PRO ADM 226/14 Balloon forms; *To Ride the Storm*, Sir Peter Masefield (William Kimber, 1982), 441.

15 Museum of Army Flying, www.flying-museum.org.uk/the early days.htm; Royal Engineers Museum, www.remuseum. org.uk/specialism/rem spec aero.htm.

16 *The British Airship at War, 1914–1918*, Patrick Abbott (Terence Dalton, 1989), 11; www.raescardiff.innerdown.co.uk/ willows.htm, Willows (website Royal Aeronautical Society's Cardiff branch); *Twenty-One Years of Airship Progress*, Lieutenant Colonel W. Lockwood Marsh (*Flight*, 3 January 1930), 86; www.flightglobal.com/pdfarchive/view/1930, retrieved from http://en.wikipedia. org/wiki/ernest willows.

17 www.bbc.co.uk/dna/h2g2/A10358796; www.remuseum.org.uk/specialism/rem spe aero.htm (Royal Engineers Museum); www.flying-museum.org.uk/the early days.htm (Museum of Army Flying); *Wings*, Roe, 149–50.

18 Fisher, John Arbuthnot (1841–1920). Submarine and airship believer. Introduced *Dreadnought* battleships and *Invincible* battlecruisers in readiness for war with Germany. *Chambers Biog.*, 519; his supporters, technically-minded progressive naval officers, often described as being in Fisher's 'fishpond'.

19 Bacon, Captain, later Admiral Reginald (1863–1947). 'brilliant protégé of Fisher ... played a major role in the early development of British submarines'; *Giants*, Robinson, 146; friend and biographer of Admiral Sir John Jellicoe; *The Naval Air Service Vol.1, 1908–1918* ed. Captain S. W. Roskill (The Navy Records Society, 1969), 6.

20 Sueter, Rear Admiral Sir Murray Fraser (1872–1960). Roskill quoted in *Giants*, Robinson, 145, revealing in December 1917 Sueter wrecked his career by writing to King George V suggesting he (Sueter) be decorated for his role in developing the tank. In 1914

Sueter initiated the reorganisation of the RN Air Service as an integral part of the Navy; see Roskill, 5. Sueter's *The Evolution of the Submarine Boat, Mine and Torpedo, from the Sixteenth Century to the Present Time* (J. Griffin & Co., Portsmouth, 1907) in Admiral Sir Alexander Edward Bethell's papers in King's College Liddell Hart Centre. Sueter in the 'fishpond', technically minded young officers who surrounded Fisher; Sueter said 'it was impossible to get new ideas into old men's heads'. *Icarus over the Humber*, T. W. Jamison (Lampada Press, 1994), 35.

21 Submarines were analogous to airships in floating by displacement of a medium in that they were totally submerged; *Giants*, Robinson, 146.

22 Vickers archives Historic Document 524, pp 77–8; *Giants*, Robinson, 146–7; PRO ADM 131/164 Airships & Balloons 1914–1918; PRO ADM 226/14 Balloon forms and sundry details.

23 *Naval Air Service*, Roskill, Navy Records Society, 6.

24 Vickers, Register of Investments; *Vickers History*, J. D. Scott, (Weidenfeld & Nicolson, 1962).

25 Sueter interview Scott, notes dated 21/10/58 for *Vickers History*, Vickers His. Doc. 524.

26 Vickers His. Doc. 5324 71/13, May 10 1911.

27 Hartley Pratt, influential, technically accomplished, urbane, early friend of famed designer Barnes Wallis, with whom he worked closely; wrote *Commercial Airships*, H. B. Pratt (Thomas Nelson & Sons Ltd., 1920); *Barnes Wallis: A Biography*, J. E. Morpurgo (Longman, 1972).

28 Sturdee, Admiral Sir Frederick Charles Doveton (1859–1925). Six years after the *Mayfly* inquiry he commanded the battlecruiser *Invincible* in the action that wiped out the German squadron under von Spee off the Falklands in 1914. *Chambers Biog.*, 1413.

29 Vickers. His. Doc. 524; Liddell Hart papers, Bethell.

30 Asquith (1852–1928) succeeded Campbell-Bannerman as Prime Minister 1908; *The War in the Air, Vol.1* (Oxford, 1922), 181, quoted in *Battlefronts*, Kildare, 66, saying Britain should construct at least two Zeppelins.

Count von Zeppelin's name became the generic for all airships, not just those constructed in Germany.

31 Churchill Archive, CHAR 13/22a/126-7, June 12 1913.

32 Appendix D

33 Vickers. His. Doc. 524; *Storm*, Masefield, 443.

34 NMM 1 DEY/34.

35 Tennyson-d'Eyncourt, Sir Eustace (1869–1951). Director Admiralty Naval Construction 1912–23. Designed HMSS *Nelson* and *Rodney* and cruisers *Frobisher* and *Effingham*. In First World War designed 40-knot motor boats, with skimming hulls, designs influenced by experiments into stress and drag using test tanks and models by naval architects/engineers William Froude and son, T. E. Froude in the nineteenth century. *Obituaries from The Times, 1951–60* (Newspaper Archive Developments, 1979).

36 NMM DEY/34/MSS72/030.

37 *Storm*, Robinson, 443.

38 *British Airship*, Abbott, 83–4, 89; *Airship Pilot No.28*, Lord Ventry (Blandford Press, 1982). Ventry was adjutant at Howden airship station 1919. Owned his own ship *Bournemouth* 1946–52. Details *Bournemouth* and British Airship Club PRO DR 16/71, PRO DR1/27, PRO DR 33/530. A friend of Ventry was Squadron Leader T. P. York-Moore, airship captain May 1915–19; papers in National Maritime Museum NMM M58/031.

39 CHAR 13/29/141, September 10 1914.

40 CHAR 13/29/141.

41 Phipps-Hornby papers include War Office reports of anti-submarine activities dated December 16 1916, NMM PH 210B.

42 Papers of airshipman Wing Commander T. R. Cave-Browne-Cave refer to *SS* airships in Imperial War Museum archives. Handwritten note by Sueter (difficult to read) headed *How we defeated the Zeppelins*, IWM Misc. 215 item 3116. Assorted airship papers, some anonymous and undated, IWM Misc. 155.T. Box 8.

43 PRO ADM 1/8488/97 submarines spotted by airships, Dover 1917; *Airship Pilot*, Ventry.

44 Vickers Hist. Doc. 524 enc.89/96 notes for article by J. D. Scott, October 1958; also *Brassey's Naval Annual 1916* (B187) Chapter

IV *Aircraft and War* pp 88–107 and *Brassey's 1918 raids/limitations*, 103.

45 PRO ADM 116/1335 airship service improved; airshipman Captain T. B. Williams supervised building of early masts. Logbooks mention sailing over Hackney Marshes and Shoreditch in fog, navigating by following railway lines; IWM DS/Misc/96; T. B. Williams papers, RAF Museum archives, Hendon.

46 Geddes, Sir Eric Campbell (1875–1937) politician, businessman. First Lord 20 July 1917. 'Geddes Axe' 1921–2 cut education, transport, proposed single ministry to replace three service ministries. Unfairly dismissed Jellicoe after a disagreement.

47 PRO ADM 116/1915 memo Geddes to War Cabinet 27 August 1918.

48 PRO ADM 116/1915 (1919, 1923–5) August 30 1917.

49 Wright brothers made first heavier-than-air flight recognised by standards body Fédération Aéronautique Internationale, Kitty Hawk, 17 December 1903.

50 *Giants*, Robinson, 84–90.

51 PRO ADM 137/4168, Notes on disposition of German airships and submarines.

52 Joffre, Joseph Jacques Césaire (1852–1931). French Chief of Staff 1914; Commander-in-Chief 1915–16.

53 CHAR 13/41/49 & CHAR 13/42/37; *Wings*, Roe, 95.

54 *The Oxford Companion to the Second World War*, ed. I. C. B. Dear (Oxford University Press, 1995), 24.

55 Interview author and Brad King, 5 May 2004, director HMS *Belfast*, specialist early aviation, author *The Royal Naval Air Service* (Hikoki publications, 2001).

56 Phipps Hornby, Admiral Robert Stewart, (1866–1956). Phipps-Hornby correspondence throws light on Zeppelin defences; correspondence with Admiralty and Royal Commission on awards to inventors (1915–20); Phipps-Hornby had Co-op shop in Westminster send him fishing line (still in files) to suspend anti-Zeppelin net around London from tethered small airships. The net would be laced with grenades. The Admiralty felt exploding aerial grenades posed a threat to citizens below even greater than that of the Zeppelins. Net turned down for a prize by

Inventions Board: somebody else thought of it first. National Maritime Museum NMM/PHI 210 A/B H1/210/E papers Admiral Phipps-Hornby.

57 Detailed map airship dispositions Europe 1914; PRO FO 925/30036.

58 *Zeppelins and Super Zeppelins*, R. P. Hearne (Bodley Head, MCMXV1), 9.

59 PRO ADM 186/559, German airships 1917–18; *The Zeppelins*, Captain Ernst A. Lehmann and Howard Mingos (G. P. Putnam, 1927), 45–53. Lehmann was German naval officer who later assisted Eckener, Zeppelin's protégé. According to *Giants*, Robinson, 251, Lehmann in 1917 conducted experiments to test airship lift and crew endurance. He loaded a ship with 2,650 pounds worth of bombs, 7,700 pounds of water-ballast, 6,600 pounds of machine-guns and ammunition, 29 men, 2,400 pounds of oil, and 37,300 pounds of petrol. Dodging thunderstorms, he flew non-stop for 101 hours to see if the crew, divided into watches and sleeping in 20 hammocks, could tolerate prolonged sailing and sleep deprivation. The success of the experiment encouraged the epic journey by Zeppelin *L59* from Bulgaria to the Sudan.

60 *Flight*, Grant, 97.

61 PRO/FO 881/10300, papers on incendiary bullets. A. J. P. Taylor, *English History 1914–45* (Oxford, Clarendon Press, 1965), 4, writes 1,117 civilians; 296 combatants lost lives through Zeppelin bombing: 'The raids caused much dislocation and outcry; U-boats and Zeppelins heightened popular hysteria.'

62 *The Zeppelins*, Lehmann and Mingos, 52.

63 *Up Ship*, Robinson and Keller, 5.

64 Strasser, Peter, ensured the future of German airships after negotiating with Tirpitz (1849–1930), Grand Admiral of the German Fleet, commander of the German navy August 1914 to March 1916; *Naval Warfare*, ed. Richard Humble (Little, Brown, 2002). Strasser disliked Schütte-Lanz wooden ships calling crews 'glue-potters'; *Giants*, Robinson, 91. Worked with Scheer (1863–1928) Commander-in-Chief of the High Seas Fleet; according to Robinson, the two met in 1916 to plan a Strasser-led Zeppelin raid on the Midlands that led to the reorganisation of British home defences.

65 *Pulham Pigs*, Gordon Kinsey (Terence Dalton,1988), 46

66 *First Blitz*, Neil Hanson (Doubleday, 2008) 312–13; *Over the Battlefronts*, Peter Kilduff (Arms & Armour, 1996), 66.

67 *Pulham Pigs*, Kinsey, 47.

68 *Pulham Pigs*, Kinsey, 47, quoting *The Story of a North Sea Air Station*, C. F. Snowden Gamble (Oxford University Press, 1928) and Neville Spearman, 1967. The entire crew of 22 died in Strasser's ship.

2. The Airship Stations

1 Conversation author and Jeffrey Bowles, 18 September 2009.

2 *Pulham Market Society* paper, 1989, Jocelyn Rawlence, Norman Peake, *70th anniversary R34's double Atlantic crossing 1919*; conversation author and Graham King and Hilary Hardy, 9 June 2009; extensive further research by the late Dr. Patrick Rawlence. http://pennoyers.org.uk.

3 *Pulham* paper, Rawlence, Peake.

4 *Pulham* paper, Rawlence, Peake.

5 *Pulham Pigs – History of an Airship Station*, Gordon Kinsey (Terence Dalton, 1988), 26.

6 Nigel Caley letter to author, 2 June 2007.

7 Air Commodore E. M. Maitland began career as army officer Essex Regiment 1900. Took up ballooning 1908 achieving international recognition with Professor Auguste Eugene Gaudron (1868–1913), professional balloonist/maker in Paris, and Major C. C. Turner, former air correspondent *The Daily Telegraph*, flying balloon *Mammoth* Crystal Palace to Meeki Derevi, Russia, 1,117 miles, 36.5 hours. Gaudron built Barton airship 230,000 cubic feet, 50-horsepower Buchet engine, developed business team that controversially included females. In 1913 Maitland made first parachute descent from airship *Delta*. Maitland axial making parachutes crucial in airships/compulsory RAF aircraft. First Transatlantic crossing *R34*; died in *R38* calamity. www.rafweb.org/Biographies/ MaitlandE.htm; www.flightglobal.com/pdfarchive/view/1948; *Flight*, 23 December 1948, 748; Nigel Caley airship library, author/Caley interview, unpublished Caley essay, 2 June 2007; nigelcaley@live.com; http://www.ballooninghistory.com/whoswho.

8   Author/Caley interview, unpublished essay, 2007.

9   *Pulham* paper, Rawlence, Peake, 1989; *Pulham Pigs*, Kinsey.

10 *Giants*, Robinson, 178, quoting T. B. Williams, *Airship Mooring in England, The Airship*, vol. 5 No.18 April–June, 1938, 16; *The British Rigid Airship, 1908–31*, Robin Higham (G. T. Foulis & Co. 1961), 352.

11 *Jane's Pocket Book 7 – Airship Development*, Lord Ventry, Eugene Kolesnik, 1976; *Zeppelin! The German Airship Story*, Manfred Griehl, Joachim Dressel, 1990; Airship Heritage Trust, www.aht.ndirect.co.uk/R33.

12 *Pulham Pigs*, Kinsey, 137.

13 Conversation author and Peter West, 21 September 2009.

14 *Barnes Wallis*, Morpurgo, 74.

15 *Howden's Airship Station*, Kenneth Deacon (Langrick Publications, 2003), ISBN 0-9546606-0-9; *The Men and Women who Built and Flew the R100*, Kenneth Deacon (Langrick, 2008), ISBN 978-0-9540660-1-7; Airship Heritage Trust www.aht.ndirect.co.uk/sheds/Howden.htm

3. Control, Commercial Opportunity and Controversy

1   The *Naval Air Service, Captain S. W. Roskill*, Navy Records Society, 1969.

2   *Naval Air*, Roskill, 4.

3   Char. 13/20, 106-108, Roberts to Churchill, 1 December 1913.

4   Char. 13/20, 106-108, Churchill to Roberts, 4 December 1913.

5   *Voices in Flight*, Anna Malinovska and Muriel Joslyn (Pen & Sword Aviation, 2006), 55–64. Goddard served in the Royal Naval Air Service during the Great War and was a senior commander in the Royal Navy in the Second World War. In 1915 he served at Barrow-in-Furness and at Capel as an Airship Officer and met his lifelong friend Barnes Wallis. For a time he patrolled the North Sea for submarines. During the Battle of the Somme he assisted the Royal Flying Corps by using his airship to drop agents behind enemy lines at night. Later he read engineering at Jesus College, Cambridge, becoming the first instructor at Cambridge University Air Squadron. In 1941, just prior to the Japanese attack on Pearl Harbor, he

became Air Commodore Chief of the Air Staff Royal New Zealand Air Force. He commanded the RNZAF at the Battle of Guadalcanal and the Solomon Islands campaigns. Later he went to Washington as the RAF representative. The principal of the College of Aeronautics and President of the Airship Association 1975–84, he spent years investigating the spirit world; *The Airmen Who would not Die*, John G. Fuller (Puttnam, 1979) about medium Eileen Garrett and *R101* seances.

6   Smuts, Jan Christian (1870–1950). South African statesman. Entrusted during First World War with operations in German East Africa, joined Lloyd George's War Cabinet. Prime Minister South Africa 1919–24, 1939–48. *Chambers Biog.*, 1366.

7   Trenchard, Hugh Montague, 1st Viscount (1873–1956). Entered the forces in 1893 serving on the NW Frontier in South Africa. Chief of Air Staff 1919–29. Raised to peerage 1930. *Chambers Biog.*, 1473; *Trenchard*, Andrew Boyle (Collins, 1962); *The War in the Air*, Walter Raleigh (Oxford Clarendon Press, 1922) vol.1 Chapt. VIII: *The Expansion of the Air Force*, covers Trenchard, Brancker, *SS* airships pp 410–89; *War in Air*, vol. II, H. A. Jones (Oxford Clarendon Press, 1928) covers Sueter on early naval flying, 159. Also *Into Wind: A History of British Naval Flying*, Hugh Popham (Hamish Hamilton, 1969), 1–5 covers early naval air service, Bacon, Sueter.

8   Brancker, Sir William Sefton (1877–1930). Director Civil Aviation 1925. Described as 'short, dapper, monocled, high spirited'. *Dictionary of National Biography* 1922–1931 ed. J. R. H. Weaver (Oxford University Press, 1937), 105.

9   Harmsworth, Harold Sydney, 1st Viscount Rothermere. Irish newspaper magnate. Brother of Alfred Harmsworth (Lord Northcliffe) also a leading newspaper proprietor. Rothermere, whose family today owns Britain's Associated Newspapers (*Daily Mail, Mail on Sunday*) built up the *Daily Mirror* to a circulation of three million in 1922. Air Minister 1917–18. *Chambers Biog.*, 670.

10 *Naval Air*, Roskill, 609; *Trenchard*, Boyle.

11 Dr. Giles Campion, editor *Dirigible*, journal

of Airship Heritage Trust; from his PhD thesis: *Rediscovering the Arcane Science of Ground Handling Large Airships*, School of Engineering and Mathematical Science, City University, London, 2007.

12 *The British Rigid Airship, 1908–1931*, Robin Higham, (Foulis, 1961) Chapter XII.

13 *The Zeppelin*, Christopher Chant (David & Charles, 2000), 35.

14 *L59* carried 15 tons of supplies and medicines to von Lettow-Vorbeck holding out against British forces in German East Africa. The heat from the sun expanded her hydrogen causing gas to be blown off via an automatic valve. *L59* never moored in the Sudan, finding on arrival that von Lettow-Vorbeck had been defeated; *Giants*, Robinson, 254.

15 Airship company registrations are likely to be higher over a 19-year span; 14 is based on incomplete Board of Trade records.

16 PRO BT 31/14172/131375 BoT registration papers White Star Airship company.

17 Layers of skin were also glued instead of stitched. A Berlin factory began making rubberised fabric that was less costly and laborious than goldbeaters' skin.

18 PRO Avia 2/1796, 23 April 1919.

19 Unpublished paper, *R34, The First Great Transatlantic Airship*, by Grant Newman, RAF Hendon museum; interview author and Newman, 23 March 2004; Avia 2/1796 Ctte. Civil Aviation file reg.no. B11105.

20 PRO Avia 2/1796.

21 PRO Avia 2/1796.

22 J. D. Scott, author of Vickers company history, said Vickers had been treated unfairly; the company had done sterling work for the Admiralty pioneering submarines and lost over £50,000 on *Mayfly*; Vickers Hist. Doc. 524.

23 A note by Flight Lieutenant Herbert Irwin, famous later as captain of the *R101*, postmarked Royal Airship Works, Cardington, 12 February 1929, proposed that 'elephants recruited from all the wandering fairs in the country might replace the large ground handling crews if airships were to become a commercial proposition'. Imperial War Museum Archives IWM Misc. 155 T. Box 8.

24 Barnes Wallis letter to Sir Victor Goddard, 12 September 1974.

25 PRO AIR 11/161; Vickers Hist. Doc. 524; *Giants*, Robinson, 174–5; *Commercial Airships*, Pratt, 39–53.

4. Triumph, Catastrophe and Cover-Up

1 Interview author and Grant Newman, RAF Museum, Hendon, 23 March 2004; Newman is author of *The First Great Transatlantic Airship* (unpublished paper) that gives a detailed account of the *R34*.

2 PRO AIR 11/163 log *R34*.

3 Private interview between author and Brad King, 5 May 2004, author *The Royal Naval Air Service 1912–1918* (Hikoki publications, 1997).

4 *Icarus over the Humber, The Last Flight of Airship R38/ZR2*, T. W. Jamison (Lampada Press, 1994), 54.

5–9 *New York Times*, 14 July 1919, page 1, col. 7.

10 PRO BJ 5/17 & PRO 5/20 reports by Meteorological Office.

11 At 643 feet R34 was called 'tiny' by her crew. www.airshipsonline.com/airships/r34/index.html; Airship Heritage Trust is an excellent site; see also Appendix B.

12 PRO AIR 11/162 & AIR 11/163.

13 *Giants*, Robinson, 162; PRO Air/1 Cardington Aero Works 1911–39

14 'Like a cracked egg,' Len Deighton and Arnold Schwartzman's description of the *R38* disaster in *Airshipwreck* (Jonathan Cape, 1978), 44.

15–16 Interview author and Tom Jamison at his home in Anlaby, Hull, 26 August 2009.

17 Nigel Caley, airship historian, unpublished paper, June 2007.

18 *Pulham Pigs*, Kinsey, 88.

19 *Slide Rule, The Autobiography of an Engineer*, Nevil Shute (Heinemann, 1954), 55.

20 *Giants*, Robinson, 173.

21 Edward Masterman joined the Royal Navy 1894 aged 14. Britannia Naval College. On HMS *Revenge* learned about new weapon, torpedoes; involved in Navy's attempt to build an airship 1911. Commander 1912 Naval Airship section. In First World War in Royal Naval Air Service commanding Farnborough Airship Station, transferring to RAF on formation 1 April 1918. Before end of war promoted brigadier general in

command RAF No. 22 (Marine Operational) Group, rank commuted Air Commodore when current RAF ranks came into being.

22 Mary, Barnes Wallis's daughter, married Harry Stopes-Roe, son of Dr. Marie Stopes (1880–1958), pioneer advocate of birth control; father Humphrey Verdon-Roe. With brother Alliott Verdon-Roe, Humphrey founded Avro aircraft 1 January 1910; Avro 504 front line aircraft in First World War. At Cambridge Harry read astrophysics and later philosophy; Mary, historian and psychologist, worked Birmingham University; *Wings and Things*, Verdon-Roe, 24, 64.

23 Barnes Wallis letter, private collection Mary Stopes-Roe (née Wallis).

24 Guest, Captain Frederick, (1875–1937) Secretary of State Air April 1921 to October 1922.

25 PRO ADM 116/2358, *R38* findings; PRO DSIR 23/1698, *R38* accident report Aug. 23 1921–2; private papers Wing Commander T. R. Cave-Browne-Cave, Imperial War Museum; PRO H045/22869 Home Office papers, 1921, loss of *R38*.

26 *Lighter than Air*, David Owen (Quintet, 1999), 65.

27 *A Wrack Behind*, Lord Kings Norton, *Aeronautical Journal*, Kings Norton commemorative issue, **vol. 103** [?], No. 1022, April 1999.

5. An Aerial Navy

1 PRO 116/1915 Dec. 4 1918.

2 PRO ADM 116/1915 Dec. 12 1918.

3 PRO ADM 116/1915 Feb. 6 1919, Admiralty Board Minutes.

4 PRO ADM 116/1915.

5 PRO ADM 116/1915; *Giants*, Robinson, 166.

6 Amery, Lieutenant Colonel Rt. Hon. Leopold Charles Maurice Stennet (1873–1955) First Lord Admiralty October 1922 to January 1924.

7 PRO ADM 116/1915, Scott to Admiralty; PRO ADM 101/442, Pulham station.

8 PRO ADM 116/1915; PRO ADM 116/1431, seaplane and early experiments.

9 PRO AVIA 6/4417 Experiments launching planes from *R33* similar to those Scott mentioned; see also *RNAS*, King.

10 PRO ADM/1607 Case 5764, airship policy

1917–1918, cost of steel airship sheds.

11 In 1926 the US Navy built airships *Akron* and *Macon* as aircraft carriers, with hangars for five fighters. On 2 April 1933 *Akron* was lost over the Atlantic; of 73 men, three were saved; *Airshipwreck*, Deighton and Schwartzman, 60–2; *Giants*, Robinson, 221; planes off airships/lighters towed behind surface ships, *RNAS*, King.

12 ADM 116/1915, letter Scott to Amery 20 March 1922.

13 PRO AIR 1/656/17/122/547, Treasury note 3 October 1913 to Admiralty. Admiralty bought Pulham £10,500; PRO ADM 16/1915, Amery note to DCNS and ACNS March 1922 response to Scott.

14 PRO ADM 116/1915 ACNS to Amery 22 March 1922.

15 *The Dictionary of National Biography (DNB) 1961–1970*, ed. E. T. Williams and C. S. Nicholls (Oxford University Press, 1981), *Dictionary of Business Biography* vol.1, ed. David J. Jeremy (Butterworth, 1984), *The Times Obituaries 1961–1970* (Newspaper Archive Development, 1975).

16 PRO AIR 8/60, Burney to Trenchard 28 March 1922.

17 PRO ADM 116/1915, Amery to Lee, 8 April 1922.

18 After exhaustive efforts by Waley Cohen, the engine was abandoned by Wallis because it was not ready; BNWBB1/1, 21 March 1922; *Giants*, Robinson, 300.

19 House of Commons library, *Hansard* vol. 153 col. 393, 12 April 1922.

20 PRO ADM 116/3327, Admiralty note headed ACNS Bellairs to Lee, 5 May 1922.

21 PRO AIR 8/60, Burney Scheme; AIR 5/349, Burney/Admiralty agreements; PRO PREM 1/51, Burney Scheme.

22 PRO AIR 5/908; PRO AIR 19/546; PRO ADM 116/3327.

23 PRO ADM 116/3327, Burney to Admiralty, 4 May 1922.

24 PRO ADM 116/3327, Admiralty memo Amery to unknown recipient, 5 May 1922. Bonar Law (1858–1923), Prime Minister October 1922 to May 1923. *Chambers Biog.*, 868.

25 *English History*, Taylor, 195.

26 PRO ADM 116/3327; PRO ADM 1/8657/34; Roger John Brownlow Keyes

(1872–1945) May 1925, C-in-C
Mediterranean Fleet, 1926 promoted
Admiral, 1930 Admiral of the Fleet; *DNB*
1941–50, 449.

27 PRO CAB 16/41, Cabinet papers
mentioning Burney,, 1922.

28 PRO ADM 116/3327, Lee to CID, 27 May
1922.

29 PRO ADM 1/8657/34, personal papers
Keyes DCNS 1922–4; Cabinet memo
Stevenson Horne, 12 June 1922.

30 PRO ADM 1/8657/34, Cabinet paper 4053,
Churchill 21 June 1922; Minutes Defence
sub-committee 12 July 1922.

31 House of Commons debates vol.155, col.
2297, 29 June 1922.

32 HoC debates. vol. 156, col. 1705/6, 17 July
1922.

33 PRO ADM 1/8657/34, Minutes Defence
sub-committee CID, 12 July 1922.

34 Curzon was a frequent advocate of the
Burney Scheme; Curzon, Francis Richard
Henry Penn (1884–1964) Captain RNVR
from 1921. Former naval commander.
Conservative MP Battersea South 1918–29;
succeeded to peerage as Earl Howe.

35 HoC debates vol. 156, col. 1705, 17 July
1922; *Storm*, Masefield, 450.

36 Lloyd George coalition government collapsed
when Tories withdrew support. Germany
gripped by inflation; 30 October 1922
Fascists ousted Italian government; *Chronicle
of the World* (DK, 1996).

37 PRO AIR 8/60; PRO AIR 5/591; *Storm*,
Masefield, 450.

38 Thomson twice stood unsuccessfully as
Socialist MP. Chairman Royal Aero Club.
Raised to peerage as Baron Thomson of
Cardington, taking title from the
Bedfordshire village of the Royal Airship
Works. Close friend of Ramsay MacDonald;
'charming, easy-going, man of the world,'
Ramsay MacDonald, David Marquand
(Jonathan Cape, 1977), 409.

39 PRO AIR 8/60; *Storm*, Masefield, 451.

40 PRO ADM 116/3327.

41 PRO ADM 116/3327, Burney to Admiralty,
9 February 1923.

42 PRO ADM 116/1915, Amery to CID 15
February 1923.

43 PRO ADM 1/8641/124, Hemming
Admiralty, 27 February 1923.

44 PRO ADM 1/8641/124 Hemming
Admiralty 27 February 1923; Admiralty
reject Hemming, 8 March 1923; letters
Boothby to Anderson and Eckener, 30 March
1923; Admiralty reject Boothby Scheme, 1
May 1923.

45 PRO ADM 116/1915, Amery reacts to
Hoare, internal Admiralty note, 15 March
1923.

46 PRO ADM 116/1915, Amery to CID, 26
March 1923.

47 PRO ADM 116/3327 Hussey to Murray, 19
March 1923; Murray, 5 April 1923.

48 PRO ADM 116/3327, Moore to Burney, 20
April 1923.

49 PRO ADM 116/3327, Hemming to Moore,
CID, 4 May 1923.

50 BNW BB1/2; *Commercial Airways*, Pratt.

51 PRO AIR 5/591, CID on Burney Scheme,
10 July 1923.

52 PRO ADM 116/1915, Devonshire telegram,
26 July 1923.

6. Glued to the Earth

1 *The Times*, 23 August 1923, page 11 col. c.

2 PRO ADM 116/3327, memo 3 September
1923, Reg. No. gd 3192/23.

3 PRO ADM 116/1915, Boothby Admiralty
25 August 1923; Admiralty reply 9 October
1923

4 PRO AIR 5/331 Enc. 2, Admiralty memo, 6
October 1923.

5 PRO AIR 5/331, Admiralty Technical Heads
of Agreement, 6 October 1923; Admiralty to
Sir W. F. Nicholson at Air Ministry, 6
October 1923; internal Air Mininstry note
on Admiralty memo to Nicholson, 19
October 1923.

6 PRO AIR 8/60, internal Air Ministry memo,
14 December 1923.

7 Sinclair, Major Sir Archibald (1890–1970),
Liberal MP Caithness and Sutherland.

8 Sinclair, HoC debates 1923–4 vol. 161, col.
2618, 23 March 1923.

9 Burney, HoC debates 1923–4 vol. 161, col.
2620, 23 March 1923.

10 Frank Herbert Rose (1857–1928), Labour
MP West Aberdeen December 1918 to
January 1928.

11 Rose, HoC debates vol. 161, col. 164, 14
March 1923.

12 The USA had monopoly on non-

inflammable helium. Helium is marginally heavier than hydrogen, offering slightly reduced lift and vastly more expensive. Discovered by French astronomer Jannsen and British scientists Franklin and Locker in 1868. Named after 'helios', Greek for 'sun'. Found in natural gas fields in Kansas, Texas, Utah and Wyoming. *The Story of the Airship*, Hugh Allen (Goodyear Tire & Rubber, 1932); York-Moore papers contain booklet *Aviation Progress 1968 Goodyear Aviation*, with an article, 'Hot Air, Helium and History', NMM/LN/MS/81/031.

13 Caillard, Sir Vincent Henry Penalver (1856–1930). Fluent in Eastern languages, knew India well. Negotiated Vickers contracts around the world. His contacts were invaluable to Burney and AGC; *DNB* 1922–30, 151.

14 PRO Board of Trade 31/32606/194068, AGC Registration documents, 28 November 1923.

15 Vickers (VA) Historical Document (HD) 913, 5 December 1923.

16 PRO AIR/19, Thomson private office papers; *Giants*, Robinson, 257,

17 *Giants*, Robinson, 259.

18 *Story*, Allen, 17.

19 Hungarian Paul Jaray (1889–1974). Born Vienna. Joined Zeppelin 1914. Streamline expert. Set up wind tunnel. Developed teardrop shape Zeppelin, radically different to narrow cylindrical configuration. Later worked on car design. Influenced design of bicycle. Ran consultancy in Switzerland, where he lived until death.

20 *Story*, Allen, 17; *Giants*, Robinson, 257–9.

21 *Mathematics*, Stopes-Roe, 94–5.

22 Barnes Wallis archive, BNW BB1/1; BB1/2.

23 Report by Burney/Wallis on a visit to Zeppelin Works, Friedrichshafen, 25 May 1923.

24 Ibid.

25 Ibid.

26 *Mathematics with Love*, Mary Stopes-Roe, 82.

27 *Mathematics*, Stopes-Roe, 82–3

28 Ibid.

29 Ibid.

30 Ibid.

31 Ibid.

32 Burney/Wallis, Friedrichshafen, 1923, pp 4-6

33 Ibid.

34 Ibid.

35 Ibid.

36 *Mathematics*, Stopes-Roe, 94–5.

37 *The Paravane Adventure*, L. Cope-Cornford (Hodder & Stoughton, 1919), 77.

38 *Mathematics*, Stopes-Roe, pp 95, 96

39 Ibid.

40 Ibid.

41 Author, conversation with Mary Stopes-Roe, 16–17 July 2009

42 *Mathematics*, Stopes-Roe, 99–100

43 *Barnes Wallis*, Morpurgo, 114.

7. New Order

1 PRO AIR 8/60, Burney Scheme summary Thomson, 11 February 1924.

2 PRO AIR 8/60, unsigned Air Ministry memo, 20 February 1924.

3 Char 22/43, Cabinet meetings 1 May and 7 May 1924.

4 PRO PREM 1/51, 14 May 1924.

5 House of Lords vol. 57 cols. 573, 586, 21 May 1924.

6 HoC debates vol. 161, cols. 1696/7.

7 Author/Stopes-Roe, 16–17 July 2009.

8 *British Rigid*, Higham, 97.

9 *British Rigid*, Higham, 199.

10 Dr. Albert Francis Zahm, American prize-winning aeronautical scientist, academic, wind-tunnel pioneer. Chief research engineer Curtiss Aeroplanes 1914–15. Guggenheim chair of Aeronautics 1930–46; involved controversy that Wright brothers did not make first powered flight. *Wilbur and Orville*, Fred Howard (Dover, 1998), 435; *Aerial Navigation*, Albert Francis Zahm (D. Appleton & Co.,1911).

11 *Giants*, Robinson, 174–5.

12 Caley letter to author, 2 June 2007.

13 *Wallis*, Morpurgo, 67.

14 Caley letter author, 2 June 2007.

15 Author conversation Stopes-Roe, 16–17 July 2009.

16 Ibid.

17 'Innovations in *R100*: Construction Notes from a Manuscript Handbook', Norman Peake, in *Dirigible*, the journal of Airship Heritage Trust (AHT), August 1999, 13.

18 *Rigid*, Higham, 286.

19 'Innovations', Peake, AHT, August 1999, 13.

20 *Wrack*, Kings Norton, extract in *Aeronautical Journal*, April 1999, 189.

21 'Innovations', Peake, AHT, August 1999, 13–14.

22 Author/Caley, 25 August 2009.

23 'Innovations', Peake, AHT, August 1999, 13–14.

24 *Rigid*, Higham.

25 *Slide Rule*, Nevil Shute (Heinemann Ltd., 1954), 285. Shute was a Cambridge-educated engineer who later quit aviation and achieved world recognition writing 25 novels. In the Second World War he joined the RNVR and, like Burney, worked on secret weapons.

26 Author conversation Peter Davison, former aviation curator London Science Museum, member Historical Group RAeS, Kesgrave, Suffolk, 11 November 2009.

27 Author conversation Crispin Rope, Kesgrave, Suffolk, 11 November 2009.

28 Crispin Rope letter to author, 7 December 2009.

29 *Slide Rule*, Shute, 54; *The Secret War 1939–45*, Gerald Pawle (Harrap, 1956) about Admiralty Department of Miscellaneous Weapon Development, known as 'Wheezers and Dodgers'.

30 BNW BB8/5 article Nevil Shute, *The Airship Venture*, 2 May 1933; see also *Slide Rule*, 58. Shute's company Airspeed made the *Courier* aircraft, notable for first retractable undercarriage, and other aeroplanes with important roles in the Second World War: the *Oxford* trainer, of which 8,586 were built, and the *Horsa* military glider. *Airspeed: the Company and its Aeroplanes*, D. H. Middleton (Dalton, 1982); *British Gliders and Sailplanes 1922–1970*, Norman Ellison (Adam & Charles Black, 1971), 57. Airspeed moved to Portsmouth's new airport in 1932; Germany's airship *Graf Zeppelin* flew over to mark the occasion and to reconnoitre naval dockyard. *Airspeed*, Middleton, 26.

31 Author conversation Mary Stopes-Roe, 16–17 July 2009, Birmingham

32 Author conversation Mary Stopes-Roe, 16–17 July 2009, Birmingham.

33 Letter Molly Wallis to Mary Turner, 10 April 1926.

34 Molly Wallis/Turner, 7 May 1926.

35 Wallis/Turner, 14 May 1926.

36 Author conversation Mary Stopes-Roe, 16–17 July 2009.

37 Wallis/Turner, 11 July 1926.

38 *Slide Rule*, Shute, 72–3.

39 Author conversation Nigel Caley, 31 July 2009.

40 Author/Stopes-Roe, 16–17 July 2009.

41 Wallis/Turner, 14 March 1927.

42 Wallis/Turner, 3 June 1927.

43 Author/Stopes-Roe, 16–17 July 2009.

44 Wallis/Turner, 5 August 1927.

45 *Barnes Wallis*, Morpurgo, 15.

46 Wallis/Turner, 9 September 1927.

47 Wallis/Turner, December 1927.

48 M.Wallis, 'Red Stocking', *Wycombe High School Magazine*, undated, 1927.

49 *Commemorative booklet, R100, July 5, 1928*, facsimile republished Barnes Wallis Memorial Trust, 7–8.

50 Wallis/Turner, 30 June 1928.

51 Author/Stopes-Roe, 16–17 July 2009.

52 Author/ Caley, 23 September 2009

53 *Lloyd Loom woven fibre furniture*, Lee J. Curtis (Salamander, 1991), 7–13; airship lounge photograph Hulton Deutsch collection *c*.1929.

54 *Slide Rule*, Shute, 73.

55 Author/Stopes-Roe, 16–17 July 2009.

56 Wallis/Turner, 13 January 1928.

57 *Flight*, review E. F. Spanner's 'This Airships Business', 26 January 1928, 51.

58 Letter J. E. Temple to Barnes Wallis, undated, believed 1927, in *Barnes Wallis*, Morpurgo, 145.

59 Wallis/Turner, 22 January 1928.

60 Wallis/Turner, 10 February 1928.

61 Wallis/Turner, 21 September 1928.

62 Wallis/Turner, 5 November 1928.

63 Wallis/Turner, 10 November 1928.

64 Wallis/Turner, 18 February 1929.

65 Wallis/Turner, 14 March 1929.

66 Wallis/Turner, April 1929.

67 Author/Stopes-Roe, 16–17 July 2009.

68 Wallis/Turner, 5 May 1929.

69 Author/Stopes-Roe, 16–17 July 2009.

70 Author/Stopes-Roe, 16–17 July 2009.

71 Wallis/Turner, 2 August 1929.

72 Wallis/Turner, 11 August 1929.

73 Wallis/Turner, August 1929.

74 Wallis/Turner, 6 September 1929.

75 Wallis/Turner, 20, September 1929.

76 Wallis/Turner, 4 October 1929.

77 Wallis/Turner, 25 October 1929.

78 Wallis letter to editor *Red Stocking*, undated, 1930.

79 *Airships-Cardington*, Geoffrey Chamberlain (Terence Dalton, 1984) 140; Mitchell, designer of the Spitfire, was chief designer at the Supermarine Aviation Works, a subsidiary since 1928 of Vickers-Armstrong. McLean joined Vickers-Armstrong board 1929. McLean credited with name Spitfire having called his daughter Ann ' a little Spitfire;' author particularly recommends *Spitfire – Portrait of a Legend*, Leo McKinstry (John Murray, 2007) 55; *Flight* International, April 16, 1964, 597.

80 *Rigid*, Higham, 285

81 *Wrack*, Kings Norton, *Journal*, 189

8. The Design and Build of R101

1   *The British Rigid Airship*, Robin Higham (G. T. Foulis, 1961), 293.

2   Author/Caley, 2 June 2007.

3   *Rigid*, Higham, 293.

4   *Wrack*, Kings Norton, 188.

5   *Storm*, Masefield, 13.

6 ' Wing Commander Tom Cave-Browne-Cave, Some Airship Personalities, A Century of British Aeronautics' in the *Centenary Journal*, Royal Aeronautical Society, 1866–1966 (London, 1966), 53; *draft commentary R101* (believed unfinished), Cave-Browne-Cave (Imperial War Museum).

7   Meeting Institution Naval Architects, 30 March 1928, Royal Society of Arts, reported *Flight*, 12 April 1928, 252.

8   Author conversation Nigel Caley, 25 August 2009.

9–11 *A Wrack Behind*, Lord Kings Norton, *Aeronautical Journal*, Lord Kings Norton commemorative issue, vol. 103, No. 1022, April 1999, 187, 188.

12 *Boulton & Paul Aircraft since 1915*, Alec Brew (Putnam Aeronautical Books), 1993.

13 Air Chief Marshal Sir William Geoffrey Hanson Salmond (1878–1933). Director-General Supply and Research Air Ministry 1922–6, later Air Member Supply and Research; air officer commanding India, first officer to travel to overseas command by air. Command of Air Defence Great Britain Organisation 1931; air chief marshal January 1933; April 1933 made Chief of Air Staff, took over from brother John; died of cancer days after his appointment; Sir John resumed post for several weeks after his brother's

death. *From Biplane to Spitfire*, Anne Baker (Pen & Sword), 2003.

14–15 Author/Caley 25 August 2009. John Fleetwood Baker. OBE (1901–85). British scientist. Read First engineering Cambridge. World expert steel/plastic; numerous awards; invented Second World War indoor shelter designed to squash plastically, which saved countless lives. *Royal Society Biographical Memoirs, John Fleetwood Baker, Baron Baker of Windrush* (J. Heyman, 1985).

16 Dr. Giles Camplin letter to author 18 December 2009. Dr. Camplin holds a pilot's licence for commercial hot-air balloons; distinguished career in lighter-than-air; axial in numerous projects/adventures including Don Cameron's first hot-air balloon crossing of the Alps and Alan Root's voyage over Mt. Kilimanjaro. Has worked with German cargo lifter Gmbh company and their intended 150 tonne cargo airship; the Ministry of Defence *Skyship 600* airship trialled by Defence Evaluation & Research Agency, Farnborough. Assisted with launch-site selection, meteorological monitoring and development of launch procedures for Virgin round world balloon attempts.

17 Crispin Rope letter to author, 7 December 2009.

18 *Rigid*, Higham, 337.

19 *Boulton & Paul Aircraft since 1915*, Alec Brew, Putnam Aeronautical Books, 1993.

20 *Wrack*, Kings Norton, 188.

21 Ibid.

22 *Boulton & Paul Aircraft*, Brew, 125,

23 Higham letter to author, 29 December 2009.

24 *Wallis*, Morpurgo, 139, quoting F. A. de V. Robertson, *Flight*, 30 August 1920.

25 *Giants*, Robinson, 303.

26 Author/Caley, 2 June 2007.

27 *Storm*, Masefield, 164.

28 Dr. Robin Higham letter to author, 29 December 2009; Dr. Higham, of Kansas State University, is a distinguished historian. Author of the *The British Rigid Airship 1908–1931* (Foulis, 1961), he asked that his comments were prefaced by a reminder that his book was written half a century ago.

29 Dr. John Sweetman email to author, 25 March 2010. Sweetman is an eminent military historian. Former Head of Defence

and International Affairs at Royal Military Academy Sandhurst; read Modern History Oxford; PhD war studies King's College, London. Author: *The Dambusters Raid, Tirpitz: Hunting the Beast* and *Cavalry of the Clouds: Air War over Europe 1914–1918.*

30 *Hindenburg,* Mike Flynn, (Carlton, 1999), 36.

31 Wallis, Morpurgo, 139; letter Wallis to Morpurgo, 31 January 1969.

32 *Wallis,* Morpurgo, 139.

33 *Storm,* Masefield, 463.

34 *Storm,* Masefield, 463.

35 Author/Caley, 12 August 2009.

36 Author/Stopes-Roe, 1 October 2009.

37 Author/Caley, 12 August 2009.

38 Author/Stopes-Roe, 1 October 2009.

39 Author/Stopes-Roe, 16–17 July 2009.

40 Author/Stopes-Roe, 1 October 2009.

41 Molly Wallis letter Turner, 21 March 1929.

42 *Mathematics,* Stopes Roe, 169–70; letter Barnes Wallis to Molly Bloxam from New Cross, London, 28 September 1923.

43 Barnes Wallis letter to Air Marshal Sir Victor Goddard, postmarked White Hill House, Effingham, Surrey, 30 October 1974.

44 Author/Caley, 12 August 2009.

9. The R101 Disaster

1 Sir Peter Masefield interviewed by Ms Rebecca Atherstone, ITV, 1980.

2 Camplin letter to author, 18 December 2009.

3 Crispin Rope conversation author, 11 November 2009, Kesgrave, Suffolk.

4 Masefield's unpublished book *Catch the Sunlight* told of Thomson's infatuation with Marthe Bibesco. It mentions the carpet given to Thomson in the Middle East that he had at his London flat. It was taken in the works van to Cardington on 4 October 1930, the day of departure, and stowed on the *R101.* Also mentioned is the slipper. Crispin Rope: 'Just before Thomson left Bucharest to return home during the 1914–1918 War Marthe got into a primitive taxi and in her haste left a slipper behind. Thomson kept it with him always ... a woman's slipper was found in the wreckage of *R101* and gave rise to short-lived rumours that a woman had been aboard. It was Masefield's original intention to publish *Catch The Sunlight* before *To Ride the Storm.'* Crispin Rope letter to author, 11 December

2009.

5 Crispin Rope letter to author, 7 December 2009.

6 Rope conversation author, 11 November 2009.

7 Author/Caley, 12 August 2009.

8 *Dr. Eckener's Dream Machine,* Douglas Botting (Harper Collins, 2001), 233.

9 Airship LZ 127 *Graf Zeppelin* (1928–37). Named after Ferdinand Zeppelin, who held the title 'Graf' or 'Count'. Most successful airship ever built. Sailed by Eckener. Safely carried 13,000 passengers, flew a million miles, made 590 voyages, 143 across Atlantic, one over Pacific. Regular sailings to Brazil. Made round-the-world voyage sponsored by newspaper mogul Randolph Hearst; visited Arctic 1931.

10 Airship LZ 129 *Hindenburg,* captained by Max Pruss, destroyed by fire 6 May 1937 while mooring at Lakehurst Naval Air Station US. 36 perished. Radio reporter Herb Morrison in an emotional commentary included the famous phrase, 'Oh, the humanity!' The calamity ended airship development.

11 Crispin Rope letter to author, 11 December 2009.

12 Letter Wallis to Sir Victor Goddard, from Effingham, Surrey, 30 October 1974; Wallis praises Higham's excellent *The British Rigid Airship 1908–1931.*

13 Crispin Rope conversation with author, 11 November 2009, Kesgrave, Suffolk.

14 *Storm,* Masefield, 336.

15 Letter Goddard to Wallis, 10 October 1974, postmarked Brasted, Westerham, Kent.

16 Rope/author, 11 November 2009.

17 Peter Davison conversation with author, 11 November 2009, Kesgrave, Suffolk.

18 Rope/author, 7 December 2009.

19 Caley/author conversation, 15 December 2009

20 Rope/author, 11 November 2009.

21 Rope/author, 11 November 2009.

22 Davison/author, 11 November 2009.

23 Dr. Giles Camplin letter to author, 18 December 2009.

24 Rope/author, 7 December 2009.

25 Rope/author, 11 November 2009.

26 Rope/author, 11 November 2009.

27 Davison/author, 11 November 2009.

28 Rope letter author, 7 December 2009.
29 Caley/author, 15 December 2009.
30 Ibid.
31 Camplin letter author, 19 December 2009.
32 Caley/author conversation, 15 December 2009.
33 Rope letter author, 7 December 2009.
34 Davison/author, 11 November 2009.
35 Rope letter author, December 7 2009.
36 Davison/author, 11 November 2009/3 February 2010.
37 Rope letter author, 7 December 2009.
38 Rope conversation author, 11 November 2009.
39 Camplin letter author, 22 December 2009.
40 Letter Goddard to Wallis, 10 October 1974, Brasted, Westerham, Kent.
41 Letter Wallis to Goddard, 30 October 1974, Effingham, Surrey.
42 Mary Stopes-Roe conversation author, 16–17 July 2009, Birmingham.
43 Stopes-Roe/author.
44 Dr. John Sweetman, historian, email author, 14 April 2010; letter Wallis, Effingham, Surrey, to biographer, Professor J. E. Morpurgo, Leeds University, 11 January 1971.
45 Barnes Wallis, J. E. Morpurgo (Longmans, 1972), 138.
46 Reference to medium Eileen Garrett of R101 seances; The Airmen who would not die, John G. Fuller (Putnam, 1979).
47 Flight Lieutenant Sydney Nixon, chief administrative officer, Royal Airship Works.
48 Wallis letter to Goddard, 30 October 1974.
49 Report R101 Inquiry, Leakage from Gas Bags, Flight, 14 November 1930, 1238.
50 Ibid.
51 Camplin letter author, 18 December 2009.
52 Ramsay MacDonald wrote of Thomson's death: 'Gloom and sorrow came upon the world … my friend, gallant, gay and loyal … Why did I allow him to go? He was so certain there could be no mishap.' Ramsay MacDonald, David Marquand (Jonathan Cape, 1977). 568.

10. Italy, Norway and Russia

1 Chambers Biographical Dictionary (W. R. Chambers, 1990), 1085.
2 Chambers, 42; Daily Express Enyclopaedia (Daily Express Publications, 1934), 184.
3 www.biographicon.com retrieved 2 June 2010.
4 The Airship, Christopher Sprigg (Sampson Low, Marston, c.1931), 119–20.
5 Giants, Robinson, 360.
6 http://oldbeacon.com/beacon/airships/airships-Italian.htm retrieved 2 May 2010.
7 http://www.hamptonroads.com/roma-airship-disaster retrieved 3 June 2010.
8 Chambers, 477.
9 Airship, Sprigg, 35.
10 Chambers, 1318.
11 http://www.fathom.com/feature/121855 retrieved 5 June 2010.
12 Ninety Degrees North, Fergus Fleming (Granta Books, 2002), 404–15.
13 Airship, Sprigg, 121.

11. Aircraft Carriers of the Sky: America's Airships

1 Giants of the Sky: A History of the Rigid Airship, Douglas H. Robinson (G. T. Foulis & Co. Ltd, 1973), 205
2 Giants, 213–16.
3 Dept. of the Navy, Navy Historical Centre, Washington DC, www.history.navy.mil/photos/ac-usn22/z-types/zr3.htm.
4 The Airship, Its Design, history, operation and future, Christopher Sprigg (Sampson Low, Marston & Co. Ltd, c.1930–1), 122.
5 The Airship, Sprigg, 122-3.
6 Flight, R. G. Grant (DK, 2004), 173.
7 Giants, 28.
8 The Story of the Airship, Hugh Allen (Goodyear Tire & Rubber Co. 1931), 36.
9 Story, 36.
10 Ibid.
11 Story, 39.
12 Story, 38.
13 Ibid.
14 Giants, 83.
15 Giants, 183, quoting The History of Naval Aviation, vol. VI, The Development of Rigid Airships, 1. Typescript, 1923, copied and mimeographed by Charles L. Keller, 1960.
16 NASM archives, Garland Fulton Collection, Accession no. XXXX-0101, National Air and Space Museum, Smithsonian Institute, Washington DC.
17 The Airships Akron and Macon, Richard K. Smith (US Naval Institute, Annapolis, Maryland, 1965), 53.

18 Naval Historical Centre,
www.history.navy.mi.
19 www.history.navy.mi.
20 *Giants,* Robinson, 243.
21 *Giants,* 244.

12. The Mighty Graf and the Hindenburg Calamity

1 *Giants,* Robinson, 262.
2 *Story,* Allen, helium and its production, 46.
3 *Giants,* summary by the peerless Robinson, 266.
4 *Storm,* Masefield, 28 July 1930, quoting British maestro George Herbert Scott on *R100* surviving cover problems over Atlantic en route to Canada, 243.
5 *Storm;* quoting Thompson, House of Lords, June 1930, 'remarkable' Eckener, 209.
6 *Storm,* 157.
7 *Storm,* 157
8 *Airship,* Sprigg, incisive examination of airship as 'paying proposition,' 180–93.
9 *Story,* 61.
10 *Storm,* 263.
11 *Airship,* 180.
12 The *Graf Zeppelin* had coped with cover and gasbag problems, which had plagued airships from the earliest days. At the end of her world trip she was losing no more gas than at the start of her journey. *Airship,* 207.
13 *Story,* 57–60.
14 Pundits felt the airship's future was as a pleasure cruiser rather than as a scheduled carrier; it offered changing panoramic vistas rather than endless seascapes. *Airship,* 231.
15 *Giants,* Robinson, 295.
16 *Hindenburg: An illustrated history,* Rick Archbold, paintings by Ken Marschall (The Madison Press Ltd., 1994), 144–52; highly recommended by the author. Also Daniel Grossman's *Hindenburg* and Zeppelin site: http://www.airships.net; *Pulham Pigs,* Kinsey, 118; *Wallis,* Morpurgo, 187; www.eyewitnesstohistory.com; www.britannica.com; http://hamptonroadsnavalmuseum.blogspot.com; www.bluejacket.com.

13. Epilogue: Will the Airship Sail Again?

1 Nigel Caley email to author, 25 November 2011; from '*Recollections,*' Air Marshal Sir Thomas Elmhirst, privately published 1991,

Whitstable Litho Printers; Caley private archive.
2 Hans Paul Ströhle, pilot Deutsche Zeppelin-Reederei, email to author, 25 November 2011.
3 Ms. Wendy Pritchard, conversation with author, 5 December 2011.
4 Conversation author and Gordon Taylor, 4 January 2012.
5 Column by author, *London Evening Standard,* 17 March 1998; interview with Roger Munk, *R100–R101* sheds, Cardington, Bedfordshire.
6 Interview by author with Hardy Geisler, HAV offices, Cranfield, Bedfordshire, 3 January 2012.

Appendix A

1 *Flight,* 17 January 1918.
2 *Flight,* 19 May 1919.
3 Author conversation Rebecca Atherstone, Trimley St. Martin, Suffolk, 8 October 2009.
4–39 *Grabowsky-Atherstone Log,* 31 August 1929 to 3 October 1930.
40 Author/Caley, 12 August 2009.
41 *Log.*
42 *Log.*
43 Giles Camplin letter to author, 22 December 2009.
44 *Log.*
45 Camplin letter author, 22 December 2009.
46 *Log.*
47 Author/Rebecca Atherstone, 8 October 2009.

Appendix B

1 Author visited Brian Carr, Pulham Market Society, 1 April 2010.
2 Author visited Judy Alder/Mervyn Hickford, Harleston Museum, Norfolk, UK, 22 April 2010.
3 Watts letter to mother, RNAS Pulham, Norfolk to Worstead, Norfolk, UK, undated.
4 King's Message to RAF, 11 November 1918.
5 Watts–mother, Howden, Yorks., UK – Worstead (Harleston Museum).
6 *Yorkshire Evening Post,* 29 January 1921, 6.
7 Photo gold watch, 4 June 1925; courtesy Michael Watts, Ipswich, UK.
8 *Eastern Daily Press,* 5 June 1925.
9 Telegram copies: *R33* departs 16 April returns 17 April 1925.
10 Scott letter–Watts, RAW Cardington, Beds. UK – Watts, Worstead.

11 Letter Cardington–Watts, rent, 10 October 1924.
12 *Airways* magazine, No. 14, September 1925, 38.
13 *Airways*, No.10, May 1925, 277–81.
14 *The Engineer*, 11 March 1927, 258–61; diagram airship tower/machinery house, 270.
15 Watts–mother, Booth wedding, undated.
16 Letter Watts' sister Ida to Mrs. Joscelyn Rawlence, 14 July 1989 (Harleston Museum).
17 Two exercise books; one dated 1/3/18, stamped: 'Naval and Military Schools'.
18 *Old Pastonian* magazine, No.3, 1930, 10.
19 *R33* reunion dinner invitation, 26 September 1924.
20 Two invitations, one signed by guests, *R33* dinner, Swan Hotel, Bedford, 25 April 1925.
21 Invitation, *R33* dinner, Pulham RNAS, 25 September 1925.
22 *Daily Express*, *R33* cartoon, 18 April 1925.
23 Airship engineers licence, No.15, 17 May 1930.
24 Letter Booth to Watts, *R100* appointment, 21 May 1929.
25 Fragment, Royal Canadian Signals Radio Telegraph Service, undated.
26 HMA *R100*, Christmas card, Montreal, 1930.
27 *R100*, envelope.
28 RAW Cardington, Christmas card, airship girdling globe, 1924.
29 Notebook, vol.10,1929; poem '*The Airship*,' by Marjory Augur (Harleston museum)
30 Commemorative booklet, Department National Defence for Canada, June 1930.
31 Letter/postcard Brother Hubert, Montreal, Canada, to Watts, 12 August 1930.
32 Watts–mother from Canada, undated; envelope depicts St. James Hotel, Montreal.
33 Set of coloured postcards St. Hubert airport, Montreal, undated.
34 Letter Thomas Hicks, Croydon, to Watts, *R100*, Cardington, 17 October 1930.
35 Photograph identified by Arthur Watts, 19 April 2010.
36 *Eastern Daily Press*, 27 December 1930.
37 Invitation 'Recognition dinner', 17 November 1919.
38 *Eastern Daily Press*, 30 December 1930, 8.
39 Author in conversation with Arthur Watts, Worstead, 19 April 2010.
40 *Giants*, Robinson, 306–10.
41 Letter Captain George Meager, Penton Mewsey, Andover, Hants. to Eva Davison, Granville Watts' sister, 26 October 1971.
42 Meager, RAW Cardington – Watts's mother, Alice, 31 December 1930 (Harleston museum).
43 Author, conversation Arthur Watts, Worstead, 19 April 2010.

Appendix D
1 Caley/author, 15 December 2009.
2 Crispin Rope letter to author, 11 December 2009.

Appendix E
1 *Guide to the Church of the Holy Family and St. Michael*, Kesgrave, Suffolk, 1. Commemorative card Church/Airship Heritage Trust to Fleet Air Museum, Yeovilton.
2–3 *Guide to the Church of the Holy Family and St. Michael*, Appendix 1; extracts *Storm*, Masefield, 206.
4 Mrs Eve Atherstone, widow Lieutenant Commander Noël Atherstone, First Officer *R101*, from '*A Note on Nevil Shute's book Slide Rule*,' by Group Captain E. A. Johnston (unpublished) 29 November 1954; conversation Eva Whaley-Cohen (formerly Atherstone).
5 *Guide to the Church of the Holy Family and St. Michael*, Appendix 2, family connections; *Daily Telegraph*, 5 September 2003.
6 Christmas card commemorating 80th anniversary of the Catholic Church of the Holy Family and St. Michael 1931–2011, December 2011, sent by Crispin Rope to the author.

BIBLIOGRAPHY

Manuscript sources
Admiralty papers, Public Record Office
Air Force papers, Public Record Office
Barnes Wallis archive, The Imperial Science Museum library
Cabinet papers, Public Record Office
Churchill Archives, Churchill College, Cambridge
Imperial War Museum archives
Liddell Hart Centre for Military Archives, King's College
Maritime papers, The National Maritime Museum
Vickers Archives, Cambridge University Library

Official publications
Hansard parliamentary debates
House of Lords reports
HMSO *R38* Inquiry
HMSO *R101* Inquiry

Works of reference
Chambers Biographical Dictionary
Dictionary of National Biography
Guide to the Papers of British Cabinet Ministers 1900–1951
Handbook of British Chronology
The Macmillan Dictionary of the First World War
Oxford Companion to the Second World War
Oxford Companion to Ships and the Sea

Papers of British Cabinet Ministers 1782–1900
The Times Obituaries
The Times Newspapers
The Pall Mall Gazette

Unpublished works
Newman, Grant, *The First Great Transatlantic Airship*, RAF Museum, Hendon.

Recommended reading list
Abbott, Patrick, *The British Airship at War 1914–1918*, Terence Dalton, 1989
Allen, Hugh, *The Story of the Airship*, Goodyear Tire, 1925
Archbold, Rick, *Hindenburg*,The Madison Press Ltd/Weidenfeld & Nicolson, 1994
Asquith, T., and Deacon, K., *Howden Airship Station*, Howden Civic Society, 2006
Botting, Douglas, *Shadow in the Clouds*, Kestrel Books, 1975
— *Dr. Eckener's Dream Machine*, Harper Collins, 2001
Boyle, Andrew, *Trenchard*, Collins, 1962
Brew, Alec, *Boulton Paul Aircraft since 1915*, Putnam, 1993
Brooks, Peter W., *Zeppelin: Rigid Airships 1893–1940*, Putnam, 1992
Brown, D. K., *The Grand Fleet: Warship Design and Development*, Chatham, 1999
Bryant, Arthur, *Years of Victory 1802–1812*, Collins, 1944
Chamberlain, Geoffrey, *Airships – Cardington*, Terence Dalton, 1984
Clarke, Basil, *The History of Airships*, Herbert Jenkins, 1961
Cronin, D., *Royal Navy Shipboard Aircraft Developments 1912–31*, Air Britain, 1990
Cross, Wilbur, *Disaster at the Pole*, The Lyons Press, 2002
Curtis, Lee J., *Lloyd Loom*, Salamander, 1997
Deacon, Kenneth, *The Men and Women who Built and Flew the R100*, Langrick, 2008
Deacon, Kenneth, *Howden's Airship Station*, Langrick, 2003
Deighton, Len, and Schwartzman, Arnold, *Airshipwreck*, Cape, 1978
Deurs, Rear Admiral George van, *Wings for the Fleet*, US Naval Institute, 1966
Devine, E, ed., *Thinkers of the Twentieth Century*, St. James, Chicago, London, 1985
Dick, Harold G., Robinson, Douglas H., *The Golden Age of the Great Passenger Airships: Graf Zeppelin and Hindenburg*, Smithsonian Institute, 1985
Durr, L., *Zeppelin-Luftschiffbau*, Berlin, 1924
Eckener, Hugo, *My Zeppelins*, Putnam, 1958
Ellison, Norman, *British Gliders and Sailplanes*, Black, 1971
Fletcher, J. N., *Maintenance, Flying, Operation of Airships*, Cranwell, 1918
Frank, Wolfgang, *The Sea Wolves*, Weidenfeld & Nicolson, 1955

Fuller, John G., *The Airmen Who Would Not Die*, Putnam, 1979

Gilbert, James, *Skywriting: an aviation anthology*, M. & J. Hobbs, 1978

Grossnick, Roy A., *US Naval Aviation 1910–95*, Naval Historical Center, 1997

Gunston, Bill, ed., *The Story of Flight*, Sundial, 1978

Hackman, W., *Seek and Strike: Sonar, Anti-submarine Warfare and the Royal Navy 1914–54*, HMSO, 1984

Hardy, A. C., *From Slip to Sea*, Brown & Son, 1935

Hartcup, G., *The Achievement of the Airship*, David & Charles, 1974

Hayward, K., *The Military utility of Airships*, Royal United Services Institute for Defence Studies, 1998

Hearne, R. P. *Zeppelins and Super Zeppelins*, Bodley Head, 1916

Hezlet, Arthur, Vice Admiral, *Aircraft and Sea Power*, Peter Davies, 1970

Higham, Robin, *The British Rigid Airship, 1908–1931*, Foulis, 1961

Hoffman, Paul, *Wings of Madness*, Fourth Estate, 2003

Humble, Richard, ed., *Naval Warfare*, Little, Brown, 2002

Jackson, G. G., *The Great Book of Aeroplanes*, Oxford, 1930

Jamison, T. W., *Icarus Over the Humber*, Lampada Press, 1994

Jones, H. A., *The War in the Air, Vol. II*, Oxford, 1928

Kinsey, Gordon, *Pulham Pigs*, Terence Dalton, 1988

Lehmann, Ernst August, trs. Jay Dratler, *Zeppelin: The Story of Lighter-Than-Air craft*, Longmans, Green, 1937

— and Mingos, Howard, *The Zeppelins*, Putnam, 1927

Low, Prof. A. M., *Mine and Countermine*, Hutchinson, 1940

Maitland, E. M., *Log of HMA R34*, 1920, reprinted by Lighter than Air Institute, 1997

Marben, Rolf, *Zeppelin Adventures*, Greenhill Books (facsimile), 1920

Marquand, David, *Ramsay MacDonald*, Jonathan Cape, 1977

Masefield, Sir Peter G., *To Ride the Storm: Airship R101*, Kimber, 1982

Mason, Francis K., *The Hawker Hurricane*, Aston Publications, 1987

McKinstry, Leo, *Spitfire – Portrait of a Legend*, John Murray, 2007.

Meager, George, *My Airship Flights 1915–1930*, Kimber, 1970

Middleton, D. H., *Airspeed: The Company and its Aeroplanes*, Dalton, 1982

Morpurgo, J. E., *Barnes Wallis: A biography*, Longman, 1972

Mowthorpe, Ces, *Battlebags*, Sutton Publishing, 1997

Nield, Bernard J., *The Burney Streamline Car*, Howden Civic Society, 2008

Nowara, Heinz J., *Marine Aircraft of the 1914–18 War*, Harleyford, 1966

Pawle, Gerald, *The Secret War, 1939–45*, Harrap, 1956

Poolman, Kenneth, *Zeppelins over England*, Evans Brothers Limited, 1960

Popham, Hugh, *Into Wind*, Hamish Hamilton, 1969

Pratt, H. B. *Commercial Airships*, Nelson, 1920

Raleigh, W., *The War in the Air*, Vol.1, Oxford, 1922

Rawlence, Jocelyn, and Peake, Norman, *The Story of Pulham and its Airships*, Pulham Market Society, 1989

Robinson, Douglas H., *Giants in the Sky: A History of the Rigid Airship*, University of Washington Press, 1973

Robinson, Douglas H., Keller, Charles, L., *Up Ship! A History of the U.S. Navy's Rigid Airships 1919–1935*, Naval Institute Press, 1982

Rosendahl, Commander C. E., *What about the Airship: The Challenge to the United States*, Scribner, 1938

Roskill, Captain S. W., *The Naval Air Service*, Vol. 1, 1908–18, Navy Records Society, 1969

Russell, J., *United States Naval Aviation 1910–60*, Bureau Naval Weapons, 1960

Santos-Dumont, A., *My Airships*, 1904, reprinted University Press of Pacific, 2002

Shute, Nevil, *Slide Rule*, Heinemann, 1954

Smith, Richard K., *Akron and Macon*, Naval Institute Press, 1965

Sprigg, Christopher, *The Airship*, Low, Marston & Co, *c.*1930

Stopes-Roe, Mary, *Mathematics with Love*, Macmillan, 2005

Taylor, A. J. P., *English History, 1914–1945*, Oxford, 1965

Walker, P., *Early Aviation at Farnborough*, MacDonald, 1971

Whale, George, *British Airships, Past, Present and Future*, John Lane, London, 1919

Ventry, Lord, and Kolesnik, Eugene M., *Airship Saga*, Blandford Press, 1982

Vissering, H., *Zeppelin – The Story of a Great Achievement*, Wells, Chicago, 1922

White, W. H., *A Manual of Naval Architecture*, Murray, 1894

Williams, T. B. Captain, *Airship Pilot No.28*, William Kimber, 1974

Winter, Nancy, *Man Flies*, Ecco Press, 1998

INDEX